D0780360

Fiction, Philosophy and Literary Theory

Also available from Continuum:

On Truth and Meaning, Christopher Norris

Epistemology: Key Concepts in Philosophy, Christopher Norris

Platonism, Music and the Listener's Share, Christopher Norris

Fiction, Philosophy and Literary Theory: Will the Real Saul Kripke Please Stand Up?

Christopher Norris

continuum

Continuum International Publishing Group
The Tower Building 80 Maiden Lane
11 York Road Suite 704
London New York
SE1 7NX NY 10038

www.continuumbooks.com

© Christopher Norris 2007

All rights reserved. No part of this publication may be reproduced or transmitted in any form or by any means, electronic or mechanical, including photocopying, recording, or any information storage or retrieval system, without prior permission in writing from the publishers.

Christopher Norris has asserted his right under the Copyright, Designs and Patents Act, 1988, to be identified as Author of this work.

British Library Cataloguing-in-Publication Data
A catalogue record for this book is available from the British Library.

ISBN: PB: 0-8264-9756-X
        9780826497567
    HB: 0-8264-9755-1
        9780826497550

Library of Congress Cataloging-in-Publication Data
A catalog record for this book is available from the Library of Congress.

Typeset by YHT Ltd, London
Printed and bound in Great Britain by MPG Books Ltd, Bodmin, Cornwall

Contents

Introduction

This book has three closely related and, I hope, mutually reinforcing aims. One is to challenge the idea that 'analytic' (i.e., mainstream Anglo-American) and 'continental' (i.e., post-Kantian mainland-European) philosophy have nothing in common bar a fixed antipathy each for the other and a flat disagreement on basic issues – among them the issue as to just what constitutes genuine, serious or competent philosophy – which precludes any hope of constructive dialogue. Another is to make the two-way case for philosophy (analytic philosophy included) as warranting the careful attention of literary theorists and also – perhaps more controversially – for literary theory as meriting the interest of philosophers from both camps. The third is to offer some seasoned reflections about why there has been such entrenched resistance to the opening up of these (in my view) highly promising channels of cross-disciplinary exchange. I have argued to similar effect in numerous books and articles over the past twenty years although they have tended most often to lean one way or the other, that is, toward philosophy or literary theory, or toward the 'analytic' or 'continental' modes of philosophic thought. What I hope to do here is achieve something more like a genuine working balance, even if – for any reader who goes in *via* the endnotes or index of names – there might seem a strongly philosophical bias.

So this book represents something of a *voyage de retour au pays natale*, or a turning back (not, I trust, a regression) to topics in literary theory and related fields that were my main focus of interest up to the early 1990s, but which then gave way to a predominant concern with the kinds of issue that typify philosophy in the mainstream analytic line of descent. It seeks to re-address some of those topics from a standpoint informed by more recent developments – like the debate around anti-realism in epistemology and philosophy of language – which (as I shall argue) have a direct bearing on issues thrown up in the wake of post-structuralism and kindred theoretical debates. What I further seek to do is correct certain prevalent misunderstandings that have so far hobbled many efforts in this direction. Very often they result from the tendency of literary theorists to advance far-reaching speculative claims on a frankly inadequate philosophic basis, or from the tendency of most analytic philosophers to treat anything associated with 'literary theory' as not worth serious attention. By far the most flagrant example of this is the notion – put about by opponents who exhibit a scant acquaintance with his work – that Jacques Derrida is some kind of anti-philosopher or adept in the arts of 'textualist' sophistry who has contrived a whole range of expert techniques for muddying the conceptual waters. Chapter 1 ('Deconstruction, Analysis and Deviant Logic') most directly challenges that idea by stressing the various ways in which Derrida's work can be seen to resist, controvert or amply refute any such blanket charge. Here I examine some of his earlier texts – especially his writings on Rousseau and J.L. Austin – in relation to current debates within philosophy of logic and language. I make the case that these texts are centrally concerned with issues that have also preoccupied logicians in the broadly 'analytic' camp, among them issues with regard to modal, temporal, epistemic, deontic and other non-classical (i.e., many-valued or paraconsistent) logics. I focus mainly on his exposition of the 'logic of supplementarity' as it emerges through Derrida's deconstructive reading of Rousseau and his treatment of the various problems that arise with any attempt to develop a logically adequate or consistent theory of speech-acts on the basis of Austin's often highly elusive concepts and categories. However these claims are always arrived at through a textual close reading that adheres to the standards of bivalent logic right up to the stage where that logic encounters a strictly unavoidable moment of aporia, or a point at which the classical true/false disjunction can no longer be consistently sustained.

This is what sets Derrida's thinking apart from other, less rigorous approaches according to which we might always be warranted in revising, adjusting or abandoning the ground rules of bivalent logic – except (as most would agree) the law of contradiction – just so long as it helped to obviate some otherwise troublesome empirical anomaly or to facilitate our dealing with problem areas like quantum theory. Still less, I maintain, can the Derridean logics of 'supplementarity', 'parergonality', 'iterability' and the like be treated as a sub-class of paraconsistent or dialethic logic, one that would treat even the law of contradiction as revisable for certain purposes. On the contrary: Derrida's early essays can be shown to argue their case in strict accordance with the precepts of classical (bivalent) logic, not least – or especially – when they turn out to reveal some deep-laid aporia or counter-logic that runs athwart the manifest purport of the text under scrutiny. It is my contention that those essays have a highly distinctive contribution to make in the context of present-day analytic philosophy. Thus I have a good deal to say about his close engagement with issues in philosophy of logic, mathematics and science where Derrida's approach – first arrived at through a highly perceptive critical reading of Husserl – may differ from that adopted by most thinkers in the Anglo-American mainstream but not to the extent of blocking any useful dialogue. Chapter 2 ('Ethics, Normativity and Deconstruction') goes on to contest certain other received yet erroneous ideas about Derrida's work, among them the claim that his writings exhibit an indifference to basic standards of ethical (as well as intellectual) responsibility. Rather it is the case that Derrida's practice of meticulous textual close reading, allied to his keen analytic intelligence, is frequently the source of insights – including ethical insights – that are not to be had elsewhere. This involves a fairly extensive overview from his early studies of Husserl and Levinas to the later texts which focus more explicitly on ethical and socio-political themes. My

chief point is that Derrida has engaged certain problems in moral philosophy
that lead inescapably to deep-laid dilemmas or aporias, but has done so in a way
that relates compellingly to issues of real-world practical concern.

I trace this engagement through his encounters with a range of differing
views, whether those of downright antagonists (like Searle on the topic of
Austinian speech-act theory and Habermas on Derrida's supposed betrayal of the
'philosophic discourse of modernity') or those, like the Levinasian conception of
ethics as a discourse of absolute 'alterity', to which he has been strongly drawn
even while resisting their ultimate implications. The main purpose of this
chapter is to bring out the close relation between Derrida's thinking on the
scope and limits of classical (bivalent) logic and his thinking on the kinds of
issue that arise with regard to the antinomies of Kantian practical reason, that is
to say, the rival claims of causal determinism on the one hand and rational
autonomy, free will and moral agency on the other. I show how these issues are
pursued through his reading of Husserl on the conflicting priorities of 'genesis'
and 'structure', and also how they find expression in Derrida's deconstructive
analysis of various canonical texts. My conclusion is that analytic philosophers
have a great deal to learn from Derrida's example with regard both to the ethics of
reading and to ethical questions more generally. Where these come together is in
the need to combine a meticulous respect for matters of detail – particularities of
circumstance, content and context – with a willingness, if required, to go against
the dictates of received moral thinking or the orthodox interpretative grain.

Chapter 3 ('Saussurean Linguistics as Model and Metaphor') examines the
premises of Saussurean (structuralist) linguistics from a range of philosophical,
theoretical and wider cultural perspectives. Some have to do with Saussure's
own account of what constitutes a 'science' of language, properly conceived,
and others with the impact of Saussurean theory on various disciplines, among
them anthropology, sociology, cultural studies and literary criticism. I also
examine the place of that theory within a certain, distinctively French, critical-
rationalist philosophy of science whose chief representatives were Gaston
Bachelard and Georges Canguilhem. My purpose here is to relocate Saussure's
work in relation to those subsequent movements of thought – structuralism and
post-structuralism – which made very different use of his cardinal ideas and
which also involved very different attitudes to his conception of structural
linguistics as a scientific discipline of thought. Thus the structuralist enterprise
continued to uphold that ideal, albeit with certain reservations, while post-
structuralists routinely took to denouncing it as just a lingering symptom of the
old attachment to 'logocentric' (truth-based) methods and values. Of course I
cannot pretend to be *entirely* neutral in this matter since the post-structuralist
'take' on Saussure has been a chief source of the current turn toward cultural-
relativist or social-constructivist doctrines, a development that I have criticized
at length elsewhere and which comes in for some less than sympathetic commentary here. All the same this chapter is intended to provide readers with a
means of assessing these divergent claims and placing the project of Saussurean
linguistics in a wider scientific and philosophical context.

Chapter 4 ('Translation to Tralfamadore: Images of Science in Literary Theory') has more to say about the assimilation of various ideas from the physical sciences by literary and cultural theorists. Here again I seek to distinguish what is genuinely useful and productive in such forms of interdisciplinary exchange from the tendency – call it postmodernist – to exploit vague analogies for largely rhetorical effect. My purpose is to clarify some of the confusions that result when literary theorists overextend their claims for the ubiquity of metaphor in scientific discourse, or extrapolate too readily from fictive to other areas of discourse. In this connection I propose some useful points of contact between literary theory (especially narrative poetics) and developments in modal or 'possible-worlds' logic. This is the branch of logic having to do with matters of necessity and possibility, or truths (such as those of mathematics and logic itself) which hold good in every possible world and truths (such as those concerning historical events) which hold good contingently across just that range of worlds that resemble our own in the relevant respects. These issues have lately received much attention from philosophers – among them Saul Kripke and Hilary Putnam – who put forward a realist theory of reference based on modal-logical considerations. However they also raise interesting questions about fictive 'possible worlds', the status of truth-claims in literary criticism, and the complex relationship between history and fiction in various narrative genres. Such issues have a marked relevance – I suggest – to the kinds of debate that first arose in the wake of post-structuralism and have since then continued with regard to new historicism and other varieties of 'textualist' approach.

Chapter 5 ('Will the Real Saul Kripke Please Stand Up?') begins by laying out the main arguments for the Kripke/Putnam 'new' theory of reference, along with some relevant philosophical background including its departure from the hitherto dominant descriptivist theory proposed by Russell and Frege. I then explore the implications of modal logic in various contexts, among them that of historical enquiry (which very often proceeds by means of counterfactual-supporting explanations) and issues concerning the ontology of fictive or imaginary objects. However, my main purpose here is to put the case for modal realism – suitably construed – as a promising alternative to some of the more extreme anti-realist or discourse-relativist positions that have occupied the high ground of literary theory during the past two decades. The same applies to those fashionable *topoi* – such as quantum physics and chaos theory – that are often cited as evidence for the claim that science has itself now entered a period of 'postmodern' evolution where uncertainties and paradoxes abound, and where old-style 'classical' values (of truth, knowledge, objectivity, etc.) no longer possess the least degree of credibility. As the reader might expect I treat this claim with a high degree of scepticism and put the case that it results not only from a simplified, distorted or tendentious treatment of the scientific theories concerned but also from a limited acquaintance with relevant work in philosophy of science. At the same time I note some more encouraging recent signs that literary theorists are learning to eschew such grandiose pronouncements and focus on particular episodes or aspects of the science/literature relationship. This leads on to arguments concerning the culture-relative or socially constructed character of scientific theories and truth-claims. I examine the various sources of such arguments, from the 'strong' sociology of knowledge to Wittgensteinian linguistic philosophy, Foucault's Nietzschean genealogies of power/knowledge, and postmodernist conceptions of 'truth' as a product of linguistic or discursive representation. I suggest that there is much to be learned from the questions raised by philosophers, historians, and sociologists of science without giving way to a relativist approach that would let the main philosophical issues go by default. That is to say, one can put the case for scientific realism or inference to the best explanation while allowing that other (e.g., sociological) lines of enquiry may well have some useful and perceptive insights with regard to the cultural-historical 'context of discovery'.

Philosophy of science thus assumes the role of a moderating discourse that gives due weight to the methods and procedures of scientific thought – and hence the possibility of progress in scientific knowledge – while also making room for the genuine contributions of a non-imperialist sociological perspective. Chapter 5 goes on to substantiate this claim by way of a further, more detailed account of modal or 'possible-worlds' logic, its implications for literary theory, and – most importantly here – its bearing on the realism/anti-realism issue. It is a curious reflection on the grip exerted by professional stereotypes that anti-realism of a certain albeit rather technical or logico-semantic kind has occupied the high ground in a good deal of recent 'analytic' debate, while such sceptical claims – or their near equivalent in a non-received idiom – are taken as self-evidently false or absurd when advanced by thinkers from the other, that is, 'continental' or 'literary' side of the fence. What I therefore try to do throughout this book is chip away at the kinds of deep-laid prejudice that still (despite recent, more hopeful overtures) tend to block communication across otherwise less than drastic differences of view. This is not, perhaps, so evident in the case of intra-philosophical disputes like that between realism and anti-realism as in the case of those (in large part) professionally motivated turf wars between philosophers and literary theorists that have broken out with depressing regularity in recent years. Still I trust that my discussion will open up some useful and productive lines of debate whilst avoiding any vaguely ecumenical or 'third-way' approach of the sort that – in philosophy as likewise in present-day politics – most often has just the opposite effect.

Chapter 6 ('Extraordinary Language: Why Wittgenstein Didn't Like Shakespeare') takes a different, though related, tack in approaching the various points at dispute between philosophy and literary criticism. It is a well-known fact – often treated as something of a scandal – that Wittgenstein disliked Shakespeare and found the poet's language rebarbative, chiefly on account of its piled-up metaphors, its frequent ambiguities of lexis and syntax, and – more generally – its marked deviation from the norms of straightforward communicative usage. Here I suggest a number of reasons for this negative response on Wittgenstein's part. They include his notable ambivalence with regard to the claims of poetic 'genius' *vis-à-vis* the claims of 'ordinary language' and his kindred idea that metaphor represents a standing temptation for language to 'go on holiday' and thus lose touch with those shared sense-making norms. Along with this – more acutely – went a constant sense of how far his own writing depended on just such forms of metaphorical expression in order to exert its persuasive force or to carry philosophical conviction. Those problems were compounded, I suggest, by Wittgenstein's strongly marked desire to renounce what he saw as the false blandishments of rhetoric and the lure of any language that did not respect the sanction of customary values and beliefs. To this extent his failure (or refusal) to 'appreciate' Shakespeare bears comparison with Tolstoy's likewise negative estimate, a judgement which George Orwell put down to the novelist's pained recognition, on reading *King Lear*, of his own failure to achieve a kind of secular sainthood by renouncing all worldly pleasures and achievements, among them those of literary authorship. My chapter then traces the effect of these unresolved tensions in Wittgenstein's work on later philosophical debate, especially in relation to much-discussed topics such as rule following, 'private language', and scepticism with regard to other minds or our knowledge of the (so-called) external world. So far from 'giving philosophy peace' or 'showing the fly a way out of the fly-bottle', the chief result of his later writings has been to leave philosophers more deeply in thrall to a range of hyper-cultivated problems or dilemmas which have their source in precisely that suggestive power of certain Wittgensteinian metaphors, images and modes of analogical thinking. This is perhaps why his comments on Shakespeare echo the kinds of doubt that have often been expressed by literary critics – from Dr Johnson down – in whom a keen sense of the poet's extraordinary powers of linguistic invention went along with a deep-laid resistance to them on just such overtly stylistic but ultimately social and moral grounds. What complicates the issue in Wittgenstein's case – as he seems to have realized in advance – is the way that this figural dimension of his writing would turn out to work directly against its express therapeutic intent. No philosopher has done more to promote those forms of metaphoric/ metaphysical 'bewitchment by language' from which he hoped to deliver us once and for all. As his Viennese contemporary Karl Krauss remarked of Freudian psychoanalysis, Wittgenstein's philosophy looks very much like a symptom or even a contributory cause of the self-same disease that it purports to cure.

My point in all this is not – as often happens with 'deconstructive' readings of philosophical texts in a simplified, quasi-Derridean vein – to proclaim that those texts are pervaded by metaphor right down to their most basic, structuring concepts and hence (in a kind of belated revenge for Plato's jibes against the poets and rhetoricians) that literary critics have the edge on philosophers when it comes to deciphering that long-repressed or ignored figural dimension. Instead it is to show one particular way in which philosophy's ambivalence in this regard – or the failure to settle its account with metaphor – has likewise conduced to a particular kind of linguistic bewitchment, namely the fixation (in Wittgenstein and his exegetes) on a range of problems, such as that about 'following a rule', which have their source in the compulsive and contagious power of certain dominant figures of thought. What is needed in order to give philosophy peace is not some blanket Nietzschean affirmation to the effect that 'all concepts are metaphors', 'all reasoning rhetorical (or suasive) at bottom', 'all philosophy a sub-genre of literature' and so forth. Instead it is a heightened critical awareness of the way that certain highly specific metaphors can lead thinking astray in certain highly specific contexts of argument. I make this point in Chapters 1 and 2 with regard to Derrida's work and to the widespread misinterpretation of it, whether by champions like Richard Rorty, who admire him for supposedly having no truck with such old-hat philosophical distinctions, or by opponents in the analytic mainstream, like Searle, who attack or routinely dismiss that work on the same erroneous grounds. By turning to Wittgenstein in Chapter 6 I have sought to point up the salient contrast between a mode of philosophizing (Derrida's) that remains intensely and intently alive to those problems and another – Wittgenstein's – that claims to have resolved them while in fact strengthening and deepening their hold through a failure to acknowledge its own metaphorical commitments. Thus my discussion brings together the three main themes of this book: the relationship between philosophy and literary theory, the stand-off between 'analytic' and 'continental' schools of thought, and the question as to whether – or just how far – these various conflicts of aim and priority can be tempered or resolved through an opening up of hitherto entrenched disciplinary borders. As in previous chapters, so here: my conclusion is that all parties stand to gain by dismantling some of their defensive outworks though not (most emphatically) if that process goes so far as to fall in with Rorty's prescription for a postmodern-pragmatist, post-disciplinary and, to this extent, post-philosophical culture.

Chapter 7 argues to similar effect from a different angle of approach by examining various, sharply contrasted ways in which the 'linguistic turn' across various schools of recent (post-1960) philosophical thought has influenced debate on the issue of free-will versus determinism. It puts the case that this issue has very often been marginalized, finessed or effectively shunted out of sight by regarding it either (after Wittgenstein) as a pseudo-problem amenable to treatment in the linguistic-therapeutic mode or else – amongst those of a more 'analytical' leaning – as best resolved through the application of methods derived from a range of other disciplines including theoretical linguistics, cognitive psychology or neuroscience. The middle ground is occupied by Austin's appeal to the insights attainable through analysis of (so-called) 'ordinary language', that is to say, by application of the common-sense precept that instances of everyday, natural usage are likely to yield more nuanced and valuable insights into philosophy of mind, morals and action than any amount of mere 'armchair' theorizing. My chapter seeks to demarcate the scope and limits of these approaches, and also to evaluate the claims of an alternative, 'continental' (or post-Kantian mainland-European) line of philosophical descent which goes by way of Husserlian phenomenology and its subsequent refinements and critical elaboration by thinkers such as Merleau-Ponty and Derrida. I suggest that analytic philosophy has much to gain through a closer engagement with that 'other' tradition on account of its more sustained, open-minded, yet nonetheless rigorous treatment of the various antinomies – like those between free-will and determinism or expressive *vis-à-vis* purely indicative modes of utterance – that analytic philosophers of whichever persuasion tend to ignore or downplay. My claim is not that such thinking might offer a definitive solution to problems that surely go as deep as any in the history of Western philosophy but rather to indicate some paths unexplored in the context of current analytical debate. In one sense this is the chapter most remote from the 'fiction, philosophy and theory' theme that has run through my book in various forms and with increasing centrality and emphasis toward the end. However its relevance should not be missed by those who have followed the argument so far and registered my general point about the benefits brought by a creative or conceptually inventive mode of philosophical thinking such as tends to be more typical of work in the mainland-European than the mainstream Anglo-American line of descent. Thus it is not so much a matter of sinking the difference between philosophy and literature – as Rorty recommends and Habermas (wrongly) lays to Derrida's charge – but rather a question of remaining open to the kinds of exploratory or speculative thought that are sometimes better able to point a way forward from the doldrums of pure-bred conceptual analysis or of ordinary-language philosophy when raised to a high point of common-sense dogma.

As usual I have amassed a great number of debts, intellectual and personal, in the course of writing this book. I should like to thank my colleagues and postgraduate students in the Philosophy Section at Cardiff University for no end of helpful advice, intellectual stimulus and practical support along the way; also the various people (interlocutors, correspondents, seminar participants, conference organizers and others) who have provided a series of welcome opportunities for discussing work in progress. Among them let me give special mention to Manuel Barbeito and Alison Scott-Baumann for their constant encouragement and friendship as well as constructive criticism. Alison, Clare and Jenny were patient and supportive as ever, which is no small tribute after so many years of skewed priorities on my part. Above all I am indebted to Jacques Derrida – the fact of whose cruelly premature death it is still hard to take in – for his unfailing generosity, friendship, philosophical genius and (in these as in so many ways) his truly inspirational example.

Some parts of this book have appeared previously in journals and edited volumes. For permission to reprint that material in revised form I am grateful to Cambridge University Press, Edinburgh University Press and Routledge; also to the editors of *Southern Humanities Review* and *Harvard Review of Philosophy*.

Cardiff, November 2006

I

Deconstruction, Analysis and Deviant Logic: Derrida 'At the Limits of Thought'

I

My aim in this chapter is to make good the case that Derrida's writings – especially those of his earlier (pre-1980) period – are such as would repay the closest attention from philosophers of a broadly 'analytic' mind.[1] This case has been put by a number of recent commentators, among them (from various angles of approach and with varying degrees of conviction) Stanley Cavell, Newton Garver, Simon Glendinning, Marian Hobson, Stephen Mulhall, Graham Priest, A.W. Moore and Samuel C. Wheeler.[2] Indeed there is now a growing sense that the reception of Derrida's work has been badly skewed by certain contingent or largely extraneous cultural-historical factors. These would include its initial, highly enthusiastic take-up by anglophone literary and cultural theorists rather than professional philosophers and also the much-publicized exchange (the 'determined non-encounter', as Derrida described it) between himself and John Searle on the topic of Austinian speech-act philosophy.[3] One result of this episode was to convince many analytic philosophers – often, one suspects, on the basis of hearsay or second-hand polemical accounts – that Derrida simply had not grasped (or was out to subvert) all the standards of serious responsible debate.

That impression was further reinforced by Richard Rorty's claim, first advanced in an influential 1982 essay, that the chief value of Derrida's texts lay in their brilliantly inventive demonstration of what philosophy might become if it would just set aside its deluded quest for truth, rigour and constructive solutions to well-defined philosophic problems.[4] Thus we should read those texts as pointing the way toward a post-analytic (or 'post-philosophical') culture wherein such problems and wished-for solutions would no longer strike us as possessing the least degree of relevance or interest. Derrida had performed the great service of showing that philosophy was just another 'kind of writing' – along with poetry, fiction, history, anthropology, sociology and literary criticism, not to mention all the other human as well as natural sciences – whose chief merit was to come up with striking new metaphors, language-games or favoured modes of description rather than purporting to get things right in some ultimate, objective way. All the more unfortunate – in Rorty's view – that Derrida was prone, on occasion, to fall back into old philosophical ways of talking that merely replaced one set of false absolutes ('truth', 'reason', 'knowledge', 'correspondence', etc.) with another set of terms ('*différance*', 'supplement', 'trace', and so forth) which took on the same kind of privileged status, albeit in a shiny new deconstructive idiom. So likewise with his talk of 'logocentrism' and the Western 'metaphysics of presence', the effect of which – despite and against its professed intent – was to eke out philosophy's dwindling resources in a last, vain attempt at thinking on the grand scale. Nor should we be over-impressed when Derrida's earnest-minded disciples seek to reclaim his texts for philosophy by imputing to them a distinctive form of 'negative-transcendental' argument, or taking them to bring out a covert strain of deviant, non-classical or paraconsistent logic that has marked the discourse of 'Western metaphysics' from Plato to Husserl and beyond.[5] Much better, Rorty thinks, to ignore these misguided efforts on Derrida's behalf – even if they find warrant in some of his more 'philosophically' inclined texts – and just enjoy the new freedoms for creative 'redescription' opened up by his witty and metaphorically inventive style of writing. For we shall otherwise miss what is most valuable about that writing, namely its capacity to point a way beyond all those futile debates that have preoccupied philosophers in the mainstream (call it 'logocentric') tradition from Plato, *via* Descartes and Kant, to their present-day analytic progeny.

Thus, despite their sharply opposed valuations, Searle and Rorty are pretty much in agreement with regard to the character of Derrida's work and – more specifically – what sets it apart from the kinds of work carried on by those thinkers in the orthodox, reputable line of descent. Where Searle thinks it an affront to every standard of logic, reason and plain good sense, Rorty holds Derrida up as an example of the way that philosophy can and should go once relieved of such burdensome constraints. And again: where Searle sees nothing but confusion (or intellectual bad faith) in Derrida's habit of perversely raising problems or discovering logical anomalies at every turn, Rorty thinks it just a propaedeutic exercise which can best be left off – along with all those notions of philosophy as a constructive, problem-solving business – once we have taken Derrida's point. Such is the background, or a major part of it, to the reception of his work during the past three decades by most analytic philosophers, a reception marked chiefly by attitudes ranging from studied indifference, through curt dismissal, to unrelenting and (at times) near obsessive hostility.[6] Anyone who ventures into this zone with the idea of finding common ground or persuading analytic philosophers to take a second look is liable to feel – as Frank Kermode once wrote in a different though related context – like a pacifist who wanders onto no-man's land offering cigarettes all round and then gets shot at by both sides. Still there is every reason to make the effort since, in this case, the warring parties (analytic philosophers and 'continental' types with an equal and opposite aversion) have much to gain from a better understanding of just how Derrida's work relates to developments in the other tradition. That is to say it brings a sharp, a highly distinctive, and – in the best, non-parochial sense – a strongly *analytical* focus to bear on issues that are often viewed as the exclusive preserve of mainstream anglophone philosophy. Indeed there is a strong case to

be made that Derrida has raised some of those issues with a pertinence and force
– not merely (as critics like Searle would have it) a kind of perverse ingenuity –
that might yet shift the debate onto different and perhaps more fertile ground.

II

Such is at any rate the case put forward in this chapter. While my aim is not at
all to scratch at old sores by inveighing against a typecast 'analytic' opposition I
shall nonetheless seek to represent his work in a way that resists those distorted
characterizations. More constructively, I shall try to explain where Derrida's
thinking engages issues in two heartland regions of the analytic enterprise, that
is, philosophy of logic and philosophy of language. This will involve looking
closely at what he has to say concerning the status of classical (bivalent) logic vis-
à-vis certain non-classical, 'deviant', many-valued or paraconsistent alternative
systems, along with the question as to whether – or just how far – the classical
axioms might be suspended in response to counter-evidence of various kinds. In
each case Derrida's work offers something more than a contrasting 'view from
elsewhere', or a different way of approaching these topics unconstrained by the
dominant conventions of analytic discourse. Rather it can serve to reopen critical
perspectives on the mainstream analytic agenda which have been closed off since
that famous parting of the ways signalled by Frege's criticism of Husserl on
account of the residual psychologism that supposedly marked the phenomenological project, along with that other, more wholesale strain of anti-
'continental' thinking which first found expression in Russell's and Moore's
rejection of Hegelian idealism.[7]

To be sure, there is already a growing interest amongst some analytic (or
analytically trained) philosophers in the various points of contact – as well as the
missed opportunities or paths not taken – which must find a place in any
adequate account of that history. Thus, for instance, Michael Dummett and
others have made a start in re-assessing the relationship between Frege and
Husserl from a more balanced and open-minded even if (in Dummett's case) a
still markedly pro-Fregean standpoint.[8] Meanwhile Michael Friedman has cast
some revealing light on the famous 1929 Davos 'Disputation' between Heidegger and Ernst Cassirer which was also attended – and followed with keen
interest – by Rudolf Carnap, a leading figure in the emergent school of Vienna-
based logical positivism.[9] Friedman's purpose, in brief, is to question the
received, drastically dichotomist view first by showing that the two traditions –
or two of their most prominent figures – had at least some early interests in
common, and second by explaining the subsequent rift as a product of deep-laid
political and socio-cultural as well as more purely philosophical differences. So
there is now a fair amount of detailed work from a range of disciplinary perspectives that has helped both to clarify and to complicate the picture with
regard to such formative episodes. Beyond that, as I have said, there is a small
but growing literature which seeks to carry this project forward to the point

where Derrida's work can likewise be seen as a challenge and, in some ways, a source of disquiet but not just a standing provocation to thinkers in the analytic camp.[10]

However there is little agreement as to the precise nature of that challenge or where exactly it impinges on those thinkers' main interests and established topics of concern. One proposal – well short of the Rortian wholesale 'post-analytic' line but tending somewhat in that direction – is that Derrida's texts, especially his approach to Austinian speech-act theory, can be seen as espousing a kind of 'minimalist semantics', that is to say, an account of meaning, utterer's intention and communicative uptake that involves the least possible commitment in theoretical or philosophic terms.[11] On this view Derrida's thinking falls square with Donald Davidson's idea, in his essay 'A Nice Derangement of Epitaphs', that we get along for most communicative purposes through a process of largely ad hoc, context-specific, one-off intuitive grasp – a mixture of 'wit, luck and wisdom' – which relies hardly at all on 'prior theories' of the type that philosophers and linguists typically propound. Rather it draws upon 'passing theories' or hunches with regard to speaker's intent that are worked up pretty much from scratch on each occasion and require just a knack for guessing what people most likely have in mind (quite apart from what a prior theory would have them mean) on the evidence of various contextual clues and cues. It is to much the same effect, these thinkers maintain, that Derrida defines speech-act 'iterability' as simply what is left – the bare minimum of communicable sense – when one has deconstructed the Austinian notions of sincere, good-faith performative utterance and of appropriate context as that which decides whether or not a speech-act should be counted successful (or 'felicitous') in the absence of such criteria.[12]

Thus Derrida can best, most usefully, be understood as adopting a minimalist-semantic approach that finds little use for the kinds of large-scale, systematic theorizing indulged in by many linguists and philosophers of language, for example, those who advocate a representationalist theory of mental content or an account of propositional beliefs and attitudes based on that type of theory.[13] All we need in its place is a notion of communicative uptake which leaves enough room for the various ploys – the non-theorizable (since context-specific) adjustments, allowances and mutual accommodations – that speakers and listeners typically devise in figuring out each others' meanings and motives. Likewise, it is suggested, Derrida comes up with such a range of counter-instances and problematic or borderline cases as regards Austin's criteria for valid performative utterance that the sole remaining option is a kind of theory to end all theories, or a pragmatist approach that involves no more than contextually informed guesswork plus a readiness to apply the principle of charity (i.e., to maximize sense and relevance) where needed.[14] Thus deconstruction works out as a somewhat more circuitous route to the moderate post-analytic conclusion that much (not all) of what philosophers of language and speech-act theorists have laboured to provide is off-the-point for practical purposes and really, truth to tell, just a source of needless complications.

I have argued against this basically deflationist reading of Derrida's work on the grounds that it has to ignore such a deal of elaborate and often (*pace* Searle) logically exacting argument.[15] Besides, one may doubt that Davidson's approach – his idea that 'there is no such thing as a language', if by 'language' is signified what philosophers mostly have in mind when they attempt to provide an adequate theory of meaning or utterer's intent – can come close to explaining the complexities of everyday communicative discourse, let alone what transpires in episodes of cross-cultural or inter-lingual exchange. This understanding of Derrida ignores both the problems with that whole Davidsonian line of argument and also the extent to which Derrida's texts controvert any claim that such issues in philosophy of mind, language and logic can be simply got over by declaring them no longer a topic of serious concern. Thus Derrida is not merely poking fun – or trying to turn the tables – when he takes issue with Searle's indignant claim that he (Derrida) has muddied the waters of Austinian speech-act theory by demanding too much conceptual rigour in an area ('ordinary language') where one cannot reasonably make such demands, or not without knowing full well in advance that they will not be met.[16] According to Searle it is only by means of this well-tried sophistical device that Derrida is able to catch Austin out in the various (supposed) anomalies, non-sequiturs and deviant instances which then become the basis – or a handy pretext – for his deconstructive reading. Had he just taken Austin's sensible point and acknowledged the limits to conceptual precision or the due allowance for borderline cases that is always required in dealing with matters of everyday, non-philosophical usage then Derrida could scarcely have pressed so far with his misconceived claims for the radical 'undecidability' of speaker's intent or contextual warrant.

Yet Derrida then comes back against Searle with a series of shrewdly aimed remarks to the effect that philosophy is no place for such vague or merely 'approximative' notions; that when addressing those issues there is always a need for the maximum degree of conceptual precision; that a classical (bivalent) logic of truth and falsehood is the *sine qua non* for any theory that would clarify the nature of speech-act meaning or intent; and hence that Searle's over-ready resort to a quasi-'logic' of vague, indeterminate or fuzzily defined pseudo-'concepts' is a move that defeats his self-professed aim of constructing just such a theory.[17] To be sure, the outcome of Derrida's reading is to reveal certain stress points or logical anomalies, that is to say, passages in Austin's text where the theory runs up against recalcitrant examples or resistance to its own more categorical claims. These eventually require the adoption of a different, non-classical or 'supplementary' logic, one that can accommodate the various problems that result from the attempt to lay down clear-cut (true-or-false) criteria for what properly counts as an instance of sincere, good-faith performative utterance or – failing that – as the right sort of context for deciding the issue either way. However, Derrida insists, a deconstructive approach is very far from suggesting that we simply abandon those classical standards and adopt the 'approximative' logic or pragmatist line of least resistance recommended by Searle as an answer to all these problems. Rather it entails thinking them through with the utmost logical rigour and conceptual precision right up to the point where speech-act theory encounters some strictly unavoidable dilemma that cannot be resolved (merely shunted aside or declared off-limits) by any such face-saving device. Only at this point – where reading comes up against anomalies unthinkable in bivalent terms – can the theorist be justified in resorting to a non-standard, 'supplementary' logic which, so far from resolving these issues, serves to keep them very much the chief focus of attention and emphasize the challenge they pose to any straightforward, classically consistent exposition of speech-act theory. Otherwise it becomes just a shifty, all-purpose device for avoiding the kind of patient, meticulous, probing analysis that seeks to locate precisely those passages where a text exhibits its most problematic but also, by the same token, its most philosophically revealing aspects.

III

So it is not just a show of mock outrage or pious regard for the analytic virtues when Derrida declares himself frankly bewildered at Searle's willingness to set such problems aside by relaxing the standards which should always apply wherever it is a question of getting straight about the logical grammar of our speech-acts, performative commitments, appeals to validating context and so forth, as opposed to a question of what makes sense for everyday-communicative purposes. Thus:

> From the moment that Searle entrusts himself to an oppositional logic, to the 'distinction' of concepts by 'contrast' or 'opposition' (a legitimate demand that I share with him, even if I do not at all elicit the same consequences from it), I have difficulty seeing how he is nevertheless able to write [that] phrase ... in which he credits me with the 'assumption', 'oddly enough derived from logical positivism', 'that unless a distinction can be made rigorous and precise, it is not really a distinction at all'.[18]

On the contrary: it is only by maintaining such distinctions to the limit of their applicability – to the point where they run up against textual aporias beyond their power to conceptualize in clear-cut (bivalent) terms – that philosophy can claim genuine warrant for raising these issues with regard to the scope and status of classical logic. Thus, as Derrida puts it (again *contra* Searle): 'not only do I find this logic strong, and, in conceptual language and analysis, *an absolute must [il la faut]*, it must ... be sustained against all empirical confusion, to the point where the same demand of rigour requires the structure of that logic to be transformed or complicated'.[19] This claim is borne out, as I have argued elsewhere, by Derrida's analysis of sundry canonical works – from Plato and Aristotle to Rousseau, Kant, Husserl and Austin – which resist the application of classical logic yet can be shown to do so only on condition that they are held accountable to just such a reading until it breaks down on certain recalcitrant passages or textual details.[20] That is to say, Derrida rejects any version of the revisability thesis with regard to such axioms as bivalence, excluded middle or (at the limit) non-contradiction that would countenance adopting some alternative logical system as a matter of pragmatic convenience or choice, rather than as the outcome of a process of rigorously argued conceptual exegesis. This puts him decidedly at odds with those philosophers in the analytic tradition who take an altogether more relaxed and accommodating line on this issue, that is, a revisionist approach that sets a much lower threshold of acceptability for what justifies the switch to one or another non-classical or 'deviant' system.

Among them are Quine, who famously proposed that changing our logic might sometimes be the best, most pragmatically efficacious policy when a cherished scientific theory is under threat from anomalous empirical data, and Hilary Putnam, who has put the case (following von Neumann, Reichenbach and others) for adopting a three-valued logic in response to certain otherwise problematical phenomena such as quantum superposition and wave/particle dualism.[21] Then there are philosophers of logic who suggest various ways of refining, extending or (again at the limit) abandoning the classical axioms so as to create a more flexible system, one that more readily stretches around the kinds of everyday, practical reasoning whose methods elude such formal regimentation. Their proposals range from a many-valued logic that relativizes truth to degrees of probability or epistemic warrant – so that the value for any given statement would fall somewhere on the scale of real numbers between '1 = true' and '0 = false' – to a fuzzy logic that approximates an analogue (i.e., continuously varying) rather than digital (discrete, either/or) mode of computation.[22] Also there are systems which conserve a good part of the standard apparatus (i.e., the first-order propositional and predicate calculi) but go beyond it to encompass modal aspects of necessity and possibility, or which make allowance — as in tense-logic — for temporal relations that are held to bear crucially on issues of assertible truth and falsehood.[23] In addition there are epistemic or doxastic logics designed to distinguish valid from invalid inference with respect to particular, more-or-less adequate states of knowledge or belief, and deontic logics concerned to specify the precise order of relationship between statements containing such ethically salient expressions as 'ought', 'can', 'must', 'should', 'is capable of' and so forth.[24] Advocates of relevance logic maintain that the premise and conclusion of any valid inference must be linked in a germane, that is, substantive or non-arbitrary way since there is something absurd about a system – like the classical deductivist model – that leads to such plainly counter-intuitive results as the law of contradiction according to which any statement of the form $p.\neg p$ entails the truth of every statement whatsoever along with that of its negation.[25] Other thinkers, notably Graham Priest, have pressed even further with the strong-revisionist case and recommended the adoption of a dialethic or paraconsistent approach that admits contradictions (and suspends other classical axioms) for various argumentative purposes.[26]

It is against this background of currently very active debate concerning the scope, limits and pertinence of formal logic that Derrida's exchange with Searle can most usefully be viewed. On the one hand Searle is in good, if somewhat motley company when he protests – with warrant from Aristotle – that logical rigour and conceptual exactitude are not so much absolute virtues as standards which can and should apply in some contexts, but not (or at any rate not so strictly) in others. Nevertheless Derrida makes a strong case for the indispensability of classical (bivalent) logic as a means of locating those stress points or moments of strictly inescapable aporia that emerge through a deconstructive reading of texts from Plato to Husserl and Austin. Thus he takes a more conservative view of these issues than thinkers like Quine, Putnam and especially Priest who would endorse the revisability thesis – whether on principled, pragmatic or science-led grounds – as a ready-to-hand option rather than an option of strictly last resort in the face of certain otherwise intractable problems with the logical or argumentative structure of those same texts. That is to say, Derrida rejects the idea (the 'empiricist confusion', as he would call it) that we could ever claim *rational* warrant for suspending the ground rules of bivalent logic in response to some anomaly turned up in the course of scientific investigation, or some conflict between a well-entrenched theory and a discrepant empirical finding. Still less would he accept the Quinean dictum that changes in our logic should best be viewed as a matter of 'pragmatic convenience', or of working an intelligible structure into the chaos of sensory stimuli while seeking to avoid such conflicts by making adjustments where needed and thereby conserving maximum coherence across the entire current 'fabric' of beliefs-held-true.[27] For this strain of radical empiricism suffers from a marked normativity deficit, that is, an ultimate failure to explain how any given episode of scientific theory change could ever be counted a *rational, constructive and knowledge-conducive* answer to problems with the precursor theory, rather than a kind of ad hoc manoeuvre for defusing conflicts as soon as they arise.[28]

The same charge can be levelled against other revisionist proposals, like the notion of a non-classical 'quantum logic' that would offer an escape route from the various conceptual problems thrown up by quantum mechanics on the orthodox interpretation through the simple expedient of introducing a third (indeterminate, 'both-true-and-false' or 'neither-true-nor-false') value just in order to avoid those problems.[29] Here again, the result of adopting such a view – clearly visible in many debates on this topic – is to deflect any challenge from the realist quarter that would hold quantum theory duly accountable to standards of valid logical argument and inference to the best, most rational or adequate causal-realist explanation. Hence the case against quantum logic often mounted by those in the dissident tradition, like David Bohm, who have considered it just a shifty device for disguising the radical 'incompleteness' of the orthodox theory and excusing its failure – indeed, its doctrinaire refusal – to go beyond the empirical-predictive data and offer a credible realist ontology.[30] Hence also Derrida's case against Searle with respect to the risk of 'empiricist confusion', the inadmissibility of ill-defined or fuzzy concepts in philosophy of language or logic, and the absolute need for 'precise and rigorous distinctions' where these disciplines are concerned. At any rate there is much of interest to be found in Derrida's engagement with these issues and, more specifically, his way of engaging them through a close exegesis of texts which is no less rigorous and cogently argued for its raising crucial questions with regard to the scope and limits of classical logic.

One useful way of making this point is to read Derrida's own texts with the same attentiveness to matters of detail and to longer-range structures of logico-semantic implication that typifies his commentaries on Plato, Rousseau, Husserl, Austin and others. What then emerges – as I have argued at length elsewhere – is a remarkably rich and sustained meditation on precisely those forms of non-standard (e.g., modal, epistemic, doxastic, deontic and temporal) logic that have been much discussed by analytic philosophers during the past few decades.[31] Nowhere is this more apparent than in the reading of Rousseau that dominates *Of Grammatology*, a reading focused on precisely the range of complex and (at times) tortuous locutions that Rousseau is compelled to adopt when attempting to make good his claims for the intrinsic priority of nature over culture, speech over writing, melody over harmony, passion over reason, metaphor over concept, the primitive over the civilized and so forth.[32] In each case Rousseau's express declarations – what he clearly 'wants to say' on a straightforward (intentionalist) account – are overtaken and thrown into doubt by a 'supplementary' logic whose regular effect is to invert, unsettle or desta-bilize that order of priorities.

What a deconstructive reading thus seeks to bring out is 'a certain rela-tionship, unperceived by the writer, between what he commands and what he does not command of the patterns of the language that he uses'.[33] In Rousseau this most often takes the form of a swerve from the indicative to the subjunctive mood, or from factual statements to speculative claims and hypotheses, or from modal expressions asserting some (purported) necessary truth to expressions whose modality seems to concern what *might* (possibly) or *should* (ideally) have been the case. Also there is a frequent switching about from one tense to another, as for instance when Rousseau gestures toward that idyllic state of social (more precisely: of pre-social) existence that serves as a foil to the corrupting effects of latter-day 'civilized' life yet the historical location of which – even its reality as anything other than a wishful mythic projection – is constantly called into doubt. These complications of tense combine with the other, above-mentioned shifts of mood, modality and assertoric force so as to create quite extraordinary tensions between what Rousseau clearly *means to say* in any given instance and what his statements are *constrained to mean* by the logic of his own discourse. Such is '[the] difference between implication, nominal presence, and thematic application' that runs like a single though intricately knotted thread through the entire corpus of Rousseau's writings on nature, culture, history, civil society, ethics, language, music and the various (especially sexual) aspects of his life-experience as narrated in the *Confessions*.[34]

IV

Thus Rousseau stands as a particularly striking example of the more general truth: that 'the writer writes *in* a language and *in* a logic whose proper system, laws, and life his discourse by definition cannot dominate absolutely [since] he uses them only by letting himself, after a fashion and up to a point, be governed by the system'.[35] Again it is worth noting the distance between this and the Davidsonian 'minimalist-semantic' line espoused by some post-analytic philosophers who take it to converge rather nicely with Derrida's thoughts about 'iterability' as the likewise minimalist, that is, 'metaphysically' unencumbered, basis for a theory of linguistic meaning and communicative grasp.[36] For if one thing is clear from Derrida's deconstructive reading of Rousseau it is that he goes some highly complex logical, as well as exegetical, ways around in bringing out the sheer resistance of Rousseau's text to a reading premised on classical (bivalent) modes of thought.

Such is indeed the 'logic of supplementarity' as it works to destabilize those various binary oppositions or conceptual distinctions which are nonetheless strictly indispensable to any adequate critical account. 'It is a matter', Derrida writes, 'of Rousseau's situation within the language and the logic that assures to this word or this concept sufficiently *surprising* resources so that the presumed subject of the sentence might always say, through using the "supplement", more, less, or something other than *he would mean* [*voudrait dire*].'[37] Nothing could be further from Davidson's idea that, for everyday communicative as well as philosophical purposes, we are better off dumping all that otiose stuff about propositional contents, attitudes, beliefs and so forth, and accepting that what people mean *just is* whatever we take them to mean on the best circumstantial evidence to hand plus a sense-optimizing 'principle of charity' and – beyond that – our normal, practically acquired supply of intuitive 'luck, wit and wisdom'.[38] On this view, as on Rorty's, a large pinch of salt is required when Derrida starts up about topics like the 'logic of supplementarity' (along with 'logocentrism', '*différance*', or the ubiquitous 'metaphysics of presence') since they are really just a sign of his falling back into the discourse of old-style system-building philosophy, albeit with a negative or deconstructive spin.

The alternative view is that Derrida, at least in a good proportion of his earlier writings, can usefully and justifiably be read as a thinker with original contributions to make in philosophy of logic and other central areas of recent analytic debate. This is *not* to say – as his detractors (or most of them) would have it – that analytic philosophy in the received, parochial sense of that term straightforwardly equates with all the virtues of rigorous, conceptually and logically disciplined thought as distinct from the typecast 'continental' excesses to which it stands squarely opposed. Rather it is to say that all good philosophy partakes of those virtues by very definition and that Derrida's work is no exception to this rule even while it raises questions and explores issues – not least in philosophy of logic – that have received nothing like this kind of attention from mainstream analytic thinkers. Take for instance the following, fairly typical passage where Derrida remarks on the various complications of modality and tense-logic that characterize Rousseau's attempt to explain how language and music both took rise from a common source, that is, the natural wellspring of passionate speech-song. Somehow we are to think that this source would not yet have been corrupted by the adventitious 'supplements' of grammar and harmony despite Rousseau's implicit acceptance — signalled by those same complications — that grammar and harmony *are and always were* integral to the very nature of language and music. Thus:

> Instead of concluding from this simultaneity [i.e., their common point of origin] that the song broached itself in grammar, that difference had already begun to corrupt melody, to make both it and its laws possible at the same time, Rousseau prefers to believe that grammar *must (should) have* been comprised ... within melody. There *must (should) have* been pleni-tude and not lack, presence without difference. From then on the dan-gerous supplement, scale of harmony, *adds itself from the outside as evil and lack* to happy and innocent plenitude. It would come from an outside which would be simply the outside. This conforms to the logic of identity and to the principle of classical ontology (the outside is outside, being is, etc.) but not to the logic of supplementarity, which would have it that the outside be inside, that the other and the lack come to add themselves as a plus that replaces a minus, that what adds itself to something takes the place of a default in the thing, that the default, as the outside of the inside, should be already within the inside, etc. What Rousseau in fact describes is that the lack, adding itself as a plus to a plus, cuts into an energy which *must (should) have* been and remain intact.[39]

What this passage brings out to striking effect is the way that Derrida reads against the grain of Rousseau's overt intent — against what Rousseau quite plainly and self-evidently meant to say — yet does so always with the strictest regard both for matters of textual detail and for standards of logical consistency and truth. Indeed it is precisely by respecting this double and, as it might seem, contradictory imperative that Derrida is able to develop his case with regard to the 'supplementary' logic at work in Rousseau's text, or what he calls '[the] difference between implication, nominal presence, and thematic application'.

Moreover — as this last phrase strongly suggests — that case has a bearing not only on issues in philosophy of logic and language but also on the way such issues connect with matters of real-world, empirical or experiential import. Thus it is a truth borne out by reflection on the nature and structure of musical experience, as well as through a deconstructive reading of Rousseau's text, that any claim for the absolute priority of melody over harmony will prove unsus-tainable once subject to critical questioning. That is to say, our perceptions of melody are ineluctably shaped, informed and made possible by the element of harmony that goes along with any sense of melodic outline or character, even in the case of that unadorned (monodic) singing line that Rousseau takes to be the source and perfection of music's expressive power. Together with this basically phenomenological argument (i.e., one grounded in the modalities of human perceptual and cognitive response) there is also an argument from the properties of music as a physical-acoustic phenomenon, among them – crucially – the fact that any single note sounded in apparent isolation will always be accompanied by a whole complex series of more or less remote harmonic overtones, ascending and descending through the circle of fifths. So when a sequence of notes is sung or played then the resultant melody (and our perception of it) cannot be conceived as existing apart from this constant and strictly inseparable sense of harmonic implication. In short, contrary to Rousseau's overt claim, harmony is an absolute prerequisite or condition of possibility for melody, a 'supplement' not in the depreciative sense 'that which can always (yet should not) be added on as a mere accessory or optional extra', but in the opposite, palliative sense: 'that which alone makes up or makes good some otherwise irremediable lack in what purports to be perfectly autonomous and self-sufficient'.

It is this same curious but nonetheless powerful and insistent double logic that Derrida pursues through Rousseau's writings on the origin and development of language where it involves the 'supplementary' role of grammar, structure and 'articulation' *vis-à-vis* the supposed self-sufficiency of passional or purely expressive speech. So likewise with his outlook on the history of civilization where it has to do with the imaginary ideal of a long-lost organic community as yet untouched by the evils of cultural and socio-political distinction, and on the wished-for return to a state of nature that would somehow restore that idyllic state while remaining a *society* and hence (by definition) embodying a cultural rather than a natural order of existence. It is through Rousseau's effort to negotiate these various deep-laid aporias – and through Derrida's tenacious, logically acute attempt to make rational sense of them – that we grasp certain basic (if easily forgotten) truths about language, music and society that would otherwise achieve nothing like the same degree of thematic and philosophic salience.

This is why, as I have said, Derrida holds out against the 'strong' revisability thesis with regard to non-bivalence, excluded middle or any axiom of classical logic that might come into conflict with this or that item of (presumed) empirical evidence. Where such proposals break down – as with Quine's ontological-relativist doctrine of wholesale pragmatic adjustment – is in leaving no room for rational theory choice or for any principled, that is, non-arbitrary verdict as to which, amongst two or more competing theories, most closely conforms to well-tried methods of scientific reasoning or inference to the best explanation.[40] Hence (to repeat) the chief objection to that idea for 'resolving' the conceptual problems with quantum mechanics that would recommend switching to a three-valued logic in order to conserve the empirical-predictive data, but which thereby renounces not only the most basic standards of rational consistency and truth but also the prospect of advancing beyond those same empirical data to a credible realist ontology.[41] What Derrida's readings show, by contrast, is the fact that a sufficiently close attention to the detail of certain texts, joined to an adequately rigorous account of their logical blind spots or aporias, can yield certain highly revealing insights into the nature and structure of real-world situated human perceptual and cognitive experience. Thus, despite his typically 'French' mistrust of empiricism in any form, Derrida is very far from taking the line – adopted most forcefully by Frege in his famous riposte to J.S. Mill – that logic and the formal sciences have to do with a realm of absolute, ideal objectivities which intrinsically transcend any possible reference to matters of empirical warrant.[42] On the contrary: a striking feature of Derrida's texts is the way that they bring out precisely that connection, so repugnant to Frege, between matters of logical validity and truth (in this case, the logical *impossibility* of consistently maintaining certain value-laden conceptual oppositions) and matters of empirical fact, such as the necessary imbrication of harmony with melody or the elements of structure that are present in all, even the most 'primitive' forms of language and social existence. That is to say, his readings never ignore the priority of logic – and classical, bivalent logic at that – as the *sine qua non* of conceptually precise (as opposed to vaguely 'approximative') argument even while they acknowledge, as can scarcely be denied, that the ground rules of valid inference are directly involved with manifold aspects of our everyday practical lives.

My point, briefly put, is that Derrida's writings on (among others) Rousseau and Austin are none the less rigorous and closely observant of those ground rules for the facts (1) that he discovers certain logical anomalies which complicate any straightforward exegesis in classical or bivalent terms, and (2) that he makes a point of relating such anomalies to certain likewise problematic but strictly unignorable aspects of our cultural, historical and linguistic-communicative modes of understanding. In other words – pursuant to both these claims – Derrida sees no merit in adopting an approach that would slacken or relax the requirements of logical precision to the point where they become little more than convenient rules of thumb, to be followed just so far as they promote coherence amongst our various theories, observations and standing beliefs but revised or abandoned as soon as they generate some otherwise intractable conflict. 'When a concept is to be treated as a concept', Derrida insists,

> [o]ne has to accept the logic of all or nothing ... at any rate, in a theoretical or philosophical discussion of concepts or of things conceptualizable. Whenever one feels obliged to stop doing this (as happens to me when I speak of *différance*, of mark, of supplement, of iterability and of all they entail), it is better to make explicit in the most conceptual, rigorous, formalizing, and pedagogical manner possible the reasons one has for doing so, for thus changing the rules and the context of discourse.[43]

What I have sought to show here is that there is indeed a 'logic of deconstruction' and that it shares certain features with other recently developed forms of deviant, many-valued or non-classical logic. However I would once again emphasize the point that Derrida's various, closely related expositions – of 'supplementarity' in Rousseau, 'parergonality' in Kant, '*différance*' in Husserl, and so forth – are able to articulate their terms and conditions only by meticulously thinking through those problems that arise in the reading of texts which turn out to resist the best efforts of bivalent truth-functional analysis.[44] It seems to me that there is much to be learned from his example by analytic philosophers with an open mind and a willingness to bring something like that same degree of close-focused logical acuity to the reading of Derrida's work. Very often they tend to raise these issues either in a highly speculative form with minimal reflection on their pertinence to questions of practical applicability or else with reference to disputed areas of physical theory – such as quantum mechanics – where the effect of adopting a non-standard logic is to shunt aside more substantive (e.g., causal-explanatory) concerns for the sake of upholding a received account or saving empirical appearances. Such has been the chief objection to quantum logic, whether voiced by more 'conservative' logicians or by philosophers of science – like Popper and other opponents of the orthodox (Copenhagen) theory – who see it as just a handy device for staving off awkward or maybe insoluble problems.[45]

V

I should acknowledge that my reading of Derrida here, especially my alignment of his work with certain aspects of that anti-revisionist case, might not find favour with some commentators. Of course it will be rejected outright by those, like Searle, who would deny him the right to a serious hearing on matters of language, logic or philosophy in general. Nor will it carry much weight with those – like Rorty – who would urge us to regard all that technical-sounding stuff as just a tedious irrelevance, unlikely to detain readers who have come to appreciate the liberating power of Derrida's stylistic genius. I have perhaps said enough about the skewed understanding of his work that unites these two, otherwise sharply opposed, perspectives. What I have in mind here is that alternative view according to which Derrida has indeed made valid contributions to philosophy of language and logic, but only in so far as we accept some version of the strong revisability thesis. This might have to do with the bearing of a deconstructive ('supplementary') logic on issues in quantum theory and with their joint implication for our thinking about questions of scientific knowledge and truth. Or again, it might concern the relevance of Derrida's work on Plato, Rousseau, Austin and others to the idea of a paraconsistent (or dialethic) logic that would dispense not only with bivalence and excluded middle but also – more drastically – with the law of contradiction.

Thus, for instance, Arkady Plotnitsky has argued that Derrida's broaching of a 'general' as opposed to a 'restricted' economy of logic, language and representation is one that brings him out on the same conceptual (or post-conceptual) terrain as was occupied by Niels Bohr in his likewise radical break with all the governing assumptions of a 'classical' realist ontology and epistemology.[46] From this point of view it is a downright retrograde move – that is to say, a reversion to pre-quantum and pre-deconstructive ways of thinking – that would represent Derridean logic as still respecting those classical standards even where they are forced up (as I have sought to show here) against their limits of logical intelligibility. Yet there is a great deal of evidence in Derrida's texts – in the detailed working out of his arguments as well as in the various explicit disclaimers that I have cited from his second-round rejoinder to Searle – that he rejects the ultra-revisionist line on such matters that Plotnitsky regards as strictly unavoidable once we have followed Derrida and Bohr beyond the utmost range of those classical resources.

The same may be said of proposals, such as that of Graham Priest, for treating Derrida's 'supplementary' logic (along with its various cognates) as a para-consistent or dialethic mode of reasoning that might always entail the suspension or abandonment of the law of non-contradiction.[47] For there is a crucial difference – here as in quantum-theoretical debate – between entertaining such drastic revisions as a matter of policy or choice and allowing that they might (disturbingly) emerge at some point in the course of striving to make better sense of a complex philosophical text or seeking a solution to the problems and paradoxes of orthodox quantum theory. In these latter sorts of case what results is more like a form of *reductio ad absurdum*, that is, a drawing out of logical implications arrived at by applying the strictest standards of bivalent logic but yielding a pair of contradictory results or an outcome sharply at odds with those same standards. Thus when Derrida reads Austin he does so not (like Searle) on the assumption that, in dealing with 'ordinary language', one must suitably relax one's operative standards for what should count as an adequate, well-defined conceptual distinction with regard to (say) valid as opposed to invalid forms of speech-act utterance, or proper as opposed to improper contexts within which those speech-acts may be thought to occur. Rather he does so on the contrary assumption – one that puts Derrida (ironically enough) more in the company of 'hard line' analytic than of typecast 'ordinary-language' philosophers – that when it comes to the business of *theorizing* speech-acts or examining the *logic* of our everyday linguistic practices then one had better maintain the most exacting criteria of logical accountability right up to the point where they encounter some strictly unavoidable anomaly or counter-instance. For otherwise those problems simply will not register, subject as they would be to a Quinean process of pragmatic re-adjustment across the whole web of beliefs (including logical axioms) currently held true, or a paraconsistent conjuring away of any looming contradiction, or the quantum-logical introduction of a third (indeterminate) truth-value that 'resolves' the anomalies of superposition and wave/particle dualism.

To this extent – *contra* widespread report – Derrida can be seen to side with those (whether realists about quantum mechanics or sceptics about the more radical varieties of deviant logic) who argue that the chief result of adopting such views would be to stifle criticism, neutralize productive disagreement, and thereby block any prospect of advance in science and other fields of enquiry.[48]

Moreover, there is a strong (if heterodox) case to be made that Derrida's deconstructive readings of texts in the Western 'logocentric' tradition from Plato to Descartes, Kant, Husserl and Austin have much in common with the kinds of 'rational-reconstructive' approach adopted by analytic philosophers from Bertrand Russell to Jonathan Bennett.[49] This is not to deny the obvious differences, among them the analytic presumption that philosophical arguments – their purport, content, structure, truth-conditions, modes of valid inference and so forth – may indeed be 'textual' in the straightforward sense of depending on forms of written communication and yet be subject to rational debate without constantly adverting to this fact as a high point of deconstructive principle. That difference no doubt goes deep, involving as it does the further presumption that, although the concern with issues of language has become a virtual trademark of analytic philosophy (even, as Dummett maintains, its chief constitutive feature) still there are concepts, logical relations and validity-conditions which cannot be reduced without remainder to their forms of linguistic expression.[50] Such, after all, is the tension that has characterized analytical philosophy during the past half-century and more, namely that between an *echt*-analytic approach in the Frege–Russell mode which strives to disambiguate everyday usage by revealing its subjacent logico-semantic structures and, on the other hand, an 'ordinary language' approach (deriving from Wittgenstein or Austin) which rejects that programme as a chronic misconception of philosophy's proper role.[51] I have written elsewhere about the problems that arise – notably in Dummett's case – with the attempt to combine these two, radically divergent views in the form of an anti-realist (or updated verificationist) theory of meaning and truth.[52] My point here, in relation to Derrida, is that there do exist other modes of analysis that have likewise taken the linguistic turn and followed out its far-reaching critical implications for the logocentric 'way of ideas' yet have also retained (unlike more orthodox versions of the Wittgensteinian approach) a keen sense of those conceptual problems which cannot be wished away by any amount of applied linguistic therapy.

It is for this reason also that Derrida's work very firmly resists Rorty's characterization of it as a post-philosophical new 'kind of writing' that is best, most rewardingly read for the sake of its inventive metaphors, narrative games and elaborate textualist jokes at the expense of all that earnest seeking after truth from Descartes to the analytic schools. Very often differences of view about this are aired through debates as to whether or not Derrida is a 'transcendental philosopher', that is to say, whether or not he deploys a form of transcendental reasoning from the conditions of possibility for some given aspect of human experience, knowledge or judgement.[53] More precisely, what is at issue is a negative twist on this Kantian mode of argument whereby a deconstructive analysis sets out to demonstrate the logically necessary conditions of *im*possibility for maintaining certain conceptual distinctions, such as those that Derrida locates in his readings of (among others) Rousseau and Austin. Thus Rorty's claim that there is no such thing as a transcendental argument – since any appeal to such demonstrative, *a priori* grounds for asserting this or that to be the case is really just a species of rhetorical hand waving – goes along with his view of Derrida's work as a kind of writing occasionally prone to delusions of episte-mological grandeur but otherwise an excellent remedy for them.[54] I would suggest, on the contrary, that it is just this form of negative-transcendental reasoning that undergirds Derrida's various demonstrations of the way in which a textual close reading premised on the axioms of classical (bivalent) logic gives rise to contradictory entailments that are strictly unthinkable within that logic. This is why I have risked raising a few hackles with my argument that Derrida's work not only merits the title 'analytic philosophy' but in some respects lays a stronger claim to it than much of what currently bears that description. It is also why I suggested that his deconstructive approach to texts shows a certain kin-ship – unlikely as this may seem at first blush – with the kinds of rational-reconstructive commentary that hard-headed analysts such as Jonathan Bennett provide when they read the work of past philosophers with a view to sifting what is valid in their thought by present-day philosophic lights from what belongs to the history of bygone, false or now discredited ideas.[55]

Not that I would wish to push this comparison too hard, given their marked divergence of views when it comes to the question of just how much can be imputed to a text in the way of oblique philosophical insight if one follows Derrida (as against Bennett) with regard to the potential yield of an approach that goes beyond the warrant of express authorial intent to the various, often unlooked-for implications that emerge through a deconstructive reading. Hence, to repeat, Derrida's assertion in *Of Grammatology* that such readings have to do with 'a certain relationship, unperceived by the writer, between what he com-mands and what he does not command of the patterns of the language that he uses'.[56] And again, more specifically, the work of deconstruction,

[c]annot consist of reproducing, by the effaced and respectful doubling of commentary, the conscious, voluntary, intentional relationship that the writer institutes in his exchanges with the history to which he belongs thanks to the element of language. This moment of doubling commentary should no doubt have its place in a critical reading. To recognize and respect all its classical exigencies is not easy and requires all the instru-ments of traditional criticism. Without this recognition and this respect, critical production would risk developing in any direction at all and authorize itself to say almost anything. But this indispensable guardrail has always only *protected*, it has never *opened*, a reading.[57]

None of which – one imagines – would cut much ice with Bennett, committed as he is to the analytic premise that concepts, propositions, arguments, truth-claims, justificatory criteria and so forth are up for philosophical assessment on their merits and not through some super-subtle technique of reading that brings them out more closely in accord with the interpreter's own predilections. Thus Bennett – like Russell – comes at the business of learning from past thinkers very much on a basis of 'credit where credit's due', that is, by readily acknowledging their positive achievements (as gauged by our current best philosophic lights) but also by remarking on the errors and confusions which (again from a present-day perspective) can often be seen to have resulted from their under-developed logical resources or their limited powers of analytic grasp.

What would seem to set this approach squarely apart from Derrida's as described in the passage cited above is Bennett's confidence that one can indeed have access, by way of careful reading, to the 'conscious, voluntary, intentional relationship that the writer institutes in his exchanges with the history to which he belongs thanks to the element of language'. Moreover it is clear that, for Bennett, there is no real problem about combining the tasks of exegesis and critique, or on the one hand that of seeking to establish what a thinker originally had in mind through application of the best scholarly interpretative methods, and on the other that of showing where and how their intentions may have missed the philosophic mark. Least of all does it strike Bennett, or other exponents of the rational-reconstructive approach, that one might have to tread a precarious path between the 'effaced and respectful doubling of commentary' and the risk that, 'without this recognition and this respect, critical production would risk developing in any direction at all and authorise itself to say almost anything'. Thus whereas, for Derrida, the notion of fidelity to author's intent as an 'indispensable guardrail' is one that poses all sorts of hermeneutic problems, for Bennett it is more simply a matter of first getting straight about just what it was they were trying to say, and then getting straight about just how successfully (or otherwise) they managed to argue their case.

Nothing, it seems, could more plainly illustrate the contrast between a 'continental' approach schooled in the complexities of textual understanding and an 'analytic' mode which takes it for granted that conceptual precision is the chief virtue of philosophic language, and hence that there is no difficulty in principle – whatever the occasional problems in practice – about the method of rational reconstruction. Yet I would venture that nobody could complete an attentive, intelligent and (above all) unprejudiced reading of Derrida on Plato, Rousseau, Kant, Husserl or Austin and of Bennett on Descartes, Spinoza, Leibniz, Locke, Berkeley, Hume and Kant without coming around to the view that these thinkers do after all have a good deal in common.[58] What they share, in brief, is a highly focused awareness of textual complications and a willingness to press hard on problematical passages where a reading of this kind may go sharply against the received or canonical view, yet for just that reason be a source of philosophical insights unobtainable by other, more conventional means. That is to say, it is a fallacy – albeit one strongly underwritten by likewise conventional views of the analytic/continental split – that one can *either* have the benefits (if such they are) of clear-headed logical rigour, *or* the rewards (if such they are) of deconstructive close reading, but surely not both since they owe allegiance to totally different, conflicting standards of reputable philosophic thought.

Such views in fact have a lot less to do with what has actually been going on in the 'two traditions' over these past few decades than with a certain culturally or professionally driven idea of what sets them apart. This is not to deny that Derrida and Bennett – taken as thinkers representative of each tradition at its most characteristic or (at times) its most extreme – do approach the business of conceptual exegesis with differing emphases and aims in mind. Thus Bennett could scarcely be brought to accept some of Derrida's more radical pronouncements with regard to the intrinsically figural character of philosophic discourse and the extent to which texts can be shown to complicate, challenge or deconstruct their own grounding premises while Derrida would likewise be quick to question some of Bennett's more confident statements with regard to the project of rational reconstruction as an exercise in applied critical thought. Indeed, as I have said, this difference goes deep – involving some basic issues in philosophy of language, logic and mind – and thereby does much to explain the highly cautious character of recent moves toward a certain *rapprochement* between the two traditions. Still it is worth citing a couple of passages from Bennett which might give pause to anyone who thinks that this is no more than ought to be expected, given their fundamental conflicts of interest. Thus:

> A scholar whose thought is continuously informed by a clear strong view about a work's overall purposes may overlook textual episodes that do not fit the pattern. When that happens, something is lost. Such a misfit passage can be the philosopher's fragmentary response to a half-recognised difficulty in his position, or his expression of a half-conscious insight that he hasn't turned into doctrine. One can learn from exploring a great philosopher's subliminal sensitivities as well as from studying his declared doctrinal programme. Certainly there is value in knowing all about a studied work's unity of purpose, but there is value of a different kind – less sedate and often more interesting – in approaching a masterpiece more openly and vulnerably, more ready to be surprised by it, never comfortable with it.[59]

This strikes me as an admirable brief statement not only of Bennett's aims and priorities in the project of rational reconstruction but also – though Bennett might wish to demur – of what Derrida achieves in his reading of texts from Plato to Austin. That is to say, if one places it alongside Derrida's above-cited passage concerning the issue of exegetical fidelity and the way that deconstruction seeks to bring out a 'certain relationship, unperceived by the writer, between what he commands and what he does not command of the patterns of the language that he uses', then one is likely to conclude that their two approaches are not, after all, so drastically at odds.

VI

This suggestion gains further credibility when Bennett goes on to offer some remarks very much in keeping with Derrida's point about respect for authorial intention, that is, that such respect may serve as an 'indispensable guardrail' which prevents interpretation from 'developing in any direction at all', and yet that it 'has always only *protected*, it has never *opened*, a reading'.[60] Bennett's main concern in raising this question is with the issue of how we can best, most profitably, try to comprehend both the original (intended) meaning and the present-day value or significance of a past thinker's work. 'Should we look', he asks, 'for the interpretation which (1) fits best with his intentions at the time of writing? (2) comes closest to making what he says true? (3) makes what he wrote most philosophically interesting and instructive?'[61] I would hope to have shown by now that Derrida is very far from summarily rejecting any of these approaches, even though – like Bennett – he sees then as involving a sometimes complex and difficult choice of priorities. As regards option (1), the idea is, in Bennett's words, that 'one's best chance of getting help from a great philosopher of the past is to plug into his mind, rather than dancing around in its vicinity waiting for lightning to strike'.[62] One could imagine many analytic philosophers, Bennett perhaps among them, taking this latter metaphorical turn as a fair description of Derrida's practice in the deconstructive reading of texts. Nevertheless, as we have seen, it would be wide of the mark since it ignores Derrida's engagement not only with the issue of authorial intent (how far it can or should constrain interpretation) but also with the closely related issue as to whether the truth-content of a text is best served by a reading which seeks to maximize that content on a Davidsonian principle of charity or by a critical reading alert to those truths which the text is unable fully or clearly to articulate. On this point Bennett is strikingly in accord with Derrida, since he sees no virtue in the kind of fideist reading that would deny itself such hard-won and hence (very often) intensely revealing critical insights in the name of a somewhat pious respect for authorial intent. Thus it may well be, Bennett writes, that 'the primary way to plug into [an author's] mind is of course to establish what he consciously wanted to communicate when he wrote'. However, '[this] objective is too narrow, because some of what is most instructive and revealing ... is to be found not in his consciously intended and openly proclaimed doctrines, but rather in the margins, between the lines, just beneath the surface'.[63]

One could hardly wish for a better formulation of Derrida's deconstructive way with texts, that is to say, his manner of combining a sedulous attention to matters of detail (often 'marginal' detail, at least by orthodox interpretative lights) with an acute awareness of those logical complexities that may turn out to harbour implications at odds with the manifest purport. Indeed, Bennett's phrasing catches precisely the tenor of Derrida's remarks about the problems of appealing to authorial intent as a source of interpretative guidance and the need to go beyond that restrictive (though doubtless 'indispensable') criterion if reading is to achieve any measure of critical insight. Thus we are perfectly justified, from a rational-reconstructive viewpoint, in questioning received, canonical ideas of what a thinker 'self-evidently' had to say as opposed to what he might have been constrained to imply (to concede 'in the margins' or admit 'between the lines') by the deviant logic of his own argument. Here it is worth noting that the term 'deviant' has a double signification. On the one hand (as in standard philosophical parlance) it can be taken as referring to any non-classical logic that suspends or abandons such precepts as bivalence or excluded middle. On the other – as with Derrida's and also, I would suggest, with Bennett's exegetical approach – it describes those presumably unconscious or at any rate involuntary swerves from express argumentative intent that characterize certain crucial, problematic, and (for just that reason) especially revealing passages in philosophic texts. What they are both keen to stress is that such problems in the way of a straightforward intentionalist account are by no means indicative of mere intellectual confusion or, even less, of these thinkers' relegation to the history of downright false or philosophically irrelevant ideas. Thus Bennett recalls how Austin once remarked to him, concerning an idea of Leibniz, that 'it is a very great mistake, and only a very great philosopher could have made it'. To which he adds the approving gloss: 'a philosopher can be led into error by the very power of his thought, making serious mistakes that he might not have made if he had seen less and probed less deeply'.[64] Perhaps Bennett might have followed Paul de Man in distinguishing 'errors' from 'mistakes', the former denoting those cases where indeed it is a question of getting things wrong in some deep, philosophically significant and motivated way while the latter have to do with mere carelessness, inattention or faulty reasoning.[65]

Some such distinction is anyway implicit throughout Bennett's writings on the work of those early modern philosophers whose continuing claim to our interest and attention – as philosophers rather than figures in the history of ideas – he takes to consist in their often having got things right but elsewhere more frequently fallen into 'error' than into plain or easily rectified 'mistakes'. It is likewise implicit in Derrida's deconstructive analyses, starting out as they do from the basic assumption – made good in the course of close reading – that the text under scrutiny is (1) sufficiently complex to warrant such intensive critical treatment and (2) sufficiently rewarding in terms of the insights to be gained by attending to its various blind spots, contradictions or aporias. This is why, as Bennett says, 'a philosopher's proclaimed doctrine may be better understood as a misformulation of something different, more interesting, and closer to the truth'.[66] Or again, in what is perhaps his most suggestively Derridean passage.

> Mistakes, tangles, and the like can reflect credit on their authors … The trouble they get into often comes from how much they have noticed: they have subliminally felt conceptual pressures of various kinds, and have subtly responded to them, without always managing to bring them into the open to be dealt with theoretically. That is why my kind of interpretation, in which error and confusion and contradiction are often alleged, is more respectful towards the studied philosopher than the kind which makes him right but trite.[67]

This could just as well stand as a summary statement of Derrida's working principles with regard to what counts as an adequate, responsible, philosophically valid, perhaps highly critical but nonetheless 'respectful' reading of texts that lay claim to such treatment. It is borne out constantly in his essays on Plato, Rousseau, Kant, Husserl and others, but perhaps to most striking effect in his engagement with Austinian speech-act theory. After all, Derrida's commentary here has to do with a mode of argument which raises such issues – of truth, meaning, intention, validity, 'constative' *vis-à-vis* 'performative' criteria of truthful (or felicitous) utterance and so forth – not only between the lines but as a matter of explicit and primary philosophical interest. Moreover, it does so in such a way as to reflect on those issues in and through a text that self-consciously rehearses their implications and which thereby brings out the impossibility – as Derrida sees it – of treating them from a purely constative (i.e., theoretical or metalinguistic) vantage point outside and above the complexities of so-called 'ordinary' language.

It is here that my comparison might seem to break down since this particular aspect of Derrida's writing is one that is apt to strike not only die-hard opponents like Searle but most analytic philosophers (Bennett probably included) as beyond the pale of acceptability. That is, they are still committed in some degree – even after Quine's vaunted demolition job in 'Two Dogmas of Empiricism' – to the notion that philosophy can and should preserve a certain methodological distance between its own discourse (or the standards of conceptual and analytic rigour properly pertaining thereto) and the various first-order or natural languages that constitute its object-domain.[68] And indeed it is far from clear that they are wrong in this, or that Quine got it right with his radically holistic, non-normative and (I would argue) grossly implausible account of 'epistemology naturalized'.[69] Nor again should we too readily assume that Derrida is likewise out to demolish those distinctions that Quine so resolutely laid under siege. On this view deconstruction amounts to just a somewhat more refined, 'philosophical' version of the wider postmodernist attack on every last vestige of that old metalinguistic (or 'meta-narrative') delusion which seeks to attain a critical perspective above and beyond the currencies of in-place consensus belief.[70] This chapter has been mainly devoted to putting the case against that idea of what Derrida is all about, whether advanced by hostile commentators or by others – like Rorty – who admire him for precisely those reasons. On the contrary: it is just in so far as his work resists or repudiates such a reading that it also provides a strong counter-argument to any philosophical approach, including that espoused by the later Wittgenstein, that would relativize standards of validity and truth to the norms of some given language-game or cultural 'form of life'.[71]

To be sure, Derrida's writings do much to complicate the language /metalanguage distinction, along with the performative/constative dichotomy, especially where this is propounded (as by Searle) in the form of a systematized speech-act theory designed to keep those complications safely out of view.[72] In this respect Derrida can rightfully claim to be following Austin's lead, since after all it was Austin himself – at a famous turning point in *How to Do Things With Words* – who first acknowledged the impossibility of fixing such a clear-cut distinction.[73] However, as I hope to have shown, Derrida always comes at these issues through a reading that is maximally alert to salient (even if 'marginal') details of the text in hand and that is conducted according to the strictest protocols of logical argumentation. This is why recent overtures in a Derridean direction by those, like Priest, who take him to adopt a paraconsistent logic which suspends not only bivalence and excluded middle but even (conceivably) the law of non-contradiction are welcome as signs of a new open-mindedness on the part of analytic philosophers but distinctly wide of the mark as concerns the true significance of Derrida's thought. What his work most strikingly exhibits is a unique combination of interpretative flair with logical acuity and philosophic insight which might yet stimulate some new lines of thought in that other, up to now just as strikingly resistant tradition. In Chapter 2 – and again in Chapter 7, albeit from a somewhat different angle – I shall pursue this argument by suggesting further reasons why analytic philosophers should take more account of Derrida's thinking about issues in the sphere of ethics, law and politics.

NOTES

1   See especially Jacques Derrida, 'Speech and Phenomena' and Other Essays on Husserl's Theory of Signs, trans. David B. Allison (Evanston, IL: Northwestern University Press, 1973); Of Grammatology, trans. Gayatri. C. Spivak (Baltimore, MD: Johns Hopkins University Press, 1974), Writing and Difference, trans. Alan Bass (London: Routledge & Kegan Paul, 1978); Dissemination, trans. Barbara Johnson (London: Athlone Press, 1981); Margins of Philosophy, trans. Alan Bass (Chicago: University of Chicago Press, 1982).

2   See especially various contributors to Simon Glendinning (ed.), Arguing with Derrida (Oxford: Blackwell, 2001); also Reed Way Dasenbrock (ed.), Re-Drawing the Lines: Analytic Philosophy, Deconstruction, and Literary Theory (Minneapolis: University of Minnesota Press, 1989); Newton Garver and Seung-Chong Lee, Derrida and Wittgenstein (Philadelphia, PA: Temple University Press, 1994); Marian Hobson, Jacques Derrida: Opening Lines (London: Routledge, 1998); Christopher Norris and David Roden (eds.), Jacques Derrida, 4 vols. (London: Sage, 2003); Christopher Norris, 'Derrida on Rousseau: Deconstruction as Philosophy of Logic', in Norris and Roden (eds.), Jacques Derrida, Vol. 2, pp. 70–124; Graham Priest, 'Derrida and Self-Reference', Australasian Journal of Philosophy 72 (1994), pp. 103–111 and Beyond the Limits of Thought (Cambridge: Cambridge University Press, 1995); Henry Staten, Wittgenstein and Derrida (Oxford: Blackwell, 1986); Samuel C. Wheeler, Deconstruction as Analytic Philosophy (Stanford, CA: Stanford University Press, 2000).

3   See Jacques Derrida, 'Signature Event Context', Glyph 1 (1975), pp. 172–97; John R. Searle, 'Reiterating the Differences', Glyph 1 (1975), pp. 198–208; Derrida, 'Limited Inc abc', Glyph 2 (1977), pp. 75–176; also Derrida, 'Afterword: Toward an Ethic of Conversation', in Gerald Graff (ed.), Limited Inc (Evanston, IL: Northwestern University Press, 1989), pp. 111–54.

4   Richard Rorty, 'Philosophy as a Kind of Writing: An Essay on Jacques Derrida', in Consequences of Pragmatism (Brighton: Harvester Press, 1982), pp. 89–109 and 'Is Derrida a Transcendental Philosopher?', in Essays on Heidegger and Others (Cambridge: Cambridge University Press, 1991), pp. 119–28; also Christopher Norris, 'Philosophy as Not Just a "Kind of Writing": Derrida and the Claim of Reason', in Dasenbrock (ed.), Re-Drawing the Lines, pp. 189–203 and Rorty, 'Two Versions of "Logocentrism": A Reply to Norris', in Dasenbrock (ed.), Re-Drawing the Lines, pp. 204–16.

5   See for instance Rodolphe Gasché, The Tain of the Mirror: Derrida and the Philosophy of

Reflection (Cambridge, MA: Harvard University Press, 1986); Christopher Norris, *Jacques Derrida* (London: Fontana, 1987) and *Deconstruction and the Unifinished Project of Modernity* (London: Athlone, 2000).

6   For further discussion, see Christopher Norris, 'Of an Apoplectic Tone Recently Adopted in Philosophy', in *Reclaiming Truth: Contribution to a Critique of Cultural Relativism* (London: Lawrence & Wishart, 1996), pp. 222–53.

7   See Gottlob Frege, 'Review of Edmund Husserl's *Philosophie der Arithmetik*', trans. E.-H. W. Kluge, *Mind* 81 (1972), pp. 321–37; also Gilbert Ryle, 'Phenomenology' and 'Phenomenology versus *The Concept of Mind*', in Ryle, *Collected Papers*, vol. 1 (London: Hutchinson, 1971), pp. 167–78 and 179–96; Leila Haaparanta (ed.), *Mind, Meaning, and Mathematics: Essays on the Philosophical Views of Husserl and Frege* (Dordrecht and Boston: Kluwer, 1994).

8   Michael Dummett, *The Origins of Analytic Philosophy* (London: Duckworth, 1993).

9   Michael Friedman, *A Parting of the Ways: Carnap, Cassirer and Heidegger* (Chicago: Open Court, 2000); also *Reconsidering Logical Positivism* (Cambridge: Cambridge University Press, 1999).

10 See Note 2, above.

11 See Derrida, 'Signature Event Context' and Donald Davidson, 'A Nice Derangement of Epitaphs', in R. Grandy and R. Warner (eds.), *Philosophical Grounds of Rationality*: *Intentions, Categories, Ends* (Oxford: Oxford University Press, 1986), pp. 157–74; also Ernest LePore (ed.), *Truth and Interpretation: Essays on the Philosophy of Donald Davidson* (Oxford: Blackwell, 1986); W.J.T. Mitchell (ed.), *Against Theory: Literary Theory and the New Pragmatism* (Chicago: University of Chicago Press, 1985); Christopher Norris, *Resources of Realism: Prospects for 'Post-Analytic' Philosophy* (London: Macmillan, 1997); S. Pradhan, 'Minimalist Semantics: Davidson and Derrida on Meaning, Use, and Convention', *Diacritics* 16 (Spring 1986), pp. 66–77; Wheeler, *Deconstruction as Analytic Philosophy*.

12 See Note 3, above; also J.L. Austin, *How to Do Things With Words* (Oxford: Oxford University Press, 1963).

13 For further discussion, see Norris, *Resources of Realism*; also Jerry Fodor, *Representations* (Cambridge, MA: MIT Press, 1981), *Psychosemantics: The Problem of Meaning in the Philosophy of Mind* (Cambridge, MA: MIT Press, 1987), and *A Theory of Content and Other Essays* (Cambridge, MA: MIT Press, 1992).

14 See Notes 3 and 11, above; also Donald Davidson, *Inquiries into Truth and Interpretation* (Oxford: Clarendon Press, 1984).

15 See Norris, *Resources of Realism*.

16 Searle, 'Reiterating the Differences'.

17 Derrida, 'Afterword'.

18 Ibid., p. 123.

19 Ibid., pp. 122–3.

20 See Notes 1, 5 and 6, above.

21 See W.V. Quine, 'Two Dogmas of Empiricism', in *From a Logical Point of View*, 2nd edn (Cambridge, MA: Harvard University Press, 1961); also G. Birkhoff and J. von Neumann, 'The Logic of Quantum Mechanics', *Annals of Mathematics* 37 (1936), pp. 823–43; Martin Gardner, 'Is Quantum Logic Really Logic?', *Philosophy of Science* 38 (1971), pp. 508–29; Peter Gibbins, *Particles and Paradoxes: The Limits of Quantum Logic* (Cambridge: Cambridge University Press, 1987); Hilary Putnam, 'How to Think Quantum-Logically', *Synthèse* 74 (1974), pp. 55–61.

22 See for instance D. Gabbay and F. Günthner (eds.), *Handbook of Philosophical Logic*, 2 vols (Dordrecht: D. Reidel, 1984); Susan Haack, *Deviant Logic: Some Philosophical Issues* (Cambridge: Cambridge University Press, 1974); B. Kosko, *Fuzzy Thinking* (New York: Hyperion, 1993); Jan Lukasiewicz, *Selected Works*, ed. L. Borkowski (Amsterdam: North-Holland, 1970); R.L. Martin (ed.), *Recent Essays on Truth and the Liar Paradox*

(New York: Oxford University Press, 1984); Priest, *Beyond the Limits of Thought*; Nicolas Rescher, *Many-Valued Logic* (New York: McGraw-Hill, 1969).

23 See especially A.N. Prior, *Past, Present and Future* (Oxford: Oxford University Press, 1967); also N. Rescher and A. Urquart, *Temporal Logic* (New York: Springer Verlag, 1971).

24 Raymond Bradley and Norman Swartz, *Possible Worlds: An Introduction to Logic and its Philosophy* (Oxford: Blackwell, 1979); Rod Gierle, *Modal Logics and Philosophy* (Teddington: Acumen, 2000) and *Possible Worlds* (Teddington: Acumen, 2002); G. Hughes and M. Cresswell, *A New Introduction to Modal Logic* (London: Routledge, 1996); L. Linsky (ed.), *Reference and Modality* (Oxford: Oxford University Press, 1971); M. Loux (ed.), *The Possible and the Actual: Readings in the Metaphysics of Modality* (Ithaca, NY; Cornell University Press, 1979).

25 See for instance Stephen Read, *Relevant Logic* (Oxford: Blackwell, 1988).

26 Priest, *Beyond the Limits of Thought*.

27 Quine, 'Two Dogmas of Empiricism'.

28 For further argument to this effect, see Jaegwon Kim, *Supervenience and Mind* (Cambridge: Cambridge University Press, 1993), also Norris, *Resources of Realism* and *New Idols of the Cave: On the Limits of Anti-Realism* (London: Macmillan 1997)

29 See Gardner, 'Is Quantum Logic Really Logic?' and Gibbins, *Particles and Paradoxes*; also Christopher Norris, *Quantum Theory and the Flight from Realism: Philosophical Responses to Quantum Mechanics* (London: Routledge, 2000).

30 See especially David Bohm, *Causality and Chance in Modern Physics* (London: Routledge & Kegan Paul, 1957); also David Bohm and B.J. Hiley, *The Undivided Universe: An Ontological Interpretation of Quantum Theory* (London: Routledge, 1993); Evadro Agazzi (ed.), *Realism and Quantum Mechanics* (Amsterdam and Atlanta: Rodopi, 1997); Peter Holland, *The Quantum Theory of Motion* (Cambridge: Cambridge University Press, 1993).

31 Norris, 'Derrida on Rousseau: Deconstruction as Philosophy of Logic'; also *Language, Logic and Epistemology: A Modal-Realist Approach* (London: Macmillan, 2004).

32 Derrida, *Of Grammatology*.

33 Ibid., p. 158.

34 Ibid., p. 135.

35 Ibid., p. 158.

36 See Notes 3 and 11, above.

37 Derrida, *Of Grammatology*, p. 158.

38 Davidson, 'A Nice Derangement of Epitaphs'.

39 Ibid., p. 215.

40 See Notes 21 and 28, above: also W. V. Quine, *Ontological Relativity and Other Essays* (New York: Columbia University Press, 1969).

41 See Notes 29 and 30, above.

42 See Note 7, above.

43 Derrida, 'Afterword', p. 117.

44 See entries under Note 1, above; also Jacques Derrida, 'Parergon', in *The Truth in Painting*, trans. Geoff Bennington and Ian McLeod (Chicago, IL: University of Chicago Press, 1987), pp. 15–147.

45 See Note 29, above; also Karl Popper, *Quantum Theory and the Schism in Physics* (London: Hutchinson, 1983).

46 Arkady Plotnitsky, *Complementarity: Anti-Epistemology after Bohr and Derrida* (Durham, NC: Duke University Prerss, 1994).

47 Priest, *Beyond the Limits of Thought*; also 'Derrida and Self-Reference', *Australasian Journal of Philosophy* 72 (1994), pp. 103–11.

48 See Notes 29 and 45, above.

49 See especially Jonathan Bennett, *Learning from Six Philosophers: Descartes, Spinoza, Leibniz, Locke, Berkeley, Hume*, 2 vols (Oxford: Clarendon Press, 2001).

50 Michael Dummett, *Truth and Other Enigmas* (London: Duckworth, 1978) and *The Logical Basis of Metaphysics* (Duckworth, 1991).

51 See Richard Rorty (ed.), *The Linguistic Turn* (Chicago: University of Chicago Press, 1967) for a useful anthology of essays from both traditions. In his Preface to the volume Rorty concludes – in a manner prefiguring his later neo-pragmatist turn – that they embody such radically different ('incommensurable') aims, interests and priorities as to rule out any hope of agreement, and moreover that this stalemate situation must be seen as spelling an end to the very idea of philosophy as a constructive, problem-solving enterprise. As so often with Rorty, what looks like an even-handed deconstruction of two opposed lines of argument in fact offers a covert endorsement of one, i.e., the 'post-analytic', neo-pragmatist or thoroughly 'linguistified' approach. See Christopher Norris, *The Truth About Postmodernism* (Oxford: Blackwell, 1994) for further argument to this effect.

52 See Norris, *Language, Logic and Epistemology* and *Philosophy of Language and the Challenge to Scientific Realism* (London: Routledge, 2004).

53 See Note 4, above; also Richard Rorty, 'Transcendental Arguments, Self-Reference, and Pragmatism', in P. Bieri, R. Horstmann and L. Krüger (eds.), *Transcendental Arguments and Science* (Dordrecht: D. Reidel, 1979), pp. 77–103.

54 Rorty, 'Philosophy as a Kind of Writing'.

55 Bennett, *Learning from Six Philosophers*.

56 Derrida, *Of Grammatology*, p. 158.

57 Ibid., p. 158.

58 See Notes 1 and 49, above.

59 Bennett, *Learning from Six Philosophers*, pp. 1–2.

60 Derrida, *Of Grammatology*, p. 158.

61 Bennett, *Learning from Six Philosophers*, p. 7.

62 Ibid., p. 7.

63 Ibid., p. 7.

64 Ibid., p. 5.

65 See Paul de Man, 'Heidegger's Exegeses of Hölderlin', in *Blindness and Insight: Essays in the Rhetoric of Contemporary Criticism*, 2nd edn (London: Routledge, 1983), pp. 246–66.

66 Bennett, *Learning from Six Philosophers*, p. 8.

67 Ibid., p. 9.

68 Quine, 'Two Dogmas of Empiricism'.

69 See Notes 28 and 40, above.

70 See especially Jean-François Lyotard, *The Postmodern Condition: A Report on Knowledge*, trans. Geoff Bennington and Brian Massumi (Manchester: Manchester University Press, 1984); also – for some opposing arguments – Norris, *The Truth About Postmodernism* and *What's Wrong with Postmodernism* (Baltimore, MD: Johns Hopkins University Press, 1990).

71 See especially Ludwig Wittgenstein, *Philosophical Investigations*, trans. G.E.M. Anscombe (Oxford: Blackwell, 1953) and *On Certainty*, trans. and ed. Anscombe and G.H. von Wright (Oxford: Blackwell, 1969).

72 See Searle, 'Reiterating the Differences'; also *Speech Acts: An Essay in the Philosophy of Language* (Cambridge: Cambridge University Press, 1969).

73 Austin, *How to Do Things With Words*.

2

Ethics, Normativity and Deconstruction

I

Analytic philosophy has often tended to veer back and forth in its attitude toward developments in the other, that is, 'continental' or (more accurately) post Kantian mainland European line of descent. That is to say, it has either dismissed those developments pretty much out of hand as so much 'metaphysical' (for which read: empirically vacuous and logically unwarranted) pseudo-philosophy, or – very often the minority view – conceded that it might after all have something of interest and importance to offer. The former reaction is typified by A.J. Ayer's breezily dismissive treatment of existentialism for its supposed logical blunders, among them its unfortunate habit of making such a fuss about matters – like the fact/value dichotomy – which we had better just accept (like philosophers from Hume to the logical positivists) as problems that will not go away for any amount of *Angst*-ridden melodramatics.[1] It is also very evident in Searle's rejoinder to Derrida on the topic of Austinian speech-act theory, one which either fails or steadfastly refuses to see that Derrida is here raising crucial questions about the scope and limits of performative account-ability which *cannot but* arise through any close and attentive critical engagement with Austin's texts.[2] The second mode of response amongst some analytically trained philosophers is that which accepts the very real differences of interest, emphasis and priority between the 'two traditions' but none the less takes them as a welcome spur to deeper, more intensive or self-critical reflection on its own part. Just recently this open-minded attitude has begun to gain ground in various quarters – including philosophy of language and logic – where hitherto the orthodox line (at least since the time of Frege's falling out with Husserl) had been one of mere indifference or downright hostility.[3] 'Continental' philosophy can then be seen as offering an added resource – at very least a useful, since provocative, stimulus – to those working in the other main line of descent.

Thus Derrida's later writings on ethical themes contain passages that may strike an alien note (too 'existentialist' by half) to philosophers of an analytic mind and yet raise issues that cannot be ignored unless by evading the central problem with regard to the scope and limits of our moral, intellectual or doxastic responsibility.[4] Take for instance the following, fairly typical remark from his 1992 essay 'Force of Law':

> Law is the element of calculation, and it is just that there be law, but justice is incalculable, it requires us to calculate with the incalculable; and aporetic experiences are the experiences, as improbable as they are necessary, of justice, that is to say of moments in which the decision between just and unjust is never ensured by a rule.[5]

This theme is taken up more explicitly in *Aporias*, a text where Derrida meditates at length on the various kinds of strictly 'unthinkable' experience – such as that of one's own death – which cannot be brought under any adequate concept or subsumed by any other, for example, dialectical or phenomenological mode of thought. Here again the argument goes by way of a prefatory section where Derrida insists on the moment of dizzying aporia – the suspension of all operative rules or guidelines – that he takes to distinguish the 'experience' of authentic ethical choice, as distinct from mere action in accordance with this or that moral code. Yet surely (and just as problematically) there *must* be a sense in which our choices can count as ethical only if they represent the outcome of reasoned, deliberative thought and hence of procedures that *do* have precisely such a given prescriptive or regulative force. 'In order to be responsible and truly decisive', Derrida writes,

> [a] decision should not limit itself to putting into question a determinable or determining knowledge, the consequence of some preestablished order. But, conversely, who would call a decision that is without rule, without norms, without determinable or determined law, a decision? Who will answer for it as if for a responsible decision, and before whom? Who will dare call duty a duty that owes nothing, or, better (or, worse), that *must owe nothing*? It is necessary, therefore, that the decision and responsibility for it be taken, interrupting the relation to any *presentable* determination but still maintaining a presentable relation to the interruption and to what it interrupts. Is that possible? Is it possible once the interruption always resembles the mark of an orderly edge, the mark of a threshold not to be trespassed?[6]

Now there are various things about this that philosophers might wish to dispute, not least the idea of a drastic dichotomy between judgements arrived at on the basis of some 'rule', maxim, case-law precedent or rational decision procedure and those other, properly ethical judgements that are made without reference to any such existing guidelines. What is perhaps most striking (and disconcerting for some of his long-term disciples) is the way that 'late' Derrida broaches this question of ethical responsibility in terms strongly reminiscent of Sartrean existentialism, an outlook that he had once rejected – along with other leading representatives of *la pensée soixante-huit* – as merely a kind of last-gasp humanist illusion.[7] Moreover these writings seem to point back beyond Sartre's secularized version of that project to something very like the Kierkegaardian 'leap of faith' that requires us to suspend all the normative values of our everyday, 'inauthentic' social existence for the sake of achieving authentic religious belief.[8]

I should say straight off that I also have problems with this aspect of Derrida's later thought.[9] Thus I agree with those who would argue for a much greater degree of continuity between our rational, deliberative, rule-guided (if not entirely rule-governed) processes of thought and the way that we act or decide in extreme situations or under pressures of circumstance that seem to preclude any falling back on such customary sources of assurance. No doubt there is a sense, as Derrida says, in which acts and decisions may be thought of as genuinely ethical just in so far as they involve some element of strictly 'incalculable' choice that takes us beyond any straightforward appeal to pre-established laws, rules or conventions. Such would be the case with conscientious objectors or with those who transgress the legal codes or the received moral wisdom of their time in the name of some other, incompatible and (to them) overriding ethical imperative. One of Derrida's great exemplars here is Nelson Mandela, whom he takes to personify not only the highest degree of moral courage but also – especially in view of his early professional training as a lawyer – the very embodiment of justice in an unjust or wicked (apartheid based) legal system.[10] Hence the claim – again a source of some disquiet to Derrida's followers – that 'justice in itself, if such a thing exists, outside or beyond law, is not deconstructible'.[11] That is to say, it is something very like a 'regulative idea' in the Kantian sense, an idea (rather than a well-defined, empirically applicable concept) which orients our thinking toward certain ultimate values such as justice, equality, democracy, freedom or 'perpetual peace'. That they are notable for possessing an as-yet-unachieved – perhaps strictly speaking unachievable – character does nothing to diminish their claims on our ethical or socio-political conscience.[12] According to Derrida this is what places such an absolute, non-negotiable distance between 'justice' and 'law': that the principles of justice cannot be discredited, impugned or even 'deconstructed' (i e , shown up as inconsistent or contradictory), whereas those of law remain forever open to such treatment since they embody a par ticular, historically and culturally given set of juridical practices. And indeed there is nowadays quite an academic industry of 'deconstructive' legal theorists who specialize in the constant teasing out of just such conflicts and anomalies.[13]

So there is something to be said for Derrida's emphasis on maintaining this absolute and principled distinction between, on the one hand, those various enactments (whether statutes, constitutional provisions or case-law precedents) which determine what is lawful as a matter of juridical warrant and, on the other, the idea of justice as that which inherently transcends the limits of any past or present – and perhaps any future – legal system. By the same token it can hardly be denied – if one considers the record of moral and socio-political history to date – that 'best opinion' as a matter of general consensus or even amongst those presumptively best qualified to judge has very often been sharply at odds with what nowadays counts as such. (The instances of slavery and sexual dis-crimination are two that would carry decisive weight with any but the most extreme conservatives or exponents of cultural relativism.[14]) Still one may doubt that reflection on such matters is well served by any doctrine that imposes a radical disjunction between law and ethics, practice and principle, or indeed fact and value. That is to say, those dichotomies offer no help in explaining the complex mixture of principles, practices, theories, beliefs, ideologies, historical situations, motivating interests and so forth, which must find a place in any adequate account of moral progress to date and also – more importantly – in the process of reflective and critical self-reckoning that offers the sole hope of future improvement. So one can take the point of those critics – Merleau-Ponty among them – who objected to Sartre's more extreme, all-or-nothing formulations of existentialist authenticity or good faith, as likewise (in the current context of debate) to Derrida's insistence on the absolute distinction between law as a discourse of socially approved or instituted values and justice as that which intrinsically transcends any such ground of appeal.[15] To place so exclusive an emphasis on the strictly 'undecidable', that is, the rationally non-justified and hence radically under-motivated character of ethical choice is to risk falling prey to a whole range of emotivist, decisionist or downright irrationalist ethical doctrines.

And yet, as I have said, there is a clear sense in which Derrida's reflections on the aporetic character of ethical choice and responsibility – like Sartre's before him – capture something that goes to the heart of this issue and that cannot be resolved (or wished away) by any amount of conceptual analysis or linguistic therapy. What his writing brings out with singular eloquence and force is the impossibility of thinking these problems through to an adequate or ethically responsible conclusion on anything like the terms provided by deontological (rule-governed, e.g., Kantian) theories or communitarian approaches in the Wittgensteinian mode.[16] One might remark that his case is strongly borne out – albeit obliquely so – by the current debate about rule following and by Saul Kripke's pyrrhic claim that the only standard of correctness in such matters (in arithmetic, logic and the formal sciences as well as in matters of inductive or empirical warrant) is one that involves precisely this appeal to communal acceptance or 'agreement in judgement' as all we can have in the way of probative or justificatory warrant.[17] Thus the best that Kripke is able to offer in response to Wittgenstein's 'sceptical problem' is a communitarian 'sceptical solution' which renders the truth of '2 + 2 = 4' (or the falsehood of '2 + 2 = 5') just a matter of what normally, routinely or properly counts as good arithmetical practice amongst those presumed to know. And of course, if this argument is thought to go through even in respect of elementary arithmetic or the basic axioms that underpin all our logical reasoning, then the way is wide open to a standpoint of out-and-out scepticism as regards the foundations of empirical knowledge, inductive warrant, causal explanation and every other branch of scientific or everyday enquiry. Moreover – returning to our main topic here – it cannot but raise the question as to how moral agents could ever be justified in performing some action, taking some decision or adopting some principled ethical stance that went against the communal practices or values of their own time and place.

What Kripke's 'sceptical solution' really amounts to – as I have argued at length elsewhere – is not so much a knock-down case for accepting his own and

Wittgenstein's 'sceptical solution' but rather a *reductio ad absurdum* of this whole line of thought.[18] That is to say, he shows that it must have started out from some mistaken premise – or else gone wildly off the rails at some point – if it leads to what Kripke himself regards as frankly 'bizarre' or 'unthinkable' conclusions, like that concerning the non-existence of standards of correctness in logic or arithmetic beyond those endorsed by some like-minded community. Such a reading acquires even greater diagnostic force when one takes Kripke's point that, if his argument succeeds, then it applies not only to the range of formal rule-following procedures examined in his book but also to the entire body of our putative knowledge (or supposed justificatory grounds for that knowledge) across every field of scientific, historical and everyday practical enquiry. At least this would seem to be the case in so far as one shares his leading assumption that Wittgenstein's sceptical paradox looms unavoidably at the end of the road that analytic philosophy has been travelling from Frege and Russell to Quine and beyond. Even if one rejects it as just too bizarre still there is reason to think (or so the argument might go) that some such outcome – a 'sceptical solution' that is really no solution at all – was always just a few steps on from the various intractable problems and dilemmas that emerged within that tradition.

II

For some commentators, Richard Rorty among them, this is where the 'other', continental (or mainland-European) tradition kicks in: as a welcome reminder that philosophy need never have taken that analytic path and conceived itself as a specialized, conceptually rigorous mode of discourse whose proper business was to offer constructive solutions to genuine philosophic problems. Once rid of that false self-image, so Rorty thinks, philosophers will at last be content to assume their strictly non-privileged role as participants in the ongoing 'cultural conversation', along with the novelists, poets, literary critics and others whom they would do well to emulate since these latter have no such unfortunate delusions of epistemological grandeur.[19] Hence his admiration for those 'literary' aspects of Derrida's work which might help persuade us to approach philosophy as just another 'kind of writing', one whose chief virtue lies not at all in its problem-solving power but rather in its capacity to create new 'metaphors we can live by' or novel, more adventurous ways of recounting its own history to date.[20] Hence also his professed aversion to those other, distinctly 'philosophical' texts where Derrida not only argues a case but does so through a deconstructive reading of various philosophers, from Plato to Husserl, which lays claim to a high degree of analytic and conceptual rigour.[21] So far as Rorty is concerned this is just a throwback to the same old Platonic–Cartesian–Kantian–analytical obsession with issues (such as the 'problem of knowledge' or the status of ethical value-judgements) which cannot be resolved – and do not merit our continued interest – since they were pseudo-problems or artificial dilemmas in the first place. However this reading of Derrida is so tendentious (not to say narrowly selective or downright distorted) as scarcely to count as a 'reading' on any but 'strong'-revisionist or 'literary' terms.[22] Quite the contrary: what sets his work decisively apart from any such wholesale debunking view of philosophy's aims and pretensions is Derrida's absolute insistence on the need to think these problems through with the utmost attentiveness to just those moments of conceptual strain when thinking runs up against the limits of its power to contain their disruptive effects. Nothing could be further from Rorty's blithely dismissive approach to such issues or his idea of a 'post-philosophical' culture where the aim is simply to let them go and move on to more 'edifying' (that is to say, culturally salient or socially uplifting) topics of debate.

There is also a notable contrast between Derrida's insistence, in essays like 'Force of Law', that any rule-based or procedural approach to matters of ethical choice must always fail to capture what is properly, distinctively ethical about them and the kinds of debate that have ensued from Kripke's ultra-sceptical account of Wittgenstein on the topic of rule-following.[23] Thus Kripke might appear to be making a similar point in a different but related context, that is, that any given rule (such as those for addition or continuing the series 'n+2') must always be open to a whole vast range of other possible interpretations. No doubt some of them will strike us well-drilled orthodox types as decidedly bizarre, like the student who interprets '+' as meaning 'add 2 up to 1,000, then 4 up to 2,000, 8 up to 3,000, etc.', and whose response when asked why he has not applied the same rule correctly and consistently throughout is that indeed he has done just that, since the above operation was exactly what he had in mind from the outset. I shall not rehearse the many ingenious variations on this theme that Kripke produces in the course of showing that the student need never be stumped for a reply since he can always devise an alternative, more or less complicated rule that will bring him out correct for any non-standard answer to a question in basic arithmetic or any (as it might seem) mistaken or downright crazy way of continuing a number series. Kripke's point, in brief, is that *no* answer to such questions can be proven objectively right or wrong since it is only by the standards of a certain community – in this case, the community of orthodox arithmeticians – that the question makes sense and the answer is subject to agreed-upon truth/falsehood criteria. Nor is it any use appealing to concepts like that of recursivity, or telling the student: 'just keep on adding 2 the same way you did up to 1,000', since of course he will reply: 'no, you do not understand, I was working on the same (correct) rule from the start, and that rule says "double the increment after 1,000" ' (etc.). Besides, Kripke has a second line of attack which involves linking Wittgenstein's thoughts on the topic of rule following with his thoughts about 'private language', that is to say, about the impossibility of there being (or our having access to) any such realm of inner, publicly non-communicable goings-on. Put these arguments together, so Kripke claims, and we can see how futile is the notion that anyone could check their own performance against what they supposedly once 'had in mind' (or even what they are presently minded to do) when following this or that rule. In Wittgenstein's simile, it is like buying a second copy of the daily newspaper just to make sure that what the first copy says is true.[24] In which case there is no adequate criterion – no 'fact' concerning what we (or the student) might have meant by 'plus' on any previous occasion – that could possibly serve to adjudicate the issue between his and our own way of adding up or continuing a number sequence. Or, rather, we can and do so decide but only on the basis of 'agreement in judgement', and not (as realists or objectivists would have it) in accordance with standards that inherently transcend any such communal court of appeal.

As I have said, there is a great difference between this 'Kripkensteinian' treatment of the rule-following paradox and Derrida's point about the non-rule-governed, that is, the procedurally unconstrained and hence – to this extent at least – the rationally under-motivated character of genuine ethical decisions. Kripke's approach is to press hard on the sceptical paradox, to the point where it strikes him as unthinkably 'bizarre', and then fall back on a 'sceptical solution' which does not so much resolve the problem as effectively shunt it off into some branch of group psychology or the sociology of knowledge. To this extent, whatever their specific bearing on interpretative issues in late Wittgenstein, the paradox and quasi-'solution' alike are prime examples of what Rorty has in view when he chides philosophers in the analytic mainstream for always mulling over the same old questions without the least hope of coming up with new answers unless by his preferred conversational expedient of simply 'changing the topic'. Thus, despite Rorty's lumping Kripke together with the old-guard analytic types, he can better be seen – like Wittgenstein – as a kind of latter-day sophist, the effect of whose thinking is to block the appeal to any standards of truth or rationality beyond those that happen to accord with our shared practices and beliefs. It is here that Derrida's work offers the sharpest possible contrast, devoted as it is – early and late – to a detailed traversal of precisely those passages in Plato, Aristotle, Descartes, Kant, Husserl and others where philosophy is brought up against the limit of received opinion or its own pre-existing conceptual resources, but is thereby impelled to raise further questions which are no less 'philosophical' for that.[25]

To be sure, there is a sense in which my Derrida/Kripke comparison may appear wildly off the point, since when Derrida raises the issue about rules and the limits on their valid application he is doing so chiefly in an ethical context and not – like Kripke – by way of reflection on the problem of knowledge and its justificatory grounds. However it will seem less strained if one goes back to Derrida's earlier work (especially his detailed and intensive studies of Husserl) and registers the way that these studies bring out the close, indeed strictly indissoluble, relation between epistemological and ethical issues.[26] What sets his thinking so firmly apart from the analytic mainstream – and especially from the kinds of debate sparked off by Kripke's reading of Wittgenstein – is its absolute rejection of any idea that such issues can be settled (or conjured away) by invoking the authority of ordinary language or communal 'agreement in judgement'. Rather it is the case, as emerges very clearly from Derrida's essay on Austin, that they are apt to arise with inescapable force as soon as one abandons the safe ground of an orthodox appeal to these values and focuses instead (like Austin at his best) on the way that a close examination of language can challenge or unsettle our routine, conventional habits of belief.[27] This is where a deconstructive reading such as Derrida's brings out aspects of Austin's work that pass altogether unnoticed by other exegetes, whether those who would assimilate his thinking to a Wittgenstein-derived communitarian approach or those – Searle among them – who seek to erect a systematic theory of performative utterance or speech-act implicature on the basis of Austin's much subtler, more nuanced and (often) deeply problematical remarks.[28] It is also why Derrida is justified in claiming that we shall come much closer to the spirit, as well as the letter of Austin's text if we follow his proto-deconstructive lead and acknowledge the extent to which Austin himself was prone to raise questions with regard to the authority of 'ordinary language' and the adequacy of his own theoretical terms and distinctions. Thus Derrida's reading has the signal virtue of rescuing Austin from the sorts of charge sometimes levelled against him, that is, that his approach amounts to no more than a covert endorsement of the *status quo* as enshrined in a certain, supposedly 'common-sense', but in fact highly culture-specific range of verbal practices and customs.[29] More than that: it stresses precisely those disruptive or anomalous passages in Austin's text which put up resistance to the kinds of take-over bid regularly mounted by partisans of a Wittgensteinian or neo-pragmatist (Rortian) approach.

It is the same resistance that characterizes Derrida's writing, especially if one comes to it with Rorty's advice in mind – that is, that we should read him as simply 'circumventing' all the problems of old-style philosophic discourse – only to be struck by the extreme contrast between this and what actually goes on when Derrida reads Austin (or, for that matter, Plato, Aristotle, Rousseau, Kant or Husserl).[30] For it is precisely through his own Austinian attentiveness to nuances of textual detail, joined to a keen analytical grasp of their logico-semantic implications, that Derrida is able to raise such distinctly *philosophical* issues about meaning, intention, validating context and (not least) the question concerning our ethical responsibility for holding certain beliefs or acting in accordance with certain principles. Besides, his particular way of raising them – especially with regard to the criteria for speech-act commitment over time or the validity-conditions for future satisfaction of past promises, contractual agreements or other such performative undertakings – is very much of a piece with the kinds of question posed by a thinker like Derek Parfit in his much-discussed book *Reasons and Persons*.[31] That is to say, it asks us to consider the degree to which certain changes in a person's character, interests, priorities, circumstances or life-history may complicate the matter of just what it means to require that promises be kept or that people should in future remain true to their past or present declarations of intent. For, as Parfit remarks, 'we may regard some events within a person's life as, in certain ways, like birth or death. Not in all ways, for beyond these events the person has earlier and later selves. But it may be only one out of the series of selves which is the object of some of our emotions, and to which we apply some of our principles.'[32] Thus his case for loosening our normal, strongly individualist conception of personhood – for rejecting the idea of some 'deep further fact' that anchors our sense of uniqueness, identity, and perduring existence over time – goes along with Parfit's consequentialist claim that this offers a better, more socially responsive and ethically desirable (since less self-centred) approach to such issues.[33]

Of course Derrida comes at them from a different angle, concerned as he is – in this particular case – with the aporias of Austinian speech-act theory and the problems that Austin runs up against in trying to fix the normative criteria for properly (sincerely, in the right sort of context) meaning what one says and saying what one means. Still there is a clear sense in which Derrida, like Parfit, is centrally concerned with metaphysical questions concerning the nature of the self, the extent of our trans-temporal responsibility for past (as well as future) commissions or omissions, and – above all – the ethical implications of adopting such a scaled-down, basically Humean, conception of individual personhood. That he raises these questions in a 'textualist' or deconstructive mode rather than through Parfit's preferred kind of thought-experimental approach should not disguise the extent of common ground between them or – *contra* critics like Searle – the fact that Derrida is here engaged with issues of a genuinely ethical import. Thus he would have no reason to dissent from Parfit's defence against the charge that, 'if the Reductionist view is true, we can never be bound by past commitments'. After all,

[w]hen we are considering commitments, the fact of personal identity enters twice. We must consider the identity both of the maker of some promise, and of the person to whom it is made. The weakening of connectedness may reduce the *maker's* obligation. But, in the case of the person who *received* the promise, any implications of the Reductionist view could be deliberately blocked. We could ask for promises of this form, 'I shall help you, and all of your later selves'. If the promises made to me take this form, they cannot be held to be later undermined by any change in my character, or by any other weakening, over the rest of my life, in psychological connectedness.[34]

And again, more generally:

It may be objected that, by distinguishing successive selves in convenient ways, we could unfairly escape our commitments, or our just deserts. This is not so. I might say, 'It was not I who robbed the bank this morning, but only my past self. But others could more plausibly reply, 'It was you'. Since there are no fixed criteria, we can choose when to speak of a new self. But such choices may be, and be known to be, insincere. And they can also sincerely express beliefs – beliefs that are not themselves chosen.[35]

I do not want to press too hard on this Parfit/Derrida comparison, except to make the point – again with critics like Searle chiefly in mind – that when

Derrida questions the precepts of orthodox (Searlean) speech-act theory it is with ample warrant from Austin's texts and also with a view to addressing such issues as regards the metaphysics of personal identity and the ethical implications of adopting a Parfit-type, reductionist and consequentialist approach. Nor should we conclude that Derrida is just having fun at Searle's (or Austin's) expense when he brings out the difficulty of distinguishing 'serious' from 'non-serious' performatives, that is to say, authentic or genuine samples of the kind from speech-acts that are cited, uttered on the stage, spoken by characters in novels, taken 'out of context', meant in jest or whatever.[36] For here again, what is involved is an important point about the conventional character of all speech-acts and hence not only the open (non-denumerable) range of contexts in which they can function but also the lack of any principled basis for defining what should count as a proper, 'serious', not *merely* conventional but authentically committed first-person mode of utterance. To raise such questions – even, at times, in a self-consciously performative style that scores various points at Searle's expense – is not to give up on the whole business of responsible philosophical thought but rather, like Parfit, to challenge certain rooted individualist assumptions which may exert an otherwise restrictive pressure on our moral, intellectual, and everyday practical lives.

III

A joke doing the conference rounds a couple of years ago asked 'What do you get if you cross a deconstructionist with a mafia boss?', to which the answer was: 'an offer you can't understand'. In fact, as I have argued, Derrida's approach is one that crosses an extreme sensitivity to language with an acute (almost hyper-developed) sense of the problems that arise when one looks beyond its surface conventions or routine assurances. That is to say, it involves neither the placid Wittgensteinian resort to customary usage as an end-point of all our questioning, nor the Kripkean ultra-sceptical argument that eventually falls back on that same pseudo-solution, nor again the Searle-type confidently orthodox appeal to a generalized theory of language and intentionality that would count such problems merely irrelevant for all serious, constructive or properly philosophical purposes. Between them, these alternatives stake out much of the contested ground in recent (post-1970) analytic debate. What they tend to exclude – in practice if not as a matter of express principle – is any notion that philosophy might take the 'linguistic turn' yet continue to engage those problems in a way that acknowledges their deep and ineluctable character, rather than claiming to dissolve them altogether through linguistic therapy or resolve them outright through some form of conceptual analysis.[37] If there is one good reason (apart from group loyalty or professional self-image) for retaining the 'two traditions' idea, it is the contrast between an 'analytic' mode of thought which adopts one or other of those standard techniques for avoiding questions beyond its customary remit and a 'continental' approach that persists in raising such questions even when – as with Derrida – this takes the form of a close reading of texts which draws out their moments of conceptual strain or aporia. For it is at just such moments that philosophy itself has to face the issue of doxastic responsibility, that is to say, of its ultimate need to decide between the claims of an orthodox, traditional approach to those texts and one that takes the risk of reading them against the received doctrinal grain. In Derrida's case this latter disposition is not, as opponents like Searle would have it, merely the sign of a wilful or perverse desire to find problems where no such problems exist. Still less, *pace* Rorty, can it be put down to boredom with the old way of doing things, or a desire simply to 'change the conversation' and leave all those pointless (since unanswerable) problems behind. Rather it is the upshot of a principled commitment to standards of interpretative fidelity and truth that require nothing less than a willingness to question the received or canonical view of things.

Of course this claim will be seen to raise all the same conceptually intractable issues that have always emerged in the context of debates about free-will and determinism, or with regard to the volitional or non-volitional character of actions and beliefs. They are posed most explicitly in Derrida's later writings on ethical themes, where he takes – I would suggest – an overly extreme and paradoxical view (one with distinct Kierkegaardian echoes) of the absolute gulf between authentically ethical decisions and those arrived at on the basis of evidence, rational deliberation, appeals to precedent or any kind of calculative (i.e., consequentialist) reasoning.[38] However they are already present in those passages of his early work where Derrida reflects on the scope and limits of interpretative licence, the constraints on any reading that would claim good philological, textual or scholarly warrant, and the complex interplay of freedom and necessity that he takes to characterize all such forms of 'respectful' yet 'productive' (hence to some extent heterodox) relationship between philosophy and its past. After all, as he remarks, 'the writer writes *in* a language and *in* a logic whose proper system, laws, and life his discourse by definition cannot dominate absolutely'.[39] In which case there is a problem – one much emphasized by literary theorists – about any appeal to authorial intention that treats it as a source or validating ground for this or that preferred interpretation.[40] On the other hand, as Derrida brings out with exemplary force in his early writings on Husserl, one also has to recognize the limits of any such downright anti-intentionalist approach and the extent to which meaning – the expressive potential of language – must be thought to exceed or elude the utmost efforts of a purely structuralist account.[41]

What is in question here is recognizably the 'old' free-will/determinism issue, though recast in terms of a particular debate within philosophy of language which allows that issue to be raised more pointedly through the close reading of various passages from Rousseau, Saussure, Lévi-Strauss and others. Thus a deconstructive reading 'must always aim at a certain relationship, unperceived by the writer, between what he commands and what he does not command of the language that he uses'.[42] As Derrida conceives it, this relationship pertains just as much to the reading itself, or to the text that is produced by way of that reading, as it does to the 'original' or 'primary' text whose complications are under scrutiny. In each case one has to acknowledge *both* the extent to which language is inevitably constrained by pre-existing norms, conceptual oppositions, logico-semantic structures and so forth, *and* the extent to which it nonetheless offers some leeway for readings that go beyond mere paraphrase or (in the limit-case) straightforward literal transcription. Where Derrida locates the ethical 'moment' of reading is in precisely this space between the twin poles of an interpretative freedom that is responsible only to itself and an outlook of extreme conservatism in that regard which totally renounces any such freedom – any room for the exercise of autonomous judgement, within whatever 'responsible' constraints – for the sake of absolute fidelity to the text in hand. Of course it may be said, with Searle's critique in mind, that this way of setting up the issue by playing off two equally extreme and preposterous positions is just another instance of Derrida's deplorable penchant for muddying the philosophical waters. To be sure, they are not the kinds of position that one is likely to encounter in practice, or perhaps anywhere outside the fictions of Jorge Luis Borges. Yet it is just Derrida's point *contra* Searle that philosophy *can and should* concern itself with issues that may seem marginal – even absurd – from a common-sense (or philosophically orthodox) view, yet which thinking is sure to confront once it leaves the safe ground of a confident appeal to 'ordinary language' or the way we routinely and conventionally 'do things with words'.

Nowhere is this more clearly the case than in debates about free-will and determinism, issues which are taken up and developed to singular effect in Derrida's remarks about reading. 'To produce this signifying structure', he writes,

> [o]bviously cannot consist of reproducing, by the effaced and respectful doubling of commentary, the conscious, voluntary, intentional relationship that the author institutes in his exchanges with the history to which he belongs thanks to the element of language. This moment of doubling commentary should no doubt have its place in a critical reading. To recognise and respect all its classical exigencies is not easy and requires all the instruments of traditional criticism. Without this recognition and this respect, critical production would risk developing in any direction at all and authorise itself to say almost anything. But this indispensable guardrail has always only *protected*, it has never *opened* a reading.[43]

What I should wish to emphasize here is the way that this passage so pointedly raises questions concerning intellectual and ethical responsibility – or the issue of doxastic voluntarism – in the context of querying just how far and with what necessary qualifications we are entitled to equate textual meaning with authorial intent. His answer is one that will scarcely satisfy those (whether literary theorists or philosophers) for whom such questions are not worth pursuing if there is no prospect of a clear-cut solution or straightforward guidance on how to proceed. Nor will it go down well with those others – Wittgensteinians, followers of Rorty, and some (not all) readers of Austin – who take them to be simply insoluble except through a course of linguistic-therapeutic counselling that would lead us back, in Stanley Cavell's soothing words, 'via the community, home'.[44] Indeed these have been the two main lines of attack amongst Derrida's opponents, namely the charge – as by Searle – that his misunderstandings of Austin result from a straightforward failure of theoretical grasp, and the idea that all these hyper-cultivated problems can always be resolved through a sensible acceptance that we *just do* (normally or properly) mean what we say through this or that communally warranted mode of expression.[45] However there is no reason to endorse this placidly consensualist account of philosophy's legitimate role if one takes the contrary (non-Wittgensteinian) view that its responsibilities are best discharged through a close attentiveness to just the sorts of issue like those concerning the scope and limits of doxastic voluntarism – which cannot be wished away by any such emollient strategy. For if one thing is clear it is the fact that these deeply puzzling questions are no likelier to find their quietus in some version of the ordinary-language mantra 'don't ask for the meaning, look at the use' than through the advent of some startling new discovery in neurophysiology or cognitive science.

I trust that this will not be misconstrued as lending support to the 'mysterian' idea that such problems are insoluble since we are congenitally just not bright enough to figure out a solution.[46] Rather it is to say that at present, as things stand with those disciplines, we are not remotely within sight of achieving any such solution or even capable of suggesting the likeliest terms on which it might be had. Indeed the most striking feature of such debates – at least as concerns the issue of free-will/determinism or doxastic responsibility – is the fact that they display so impressive a degree of advancement on various specialist fronts (psychological, cognitive-scientific, neuro-scientific, and so forth) while finally failing to get any closer to an answer on the basic philosophical question. Hence the persistent explanatory gap that mysterians are so readily able to exploit, that is, the gap between what we might know if we possessed a complete science of the brain and a knowledge of its physically specifiable state at any given time and, on the other hand, those salient aspects of our first person, subjective or phenomenological experience that seem to elude any such specification.[47] The equivalent problem in doxastic or volitional terms is that which arises if one asks what is missing from a theory of rational belief-formation or rationally motivated acts and decisions that adopts a purely formal (inferentialist) perspective on the reasoning processes involved and thus self-defeatingly omits any reference to the workings of conscious agency or will. Mark Bevir makes the point most succinctly when he comments that 'not all pro-attitudes lead to intentions, so we need a concept such as intention to denote the special stance we adopt towards a pro-attitude when we decide to act on it'.[48] After all, he goes on, 'practical syllogisms give us only grounds for doing things, where there might be grounds for not doing them, or for doing different things, and this means that the conclusions of practical syllogisms cannot be actions'. In which case – the upshot of his own subtly but crucially distinct form of syllogism – 'there is a gap between the two, a gap we can fill only by evoking the operation of the will'.[49]

Bevir is one of those among the younger generation of analytically trained philosophers who have not gone 'post-analytic' in a wholesale Rortian fashion but who have found themselves up against problems with that way of thinking which compel them to take some account of developments in the 'other' tradition.[50] Most significant here is that parting of the ways after Kant which eventually gave rise to the analytic emphasis on issues of conceptual understanding and, as the text-book account would have it, to a typically 'continental' emphasis on the role of intentionality, agency and choice. However it is becoming steadily more apparent that this was a false or at any rate a heavily skewed perspective, and that the various problems encountered by analytic philosophy over the past eight decades have also been engaged to revealing effect by thinkers in the continental line of descent.[51] Above all, they have offered a series of provocative reminders – 'provocative' in every sense of the term – that conceptual analysis, though strictly indispensable to any kind of philosophical reasoning worth the name, nevertheless turns out to have certain limits when it comes to issues of ethical or doxastic responsibility. Indeed, as Bevir pointedly suggests, if the term 'post-analytic' is to gain any useful descriptive purchase then it is perhaps best thought of as encompassing all those developments – at least since Quine's 'Two Dogmas of Empiricism' – which have cast doubt on the very possibility of drawing a sharp, categorical distinction between analytic 'truths of reason' and empirical (or synthetic) 'matters of fact'.[52] That all philosophy in some sense aspires to the condition of the analytic statement was the unspoken Leibnizian subtext of much work from the heyday of logical positivism, whatever its allowance for those other kinds of statement (prototypically in the natural sciences) whose truth-conditions were a matter of straightforward empirical or observational warrant.[53] For, of course, it was just the validity of that distinction – along with the idea that such statements could be tested one by one against likewise discrete items of empirical evidence – that Quine set out to deconstruct in his landmark essay.

Since then the term 'analytic philosophy' has become ever more loosely defined, to the point where very often it seems to mean nothing more specific than 'philosophy having some connection (at whatever "post-analytic" remove) to the earlier analytic mainstream', or 'philosophy that steers well clear of those pesky "continental" types'.[54] My own view – as will be evident by now – is that the latter sort of prejudice has done great harm and helps to explain the impression given by so much recent work in the (broadly) analytic line that it has entered some prolonged, perhaps terminal phase of intellectual exhaustion. Hence the ease with which Rorty can set out his prospectus for a version of the post-analytic turn which counts all that earnest seeking after truth (whether in Descartes, Kant, Husserl, Frege, Russell or a certain retrograde aspect of Derrida's work) as a world well lost in comparison to the new-found freedoms afforded by a view of philosophy as just another 'kind of writing', one that does best when it exploits the full range of fictive, metaphorical or literary themes and devices.[55] To be sure, there are certain texts of Derrida that do answer to something very like this description, and which make a strong point – like Kierkegaard before him – of drawing attention to the presence and the workings of precisely such elements, not only in the texts that he examines but also, by way of example, in his own deconstructive reading of them.[56] This is nowhere more apparent – and nowhere more strongly allergenic to philosophers of a mainstream analytic persuasion – than in Derrida's treatment of Austinian speech-act theory and his subsequent rejoinder to Searle on that topic, devoted as it is to an extraordinary set-piece performative rehearsal of the various aporias, that is, the problems and unresolved conflicts that afflict any orthodox approach (like Searle's) based on the assumed possibility of distinguishing sharply between constative and performative, 'felicitous' and 'infelicitous', or 'normal' and 'deviant' samples of the kind.[57] All the same there is a singular demonstrative force about Derrida's way of raising these issues which, *pace* Searle, loses nothing of its philosophic strength and conceptual precision through its often being couched – textually enacted – in performative rather than constative (i.e, straightforwardly propositional) terms.

So when Derrida talks about 'playing old Harry' with the truth/falsehood 'fetish' it is important to note firstly that he is citing Austin's use of just that phrase in just that context and, secondly, that it raises the pertinent issue as to whether Searle's tidying-up endeavours on Austin's behalf – his attempt to provide a clear-cut regimentation of speech-act theory – can possibly cope with those textual complications that Derrida's reading brings out to such striking effect. This is not say – far from it – that Derrida rejects or disregards the need for logical rigour in argument or for defining one's operative terms and distinctions with the greatest possible degree of conceptual clarity. Indeed, he rather mischievously turns the tables by declaring himself shocked by Searle's claim that he (Derrida) has contrived to come up with all these pseudo-problems about meaning, intention, validating context and so on, only by applying inappropriate (overly rigorous) standards of what should count in this context as an adequate, clear-cut or philosophically precise distinction. Thus:

> From the moment that Searle entrusts himself to an oppositional logic, to the 'distinction' of concepts by 'contrast' or 'opposition' (a legitimate demand that I share with him, even if I do not at all elicit the same consequences from it), I have difficulty seeing how he is nevertheless able to write [that] phrase ... in which he credits me with the 'assumption', 'oddly enough derived from logical positivism', 'that unless a distinction can be made rigorous and precise, it is not really a distinction at all'.[58]

However this is not just a point-scoring exercise at Searle's expense or another case of Derrida playing wilful games with the concepts and protocols of serious philosophical debate. Rather it is a statement of the principle – borne out by his reading of numerous texts, Austin's among them – that *even though* deconstruction may complicate matters with regard to any straightforward, logically consistent exposition of those same texts, it can do so only by respecting the constraints of classical (bivalent) logic as far as possible and thus showing where it runs up against such moments of strictly irresolvable aporia. 'When a concept is to be treated *as* a concept', Derrida writes:

> One has to accept the logic of all or nothing ... at any rate, in a theoretical or philosophical discussion of concepts or of things conceptualizable. Whenever one feels obliged to stop doing this (as happens to me when I speak of différance, of mark, of supplement, of iterability and of all they entail), it is better to make explicit in the most conceptual, rigorous, formalizing, and pedagogical manner possible the reasons one has for doing so, for thus changing the rules and the context of discourse.[59]

These passages very forcefully make the point (as against Searle) that deconstruction has nothing whatever in common with the kinds of all-licensing interpretative 'free-play' sometimes invoked in its name. Nor again should it be confused – as I have argued at length elsewhere – with over-ready or premature appeals to various forms of non-classical, 'deviant' or many-valued logic.[60] No doubt there is a valid case to be made for regarding Derrida's deconstructive logics of 'supplementarity', 'parergonality' and their various cognates as further, distinctive and legitimate additions to the above-mentioned class.[61] However it is a case that requires significant qualification in so far as a deconstructive reading would lack any critical purchase – any standard by which to register those moments of textual conflict or aporia – without this ultimate presumption in favour of a bivalent (true-or-false) logic.

It is worth quoting one more passage from Derrida's second-round response to Searle so as to clarify the issue between them and avoid leaving any impression (such as Searle is keen to convey) that it is merely another instance of perverse and irresponsible gamesmanship on Derrida's part. 'To this oppositional logic', Derrida writes,

> [w]hich is necessarily, legitimately, a logic of 'all or nothing' and without which the distinction and the limits of a concept would have no chance, I oppose nothing, least of all a logic of approximation [*à peu près*], a simple empiricism of difference in degree; rather I add a supplementary complication that calls for other concepts ... or rather another discourse, another 'logic' that accounts for the impossibility of concluding such a 'general theory'.[62]

This helps to bring out the crucial difference between, on the one hand, a properly deconstructive reading of texts that reveals their logical anomalies or blind spots by holding them accountable to rigorous (bivalent) truth/falsehood conditions and, on the other, an 'approximative' pseudo-logic that takes the path of least resistance by pragmatically adjusting or relaxing those conditions in response to any such anomalies. There is a similar problem about other proposals – most famously, that of Quine in 'Two Dogmas of Empiricism' – that the axioms or ground rules of classical logic might have to be revised, suspended or abandoned in face of empirical counter-evidence, such as (perhaps) the phenomena of quantum superposition or wave/particle dualism.[63] Simply put: this prescription, if consistently applied, would spell an end to all progress (indeed, to all rational debate) in science, philosophy and every discipline where issues of truth are not straightforwardly reducible to issues of direct observational or empirical warrant. Taken together with Quine's twin theses of the underdetermination of theory by evidence and the theory-laden character of observation statements it amounts to a form of radically holistic or paradigm-relativist thinking which blocks any possible appeal to objective, that is, verification-transcendent and non-framework-internal standards of validity and truth.[64] This is, I think, a chief reason for Derrida's insistence on the need to maintain an 'all or nothing' (bivalent) conception of logic, and also for his taking so strong a line on what he sees as Searle's disreputable recourse to a 'logic of approximation', a 'simple empiricism of difference in degree'. Such recourse may perhaps be justified in certain, pragmatically oriented contexts of everyday linguistic exchange where conceptual precision of the kind that Derrida here demands is neither attainable nor (perhaps) much to be desired. However it has no place in that other type of discourse – speech-act theory or philosophy of language – where indeed it is the case that 'unless a distinction can be made rigorous and precise, it is not really a distinction at all'. Thus when Searle charges Derrida with having wilfully muddied the waters by applying inappropriate standards – 'oddly enough, derived from logical positivism' – for what should count as an adequate, precise or rigorous distinction, Derrida can turn this charge straight around and remark on its oddity when issued by one whose professed aim is exactly to provide a more adequate, precise and rigorous treatment of Austin's often rather ad hoc and unmethodical mode of address.

IV

Still I am not so much concerned with these issues in philosophy of language and logic but more with their bearing on the question of doxastic responsibility. This, to repeat, is the question as to whether – or just how far – we can reconcile the claims of doxastic voluntarism with a due recognition of those various factors (causal, circumstantial, psycho-physical, socio-cultural, etc.) which restrict or, as hard-line determinists would have it, utterly negate any scope for the exercise of free yet responsible choice in our various commitments.[65] What Derrida has achieved is a recasting of this question that takes full measure of the present-day linguistic 'turn' but which nonetheless retains – unlike other versions – an acute awareness of those problems and antinomies that cannot be resolved by any appeal to language-games or cultural 'forms of life' as the furthest we can get toward rational or ethical justification. That he raises these issues in a 'textualist' mode – through the close reading of philosophers from Plato to Austin – should not blind us to the fact that they emerge through such reading with a clarity and force that refutes any charge of mere gamesmanship on Derrida's part. Here one might recall the above-cited passage in which he denies that a deconstructive commentary can consist of simply 'reproducing ... the conscious, voluntary, intentional relationship that an author institutes in his exchanges with the history to which he belongs thanks to the element of language', then qualifies this with the statement that authorial intention must play some guiding or regulative role since otherwise 'critical production would risk developing in any direction at all and authorize itself to say almost anything', only to add – by way of further qualification – that 'this indispensable guardrail has always only *protected*, it has never *opened* a reading'.[66] Nor are these remarks mere statements of abstract principle or defences raised against the likely charge – one much bandied about among Derrida's critics – that deconstruction amounts to nothing more than a kind of free-for-all interpretative licence. On the contrary: they describe exactly that unique combination of extreme attentiveness to textual detail with logical rigour and conceptual acuity which leads him to read very often against the straightforward (manifest) intentionalist grain but always according to standards of evidence more precise and exacting than those observed by his opponents.

Most relevant here is the close, indeed indissoluble tie between Derrida's highly nuanced approach to these hermeneutic issues concerning the scope and limits of authorial intention and the issue of free-will versus determinism as raised, in different forms or modalities, by philosophers from Plato and Aristotle to the present. Once again, it is the problem of explaining how an adequate regard for the claims of rational and ethical autonomy can go along with a likewise adequate allowance for the extent to which human actions and beliefs may be subject to various factors beyond our conscious, reflective or deliberative grasp. Such is one version of the deep-laid aporia – the moment of strictly irresolvable conflict or dilemma – that Derrida locates at those various textual stress points where thinking is brought up against the limits of its own self-assured concepts and categories. In his later work such themes become more explicit, as for instance when Derrida advances his idea of the ethical 'moment' as that which by very definition involves a leap beyond any justificatory appeal to rules, precedents, decision-procedures, maxims or imperatives and so on.[67] Hence the striking re-emergence of certain distinctly existentialist tonings in that later work, along with a tendency to cast ethical questions in crypto-theological terms which some commentators – myself included – find rather less than persuasive.[68] All the same what chiefly characterizes Derrida's thought, early and late, is its openness to questions that have no place in the mainstream analytic tradition, or that are there dealt with only by way of some well-practised coping strategy which brings them safely back within the scope of conceptual-linguistic manageability.

If 'continental philosophy' from Sartre to Derrida has figured most often as a standing provocation to thinkers in that other camp, still one should distinguish the hostile, rattled or dismissive response of antagonists like Ayer or Searle from the kinds of genuine critical engagement – whatever their salient differences of view – that have lately gained ground amongst its more open-minded exponents. No doubt one reason for this is the widespread sense, after Quine, that analytic philosophy has gone so far toward dismantling its own conceptual and methodological foundations that the term 'analytic' now has little use save as a rough descriptor for the kind of work carried on 'over here' rather than 'over there'. Still I would suggest that the distinction is worth retaining not so much in that standard (philosophically as well as geographically questionable) role but rather as a means of pointing up certain differences of interest, emphasis and orientation within each of the two (supposedly) separate lines of descent. Thus it is better to think of the 'continental' strain – on whichever side of the English Channel – as that which conserves a legitimate place for questions of a speculative nature that intrinsically elude or surpass the remit of conceptual-linguistic analysis as practised by most, if not all partisans of the 'other' tradition. For, as Derrida brings out in his reading of Austin, there are certain aspects of speech-act theory – or of its handling in Austin's self-consciously performative, rather than Searle's confidently orthodox and constative mode – that can be seen to display a strong elective affinity not only with his own (Derrida's) approach but also with a range of 'continental' developments after Husserl.[69] The same point is made, albeit in a more anecdotal manner, when Derrida picks up on certain suggestive analogies with Gilbert Ryle's quirkily distinctive way of treating such set-piece analytic themes as the use/mention dichotomy and the sundry vexing dilemmas – 'aporias' in deconstructive parlance – which result from the kinds of category mistake that philosophers often fall into.[70]

However what gives these comparisons a larger significance is the way that such 'continental' modes of thought tend to surface at just those moments – or in just those contexts of argument   where analytic philosophy encounters certain limits to its normal range of conceptual resources. Hence, for instance, the sharp contrast between readings of late Wittgenstein that tend in one or other of these directions, depending very largely on whether or not they are willing to pursue the sorts of question that Wittgenstein constantly provokes yet constantly claims to show up as mere products of our chronic liability to forms of self-induced perplexity or 'bewitchment by language'. On the one hand are those readings in the prevalent analytic mode that envisage the proper business of philosophy as a process of therapeutic coaxing-down from the heights of metaphysical abstraction through a routine appeal to the saving grace of (so-called) 'ordinary language'. On the other are those deconstructive or continentally inflected readings which emphasize how very *extra*-ordinary – and how deeply resistant to any such approach – are the sorts of example that Wittgenstein often brings up and which just as often figure in our everyday linguistic and social transactions.[71] Indeed one could argue, in broad-brush style, that as Husserlian phenomenology stood in relation to the discourse of 1930s logical positivism, and as existentialism stood in relation to its logical-empiricist successor movement, so deconstruction now stands in relation to the discourse of present-day analytic philosophy, at least in so far as that discourse has taken the linguistic turn toward a Wittgensteinian (i.e., a radically anti-foundationalist) conception of meaning, knowledge and truth.[72] That is to say, deconstruction keeps open certain broadly 'continental' lines of thought – certain speculative freedoms though also (as Derrida makes clear in the passages from *Of Grammatology* cited above) certain needful constraints upon their exercise in any given context – which have been effectively closed off or held within firm conceptual and linguistic bounds by the mainstream schools of analytic philosophy.

Above all, as concerns our present theme, it addresses the issue of doxastic responsibility through an intensive critical engagement with various texts which inescapably raises the question how far, and with what justification, such a reading can depart from established interpretative norms and yet claim to respect the highest standards of rigour, fidelity and truth. This question is broached more directly in Derrida's later work on the aporetic character of ethical decisions, that is to say, his idea that they involve a dizzying moment of absolute, unprecedented, non-rule-governed choice between alternatives that simply allow of no comparison on moral-evaluative grounds.[73] However it is important to recognize how closely these themes connect with the sorts of issue typically engaged in his earlier writings – texts like *Of Grammatology* and *Margins of Philosophy* – and also how those writings can serve as a corrective to accounts of the 'ethics of deconstruction' that focus exclusively on this aspect of his thought and thus ignore the complex, meticulously reasoned processes of argumentation by which he leads up to such moments of conceptual aporia.[74] Thus they tend to understate the significance of works (such as 'Violence and Metaphysics', his early essay on Emmanuel Levinas) where Derrida offers a lengthy, detailed and – in my view – extremely cogent critique of any ethics based on the notion of absolute alterity, or respect for the other as intrinsically transcending our utmost powers of mutual understanding or shared experiential and communicative grasp.[75] This critique takes the form of an elaborate defence of Husserlian phenomenology – in particular, of Husserl's attempt to establish such a realm of inter-subjective understanding in his fifth *Cartesian Meditation* – against Levinas's charge that it amounts to no more than just another variation on the subject-centred ('egological') discourse of Western philosophy right down from its ancient Greek origins.[76] Thus it offers an implicit yet powerful rebuke to those sundry postmodernist adepts of alterity, absolute difference, radical undecidability and so forth, who have raised these notions to a high point of abstract principle without subjecting them to adequate scrutiny as regards their philosophic status or their ultimate ethical implications.

However my purpose here is not to provide a detailed exegesis of those early texts where Derrida negotiates a complex path between the twin poles of phenomenology and structuralism, that is, on the one hand an approach that gives priority to the concepts of agency, expressive meaning and responsible freedom in the ethical sphere and on the other an approach that tends very strongly in the opposite (linguistic- or cultural-determinist) direction.[77] Rather it is to make the general point – as throughout this chapter – that mainstream analytic philosophy might do well to avail itself of certain descriptive, thematic and critical resources that have received their most intensive development by thinkers in the 'other' tradition, from Husserl and Sartre to Derrida. To be sure, these issues have also had a good airing in the analytic literature, as likewise in a range of other, more broadly philosophical contexts. Among them is the question posed by philosophy of mind and action as regards the relative priority of 'reasons' *vis-à-vis* 'causes', that is, of rational-justificatory versus causal-explanatory modes of argument.[78] Then of course there is the long-running debate within British sociology concerning the issue of 'agency' and 'structure', thought of – once again – as raising the free-will/determinism problem in a guise more directly amenable to treatment on its own favoured methodological terms.[79] So it would clearly be absurd to claim that 'continental' thinkers have anything like a monopoly on these topics, or on treatments that maintain an adequate sense of their resistance to any putative 'solution' that would merely collapse the relevant antinomy (free-will/determinism, reason/cause, agency/structure) in one or the other direction. Nevertheless I would hope to have convinced my readers that there are certain distinctive aspects of philosophy in the post-Husserlian line of descent that can serve not only as a spur to reflection on the part of analytic philosophers but also – more importantly – as a pointed reminder of those salient issues that are often ignored, obscured or smoothed over in some (e.g., Wittgenstein-influenced) quarters of debate. Thus Sartre presents them with a vividness and force seldom matched by the kinds of test-case example, whether 'real-life' or fictive, that are typically offered by ethical theorists of an analytic bent, while Derrida pursues them by way of an intensely critical and close-focused textual awareness that yields insights unattainable by any other means.

I should not for one moment wish to endorse the sypposed 'two traditions' idea, still less to widen the perceived (in fact much-exaggerated) gulf between post-Frege/Russell and post-Husserlian developments. Indeed I have argued to contrary effect: that there is room for much more than currently goes on in the way of reciprocal exchange, and that this can be a source of renewed intellectual stimulus even where it takes the form of conflicting priorities or mutual irritation. What has chiefly characterized this relationship over the past century or so is the Kantian legacy of unresolved issues between a speculative ('continental') impulse that drives philosophy to raise questions beyond its powers of assured conceptual grasp and a normalizing (broadly 'analytic') tendency to treat such questions as by their very nature irresolvable and hence as ill-formed, 'metaphysically' extravagant, or products of our constant tendency to forms of bewitchment by language. This Wittgensteinian diagnosis would no doubt be contested – even roundly denounced as a quietist injunction that philosophy should leave everything as it is with our everyday habits of usage – by thinkers of a more classically analytic persuasion who retain the belief that 'ordinary language' cannot be the final arbiter in such matters.[80] However, as I have said, this alternative approach still belongs very firmly to the school of thought for which philosophical problems only count as such – as genuine or well-formed, rather than spurious or pseudo-problems – to the extent that they are capable of being resolved on clear-cut conceptual terms, or through modes of analysis specifiable in advance of any particular instance. It is here that Derrida's deconstructive readings of canonical texts from Plato to Austin provide not only an object-lesson in the practice of detailed textual commentary but also, uniquely, a case-by-case enactment of the complex interplay between freedom and necessity, or 'creative', heterodox interpretation and the constraints imposed by a due regard for the protocols of scholarship and logical argumentation. Hence perhaps the mixture of bafflement and outrage expressed by critics like Searle who see nothing more to this 'performative' dimension of Derrida's writing than a desire to make trouble or a wilful disregard for the basic requirement that philosophy maintain a firm sense of the distinction between whatever goes on at the level of first-order, natural-language utterance and its own, properly constative criteria of method, validity and truth.

I hope I have said enough to justify the claim that such charges are demonstrably wide of the mark. Thus Derrida's readings are none the less rigorous, consequent and logically compelling for the fact that they raise issues of a kind – and through a mode of subtly nuanced textual commentary – which cannot but strike those opponents as yet further proof (if any were needed) of his intellectual irresponsibility. That some philosophers in the broadly analytic camp have lately seen fit to question this estimate is one hopeful sign of a larger change in the pattern of routine mistrust and hostility which has left such a damaging mark on relations between the 'two traditions' in the wake of logical positivism.[81] Where analytic philosophy has most to gain from a greater relaxation of these border controls is in the matter of rethinking those various antinomies that Kant set in place through his attempt to delimit the realm of conceptual understanding from the spheres of pure and practical reason, and that have since given rise to such a deal of trouble for epistemologists and ethical theorists alike.[82] If one thing emerges with painful clarity from recent overtures in a Kantian direction by analytic philosophers in quest of some alternative path it is the need for that quest to go by way of an intensive re-engagement with the texts of Kant – along with other texts in both (i.e., 'continental' and 'analytic') lines of descent from Kant – rather than address these problems as if *de novo* from a standpoint of pre-assured conceptual or logico-semantic grasp.[83] It is here that they have most to learn from Derrida, offering as he does some exemplary lessons in philosophy's power to open new and creative paths of thought whilst remaining faithful to the strictest standards of textual fidelity and truth. Above all he has proved its continued capacity, after and despite the 'linguistic turn', to engage the kinds of deep-laid philosophical concern that cannot be convincingly laid to rest by any application of conceptual-linguistic therapy. This is why, *pace* Searle, his encounter with Austin was among the most important and revealing episodes in recent philosophical debate. That is to say, it signalled a possible way forward from the doldrums of much mainstream anglophone philosophy since the decline of logical empiricism and the advent of a phase when the dominant influences – those of Wittgenstein and Quine – have been such as to impose tight limits on the scope for speculative thought or for any approach that threatens to exceed the bounds of pre-established linguistic or conceptual acceptability. Indeed, one could argue that some of the resourceful, intelligent and (potentially) fertile minds in recent analytic debate have been devoted to just the kinds of narrowly prescriptive philosophical agenda whose effect is to block such alternative views.[84] Now at last there are signs that thinkers in the 'other', anglophone tradition are beginning to shed their preconceptions about Derrida's work, whether based on the reports of those (like Searle) who have dismissed that work out of hand or of enthusiasts, like Rorty, who admire him for all the wrong reasons. So far from filling the Rortian bill by showing us a handy escape route from philosophy's age-old as well as its recent, analytically revamped problems Derrida has continued to engage those problems with a vigour, pertinence, conceptual creativity and depth of philosophical grasp unequalled amongst his contemporaries.

V

The phrase 'conceptual creativity' will no doubt strike an odd note to any reader whose responses are more closely attuned to the register of analytic than of recent continental philosophy. Nor is this at all surprising, given that by far the greater proportion of work carried on in the former tradition during the past near-century has been devoted to conceptual 'analysis' in the root sense of that term, that is, a chiefly clarificatory exercise aimed toward drawing out the pre-suppositions (or unnoticed implications) of our various beliefs, truth-claims, referring expressions, modes of rational inference and so forth. Of course this approach has taken some contrasting and even (on the face of it) conflicting forms, as for instance when philosophers in the 'ordinary language' line of descent from Wittgenstein or Austin reject the idea – as maintained by those in the Frege–Russell camp – that our everyday, customary habits of usage may sometimes enshrine certain errors, confusions or ambiguities of scope.[85] On the one, broadly speaking descriptivist view philosophy should either espouse the fully fledged Wittgensteinian quietist outlook and aspire to leave everything just as it is with our language-games, practices, life-forms and so on, or else follow Austin in respecting the wisdom of 'ordinary' talk while seeking to sharpen some of its less perspicuous terms and distinctions. On the other, that is, prescriptivist/revisionist account philosophy is entitled to go far beyond such a modest exercise in conceptual clarification and offer the kind of Russellian logico-linguistic analysis that purports to correct or eradicate the errors to which everyday language is so distressingly prone.[86] However that disagreement will seem more parochial – more a difference of emphasis than of principle – when compared to what these parties have in common. For here at least the two branch-lines can be seen to converge: on their conception of the proper business of philosophy as a matter of bringing analysis to bear on certain ways of speaking, thinking or judging that already have their place in our extant (whether everyday or specialized) linguistic practices.

It is for this reason, I would suggest, that the notion of 'conceptual creativity' may sound distinctly odd – even like a back-handed compliment – when applied to philosophers rather than, say, philosophically minded novelists, poets, composers or practitioners of the visual arts. Thus when Gilles Deleuze counts it a hallmark of genuine as opposed to merely academic, derivative or second-rate philosophy, his claim is apt to strike most 'analytic' types as just another case of the unfortunate penchant among French thinkers for wilfully blurring the genre-distinction between philosophy and literature.[87] Such is the charge brought against Derrida by those in the analytic mainstream (like Searle) who want to maintain a strict demarcation between performative modes of discourse and the expository standards that properly apply to the discourse of speech-act theory. It is one rehearsed in more detail by others on the 'continental' side – like Habermas – who mistakenly suppose that he (Derrida) is out to reduce philosophy to just another 'kind of writing' or sub-genre of literature and thereby revoke the hard-won gains of enlightenment or the 'unfinished project of modernity'.[88] As I have said, this idea finds absolutely no warrant in Derrida's texts and has a lot more to do with the partial – not to say grossly distorted – version of Derrida put about by Rorty and various 'literary' deconstructionists. What it registers perhaps is a grudging sense of his sheer conceptual creativity, that is to say, Derrida's extraordinary gift for the invention of new and productive ways of reading classic philosophical texts that have long been trodden into orthodox ruts by the mainstream commentators. Here it would be useful – given time – to look more closely at Derrida's thoughts concerning this term 'invention' and the way that it has moved across from its primary sense in the lexicon of ancient rhetoric ('*inventio*' = 'selection/discovery of apt topics, figures of speech, argumentative strategies', etc.) to its primary modern sense: 'invention' = 'the outcome of creative/imaginative acts of thought that inherently transcend or surpass the appeal to any such prior example'.[89] Indeed his entire life's work can now be seen as an intensive meditation on just this theme, that is, the strictly irresolvable aporia between freedom or expressive creativity as a datum of intuitive or self-conscious human experience and, on the other hand, the likewise irreducible fact that such freedom can only make sense within certain norms or pre-given structures of rational intelligibility.

Hence the typically ambivalent outcome of those early writings on Husserl where Derrida presses hard on the antinomies of 'structure' and 'genesis'. Thus 'a certain structuralism has always been philosophy's most spontaneous gesture', while at the same time 'it is always something like an *opening* which will frustrate the structuralist project', since 'what I can never understand, in a structure, is that by means of which it is not closed'.[90] Here the aporia is expressed in terms of that particular conflict of interpretations – the emergent clash between phenomenological and structuralist approaches – which was a main focus of interest in France at the time (the early 1960s) when Derrida first developed his theses with regard to their mutually incompatible but also their mutually provocative and stimulating mode of inter-relationship. However it is an issue by no means confined to that specific cultural-philosophical context but one that reaches out – as I have argued here – to some of the deepest, most intractable and longstanding problems in philosophy of mind, knowledge, action and morals. That he broaches them *via* a close reading of philosophic texts is no reason to lump Derrida with the adepts of a postmodern-pragmatist outlook that considers those problems to have long outlived their sell-by date and rejoices in the freedoms now opened up by new-found modes of creative redescription. Nor does it give any warrant for the claim – one favoured by a number of moderately well-disposed commentators – that at the end of all Derrida's ingenious argumentation we are left with just another, albeit more colourful (i.e., 'continental') version of Wittgenstein's point about the impossibility of getting outside, beneath or beyond our various language-games and cultural practices. For this is to ignore what must strike any reader not strongly predisposed toward the Wittgensteinian position, namely that far from seeking to dissolve philosophical problems or to conjure them away through some form of applied psycho linguistic therapy, Derrida is intent upon thinking them through with the utmost conceptual rigour.

Thus when he presses hard on such deep-laid antinomies as that of 'genesis' and 'structure' in Husserl, or (more generally) on the conflicting claims of phenomenology and structuralism, it is in order to reject any premature move toward synthesis or reconciliation and thereby to keep us constantly in mind of philosophy's proper role. That role is not fulfilled, as Wittgenstein would have it, at the stage where explanations run out, where the problems show up as mere products of 'bewitchment by language', and we are brought around at last to a wise acceptance that philosophy can and should leave everything just as it is.[91] In this respect Derrida's work shows more affinity with that other main 'analytic' line of descent which runs from Frege and Russell to those present-day thinkers who hold out against the notion of 'ordinary language' as a cure for all our philosophical ills, and who continue to maintain the usefulness – indeed, the necessity – of linguistic analysis as a form of conceptual rectification and critique. On the other hand, as emerges in his reading of Austin, Derrida is keenly aware of the problems that project has to confront when it turns its attention from those formalized (truth-functional) languages that represent the end point of such analysis and engages instead with the sorts of complexity that typify our natural-language transactions, even (or especially) those that may arise in the most 'ordinary'-seeming contexts. Hence, I have said, his strong resistance to Searle's highly regimented, programmatic mode of speech-act philosophy and his equally strong countervailing attraction to Austin's offbeat, witty, inventive, ironic, quizzical, anecdote-laden, theoretically inclined but doctrinally unbuttoned way of proceeding.

What Derrida shows to notable effect is the loss that philosophy suffers when analysis gets out of touch with these sources of linguistic creativity, but also the need for conceptual rigour – for the analytic virtues as commonly defined – if philosophy is not to become just a kind of ineffectual musing on our everyday speech-habits or a placid, uncritical endorsement of our customary practices and beliefs. The first danger is that which beckons when philosophical discourse aspires to the condition of the analytic statement, that is to say, when it courts the 'paradox of analysis' according to which such statements are tautologous (i.e., true by definition or simply in virtue of their logical form), and must therefore be considered vacuous or wholly uninformative.[92] Of course this claim is open to challenge on several grounds, among them the argument (*contra* Quine) that truths-of-definition are not necessarily circular or tail-chasing since they can – as for instance when consulting a dictionary – have an ampliative role in extending our knowledge through a process of incremental change. Besides, it may be said that the term 'analytic' as applied *strictu sensu* to a certain class of statements has a quite different meaning from the term 'analytic' as applied by way of descriptive convenience to certain philosophical developments whose main common feature – their close attentiveness to language – itself embraces a wide range of differing methods and priorities. All the same it is hard to escape the impression that a great deal of mainstream analytic philosophy in the wake of Quine's 'Two Dogmas' has become fixated on the kinds of issue – and been conducted at a level of specialized debate – which effectively prevent it from engaging with questions outside its narrow purview. Thus there is some justice in the charge that thinking of this sort tends toward a point where the topic is not so much a substantive philosophical issue as a matter of negotiating rival standpoints (like those taken up by recent contributors to the realism/anti-realism dispute) and then proposing a third-way alternative – such as the response-dispositional approach – whose chief or sole purpose is somehow to avoid the problems with both by steering a course between them. Indeed, as I have argued more extensively elsewhere, this particular three-sided debate is a prime example of the analytic proneness to a law of diminishing returns, that is, a version of the paradox of analysis whereby there exists an inverse relation between the formal (at the limit, the true-by-definition) character of statements, propositions or truth-claims and their specific or informative content.[93]

However there is also the second kind of danger noted above. This looms when philosophers react so sharply against what they see as the sterility or self-absorbed character of much work in the analytic mode that they swing right across – like Rorty or some followers of Wittgenstein – to an outright rejection of 'analysis' in any shape or form, and thence to some more extreme variety of the language-first doctrine. Such is Rorty's attempt at co-opting Derrida for a strong-descriptivist account of philosophy's role in present-day 'postmodern–bourgeois–liberal–pragmatist' culture, one that involves renouncing its old, delusory claims as a discourse uniquely fit to arbitrate in matters of knowledge and truth, and embracing the more modest self-image of a strictly non-privileged but fully participant voice in the 'cultural conversation of man-kind'.[94] Yet the problem is not only that this has to ignore the large proportion of Derrida's writings devoted to conceptual analysis (or textual exegesis and critique) of the highest philosophical order but also that it sells philosophy short by denying its capacity and right to raise questions beyond those that find a place in our various customary language-games and practices. Or again, more precisely, it suggests that philosophers do best by frequently 'changing the topic' or switching to some new language-game so as to keep the conversation moving and not get stuck in a routine (e.g., old-style analytic) rut. However this removes any rational grounds for seeking to promote such change save that of sheer boredom with received habits of talk and the desire constantly to shake things up. In other words it is a kind of ultra-Kuhnian outlook wherein there is no place for what Kuhn describes as the long-term periods of 'normal', constructive, problem-solving science but only for a state of perpetual revolution such that everything is always up for grabs.[95]

That Rorty's view of Derrida has been taken on board by a good many analytic philosophers – not to mention some 'continentals' like Habermas – is among the chief reasons for that widespread prejudice (reinforced by the exchange with Searle) which makes him out to be merely a wilful subverter of responsible, truth-seeking discourse. That this is nonetheless a mistaken view – that it cannot begin to account for the acuity, force and *philosophical* cogency of Derrida's work – is a case that I have made in outline here but which finds plentiful support in that work and in the commentaries of those who have engaged with it at first hand rather than through the swirling mists of polemical exchange.[96] What I have tried to suggest is the way that his thinking points beyond certain deadlocked antinomies in the discourse of mainstream anglophone debate, among them that version of the free-will/determinism issue that nowadays tends very often to surface in a curiously displaced form as a conflict between the aims and priorities of 'continental' and 'analytic' philosophy. Nobody has thought this conflict through to more telling and singular effect, perhaps because nobody (at least since Kierkegaard) has combined such a power of sustained and intensive conceptual grasp with such a gift for exploring or inventing new genres – new 'kinds of writing', in Rorty's apt though tendentious phrase – whereby to communicate the insights thus achieved. If there is indeed an 'ethics of deconstruction' then I think it is to be found quite as much in this complex interplay of freedom and constraint – or creativity and analytic rigour – as in Derrida's later, more explicit writing on ethical and socio-political themes. That is to say, it has to do with precisely those issues that were raised through his disagreement with Searle over the scope and limits of Austinian speech-act theory. Most important was the issue as to just how far a generalized or systematic (Searle-type) rendition – one that sought to lay down definite criteria for good-faith or genuine performative utterance – could possibly capture the open-ended range of meanings, intentions and validating contexts that might always be envisaged through some more-or-less inventive stretch of our conceptual and imaginative powers.

That Searle failed utterly to take the point of Derrida's argument – that it struck him as merely a frivolous exercise in 'textualist' sophistry at Austin's expense – is one (albeit extreme) indication of the distance in terms of priorities and working assumptions that continues to separate the two philosophical cultures. Still this much-publicized encounter (or 'determined non-encounter',

as Derrida mock-ruefully described it) should not be allowed to obscure the
extent and depth of his engagement with questions that are central to a good
deal of recent analytic debate. Among them, as I have said, is the issue of
doxastic responsibility – how far can we be held intellectually and morally
accountable for what we believe? – and the related issue as to just what is
involved in a reading of philosophical texts that would respect the basic
requirement of getting things right in scholarly–philological–exegetic terms
while none the less retaining the responsible freedom to criticize their blind
spots of prejudice or unexamined presupposition. The latter question is posed
with particular force by analytic philosophers, from Bertrand Russell to Jonathan Bennett, who adopt the standpoint of 'rational reconstruction', that is to
say, an approach that claims to draw the line between arguments which still pass
muster by the best current standards from those other, now discredited doctrines
which must henceforth be consigned to the history of ideas.[97] It is in this respect
that 'continental' thinkers – Derrida foremost among them – have managed to
avoid any such drastic and philosophically disabling division of labour. They
have done so chiefly by engaging the central problems of philosophy through a
close reading of various canonical texts, and moreover (as likewise emerges to
striking effect in Derrida's work) through constant reflection on the ethical
issues raised by such encounters between present and past modes of thought.
That is to say, this 'continental' way of thinking is distinguished from the
rational-reconstructive approach by its constant attempt to negotiate a path
between fidelity to the text in hand and fidelity to the principles of autonomous
judgement through a process of sustained analysis and critique.

   Such, we may recall, was Derrida's point in the above-cited passage from *Of
Grammatology* where he writes that 'without this recognition and this respect,
critical production would risk developing in any direction at all and authorize
itself to say almost anything', followed up by the crucial qualifying clause: 'but
this indispensable guardrail has always only *protected*, it has never *opened* a
reading'.[98] It is here – in the complex, overdetermined and (at times) conflictual
relationship between these two orders of responsibility – that Derrida locates the
ethical moment of deconstruction. Geoffrey Harpham puts the case well in his
book *Shadows of Ethics* when he remarks on the different meanings of 'morality'
and 'ethics', and on the way that ethical reflection may often complicate our
moral judgements to the point of preventing or suspending decision, at least
until the issue is somehow resolved. Thus:

> Morality negates ethics, and needs ethics in order to be moral. Decisions
> achieved without a passage through what Derrida would call undecid-
> ability and what a more traditional account would call the circumstance of
> free choice represent mere blindness and brutality. Ethics places impera-
> tives, principles, alternatives on a balanced scale, sustaining an august
> reticence, a principled irresolution to which, nevertheless, the limited and
> precise prescriptions of morality must refer for their authority. So while,

once again, neither ethics nor morality has any claim on our respect, their incoherent union is respect itself.[99]

One does not have to go all the way with Derrida's ultra-decisionist, quasi-Kierkegaardian conception of ethical choice to recognize in this a powerful statement of the central dilemma that has always afflicted moral philosophy and yet – for precisely that reason – defined what should count as a genuine instance of ethical thinking or reflection. Or indeed ethical *reading* since it is just the claim here advanced by Harpham on Derrida's behalf that the act of reading can appropriately serve as a test-case or striking analogue of the fraught relation between ethics and morality that has lately preoccupied philosophers like Bernard Williams. Thus: 'the injunction not to decide on a final interpretation of a text may qualify as an "ethics of reading", but it is definitely not a morality; morality does not shrink from such tasks but welcomes them as its proper responsibility'.[100] And again: 'morality is the "rigor" of ethical thought, where the rubber of a definite principle meets the road of reality'.[101]

It seems to me that Harpham is right about this and that the deconstructive ethics of reading, as Derrida presents it, is very far from the kind of 'textualist' free-for-all or crafty technique of rhetorical gamesmanship that critics like Searle would have us believe. Rather – as I have argued here – it is the point at which other, more ethically accommodating (e.g., Wittgensteinian or Rortian) variants of the 'linguistic turn' come up against a force of critical resistance or a demand for justificatory warrant that blocks any such easy resort to communal norms and values. Nor is it in any way an evasion or a trivialization of ethical issues to pose them (as Derrida most often does) as issues with regard to our responsibility as readers of philosophical texts, that is to say, as problems having to do with the complex interplay of freedom and necessity that typifies such reading at its best. If there is to be any genuine contact between the subject matter of that philosophy and the reflective, self-critical awareness that philosophy should seek to cultivate then it can only result – as Derrida insists in his rejoinder to Searle – from the kind of creative-exploratory approach (exemplified by Austin's writing and by his own speculative commentary on it) that does not take refuge in the premature certitudes of system and method. At the same time – as he also makes clear – such commentary cannot abandon the standards of logical rigour and rational argumentation in the absence of which there is simply no 'philosophy' worth the name.

Hence his professions of outrage – however ironic or mischievously point-scoring – when confronted with Searle's claim that he (Derrida) has muddied the philosophic waters by requiring such standards in a context, that is, that of speech-act theory where other, less exigent or more pragmatic criteria properly apply. This is not – I should emphasize – just a pious pretence of logical rigour on Derrida's part but a claim that is strongly and consistently borne out by his readings of a great many canonical texts from Plato to Rousseau, Kant, Husserl and Austin. Thus the claim is in no way compromised when he adduces those various deviant or non-standard logics (of the *pharmakon* in Plato, 'supplementarity' in Rousseau, 'parergonality' in Kant, *différance* in Husserl, 'iterability' in Austin) which emerge only by dint of a textual close reading that presses *as far as possible* with the logic of bivalent truth or falsehood.[102] My case (and Derrida's *contra* Searle) is that the most challenging and deep-laid problems of philosophy – like that of free-will *versus* determinism – are encountered at a certain limit point where its conceptual resources can be seen to confront some ultimate dilemma or aporia, but which cannot be arrived at except through a rigorous application of just those resources. One can trace this pattern from his earliest writings on the antinomy of 'genesis' and 'structure' in Husserl, through his engagement with Austin on various issues in the discourse of speech-act theory, to his later, more explicitly ethical concern with matters of choice and responsibility. What is crucial at every stage – and what sets his work so decisively apart from other variants of the 'linguistic turn' – is Derrida's absolute and principled refusal to adopt that Wittgensteinian line of least resistance which would count such issues merely a product of our misplaced hankering for ultimate solutions to non-existent problems.

This is also why he firmly rejects Searle's idea that any difficulty in defining the criteria or validity-conditions for speech-act utterance can be overcome by the ad hoc expedient of adopting a looser, more pragmatic or 'approximative' way with the various distinctions involved. And again: despite his detailed investigation of the various 'supplementary', that is, non-classical or non-biva- lent logics that emerge through a deconstructive reading of certain texts, Der- rida is very far from endorsing the view – maintained by philosophers like Quine and Putnam – that some axioms of logic might always be open to revision or abandonment should this prove the simplest, most expeditious way of saving empirical appearances.[103] Thus, to repeat, the laws of bivalence or excluded middle might have to go if no alternative were found to the orthodox (Copenhagen) theory of quantum mechanics, and physicists therefore had to make logical terms with such otherwise anomalous phenomena as wave/particle dualism or quantum superposition. However – as I have argued – this leaves it a total mystery how scientific progress could ever come about through the criti- cism of theories, hypotheses or even disputed empirical data on the grounds of logical consistency or rational inference to the best explanation. Indeed it is on just such grounds that Derrida takes issue with Searle as regards the latter's readiness to accept 'a logic of approximation [*à peu près*], a simple empiricism of difference in degree'.[104] Where Derrida locates the crucial point at issue between Searle's and his own approach is in the fact that deconstructive reading involves 'a supplementary complication that calls for other concepts . . . or rather another discourse, another "logic" that accounts for the impossibility of concluding such a "general theory".[105] Nevertheless that alternative (non-classical or deviant) logic is such as can only result from a process of meticulously argued textual analysis which itself presupposes – and strives to maintain – the utmost con- ceptual clarity and logical rigour. Hence Derrida's further remark: that 'when- ever one feels obliged to stop doing this (as happens to me when I speak of différance, of mark, of supplement, of iterability and of all they entail), it is better to make explicit in the most conceptual, rigorous, formalizing, and pedagogical manner possible the reasons one has for doing so, for thus changing the rules and the context of discourse'.[106]

What this amounts to is the claim that any adequate account of the various speech-act types and their respective validity-conditions will need to stretch its theoretical sights around a great range of possible meanings, intentions and operative contexts. That is to say, it will not let go of the requirement that philosophy maintain the highest standards of conceptual rigour and precision but will also – like Austin – set out to test those standards against the manifold 'deviant' (i.e., problematic or marginal) instances that defy any typecast categorization along confidently orthodox Searlean lines. This is why Derrida – much to Searle's annoyance – makes a point not simply of laying out his case in theoretical ('constative') terms but of showing it in action, so to speak, through a mode of performative utterance whereby the requirements of speech-act theory are played off against the scope for creativity that is manifest in our everyday as well as more specialized or inventive linguistic practices. It is also where the reading of Austin picks up on his early critical engagement with Husserl – concerning the antinomy of 'structure' and 'genesis' – and looks forward to his later, more expressly thematized, work on ethical and political themes. What unites them is an acute awareness *on the one hand* of those strictly unavoidable claims and constraints exerted by the act of careful, attentive close reading and *on the other* of that equally exigent demand that comes of our taking responsibility for whatever in our reading turns out to go against the received or canonical account.

It is here – I would suggest – that Derrida's work intersects most strikingly with various currents in the mainstream-analytic and 'post-analytic' lines of descent. Thus it demonstrates the continued possibility, after and despite the 'linguistic turn', of a thinking that acknowledges this pervasive feature of present-day philosophical discourse but nonetheless holds out, on principled grounds, for a critique of those ingrained values and beliefs that constitute our various acculturated language-games or communal forms of life. In so far as there is an 'ethics of deconstruction' – or an 'ethics of reading' more generally – it has to do with just this question of doxastic responsibility and (as Derrida says) with that 'relationship, unperceived by the writer, between what he commands and what he does not command of the language that he uses'.[107] If this applies to the vexed issue of authorial intention, that is, of how far we are obliged (or entitled) to suppose that authors reliably say what they mean or mean what they say then it applies just as much – and by the same token – to the reader's role in arriving at a sensitive, textually constrained but also adequately reasoned and critical approach to the work or passage in hand.

VI

As I have said, philosophers' views on this matter have differed very sharply both between and within the analytic and continental traditions. At the one extreme is a Kantian outlook of unqualified respect for an author's putative intentions whereby any failure to accord such respect would be tantamount to treating author and text as means toward the exegete's self-interested aims and desires.[108] At the opposite extreme is that Russellian 'rational-reconstructive' approach that takes whatever is deemed useful or valid for current philosophical purposes, subjects it to a frankly selective or partisan reading, and consigns what's left to the history of ideas or the scrap-heap of now-discredited doctrines. The *via media* finds its most typical expression in those hermeneutically inspired attempts to achieve common ground between past and present modes of understanding through an ultimate 'fusion' of cultural horizons that claims to annul or at any rate to reconcile such differences of view.[109] If this latter tends to issue in good-willed but somewhat vague and anodyne prescriptions then its widespread appeal – amongst 'post-analytic' as well as 'continental' thinkers – is perhaps best explained by its promising to offer a means of escape from the various dilemmas outlined above. That is to say, it very often runs close to the kind of Wittgensteinian approach – the idea of communally warranted belief as the furthest we can get toward justification in matters of knowledge or truth – which, despite all claims to the contrary, works out as a form of fully fledged epistemic, linguistic and socio-cultural relativism.

I hope I have said enough to make good the case that Derrida offers a cogently argued alternative to such ways of thinking, one that neither underestimates the problems confronting any serious, sustained engagement with the issue of doxastic responsibility nor resorts to one or other of the currently favoured problem-dissolving strategies. Above all his work provides some striking examples of the close relationship between an ethics of reading maximally alive to those problems and an ethics in the wider (personal, practical and socio-political) sense that likewise holds out against the twin temptations of systematic theory-building on the one hand and communal 'agreement in judgement' on the other. Let me here cite a lengthy passage from *Aporias* since it captures that relationship with a pertinence and force that cannot be lost on any reader who has experienced the intractable nature of genuine as opposed to set-piece or text-book ethical dilemmas.

How to justify the choice of *negative form* (*aporia*) to designate a duty that, through the impossible or the impracticable, nonetheless announces itself in an affirmative fashion? Because one must avoid good conscience at all costs. Not only good conscience as the grimace of an indulgent vulgarity, but quite simply the assured form of self-consciousness; good conscience as subjective certainty is incompatible with the absolute risk that every promise, every engagement, and every responsible decision – if there are such – must run. To protect the decision or the responsibility by knowledge, by some theoretical assurance, or by the certainty of being right, of being on the side of science, of consciousness or of reason, is to transform this experience into the deployment of a program, into a technical application of a rule or a norm, or into the subsumption of a determined 'case'. All these are conditions that must never be abandoned, of course, but that, as such, are only the guardrail of a responsibility to whose calling they remain radically heterogeneous. The affirmation that announced itself through a negative form was therefore the necessity of *experience* itself, the experience of the aporia.[110]

I have expressed reservations with regard to the way that such passages might be taken as endorsing an ultra-decisionist approach to ethical issues, one that comes disturbingly close to a Kierkegaardian conception of moral choice as involving an ultimate leap of faith beyond any humanly accountable values or standards of ethical judgement. These doubts are somewhat reinforced by his focus on *Fear and Trembling* – Kierkegaard's most extreme rendition of the absolute gulf or lack of common measure between human and religious spheres of belief – as a text that exemplifies this radical disjunction of authentic 'inwardness' on the one hand and mere observance of received moral codes or conventions on the other.[111] To put it bluntly: the last thing needed at a time of resurgent ethnic, political and religious hatreds is a notion of ethical choice or commitment that stakes its claim on the existence of values which somehow transcend the realm of shared (or at any rate inter-subjectively communicable) meanings, values and beliefs.

Such has been the charge most often levelled at Derrida by critics like Jürgen Habermas who take him to have simply renounced (or betrayed) the 'unfinished project' of modernity.[112] On this view deconstruction is just another variant of the current 'postmodernist' turn in so far as it reverts to a pre-Enlightenment outlook, one that allows no room for the progressive differentiation of discourses – scientific-cognitive, ethical and aesthetic along with all their specialized sub-genres – and thereby precludes any adequate grasp (such as philosophy ought to provide) of the complex relationship between them. Moreover, this amounts to a vote of no confidence in just that aspect of enlightened modernity – its critical-emancipatory potential – which might yet be redeemed by keeping faith with the unfinished project and attempting to rethink our way through and beyond its inherited blind spots of ignorance and prejudice. What is needed, in short, is a continued engagement with these issues from the standpoint of a theory of communicative action aimed toward the goal of an open, non-coercive, fully participant democracy wherein every voice would have an equal say and none have the power to suppress or to marginalize opposing or dissident views.[113] This theory acknowledges the linguistic (or pragmatic) turn as having finally displaced the old, for example, Kantian, epistemological paradigm. However it retains a critical edge by holding out the prospect of an 'ideal speech-situation' that can serve as an implicit rebuke to the kinds of partial or distorted dialogue which characterize the discourses of present-day social, ethical, political and inter-personal exchange. Such criticism needs to conserve and refine those various demarcations that were first put in place by Kant's metaphysically over-burdened doctrine of the faculties – cognitive understanding, pure (speculative) reason, practical reason, aesthetic judgement, and so on – and henceforth recast them in linguistic or communicative terms. It can thus hold true to the values of enlightened and progressive thought without either falling back on an outworn epistemological paradigm or else following Derrida's 'postmodernist' path (as Habermas sees it) and simply collapsing the 'genre-distinction' between reason and rhetoric, concept and metaphor, or philosophy and literature. For this leads on to a collapse of critical thought and to an outlook of unresisting acquiescence in the ideological values and beliefs of the time, even (or especially) where these involve some version of the 'end-of-ideology' thesis that has resurfaced at regular intervals during the past half-century.[114]

I scarcely need say – after so much argument to contrary effect – why I consider these charges to be quite without warrant and amply refuted by an adequate (that is, a close and attentive rather than partisan) reading of Derrida's work. Perhaps there is a certain *prima facie* force to the objection that his later work on ethical themes inclines toward an ultra-decisionist outlook, that is to say, the idea that *genuinely* ethical choices (as distinct from those that invoke some antecedent rule, precept or guiding maxim) must always be arrived at through a leap beyond anything that might find reasoned or principled justification even after the event or with the benefit of reflective hindsight. However it is a case that cannot be sustained if one considers, for instance, Derrida's early critique of Levinasian ethics for its raising 'alterity' (or absolute otherness) to a high point of ethical doctrine. His point, briefly put, is that this doctrine goes so far toward rejecting any claim to the existence of inter-subjective norms and validity-conditions that it would – if carried through consistently – amount to a denial of every last ground for mutual understanding or reciprocal respect across differences of language, culture and belief.[115] Most recent commentators on the 'ethics of deconstruction' have tended to marginalize this crucial text and to quote mainly from Derrida's later, more Levinas-influenced statements on the theme of radical alterity.[116] However this preference is one clear sign of the way that his work has been subject to a skewed reception-history under the influence of a wider postmodernist aversion to any thinking that finds some room for the subject as a locus of knowledge or autonomous (yet nonetheless other-regarding) ethical thought. Thus the point needs stressing that Derrida argues quite explicitly against the idea of an ethics that could somehow come out on the far side of all such first-person ('egological') concepts and categories. Or again: what is the use, in ethical terms, of this principled respect for the absolute 'otherness' of the other without the kind of mutual understanding, allowance and sympathy that results from my treating the other as an 'alter ego', that is to say, as one whose differences from me are balanced by an equally necessary sense of shared (inter-subjectively valid) modes of knowledge and experience?[117]

This is basically how Derrida defends Husserl against Levinas's charge that the project of transcendental phenomenology amounts to no more than a sophisticated update on the subject-centred epistemological paradigm that has dominated Western philosophy from Plato down.[118] It is also where his (Derrida's) thinking holds out against any version of the claim – whether advanced by postmodernists, Wittgensteinians or Rorty-style neo-pragmatists – that philosophy has now entered a stage of development that no longer finds room for such hopelessly outmoded 'Enlightenment' notions as truth, reason or critique. Thus Habermas quite simply gets Derrida wrong, most likely (as I have argued elsewhere) in consequence of under-exposure to Derrida's texts at first hand and over-reliance on the commentaries of those who attack him, like Searle, or who praise him, like Rorty, on the same erroneous grounds, that is, his supposed disregard for basic standards of logical argumentation and failure to engage with substantive philosophical as well as ethical and socio-political concerns.[119] Such a 'reading' ignores not only the extreme analytic acuity of Derrida's early work but also his later, more direct address to just the sorts of issue – from the aporetic relationship between law and ethics under wicked legal systems like that of South African apartheid to US foreign policy in the wake of 9/11 – which leave no doubt as to the strength of his commitments in this regard.[120] What is most impressive about these texts is the way that they lend specific ethical, social and historical content to the idea of choice as ultimately exercised in the absence of determinate guidelines or standards of right conduct. Any further misgivings – or suspicion that Derrida's ethical concerns are too often overwhelmed by his will to discover aporias at every turn – find an answer in those passionately eloquent passages from *Spectres of Marx* where he denounces the shallow triumphalist rhetoric espoused by US celebrants of the 'New World Order' at a time of unprecedented global suffering, genocidal conflict, gross inequality, resurgent ethnic and religious persecution, large-scale (including state-sponsored) atrocities and so forth.[121] Indeed the power of these statements is intensified rather than diminished by his acute awareness of the need for philosophy to confront the dilemmas of ethical discourse in a range of practical or real-world contexts that, whatever the perplexities induced by reflection on their justificatory grounds, demand nothing less than a firm and principled stance.

It is here that deconstruction makes its claim to genuine ethical import rather than seeking refuge either in the certitudes of foregone judgement or – as with much that currently passes for postmodernist ethical thought – in the endless possibilities for bad faith opened up by vague, all-purpose talk of 'undecidability' or the lack of common measure between different language-games, discourses or cultural life-forms.[122] On the one hand (to repeat): 'in order to be responsible and truly decisive, a decision should not limit itself to putting into operation a determinable or determining knowledge, the consequence of some pre-established order'. On the other, and with an equal force of intuitive self-evidence, 'who would call a decision that is without rule, without norm, without determinable or determined law, a decision?'[123] Of course these are questions that have also preoccupied analytic philosophers though rarely in a way that achieves so close (if problematical) a link between issues in the province of speculative ethical theory and issues of an urgent, real-world social and political concern. Indeed, one source of the antagonism toward Derrida's work amongst many analytic philosophers is his refusal to draw any such methodologically convenient distinction between first-order topics – those with substantive moral-evaluative import – and topics that are taken to fall within the remit of a second-order, that is, logico-linguistic or meta-ethical mode of enquiry. It is a similar refusal, as we have seen, that leads him to press even harder than Austin on the constative/performative dichotomy and the idea that any systematic theory of speech-acts could lift itself clear of the complexities involved in our various linguistic dealings with each other and the world. No doubt this complicates matters for the theorist but then, as Derrida pithily remarks in his rejoinder to Searle, 'if things were that simple, word would have gotten around'.[124] Hence what critics are apt to denounce as his tortuous, convoluted or downright impenetrable prose style should rather be acknowledged as a direct consequence of his sustained and intensive effort to articulate some of the deepest-laid quandaries of ethical thought. It seems to me that no thinker in recent times has gone so far in this direction while still maintaining a keen sense of the need for philosophy to take its stand on matters of social and political conscience.

One likely explanation for the steadfast resistance to his work is the wide-spread, though thoroughly mistaken, perception of Derrida as just another typecast 'post-structuralist' – some critics less *au fait* with the passing show would simply say 'structuralist' – who happens to have fixed his mischievous sights on a range of primarily philosophical texts. In Chapter 3 I shall take up this charge in the context of recent French intellectual history and seek to demonstrate that, while missing the mark in Derrida's case, it does nevertheless have a certain justice when applied to those other developments in the wake of Saussurean structural linguistics.

NOTES

1   See for instance A.J. Ayer, 'Novelists-Philosophers V: Jean-Paul Sartre', *Horizon* 12 (July 1945), pp. 12–26 and 13 (August 1945), pp. 101–10.

2   See Jacques Derrida, 'Signature Event Context', *Glyph* 1 (1975), pp. 172–97; John R. Searle, 'Reiterating the Differences', *Glyph* 1 (1975), pp. 198–208; Derrida, 'Limited Inc abc', *Glyph* 2 (1977), pp. 75–176; also Derrida, 'Afterword: Toward an Ethic of Conversation', in Gerald Graff (ed.), *Limited Inc* (Evanston, IL: Northwestern University Press, 1989), pp. 111–54.

3   For a range of perspectives on this parting of the ways, see Gottlob Frege, review of Edmund Husserl's *Philosophie der Arithmetik*, translated by E.-H.W. Kluge, *Mind* 81 (1972), pp. 321–37; Gilbert Ryle, 'Phenomenology', 'Review of Martin Farber, *The Foundations of Phenomenology*', and 'Phenomenology versus *The Concept of Mind*', in Ryle, *Collected Papers*, vol. 1 (London: Hutchinson, 1971), pp. 167–78, 179–96 & 215–24; Jacques Derrida, ' "Genesis and Structure" and Phenomenology', in *Writing and Difference*, trans. Alan Bass (London: Routledge & Kegan Paul, 1978), pp. 154–68 and *La problème de la genèse dans la philosophie de Husserl* (Paris: Presses Universitaires de France, 1990); also Michael Friedman, *A Parting of the Ways: Carnap, Cassirer, and Heidegger* (LaSalle, IL: Open Court, 2000).

4   See especially Jacques Derrida, *Aporias: Dying – Awaiting (One Another At) the 'Limits of Truth'*, trans. Thomas Dutoit (Stanford, CA: Stanford University Press, 1993); 'Force of Law: the "Mystical Foundation of Authority" ', trans. Mary Quaintance, *Cardoso Law Review* XI (1990), pp. 999–1045; 'At This Very Moment in This Work Here I Am',

trans. Ruben Berezdivin, in Robert Bernasconi and Simon Critchley (eds.), *Re-Reading Levinas* (Bloomington, IN: Indiana University Press, 1991), pp. 11–40; also Emmanel Levinas, *Totality and Infinity*, trans. A. Lingis (Pittsburgh, PA: Duquesne University Press, 1969) and *Otherwise Than Being, or Beyond Essence*, trans. A. Lingis (The Hague: Martinus Nijhoff, 1981).

5   Derrida, 'Force of Law', p. 1012.

6   Derrida, *Aporias*, p. 17.

7   See especially Jacques Derrida, *The Gift of Death*, trans. David Wills (Chicago: University of Chicago Press, 1995) and *Ethics, Institutions, and the Right to Philosophy*, trans. and ed. Peter P. Trifonas (Lanham, MD: Rowman & Littlefield, 2002); also Simon Critchley, *The Ethics of Deconstruction: Derrida and Levinas* (Oxford: Blackwell, 1992); Christina Howells, *Derrida: Deconstruction from Phenomenology to Ethics* (Cambridge: Polity Press, 1998); Herman Rapaport, *Later Derrida: Reading the Recent Work* (London: Routledge, 2003).

8   Derrida, *The Gift of Death*.

9   See for instance Christopher Norris, 'Postscript to the Third (2002) Edition', in *Deconstruction: Theory and Practice* (London: Routledge, 2002), pp. 156–78.

10   Jacques Derrida, 'The Laws of Reflection: Nelson Mandela, In Admiration', in Jacques Derrida and Mustapha Tlili (eds.), *Nelson Mandela* (New York: Henry Holt & Co, 1987), pp. 13–42. In this connection see also David Dyzenhaus, *Hard Cases in Wicked Legal Systems: South African Law in the Perspective of Legal Philosophy* (Oxford: Clarendon Press, 1991) and *Judging the Judges, Judging Ourselves: Truth, Reconciliation and the Apartheid Legal Order* (Oxford: Hart Publishing, 1998).

11   Derrida, 'Force of Law', p. 1013.

12   See Immanuel Kant, *Political Writings*, ed. Hans Reiss (Cambridge: Cambridge University Press, 1976) and *The Conflict of the Faculties*, trans. Mary J. Gregor (New York: Abaris Books, 1979).

13   For a critical survey, see Christopher Norris, 'Law, Deconstruction and the Resistance to Theory', in *Deconstruction and the Interests of Theory* (London: Pinter Publishers, 1988), pp. 126–55.

14   For discussion of this issue from a range of philosophical standpoints, see Christopher Norris, *Truth Matters: Realism, Anti-Realism and Response-Dependence* (Edinburgh: Edinburgh University Press, 2002); J. Haldane and C. Wright (eds.), *Realism, Representation and Projection* (Oxford: Oxford University Press, 1993); Philip Pettit, *The Common Mind: An Essay on Psychology, Society, and Politics* (Oxford: Oxford University Press, 1992), Crispin Wright, *Truth and Objectivity* (Cambridge, MA: Harvard University Press, 1992).

15   Jean-Paul Sartre, *Being and Nothingness: An Essay on Phenomenological Ontology*, trans. Hazel E. Barnes (London: Methuen, 1966); Maurice Merleau-Ponty, *Adventures of the Dialectic*, trans. Joseph Bien (Evanston, IL: Northwestern University Press, 1973) and *The Prose of the World*, trans. John O'Neill (Northwestern U.P., 1974); also Jon Stewart (ed.), *The Debate Between Sartre and Merleau-Ponty* (Northwestern U.P., 1998).

16   For further discussion, see E.F. Paul, F.D. Miller and J. Paul (eds.), *The Communitarian Challenge to Liberalism* (Cambridge: Cambridge University Press, 1996); David Rasmussen (ed.), *Universalism versus Communitarianism: Contemporary Debates in Ethics* (Cambridge, MA: MIT Press, 1990).

17   Ludwig Wittgenstein, *Philosophical Investigations*, trans. G.E.M. Anscombe (Oxford: Blackwell, 1953), sections 201–92; also Saul Kripke, *Wittgenstein on Rules and Private Language* (Blackwell, 1982); Alexander Miller and Crispin Wright (eds.), *Rule-Following and Meaning* (Aldershot: Acumen, 2002).

18   See Norris, *Truth Matters* and *Language, Logic and Epistemology: A Modal-Realist Approach* (London: Macmillan, 2004).

19   See for instance Richard Rorty, *Consequences of Pragmatism* (Brighton: Harvester, 1982);

Contingency, Irony and Solidarity (Cambridge: Cambridge University Press, 1989); *Objectivity, Relativism, and Truth* (Cambridge: Cambridge University Press, 1991).

20   Richard Rorty, 'Philosophy as a Kind of Writing: An Essay on Derrida', in *Consequences of Pragmatism*, pp. 90–109.

21   See especially Jacques Derrida, *'Speech and Phenomena' and Other Essays on Husserl's Theory of Signs*, trans. David B. Allison (Evanston, IL: Northwestern University Press, 1973); *Of Grammatology*, trans. G.C. Spivak (Baltimore, MD: Johns Hopkins University Press, 1976); *Writing and Difference*; *Dissemination*, trans. Barbara Johnson (London: Athlone Press, 1981); *The Truth in Painting*, trans. Geoffrey Bennington and Ian McLeod (Chicago: University of Chicago Press, 1987).

22   For more detailed arguments to this effect, see Christopher Norris, *Derrida* (London: Fontana, 1986); *Deconstruction and the Interests of Theory*; *Deconstruction and the Unfinished Project of Modernity* (London: Athlone, 2000).

23   See Note 17, above.

24   Wittgenstein, *Philosophical Investigations*, section 265.

25   See Notes 3, 4 and 21, above; also Jacques Derrida, *Margins of Philosophy*, trans. Alan Bass (Chicago: University of Chicago Press, 1982).

26   See Notes 3 and 21, above; also Jacques Derrida, *Edmund Husserl's 'Origin of Geometry': An Introduction*, trans. John P. Leavey (Pittsburgh: Duquesne University Press, 1978) and 'Violence and Metaphysics: an Essay on the Thought of Emmanuel Levinas', in *Writing and Difference*, pp. 79–153.

27   See Note 2, above.

28   J.L. Austin, *How to Do Things with Words* (Oxford: Oxford University Press, 1963); also John R. Searle, *Speech Acts: An Essay in the Philosophy of Language* (Cambridge: Cambridge University Press, 1969) and *Expression and Meaning: Studies in the Theory of Speech Acts* (Cambridge: Cambridge University Press, 1979). For his rejoinder to Derrida, see Searle, 'Reiterating the Differences'.

29   See for instance Keith Graham, *J.L. Austin: A Critique of Ordinary Language Philosophy* (Hassocks: Harvester, 1977).

30   Rorty, 'Philosophy as a Kind of Writing'; also 'Deconstruction and Circumvention' and 'Two Meanings of "Logocentrism": a reply to Norris', in *Essays on Heidegger and Others* (Cambridge: Cambridge University Press, 1991), pp. 85–106 and 107–18; Christopher Norris, 'Philosophy as *Not* Just a "Kind of Writing": Derrida and the Claim of Reason', in Reed Way Dasenbrock (ed.), *Re-Drawing the Lines: Analytical Philosophy, Deconstruction and Literary Theory* (Minneapolis: University of Minnesota Press, 1987), pp. 189–203.

31   Derek Parfit, *Reasons and Persons* (Oxford: Oxford University Press, 1987).

32   Ibid., p. 328.

33   For further discussion, see Jonathan Dancy (ed.), *Reading Parfit* (Oxford: Blackwell, 1997); also Kathleen V. Wilkes, *Real People: Personal Identity without Thought Experiments* (Oxford: Clarendon Press, 1988).

34   Parfit, *Reasons and Persons*, p. 327.

35   Ibid., p. 329.

36   See Note 2, above.

37   For a survey of these issues as they struck one (already somewhat jaded) commentator, see the Introduction to Richard Rorty (ed.), *The Linguistic Turn: Recent Essays in Philosophical Method* (Chicago: University of Chicago Press, 1967).

38   See Notes 4, 7 and 10, above.

39   Derrida, *Of Grammatology*, p. 158.

40   For a range of views, see Stanley Cavell, *Must We Mean What We Say?* (Cambridge: Cambridge University Press, 1969); E.D. Hirsch, *Validity in Interpretation* (New Haven: Yale University Press, 1967); P.D. Juhl, *Interpretation: An Essay in the Philosophy of Literary Criticism* (Princeton, NJ: Princeton University Press, 1980); W.K. Wimsatt

and Monroe C. Beardsley, 'The Intentional Fallacy', in Wimsatt, *The Verbal Icon: Studies in the Meaning of Poetry* (Lexington: University of Kentucky Press, 1954).

41   See Notes 21 and 26, above.

42   Derrida, *Of Grammatology*, p. 158.

43   Ibid., p. 158.

44   Cavell, *Must We Mean What We Say?*, p. 94.

45   See for instance Charles Altieri, 'Wittgenstein on Consciousness and Language: A Challenge to Derridean Theory', *Modern Language Notes* 91 (1976), pp. 1397–423; Christopher Norris, 'The Insistence of the Letter: Textuality and Metaphor in Wittgenstein's Later Philosophy', in *The Deconstructive Turn: Essays in the Rhetoric of Philosophy* (London: Methuen, 1983); Henry Staten, *Wittgenstein and Derrida* (Lincoln: University of Nebraska Press, 1985).

46   See especially Colin McGinn, *The Mysterious Flame: Conscious Minds in a Material World* (New York: Basic Books, 1999); also – for some vigorous counter-arguments – Paul M. Churchland and Patricia S. Churchland, *On the Contrary: Critical Essays, 1987–1997* (Cambridge, MA: MIT Press, 1998).

47   For a range of philosophical perspectives, see David Chalmers, *The Conscious Mind: In Search of a Fundamental Theory* (Oxford: Oxford University Press, 1996); Jeffrey A. Gray, *Consciousness: Creeping up on the Hard Problem* (Oxford: Oxford University Press, 2004); Joseph Levine, *Purple Haze: The Puzzle of Consciousness* (Oxford: Oxford University Press, 2002); William S. Robinson, *Understanding Phenomenal Consciousness* (Cambridge: Cambridge University Press, 2004); Quentin Smith and Aleksandar Jokic (eds.), *Consciousness: New Philosophical Perspectives* (Oxford: Oxford University Press, 2003).

48   Mark Bevir, *The Logic of the History of Ideas* (Cambridge: Cambridge University Press, 1999), p. 301.

49   Ibid., p. 301.

50   See for instance Simon Glendinning, *On Being with Others: Heidegger, Wittgenstein, Derrida* (London: Routledge, 1998); also various contributions to Glendinning (ed.), *The Edinburgh Encyclopædia of Continental Philosophy* (Edinburgh: Edinburgh University Press, 1999).

51   I develop this argument at greater length in Christopher Norris, *Minding the Gap: Philosophy of Science and Epistemology in the Two Traditions* (Amherst, MA: University of Massachusetts Press, 2000).

52   Bevir, *The Logic of the History of Ideas*; W.V. Quine, 'Two Dogmas of Empiricism', in *From a Logical Point of View*, 2nd edn (Cambridge, MA: Harvard University Press, 1961), pp. 20–46.

53   See for instance the essays collected in A.J. Ayer (ed.), *Logical Positivism* (New York: Free Press, 1959) and Oswald Hanfling (ed.), *Essential Readings in Logical Positivism* (Oxford: Blackwell, 1981).

54   For further discussion see Christopher Norris, *Resources of Realism: Prospects for 'Post-Analytic' Philosophy* (London: Macmillan, 1997) and *New Idols of the Cave: On the Limits of Anti-Realism* (Manchester: Manchester University Press, 1997).

55   See Notes 19, 20 and 30, above.

56   See especially Jacques Derrida, *Glas*, trans. John P. Leavey Jr. and Richard Rand (Lincoln: University of Nebraska Press, 1986); also *Spurs: Nietzsche's Styles*, trans. Barbara Harlow (Chicago: University of Chicago Press, 1979) and *Signéponge/Signsponge*, trans. Richard Rand (New York: Columbia University Press, 1984). A useful selection may be found in two volumes: Derek Attridge (ed.), *Jacques Derrida: Acts of Literature* (London: Routledge, 1992) and Peggy Kamuf (ed.), *A Derrida Reader: Between the Blinds* (New York: Columbia University Press, 1991).

57   Derrida, 'Limited Inc abc'.

58   Derrida, 'Afterword', p. 123.

59   Ibid., p. 117.

60   Christopher Norris. 'Supplementarity and Deviant Logics: Derrida versus Quine' and 'Excluded Middles: Quantum Theory and the Logic of Deconstruction', in *Minding the Gap*, pp. 125–47 and 148–71; also 'Derrida on Rousseau: Deconstruction as Philosophy of Logic', in Chrisopher Norris and David Roden (eds.), *Jacques Derrida*, 4 vols (London: Sage, 2003), vol. 2, pp. 70–124.

61   See also Graham Priest, *Beyond the Limits of Thought* (Oxford: Clarendon Press, 2002).

62   Derrida, 'Afterword', p. 117.

63   Quine, 'Two Dogmas of Empiricism'; see also Susan Haack, *Deviant Logic: Some Philosophical Issues* (Cambridge: Cambridge University Press, 1974).

64   See Christopher Norris, *Philosophy of Language and the Challenge to Scientific Realism* (London: Routledge, 2004).

65   For further discussion from a range of viewpoints, see L. Jonathan Cohen, *An Essay on Belief and Acceptance* (Oxford: Clarendon Press, 1992); Ted Honderich, *A Theory of Determinism*, vol. 1: *The Mind, Neuroscience and Life-Hopes* (Oxford: Clarendon Press, 1988) and *A Theory of Determinism*, vol. 2: *The Consequences of Determinism* (Oxford: Clarendon Press, 1988); Martha Klein, *Determinism, Blameworthiness, and Deprivation* (Oxford: Clarendon Press, 1990); J.R. Lucas, *The Freedom of the Will* (Oxford: Clarendon Press, 1970); David Owens, *Reason Without Freedom: The Problem of Epistemic Normativity* (London: Routledge, 2000); Galen Strawson, *Freedom and Belief* (Oxford: Oxford University Press, 1986).

66   Derrida, *Of Grammatology*, p. 158.

67   See Notes 4 and 7, above.

68   See Note 7, above; also Jacques Derrida, *Acts of Religion* (New York: Routledge, 2002); Jacques Derrida and Gianni Vattimo (eds.), *Religion* (Cambridge: Polity Press, 1998); also Hugh Rayment-Pickard, *Impossible God: Derrida's Theology* (Aldershot: Ashgate, 2003); Graham Ward, *Barth, Derrida, and the Language of Theology* (Cambridge: Cambridge University Press, 1995).

69   See Norris, *Minding the Gap*.

70   Jacques Derrida, *The Post-Card: from Socrates to Freud and Beyond*, trans. Alan Bass (Chicago: University of Chicago Press, 1987); also Gilbert Ryle, *Dilemmas* (Cambridge: Cambridge University Press, 1954).

71   See Note 45, above; also O.K. Bouwsma, *Philosophical Essays* (Lincoln: University of Nebraska Press, 1965); Newton Garver and Seung-Chong Lee, *Derrida and Wittgenstein* (Philadelphia, PA: Temple University Press, 1995); Reed Way Dasenbrock (ed.), *Re-Drawing the Lines: Analytic Philosophy, Deconstruction, and Literary Theory* (Minneapolis: University of Minnesota Press, 1989).

72   See Norris, *Minding the Gap* for a more developed statement of this case.

73   See Notes 4 and 7, above.

74   See especially Critchley, *The Ethics of Deconstruction*; also John Caputo, *Against Ethics: Contributions to a Poetics of Obligation, with Constant Reference to Deconstruction* (Bloomington: Indiana University Press, 1993).

75   Derrida, 'Violence and Metaphysics'.

76   Edmund Husserl, *Cartesian Meditations*, trans. Dorion Cairns (Dordrecht: Kluwer, 1995).

77   See Notes 3 and 21, above.

78   For some widely differing approaches, see G.E.M. Anscombe, *Intention* (Oxford: Blackwell, 1963); Donald Davidson, *Essays on Actions and Events* (Oxford: Clarendon Press, 1980); Fred Dretske, *Explaining Behavior: Reasons in a World of Causes* (Cambridge, MA: MIT Press, 1988); Berent Enç, *How We Act: Causes, Reasons, and Intentions* (Oxford: Clarendon Press, 2003).

79   See especially Anthony Giddens, *Central Problems in Social Theory: Action, Structure and Contradiction in Social Analysis* (London: Macmillan, 1979).

80   For further discussion along these lines, see Chrisopher Norris, 'Change, Conservation,

and Crisis-Management in the Discourse of Analytic Philosophy', in *Language, Logic and Epistemology*, pp. 227–66.

81   See Notes 48, 50 and 51, above; also Samuel C. Wheeler, *Deconstruction as Analytic Philosophy* (Stanford, CA: Stanford University Press, 2000) and various contributors to Norris and Roden (eds.), *Jacques Derrida*.

82   Immanuel Kant, *Critique of Pure Reason*, trans. Norman Kemp Smith (London: Macmillan, 1964).

83   See for instance John McDowell, *Mind and World* (Cambridge, MA: Harvard University Press, 1994); also Christopher Norris, 'McDowell on Kant: Redrawing the Bounds of Sense' and 'The Limits of Naturalism: Further Thoughts on McDowell's *Mind and World*', in *Minding the Gap*, pp. 172–96 and 197–230.

84   I put this case in Christopher Norris, *Truth Matters: Realism, Anti-Realism, and Response-Dependence* (Edinburgh: Edinburgh University Press, 2002).

85   For a representative sampling of views, see Rorty (ed.), *The Linguistic Turn*.

86   The classic examples are Gottlob Frege, 'On Sense and Reference', in Peter Geach and Max Black (eds), *Translations from the Philosophical Writings of Gottlob Frege* (Oxford: Blackwell, 1952), pp. 56–78 and Bertrand Russell, 'On Denoting', *Mind* 14 (1905), pp. 479–93.

87   Gilles Deleuze and Félix Guattari, *What Is Philosophy?*, trans. Hugh Tomlinson and Graham Burchill (London: Verso, 1994).

88   Jürgen Habermas, 'Excursus on Levelling the Genre-Distinction Between Philosophy and Literature', in *The Philosophical Discourse of Modernity: Twelve Lectures*, trans. Frederick Lawrence (Cambridge: Polity Press, 1987), pp. 185–210.

89   See especially Derrida, *Psyché: Inventions de l'autre* (Paris: Galilée, 1987).

90   Derrida, *Writing and Difference*, p. 160.

91   Wittgenstein, *Philosophical Investigations*; also *On Certainty*, ed. and trans. G.E.M. Anscombe and G.H. von Wright (Oxford: Blackwell, 1969).

92   See especially C.H. Langford, 'The Notion of Analysis in Moore's Philosophy', in P.A. Schilpp (ed.), *The Philosophy of G.E. Moore* (La Salle: Open Court, 1968), pp. 321–41.

93   For further discussion, see Norris, *Truth Matters*.

94   See Notes 19 and 20, above.

95   Thomas S. Kuhn, *The Structure of Scientific Revolutions*, 2nd edn (Chicago: University of Chicago Press, 1970).

96   See especially Rodolphe Gasché, *The Tain of the Mirror: Derrida and the Philosophy of Reflection* (Cambridge, MA: Harvard University Press, 1986) and *Inventions of Difference: On Jacques Derrida* (Cambridge, MA: Harvard University Press, 1994); Marion Hobson, *Jacques Derrida: Opening Lines* (London: Routledge, 1998); Howells, *Derrida: Deconstruction from Phenomenology to Ethics*.

97   For a particularly striking example, see Jonathan Bennett, *A Study of Spinoza's Ethics* (Cambridge: Cambridge University Press, 1984); also (should you have the time) my commentary on Bennett's mode of 'rational reconstruction' in Christopher Norris, *Spinoza and the Origins of Modern Critical Theory* (Oxford: Blackwell, 1991), pp. 73–7.

98   Derrida, *Of Grammatology*, p. 158.

99   Geoffrey Galt Harpham, *Shadows of Ethics: Criticism and the Just Society* (Durham, NC: Duke University Press, 1999), p. 30.

100 Ibid., p. 29.

101 Ibid., p. 29.

102 See Notes 2, 21 and 26, above; also Jacques Derrida, 'Parergon', in *The Truth in Painting*, pp. 15–147.

103 Quine, 'Two Dogmas of Empiricism'; also Hilary Putnam, 'How to Think Quantum-Logically', *Synthèse* 29 (1974), pp. 55–61 and various essays on the scope and limits of classical logic in Putnam, *Mathematics, Matter and Method*, 2nd edn (Cambridge: Cambridge University Press, 1979).

104 Derrida, 'Afterword', p. 117.
105 Ibid., p. 117.
106 Ibid., p. 117.
107 Derrida, *Of Grammatology*, p. 158.
108 See Note 40, above.
109 See especially Hans-Georg Gadamer, *Truth and Method*, trans. Garrett and John Cumming (New York: Seabury Press, 1975); also – for a range of views on this topic – David Newton de Molina (ed.), *On Literary Intention: Critical Essays* (Edinburgh: Edinburgh University Press, 1976).
110 Derrida, *Aporias*, p. 19.
111 Derrida, *The Gift of Death*.
112 Habermas, *The Philosophical Discourse of Modernity*; also – for a reading that rejects these various charges – Christopher Norris, 'Deconstruction, Postmodernism and Philosophy: Habermas on Derrida', in *What's Wrong with Postmodernism: Critical Theory and the Ends of Philosophy* (Hemel Hempstead: Harvester-Wheatsheaf, 1990), pp. 49–76.
113 See especially Jürgen Habermas, *Communication and the Evolution of Society*, trans. Thomas McCarthy (London: Heinemann, 1979) and *Theory of Communicative Action*, 2 vols., trans. McCarthy (Boston: Beacon Press, 1984 and 1987).
114 See for instance Daniel Bell, *The End of Ideology* (Glencoe, IL: University of Illinois Press, 1960) and, for a more recent re-cycling of the same themes, Francis Fukuyama, *The End of History and the Last Man* (London: Secker and Warburg, 1992). Amongst the most spirited and forceful rejoinders, see Alasdair MacIntyre, 'The End of Ideology and the End of the End of Ideology', in *Against the Self-Images of the Age* (London: Duckworth, 1971) and Jacques Derrida, *Spectres of Marx* (London: Routledge, 1994); also Christopher Norris, *Uncritical Theory: Postmodernism, Intellectuals and the Gulf War* (Amherst, MA: University of Massachusetts Press, 1992) and *Reclaiming Truth: Contribution to a Critique of Cultural Relativism* (Durham, NC: Duke University Press, 1996).
115 See Derrida, 'Violence and Metaphysics'.
116 See for instance Critchley, *The Ethics of Deconstruction* and other entries at Note 7, above; also – for a dissenting view – Christopher Norris, *Truth and the Ethics of Criticism* (Manchester: Manchester University Press, 1994).
117 See especially Husserl, *Cartesian Meditations*.
118 Levinas, *Violence and Metaphysics*.
119 See Note 112, above.
120 See Notes 4, 7 and 10, above; also Giovanna Borradori (ed.), *Philosophy in a Time of Terror: Dialogues with Jürgen Habermas and Jacques Derrida* (Chicago: University of Chicago Press, 2003).
121 Derrida, *Spectres of Marx*.
122 For further discussion, see Christopher Norris, *The Truth About Postmodernism* (Oxford: Blackwell, 1993).
123 Derrida, *Aporias*, p. 17.
124 Derrida, 'Afterword', p. 156.

3

Saussurean Linguistics as Model and Metaphor: The Structuralist 'Revolution' Revisited

I

In this chapter I shall look at certain aspects of the relationship between Saussurean linguistics and debates within various other disciplines, including literary theory and philosophy of science. After all it was Saussure's chief aim to place linguistics on a properly 'scientific' footing, that is, to reconfigure the field in accordance with certain well-defined principles that would constitute an adequate, rigorously theorized account of language and signifying systems in general.[1] This he took to require a decisive break with earlier (diachronic or philologically oriented) methods, and the move to a structural-synchronic approach that started out by defining its object of study (*la langue*) as a system of contrastive features, relationships and differences 'without positive terms'. Only thus, Saussure thought, could linguistics achieve the status of a genuine science, one that went beyond the mere accumulation of discrete (no matter how informative) historical data, and which thereby established itself as a discipline with its own proper standards of conceptual validity and structure. The first task was to elaborate those various distinctions that would henceforth provide its working methodology, among them the cardinal oppositions between *langue* and *parole*, synchrony and diachrony, the paradigmatic and the syntagmatic, and the orders of signifier and signified. This would open the way to a structuralist account that left no room for naive (pre-scientific) ideas about the one-to-one 'correspondence' between words and ideas or words and objects. Rather it would show how the systematic character of language – its differential structures of sound and sense – can only be described by means of a theory which itself breaks free of such delusive 'common-sense' beliefs and acquires the full range of conceptual resources whereby to articulate its own grasp of those same signifying structures.

Implicit here is something very like the doctrine of 'semantic ascent' from material to formal or from linguistic to meta-linguistic levels of description that characterized much philosophy of language, logic and science in the largely anglophone tradition of logical empiricism. Thus for any given first-order (e.g., natural) language one can devise a corresponding second-order (formal) language that translates it into more perspicuous or logically regimented terms.[2] What

these philosophers sought to achieve was a precise notation for the physical
sciences that would be subject to none of the inherent liabilities – the vagueness,
ambiguity or lack of referential precision – that were thought to vitiate natural
language. I should not wish to press too hard on this comparison between
Saussurean linguistics and the logical empiricist programme (very much in the
tradition of Frege and Russell) for reforming language so as to meet the
requirements of science and philosophy of science.[3] No doubt Saussure had very
different priorities – those of a linguist rather than a formal logician – in
proposing a structural-synchronic theory that would grant linguistics its
rightful place among the exact sciences through a process of conceptual
abstraction from the otherwise inchoate mass of data produced by earlier
methods. Still the comparison is useful up to a point since it brings out one
salient feature of Saussurean linguistics, namely the idea that any discipline
which aspires to scientific status must establish a certain formal distance between
itself and its object of study, or – more precisely – between that object as
construed on the linguist's theoretical terms and that object in its 'natural',
spontaneous or everyday occurring condition. This was the idea that exerted such
a powerful appeal upon thinkers in other fields – anthropology, historiography,
social and political theory, poetics, narratology, even 'a certain' psychoanalysis –
during the period of classic high structuralism when linguistics was hailed as the
pilot-science for a general semiology that would soon transform the entire range
of humanistic disciplines.[4] What it crucially involved, to repeat, was a claim
that those disciplines could achieve the requisite stage of semantic ascent – of
formalized meta-linguistic detachment from their first-order 'natural' object-
domain – which marked the emergence of a scientific discourse with adequate
conceptual powers.

   Such was indeed the paradigm of 'scientific' method that found voice in a
number of representative texts from that period. Among them were Lévi-
Strauss's *Structural Anthropology*, Roland Barthes's methodological postscript to
Mythologies (where he proposes an extension of structuralist concepts to the
analysis of present-day 'bourgeois' myth through a second-order deployment of
the signifier/signified dualism), and a great number of literary-critical texts
devoted to the thesis that mere 'interpretation' should now give way to a science
of literature conceived in Saussurean (systemic or synchronic) terms.[5] Hence also
Louis Althusser's claim for a 'symptomatic' reading of the Marxian text that
would sharply distinguish the elements of immature (i.e., humanist or Hegelian)
thought from the Marxist science whose advent required a decisive epistemological break, both in Marx's own thinking at a certain stage of development and
in that of his critical exegetes.[6] This structuralist 'moment' has been much
discussed by the commentators – whether in a spirit of nostalgic reminiscence or
self-distancing irony – so I shall say no more about it here.[7] Sufficient to remark
that it soon gave rise to a reactive post-structuralist trend which emphatically
rejected any notion that theory could achieve such a standpoint of conceptual
mastery outside and above the various first-order languages, discourses or signifying practices that formed its objects of enquiry.[8]

This reaction is clearly visible in Barthes's later essays where he looks back on that moment as a passing dream – an illusion of scientific method – that had once (not so long ago) captured his mind.[9] It is likewise evident in the switch of allegiance undergone by many theorists on the cultural left with the waning of Althusserian Marxism after the events of 1968 and the shift toward a more sceptical stance whose chief inspiration was Foucault's Nietzschean 'genealogy' of power–knowledge.[10] For if one thing characterized this turn against theory in the high structuralist mode it was surely the insistence that all such ideas of methodological rigour, conceptual grasp, 'scientific' warrant and so forth, were merely a product of the will-to-power disguised behind a rhetoric of pure, disinterested seeking-after-truth. Thus Barthes now took to denouncing his own early efforts in a text like *Mythologies* as an exercise in pointless theoretical abstraction, one that should henceforth be abandoned in favour of a 'semioclastic' approach, that is to say, a transformative textual practice whose aim was to 'change the object itself' through a strategy of actively subverting its structures and modes of signification.[11] Least of all could it be thought that theory might attain a critical distance on naive, 'common-sense' or naturalized (= deeply acculturated) habits of belief by aspiring to the status of a genuine 'science' with its primary source in the concepts and categories of Saussurean linguistics. Such claims merely betrayed the hankering for a discourse of reason and truth which had now been revealed – by Foucault and others – as complicit with the bad old 'Enlightenment' drive for disciplinary surveillance and control.[12]

Of course there was much debate at the time as to whether the prefix 'post' in 'post-structuralism' should be taken as marking a radical break with those same concepts and categories or whether, on a somewhat more conservative construal, it should be taken to signify a further stage in the working out of their implications for a new way of thinking about language, subjectivity and the human sciences in general. This ambivalence was especially pronounced in the psychoanalytic writings of Jacques Lacan whose literalist approach to the texts of Freud and Saussure went along with a fondness for mathematical, topological and other 'scientific' analogies but whose treatment of them was – to say the least – characterized by a certain degree of associative whimsy. Thus Lacan's notoriously obscure style can be seen as resulting in part from a certain (albeit highly idiosyncratic) idea of scientific method, and in part from his determination to escape the Cartesian 'tyranny of lucidity', itself – as he thought – a mindset very much in league with the deplorable perversion of Freudian teaching represented by US ego-psychology.[13]

Roger Smith provides a useful brief summary which captures precisely what it was about the ego-psychological approach that provoked Lacan to announce his 'return to Freud' as an antidote to all such normalizing conceptions of psychoanalytic practice. This was a theory, he writes:

That described the ego as an original mental structure with its own positive powers. They [the ego-psychologists] argued, with an optimism in tune with US meliorist values, that the psychic core of personality is a power with the capacity in a mature individual to integrate innate drives and social pressures in a genuinely self-fulfilling way ... This argument was influential in part because it made it possible to relate psychoanalysis to the academic experimental psychology of learning and adjustment ... The ego psychologists' belief that there is a natural pattern in the self's development, which makes possible the integration of all aspects of the psyche, valued aggression as necessary for competition but rejected Freud's notion of the death instinct. The psychologists encouraged optimism that maladjustment is tractable through therapy. In popular versions – incompatible with the spirit of Freud's work but in keeping with US ideals – psychoanalysis was equated with a search for personal growth and for the true self, a fantasy of personality independent of culture.[14]

Lacan, on the contrary, stressed the unattainability of any such unified ego-ideal and the late-Freudian idea that psychoanalysis was a strictly 'interminable' process, aimed toward achieving a state of mind that would always and of its very nature elude the best efforts of integrative thought. Thus ego-psychology was itself a symptom of the narcissistic or 'imaginary' drive to substitute a false notion of the integrated ego for the endless 'detours' of the signifier in quest of some sheerly impossible idealized conception of self-knowledge and fulfilment. Had Freud only read Saussure – so Lacan implies – then he would have couched his descriptions of the 'talking cure' in such a way as to prevent these gross misreadings. That is to say, he would have laid yet more emphasis on the 'bar' between signifier and signified, or 'the agency of the letter' as that which precluded any notion of psychoanalysis as a means of achieving some wished-for harmony between ego-ideals and the requirements of a balanced, well-adjusted social life. In so far as the unconscious is 'structured like a language' – subject to the constant effects of desire as a process of displacement along the chain of signifiers – it remains forever beyond reach of the specular ('imaginary') ego.

To this extent structuralism, or Lacan's interpretation of it, came out in strong opposition to received, that is, Cartesian ideas of scientific knowledge, rationality and truth. At the same time – not least in Lacan's case – it looked to Saussurean linguistics as a source of organizing concepts and distinctions (like that between *langue* and *parole*) which still bore witness to a lingering dream of properly 'scientific' method. Indeed, this is just the kind of ambivalence one might expect in a thinker much drawn to the structuralist distinction between language and meta-language (here: the first-order discourse of the analysand and the second-order discourse of the analyst), yet one whose reading of the Freudian text brought him out implacably opposed to any notion of the talking cure – like that of the despised (mostly US) ego-psychologists – as aimed toward restoring the subject to a state of lucid self-knowledge or psychic equilibrium. Moreover, as post-structuralists often remark, this dichotomy finds a curious parallel in Saussure's devotion to the project of establishing theoretical linguistics on a properly scientific basis while at the same time pursuing his strange, obsessive and (by most standards) very unscientific researches into the cryptograms or patterns of occult significance which he believed to constitute the subtext of much Greek and Latin poetry.[15] Whence the idea – attractive to some – that structuralism was itself just a dream of method whose commitment to the Apollonian ideals of science, clarity and conceptual rigour was always threatened by this Dionysiac (Nietzschean–Freudian) return of the repressed.

Nothing quite so dramatic occurred in the wake of logical empiricism, a movement of thought – as mentioned above – which shared at least one major premise with the structuralist enterprise. This was its conception of philosophy of science as requiring that a firm (categorical) distinction be drawn between first-order statements whose truth was a matter of empirical content or observational warrant and second-order (metalinguistic) statements whose truth-value could be specified in terms of their purely logical or logico-semantic form.[16] Of course the empiricist component here is sufficient to set it firmly apart from the Saussurean (rationalist) conception of scientific method, that is to say, the idea that a science of language could come into being only at the stage where thinking achieved a conceptual break with empirically derived or everyday common-sense modes of linguistic intuition. Still the comparison does hold good in one further respect. For the demise of logical empiricism came about through a likewise reactive tendency, one that took aim at the cardinal distinction between language and meta-language, or the mistaken notion (as it now seemed) that logic could be held safely immune from the prospect of eventual disconfirmation which always applied in the case of empirical statements, no matter how well-entrenched or strongly borne out by all the scientific evidence to date. Such was the tenor of W.V. Quine's landmark essay 'Two Dogmas of Empiricism' where he showed – or at any rate purported to show – that the logical-empiricist programme was flawed since this distinction failed to hold up.[17] Thus, according to Quine, there was simply no means of separating 'truths of reason' from 'matters of fact', the former construed as applying to just those statements (i.e., tautologies such as 'every bachelor is an unmarried man') whose truth was self-evident to reason on purely definitional or logico-semantic grounds, while the latter had to do with empirical claims (like most of those advanced in the physical sciences) which might always conceivably be subject to revision under pressure from conflicting or recalcitrant evidence. After all, had not certain recent developments in subatomic physics – among them wave/particle dualism and the 'superposition' of quantum states – given rise to proposals for abandoning the logical 'law' of excluded middle?

This went along with Quine's assault on the analytic/synthetic distinction, that is, his argument that any attempt to define what counted as an analytic statement would have to fall back on kindred terms (like synonymy or definitional equivalence) which themselves presupposed the notion of analyticity and thus gave rise to a vicious circle. Moreover, there was no firm line to be held between observation statements (or their empirical content) and those various higher-level theories, hypotheses, covering-law statements and so forth, which were taken – on the logical-empiricist account – as subject to different (more formalized) standards of logical consistency and truth. On the contrary:

observation statements are always 'theory-laden' and theories always 'under-determined by the evidence', so that even the simplest empirical claim will involve a vast range of implicit theoretical assumptions which might just pos-sibly be open to revision through some future (at present scarcely thinkable) change in our basic scientific beliefs.[18] Hence Quine's well-known metaphor of the entirety of knowledge at any given time as a densely woven 'fabric' whose boundary-conditions are set by experience – or by the constant 'barrage' of incoming sensory stimuli – and whose core is made up of those logical ground-rules which we take to hold good come what may but whose seeming force of *a priori* self-evidence results from their playing so central a role in our habituated modes of reasoning. Thus, just as we might be pragmatically justified in revising logic so as to conserve some recalcitrant result thrown up by empirical science, so equally we might elect to conserve some cherished scientific theory (or principle of logic) by treating our empirical observations as faulty or unreliable. In other words we can make adjustments at any point in the fabric of belief, as for instance by adducing alternative 'auxiliary hypotheses' or by redistributing truth-values and predicates in such a way as to minimize conflict and ensure the greatest measure of overall coherence. In the end such choices can be guided only by judgements of economy and 'pragmatic convenience', rather than dictated – as the logical empiricists would have it – by 'hard' empirical evidence on the one hand and on the other by a logic of scientific enquiry with its own distinct standards of rationality and truth.

What interests me here is the extent to which Saussurean linguistics likewise lay open to the kinds of charge brought against it – or 'abusive extrapolations' from it, in Perry Anderson's mordant phrase – by post-structuralists, Fou-cauldians and others with an ideological axe to grind.[19] In both cases a certain conception of scientific method proved amenable to readings of a radically contextualist, holistic or paradigm-relativist character which were strongly at odds with its original aims and ambitions. Thus Quine's assault on the two last 'dogmas' of empiricism was expressly intended as a ground-clearing exercise which would rid philosophy of its grandiose pretensions (like that of for-mulating logical ground rules for the conduct of scientific thought) and restore it to a decently scaled-down conception of its role *vis-à-vis* the physical sciences. Hence the programme of 'naturalized epistemology' – the attempt to explain how such a 'meagre input' of sensory stimuli could somehow give rise to such a 'torrential output' of statements, hypotheses, theories, etc. – which Quine saw as the sole legitimate task for philosophy of science. This could be achieved by restricting itself to the kinds of empirical observation that avoided any recourse to 'mentalist' talk about concepts, ideas or 'laws of thought', and which instead made do with a behaviourist account of what subjects (whether scientists or 'native informants') were prompted to say in some given situation or when exposed to some given range of incoming physical stimuli. In short, Quine considered that the natural sciences were our best source of guidance in such matters and that his was an approach that respected the priority of scientific method over anything that philosophers had yet come up with in the way of formalized (metalinguistic) rules or methodical constraints.[20]

Nevertheless it was largely on the basis of Quine's radical-empiricist programme that Thomas Kuhn went on to propose his more wholesale version of the paradigm-relativist case, that is, his idea that scientists living before and after some drastic paradigm change must be thought of as somehow quite literally 'living in different worlds'.[21] Thus where Aristotle 'saw' a swinging stone as an instance of matter seeking out its proper place in the order of the elements, Galileo 'saw' a case of gravitationally induced pendular motion. And likewise, where Priestley witnessed the process of combustion as involving the release of a substance (phlogiston) whose existence was proved by a decrease in the proportion of dephlogistated air, Lavoisier witnessed that 'same' process as involving the uptake of a different substance (oxygen) and hence a new conception of chemistry and physics that found no place for phlogiston amongst its range of candidate realia. In which case, according to Kuhn, it is only in the dubious wisdom of retrospect that we can take Galileo and Lavoisier to have got things right and treat Aristotle's and Priestley's theories as false on account of their referring to non-existent substances or properties. Rather we should make every effort to suspend this old-fashioned Whiggish view of things and acknowledge that such theories are strictly 'incommensurable' insofar as they involve a whole different range of object-terms, predicates and putative 'laws of nature'. Like Foucault in his early 'archaeological' period, Kuhn takes it that the process of theory change is one that comes about through such deep-laid and radical shifts of overall perspective that any talk of progress in our scientific knowledge of the world can only be the product of selective hindsight or naively 'presentist' bias.[22]

On the face of it there is little in common between Quine's hard-headed empiricist outlook and Kuhn's often rather nebulous treatment of these issues, in particular – as critics have pointed out – his equivocal usage of the term 'paradigm' in various contexts of argument.[23] Yet it is clear from Kuhn's methodological postscript to the second edition of his book that he takes Quine's radical empiricist approach as providing a source and justification for his own line of approach. Thus it allows him to answer his realist critics by acknowledging that scientists on either side of a major paradigm shift can properly be said to see 'the same thing' at least to the extent that their retinas are subject to an identical range of physical stimuli when confronted (say) with a swinging stone or a combustible substance ignited under certain (as yet unspecified) conditions. However this yields no ground to the realist when it comes to explaining why one such theory – Galileo on gravity or Lavoisier on combustion – might actually possess a superior claim to have got *things right* in descriptive, theoretical or causal-explanatory terms. For radical empiricism of the Quine/Kuhn variety starts so far back or at such an early stage in the process of sensory cognition that it places no effective (rational) constraint on the range of interpretations or physical theories that can lay equal claim to empirical warrant.

This is why Kuhn's 1969 Postscript makes a cardinal point of endorsing the

Quinean distinction between bare, uninterpreted physical 'stimuli' on the one hand and 'perceptions' (even the most basic, commonsense or pre-scientific perceptions) on the other. Thus, according to Kuhn, one can plausibly maintain that the stimuli hold firm across variant paradigms or theoretical frameworks while nonetheless arguing that what scientists *perceive* – and thereafter work up into observation statements, theories or explanatory conjectures – will vary according to the aspect (or paradigm) under which those stimuli have to be brought before they can achieve any kind of articulate expression. And from here it is no great distance to Richard Rorty's claim that 'when Galileo saw the moons of Jupiter through his telescope ... the impact on his retina was "hard" in the relevant sense', even though – when it came to interpreting the data – his idea of them as 'shattering the crystalline spheres once and for all' has to be treated (epistemologically speaking) as strictly on a par with that of his orthodox opponents, that is, as representing 'merely one more anomaly which had somehow to be worked into a more or less Aristotelian cosmology'.[24] To suppose otherwise – that Galileo got it right – is just the kind of error that realists typically make when they ignore the cardinal point that 'causation is not under a description, but explanation is'. Or again, as Rorty more picturesquely puts it: 'to say that we must have respect for unmediated causal forces is pointless. It is like saying that the blank must have respect for the impressed die. The blank has no choice, neither do we'.[25]

II

The contrast could scarcely be greater – or so it might seem – between this chapter of developments in the wake of 'old-style' logical empiricism and the kinds of thinking about science and philosophy of science that emerged as a consequence of Saussure's revolution in theoretical linguistics. After all, his proposals were squarely based on a rationalist conception of method which invoked the precedent of Descartes and the Port Royal grammarians, and whose chief philosophical premise was its claim that the study of language could be rendered truly 'scientific' only through a sharp conceptual break with the loosely empirical or fact-gathering procedures of earlier (i.e., nineteenth-century) philological enquiry.[26] Such a break was precisely that which occurred – in Saussure's estimation and that of his disciples – at the point where his own thinking underwent the decisive transformation from a diachronic (historically oriented) approach concerned with reconstructing the development of various languages to a structural-synchronic approach that acknowledged the need to reconstitute its object of study (*la langue*) in properly scientific terms. Thus Saussure criticizes Bopp and other comparative grammarians for their 'hybrid and uncertain' grasp of linguistic states, one in which such states are 'considered only in fragments and very imperfectly', since this method lacks any sound or adequate conceptual basis.[27] Hence his insistence (in Chapter Three of the *Cours de linguistique générale*) that a true science of language can come into being only by observing this rigorous distinction between diachrony and synchrony, along with the various other distinctions – chiefly that between *parole* and *langue* – that follow from this cardinal precept. In short, 'the linguist who wishes to understand this state [i.e., the "state" of *la langue* at any given point in its development] must rule out of consideration everything which brought that state about, and pay no attention to diachrony'. And again: 'only by suppressing the past can he enter into the state of mind of the language user [since] the intervention of history can only distort his judgement'.[28]

Moreover, this approach is prerequisite for a science of linguistics that achieves the break with naive (empirically based) conceptions of what constitutes a 'fact' about language. That is to say, it makes possible the moment of conceptual abstraction whereby notions of the sign as a 'positive' correlation between discrete units of sound and sense give way to a grasp of linguistic 'values' as nowhere embodied in particular (phonetic or semantic) features of language, but rather as consisting in the structural economy of differences 'without positive terms'. The Port Royal grammarians may have gone wrong in all sorts of ways but on this point at least they were on the right track and conceptually more in command of their subject than those later comparative grammarians who lapsed into vaguely diachronic and naively positivist or empiricist ways of thinking. Thus the Port Royal grammar 'attempts to describe the state of the French language under Louis XIV and to set out the relevant system of values'. In so doing, furthermore, 'it has no need to make reference to the French of the Middle Ages; it keeps strictly to the horizontal axis and never departs from it'. To this extent, Saussure maintains, 'its basis is less objectionable and its object of study better defined than is the case for the kind of linguistics inaugurated by Bopp'. Where the latter falls short of scientific rigour and method is in 'attempt[ing] to cover an inadequately defined area, never knowing exactly where it is going. It has a foot in each camp, having failed to distinguish clearly between states and sequences'.[29]

I have cited these passages at length since they bring out very clearly the extent of Saussure's allegiance to a rationalist conception of scientific method which stresses the need for linguistics to conceptualize its 'object of study' in such a way as to establish its own credentials as a discipline uniquely equipped to establish what counts as a relevant 'fact' within its own (properly specified) object-domain. Nothing could be further, on the face of it, from Quine's radical-empiricist proposal for a 'naturalized epistemology' that would take its lead from the methods and procedures of the physical sciences (among them behavioural psychology) and steadfastly eschew all rationalist ideas of setting itself up as a meta-discourse with the right to adjudicate in matters of first-order scientific practice. Thus it might well be argued that Saussure and Quine are representatives of two radically opposed traditions – French rationalism and anglophone empiricism – whose origins may be traced to a decisive parting of the ways during the seventeenth century and whose differences have lately re-emerged with particular sharpness in such fields as linguistics, philosophy of language and epistemology of science. From which it follows, on the orthodox

account, that any comparison between developments *after* Quine and Saussure –
for instance, between the Kuhnian–Rortian idea of radical paradigm-relativism
and the Foucauldian/post-structuralist conception of knowledge as a product of
various historically shifting 'discourses' – is one that blithely ignores their
provenance in two quite distinct (indeed antagonistic) lines of intellectual
descent. And this despite the plain assertions of some, Rorty included, that their
'post-philosophical' view of these matters has its source and inspiration at least
as much in the kinds of (mainly French) thinking that emerged in response to
the claims of classic high structuralism as in developments nearer home, among
them Quine's deconstruction of the two last dogmas of old-style logical
empiricism.[30] Still the view persists that such promiscuous claims are merely the
result of a failure (or a mischievous refusal) to respect the salient differences of
background history and standards of competent debate.

It is not my intention here – far from it – to advocate a Rortian view of those
standards as so many irksome and pointless constraints on the freedom of philosophers to devise new language-games or inventive modes of self-description
that will show them (at last) to have broken the hold of such antiquated ways of
thinking. What is more to the point, in this context, is the fact that Rorty can
plausibly exploit a major blind spot in the standard (doxographic) account of the
'two traditions', namely the idea of empiricism and rationalism as involving
such radically divergent theories of language, truth and logic that any comparison between them – other than for purely contrastive purposes – must be
historically and philosophically off the track. However this grossly simplified
conception is one that has been challenged by recent scholars and which hardly
stands up to close examination on either side of the supposed great rift.[31] One
result has been the growing awareness – due to the researches of Hans Aarsleff
and others – that certain of Saussure's most 'distinctive' doctrines, such as that of
the arbitrary (i.e., non-natural) relationship between signifier and signified, were
in fact just as crucial to the thinking of seventeenth-century British empiricists
like Locke, quite apart from their common source in the debate first broached in
Plato's *Cratylus*.[32] Another is the recognition that Saussure's much-vaunted
'break' with the historically-based methods of nineteenth-century philology was
less complete than some commentators (not to mention Saussure himself) are on
occasion disposed to maintain. Thus the *Cours* contains a great mass of philological evidence – grounded in his own earlier work and that of the comparative
grammarians – concerning such 'strictly' diachronic or evolutionary aspects of
language as phonetic shifts, semantic change, the disappearance of inflections,
dialectal variation, interlingual exchange, geographical diffusion, the issue of
linguistic identity across time and so forth. Maybe it is the case, as Saussure
constantly stresses, that 'the need to take account of the passage of time gives rise
to special problems in linguistics and forces us to choose between two radically
different approaches'.[33] All the same it is far from clear – even making due
allowance for the well-known problems that confronted his earliest and subsequent editors – that Saussure ever managed to respect this rigorously for-
mulated axiom of choice.

That is to say, the above-mentioned passages of philological interest are by no means so sharply or hermetically sealed off from his reflections on language in its structural-synchronic aspect as one might otherwise be led to believe by Saussure's more programmatic statements. Rather they often tend to crop up at just the point where he is making some vigorous claim about the need to keep these approaches firmly apart – and to respect the priority of a synchronic over a diachronic perspective – but where diachrony proves a vital source of evidence and thereby places a certain theoretical strain on this whole line of approach. Thus, for instance:

> Sound change ... is a source of linguistic disturbance. Wherever it does not give rise to alternations, it contributes towards loosening the grammatical connexions which link words together. It increases the sum total of linguistic forms to no purpose. The linguistic mechanism becomes obscure and complicated inasmuch as linguistic irregularities produced by sound change take precedence over forms grouped under general types; in other words, inasmuch as what is absolutely arbitrary takes precedence over what is only relatively arbitrary.[34]

Now of course Saussure is here talking about sound-change as a 'disturbance' or a 'complicating' factor insofar as it affects the communicative power and efficiency of language as a social phenomenon, or an ideally economical means of conveying information between speaker and listener. Still it is hard to ignore the further suggestion that it complicates his own theoretical programme by introducing an element of 'absolute arbitrariness' – the irruption of sheerly random or unmotivated diachronic change – into the otherwise smooth functioning of a model (*la langue*) that can find no room for such chaotic phenomena.

Hence Saussure's quickness to insist that any threat this may pose is more than adequately counterbalanced by the workings of linguistic 'analogy', that is to say, by the 'regular imitation of a model' which acts as a brake upon phonetic drift or other such internal disturbances, and is best viewed as 'responsible for all the normal modifications of the external aspect of words which are not due to sound change'.[35] Hence also – a point routinely ignored by post-structuralist exponents of Saussure – his insistence on the strictly 'limited' or 'relative' degree of arbitrariness that can be seen to characterize language as soon as one moves from the paradigmatic to the syntagmatic axis, or from the purely differential (unmotivated) order of relationship that obtains between discrete signifying elements to the order of rational motivation which obtains when those elements enter into forms of successive or linear combination. Thus there is no reason why the terms *dix* and *neuf* should signify those particular numerical values but there is every reason – arithmetically speaking – why the expression *dix-neuf* should take that particular syntagmatic form. What acts as a restriction on the 'arbitrary' character of language is precisely the requirement (again harking back to the Port Royal grammarians and the legacy of Cartesian rationalism) that linguistic structure should articulate the structures of logical thought. For if 'the entire linguistic system is founded upon the irrational principle that the sign is arbitrary', nevertheless '[a]pplied without restriction, this principle would lead to utter chaos'. However, Saussure continues, 'the mind succeeds in introducing a principle of order and regularity into certain areas of the mass of signs', such that – through the presence of 'relative motivation' – the linguist is able to 'study this mechanism as a way of imposing a limitation upon what is arbitrary'.[36] In which case the most basic precept of structural-synchronic linguistics is one that has to be given up – or at any rate subject to drastic restrictions – as soon as the focus of attention switches from language conceived *in abstracto* as a system of differential values (phonetic and semantic) 'without positive terms' to language as a means of communication between rationally motivated subjects.

This is why, as Saussure also remarks, the concept of 'difference' must likewise be kept within strict methodological limits, since 'it is suitable only for comparisons between sound patterns (e.g. *père* vs. *mère*), or between ideas (e.g. "father" vs. "mother")'.[37] Where it does not apply – although (again) post-structuralists are prone to ignore this point – is where the sign is considered as a whole, that is, as a motivated (non-arbitrary) conjunction of *signifiant* and *signifié* which alone makes it possible for language users to communicate on a basis of shared understanding. Thus 'the moment we consider the sign as a whole, we encounter something which is positive in its own domain'. And again: although signifier and signified 'are each, in isolation, purely differential and negative', nevertheless 'their combination is a fact of a positive nature'.[38] Otherwise – lacking such resources – language would indeed be a 'chaos' and not so much a *system* of differences 'without positive terms' as an undifferentiated flux devoid of intelligible structure or meaning. Yet this clearly raises problems for Saussure's claim – hammered home in numerous passages of the *Cours* – that if linguistics is ever to achieve the status of a genuine science then it must start out from the cardinal distinction between synchrony and diachrony. And it is then hard to see what room there is for compromise on those other related distinctions (*langue* vs. *parole*, the paradigmatic vs. the syntagmatic, language as a system of negative differential values vs. language as a chain of 'positive', 'rational' or 'motivated' signifying elements) where in each case methodological priority attaches to the antecedent term.

My point in all this – to recapitulate – is that Saussure's conception of linguistic science is one that encounters certain problems on its own theoretical terrain, problems that find their mirror-image in the aftermath of logical empiricism from Quine to Kuhn. With Saussure this difficulty arises chiefly from the conflict in his thinking between a realist conviction that linguistic science has to do with a well-defined object of study that should somehow – ideally – be set apart from all 'external' considerations like those of history, cultural influence, political events, conquest, colonization, etc., and on the other hand his equally firm insistence that such an object is constituted *in and by* the very act of theoretical abstraction that brings it into being. Indeed it is precisely the principled exclusion of all those extraneous factors which leads Saussure to define *la langue* in terms that would make it a product of conceptual definition

rather than a 'real' (independently existing) object of empirical study in anything like the sense envisaged by the neo-grammarians and other positivistically
inclined students of language. As Roy Harris succinctly puts it:

> A science of language, as far as Saussure was concerned, had to deal with
> linguistic *realia*, not metalinguistic fictions. And yet, as he was forced to
> admit, linguistics – unlike other sciences – had no object of study 'given
> in advance': in linguistics 'it is the viewpoint adopted which creates the
> object'. It is the tension between this admission and the claim to scientific
> status which is felt throughout the *Cours*.[39]

That is to say, Saussure's rationalist conception of scientific method could be
seen as fixing an insuperable gulf between language (*la langue*) as an object-in-
thought 'created' through an act of theoretical abstraction and whatever 'reality'
language might have as a set of 'positive facts' grounded in the actual process of
linguistic communication. In the case of logical empiricism the problem was
that most strikingly diagnosed by Quine when he showed how a more radically
empiricist approach could be seen to undermine the analytic/synthetic dualism
and, along with it, the 'metalinguistic' approach that presupposed the possibility of sharply distinguishing first-order empirical or observation statements
from higher-level theories, 'truths of reason', or self-evident logical axioms.[40]
Thus despite their deriving from two very different traditions of thought these
programmes can be seen as each falling prey to internal conflicts of aim and
method which neither was effectively able to resolve.

Moreover, as I have argued, both gave rise to a series of reactive developments
which might seem worlds apart in philosophical terms but whose underlying
kinship is not hard to discern. Thus – to take perhaps the most dramatic
example – the 'eclipse' of Althusserian Marxism came about (most commentators agree) through its failed attempt to transpose the concepts and categories of
Saussurean structural linguistics to the domain of political theory, and hence to
articulate a Marxist 'science' whose claim to such status rested on its notion of a
rigorous (theoretically elaborated) break between the 'real object' and the
'object-in-thought'.[41] As the problems with this theory came into view – not
least its commitment to what looked very like a full-blown idealist epistemology – so there emerged a post-structuralist, Foucault-inspired movement of
thought which rejected the idea of 'scientific' method as anything more than a
transient product of the various, historically shifting 'discourses' that defined its
objects of enquiry from one period to the next. This Foucauldian approach to the
'archaeology' of scientific knowledge was one that also took its bearings from
Saussurean linguistics, despite Foucault's well-known protestation that he had
never been a 'structuralist' in any – to him – recognizable sense of the term. That
is to say, it is an approach which takes for granted Saussure's claim that linguistics has no object of study 'given in advance', since in this field of investigation 'it is the viewpoint adopted which creates the object'. Where Foucault
most decidedly departs from Saussure is in extending the doctrine beyond

linguistics – which Saussure considered unique in this respect – and applying it to a wide range of other sciences whose objects are likewise thought of as constituted in and by their various modes of discursive representation.

I shall not here pursue the many problems that result from this extreme version of the paradigm-relativist or linguistic-constructivist view, among them its total inability to account for our knowledge of the growth of scientific knowledge, or – what amounts to the same thing – its failure to provide any rational account of scientific theory change.[42] Thus, as Foucault tells it, the story involves a series of decisive ruptures or 'epistemological breaks' that have totally reconfigured the field of knowledge over the past five centuries and more, but which cannot be described – let alone explained or rationally justified – through any appeal to agreed-upon criteria of truth, progress or scientific method. Rather they seem to occur through a kind of large-scale yet random subterranean drift that occasionally builds up the seismic pressure to induce vast changes in the intellectual landscape. However my two chief points in this context are first the extent to which Foucault's ultra-sceptical approach derives from certain problems and unresolved tensions in Saussure's linguistic theory, and second the marked kinship it bears to the Kuhnian account of paradigm change as a process that likewise eludes explanation in progressive or rational-reconstructive terms.

Of course there are differences that need to be noted, among them Kuhn's allowance that 'normal' science typically proceeds through various kinds of problem-solving activity on the part of scientists working within some well-established paradigm, and that it is only during periods of pre-revolutionary 'crisis' that the problems (or conflicting solutions) pile up to the point of creating a major upheaval. But this difference will appear less crucial when set against Kuhn's treatment of such problems, even those of the 'normal' variety, as themselves taking rise only within some particular paradigm and as finding (or failing to find) a 'solution' only in paradigm-relative terms. And again, the very distinction – as Kuhn draws it – between 'normal' and 'revolutionary' science is one that must appear highly problematic when taken in conjunction with his Quinean (radical-empiricist) claim for the holistic character of scientific knowledge and the lack of any ultimate, that is, other than pragmatic grounds for holding a particular statement true given the range of possible variant construals. Thus, to repeat, there is always the option of saving some cherished theory or observation sentence by invoking alternative auxiliary hypotheses, or by redistributing truth-values at any point in the overall 'fabric' of belief. In which case – given this basically conservative principle of least resistance – it is hard to see what could possibly motivate a revolution in scientific thinking. On the other hand it is just as hard to explain why strong revisionists like Rorty should be counted wrong when they adduce Kuhn's paradigm-relativist arguments in support of the view that science does best by aspiring to a state of permanent revolution and striving perpetually to break the hold of 'normal' (workaday or routine problem-solving) science.[43] So the upshot of a radical-empiricist approach is not, after all, so readily distinguished from the position arrived at by those – like Foucault and his post-structuralist disciples – who push right through with the antinomies created by Saussure's 'revolution' in theoretical linguistics.

III

Saussure himself was very firm in maintaining that most other sciences differed crucially in this respect, that is, that they required no such rigorous conceptual break between their real objects of enquiry (or the order of 'positive facts' concerning them) and those objects as defined or specified through an act of theoretical abstraction which rendered them amenable to systematic study in the structural-synchronic mode. The relevant passage is worth citing at length since it brings out very clearly the extent of Saussure's disagreement with those later thinkers (like Foucault) who chose to disregard his cautionary statements on this point. What sets linguistics apart from 'most other sciences' is their *not* being faced with the need to opt decisively for one or the other (diachronic or synchronic) approach. Thus:

> In astronomy, it is observed that in the course of time heavenly bodies undergo considerable changes. But astronomy has not on that account been obliged to split into two separate disciplines. Geology is constantly concerned with the reconstruction of chronological sequences. But when it concentrates on examining fixed states of the earth's crust, that is not considered to be a quite separate object of study. There is a descriptive science of law and a history of law: but no one contrasts the one with the other. The political history of nations is intrinsically concerned with successions of events in time. None the less, when a historian describes the society of a particular period, one does not feel that this ceases to be history. The science of political institutions, on the other hand, is essentially descriptive: but occasionally it may deal with historical questions, and that in no way compromises its unity as a science.[44]

With regard to each of these disciplines it would be forcing the issue − a misconceived theoretical issue − to require, as a criterion of 'scientific' rigour, that they adopt *either* a structural-synchronic *or* a diachronic (historical-developmental) perspective on their object-domain. Rather they can get along perfectly well by respecting that distinction − as practising astronomers or geologists do when they also take an interest in the history of their subject − but not raising it into a high point of methodological precept. For the result of transposing this precept from the science of structural linguistics (where it properly applies) to 'most other sciences' (where it has no legitimate place) is to set up a false and misleading idea of scientific method, one which effectively blocks the way to any adequate, historically informed grasp of present-day developments and what led up to them.

The most striking exception, Saussure argues, is the study of economics where the theorist is 'forced to recognise this duality' since 'political economy and economic history constitute two clearly distinguishable disciplines belonging to one and the same science'. Moreover this distinction, 'although it may not be fully recognised', is nonetheless 'required by an inner necessity of the subject', one that obliges the economist – like the linguist – to adopt wholly different methods of approach to historical, diachronic or developmental facts on the one hand and structural-synchronic considerations on the other. The reason for this is that in both cases (theoretical linguistics and political economy) 'one is dealing with the notion of *value* . . . [*with*] *a system of equivalence between things belonging to different orders* . . . in one case, work and wages; in the other case signification and signal'.[45] Thus economics, like linguistics, will run into all kinds of methodological error if it fails to heed that cardinal distinction and hence mixes up positive facts about the history of its object-domain with the workings of a system that can only be grasped in differential (structural-synchronic) terms. Which is also to say that economics, like linguistics, occupies a certain border zone between the exact or formal and the human, social and historical sciences where it is all the more imperative to keep this distinction clearly in view and not be misled into false extrapolations from one to the other domain. Saussure's firm insistence on this point stands in marked contrast to Foucault's approach in *Les mots et les choses* where the sheer historical sweep and interdisciplinary breadth of coverage results from his failing – or programmatically refusing – to acknowledge any such distinction. Thus Foucault sets out to provide a kind of historical-comparative purview of various fields of knowledge – ranging from philosophy, linguistics and economics (or the earlier 'analysis of wealth') to natural history, geology, botany and the emergent life-sciences – which treats them diachronically as characterized by periods of long-term relative stability that on occasion give way to sudden ruptures or 'epistemological breaks'.[46] However he also adopts a structural-synchronic perspective in so far as those breaks are conceived as occurring through a drastic reconfiguration of knowledge, one whose effects are registered in every field, and whose advent is no more explainable in terms of the history and development of these sciences than the state of *la langue* at some given point in time can be explained by 'extraneous' (diachronic) facts about the influence of geographical, cultural or socio-political factors.

Indeed there are several striking features of Foucault's 'archaeological' approach that are perhaps best seen as resulting from his large-scale transposition of Saussure's structural-synchronic paradigm to the comparative analysis of episodes and developments in the history of thought. One, as noted above, is its holistic tendency to level the distinction between the various formal, natural or social and human sciences, treating them all pretty much on a par as products of an overarching order of discourse (or 'episteme') which manifests its own internal economy of signifying contrasts and relationships. Thus – unlike Saussure – Foucault pays no regard to those salient differences of method and procedure that mark off (say) geology, chemistry and the life-sciences on the one hand from anthropology, philology and historiography on the other. (That he tends to favour biology among the natural sciences is probably because it occupies a middling or contested position on the standard 'hard-to-soft' scale as well as being a useful source of cross-disciplinary metaphors and analogues.) Still less is he inclined to make the kind of sharp distinction that Saussure draws between economic history and political economy, since on Foucault's account any such distinction is itself just a transient product of some period-specific 'discourse' or *episteme* wherein it happens to play a significant role. Hence his well-known dismissive reference to Marxist economic theory as belonging to the same discourse as that of earlier political economists like Smith and Ricardo, whatever the apparent (merely surface) indications of a Marxist 'revolution' in thought.[47] Another, closely related consequence is Foucault's doctrine of paradigm-incommensurability, that is to say, his ultra-Kuhnian idea that whenever there *is* such a radical theory-change or 'epistemological break' then it will surely bring about so massive an upheaval across the entire field of knowledge as to rule out any possibility of meaningful comparison between paradigms. Along with this goes the clear implication that such changes occur for no assignable reason − least of all any reason having to do with scientific progress or the advancement of knowledge − since their occurrence is a matter of seismic shifts at a level of discourse beyond the scope of rational accountability.

What is involved here is a twofold extrapolation from Saussure's model of language (*la langue*) as an object of structural-synchronic analysis. Firstly it involves treating entire 'discourses' (whether in the natural or the human sciences) as likewise subject to the 'arbitrary' link between signifier and signified, and hence as providing no possible basis for comparative judgements of truth or falsehood with regard to their various object-terms and predicates. In which case − reverting to Kuhn's well-known examples − we can have no reason for supposing the statement 'combustion involves the uptake of oxygen' to possess a stronger claim to scientific truth than the statement 'combustion involves a decrease in the volume of dephlogisticated air', or for thinking that Galileo's perception of gravitationally induced pendular movement was based on a sounder grasp of the scientific principles concerned than Aristotle's perception of matter seeking out its rightful place in the cosmic order of the elements. Rather we should see that such terms acquire their sense *and* their reference through the function they perform in some particular 'discourse' (or Quinean 'fabric' of beliefs-held-true at any given time), with the result that inter-paradigm translation or comparison becomes altogether impossible. Whence the second of Foucault's extrapolations from Saussure, namely the idea that paradigm change must be treated as wholly 'unmotivated', that is, as permitting no rational account of those drastic changes in the structural economy of knowledge which mark an 'epistemological break' whose effects extend across the entire field of discursive representation.

We have seen already that Saussure is adamant in restricting the precept of non-motivation to language considered under its structural-synchronic aspect, or as a system of purely differential relationships and contrasts 'without positive terms'. No doubt it is the case, he writes, that 'the sign always to some extent eludes control by the will, whether of the individual or of society: that is its essential nature, even though it may be by no means obvious at first sight'.[48] However, once analysis proceeds beyond that level – once it takes account of morphological, grammatical or larger-scale units of discourse – then this principle has to be abandoned or any rate qualified in various degrees. Thus:

> The fundamental principle of the arbitrary nature of the linguistic sign does not prevent us from distinguishing in any language between what is intrinsically arbitrary – that is, unmotivated – and what is only relatively arbitrary. Not all signs are absolutely arbitrary. In some cases, there are factors which allow us to recognise different degrees of arbitrariness, although never to discard the notion completely. *The sign may be motivated to a certain extent*.[49]

This restriction on the claims of arbitrariness and non-motivation would presumably apply all the more when it comes to assessing scientific theories, that is to say, instances where the 'discourse' in question (more precisely: its object-terms, predicates, inferential procedures and so forth) has been subject to intensive critical scrutiny and testing against the evidence. Thus Donald Davidson has pointed out that the argument for radical paradigm-incommensurability advanced by thinkers like Quine, Kuhn, Whorf and Foucault is one that collapses into manifest self-contradiction as soon as they purport to *describe* or to *specify* the particular differences concerned.[50] Indeed, it is a case that looks plausible only if one focuses on lexical or semantic issues (such as the famous non-translatability of certain colour terms across languages) and ignores the whole range of other linguistic functions – among them various logico-syntactic devices for conjunction, disjunction, anaphora, pronominal reference and so forth – in the absence of which no language could communicate effectively. Hence Davidson's proposal that philosophers should take more account of these invariant or trans-paradigm structures and thereby provide a more adequate basis for grasping the conditions of success (or failure) in translation.

Yet this is not to say that some version of paradigm-incommensurability is sure to result if one adopts a primarily semantic or a lexical approach to the topic of scientific theory change. Hartry Field has offered convincing evidence to the contrary by examining usages of 'mass' in Newtonian and Einsteinian physics and showing that this term can be held to exhibit a sufficient (albeit partial) continuity of reference just so long as one distinguishes various specific senses ('absolute mass', 'inertial mass', and 'rest-mass') in various, likewise specifiable contexts.[51] His main target here is the Quine–Kuhn doctrine of semantic holism and its presumptive consequence, that is, the claim that such radically different scientific theories cannot be subject to comparative evaluation since we cannot be sure that any given term will have carried across with any part of its meaning unaffected by the intervening paradigm change. However his argument also applies to Foucault's quasi-Saussurean conception of knowledge as a shifting field of discursive representations which allows for no stability of sense or reference beyond the appeal to some favoured paradigm, discourse or conceptual scheme by which to impose order on the otherwise inchoate signifying flux.

IV

It is important to stress how remote this is from anything sanctioned by Saussure since his concepts of 'arbitrariness' and the 'non-motivated' character of the linguistic sign have enjoyed (or suffered) such widespread exposure in the work of theorists who pay little heed to his precise formulations of what constitutes linguistics as a genuine science and what sets it apart from other sciences. Here it is worth noting the affinity that exists between Saussure's project and certain developments in French philosophy of science during the early to mid twentieth century which likewise emphasized the notion of a break — a *coupure épistémologique* — with hitherto dominant methods, procedures or 'common-sense' modes of thought. Gaston Bachelard and his student Georges Canguilhem were the two chief advocates of this approach, the one having devoted himself chiefly to issues in the history and philosophy of physics, the other to biology and the life-sciences.[52] Its distinctive character – described by Bachelard in qualified Cartesian terms as a kind of *rationalisme appliqué* – is one that bears detailed comparison with Saussure's linguistic theory even though it first emerged some two decades after Saussure delivered his landmark series of lecture courses in Geneva (1906–11). So if indeed there is any 'influence' here it is one that runs from Saussure to Bachelard rather than Saussure's having drawn his conception of an adequate linguistic theory from Bachelard's epistemo-critical researches into the history of science. More likely both projects took rise from the conjuncture of a lingering Cartesian tradition – the idea of truths self-evident to reason through an exercise of disciplined investigative thought – with a strong countervailing tendency (most explicit in Bachelard) to deny the existence of such *a priori* truths and conceptualize science as a constant process of revising, challenging or radically transforming our received habits of belief.

Thus Bachelard envisaged the process of theory change as one that began with an intuitive (often metaphorical) moment of insight but which then continued through stages of 'rectification and critique' to the point where science achieved the break with such 'naively' analogical, image-based or anthropomorphic residues. Among his examples was that of the tetrahedral structure of the carbon atom, an image whose usefulness or heuristic yield Bachelard was far from denying, but which marked (as he saw it) a transitional phase in the progress toward more adequate conceptions of subatomic structure. Or again, to cite one of Canguilhem's favourite instances: the cellular theory of organic tissue started out as a conjecture with strongly marked affective overtones (associations with the beehive, co-operative labour, the greater good of the organism) but was later refined and developed to a stage where those analogies became merely otiose.[53] That is to say, such advances might take rise from a state of intuitive 'reverie' which enabled thinking to perceive some resemblance – some metaphorical point of comparison – between disparate realms of knowledge or experience. However this moment had to be left behind since, in Bachelard's words, 'the danger of immediate metaphors in the formation of the scientific spirit is that they are not always passing images; they push toward an autonomous kind of thought; they tend to completion and fulfilment in the domain of the image'.[54]

Hence also his distinction between *histoire sanctionée* and *histoire perimée*, the first having to do with currently accepted theories or those that have played some contributory role in the development of scientific knowledge to date, the second with theories that have proved invalid but which might be of interest from a merely historical or socio-cultural viewpoint. Thus, for instance, Black's 'caloric' theory of heat is one that no longer enjoys scientific credence but which nonetheless – unlike Priestley's phlogiston-based theory of combustion – can be seen to have marked a crucial stage in the development of a theory (that of specific heat) which does have a place in our current best scientific thinking.[55] Bachelard's insistence on maintaining this distinction is a clear sign that he opposes any paradigm-relativist approach – such as those of Foucault or Kuhn – that would level the difference between these two kinds of history by removing any grounds for rational comparison across major episodes of theory change. It is likewise sharply at odds with the 'principle of parity' advanced by strong sociologists of knowledge and by practitioners of science- studies as a sub-branch of cultural criticism. This principle holds that one should treat *every* theory – whatever its credentials in current scientific estimation – on exactly the same terms, that is, with a view to its motivating interests, ideological values or socio-cultural conditions of emergence.[56] In other words it rejects the distinction between 'context of discovery' and 'context of justification' which formed a main plank in the logical-empiricist programme and which most philosophers of science (Bachelard included) have endorsed – albeit from differing theoretical perspectives – as the only way to make rational sense of scientific progress to date.[57]

That Saussure considered this a vital distinction in the context of linguistic methodology is evident from passages throughout the *Cours*. Thus it figures crucially in his comparison between language and games like chess where the operative rules (or 'internal' structure of the game) must be treated as 'a system which admits no other order than its own' and where one has to distinguish clearly 'between what is external and what is internal'.[58] And again: 'the fact that chess came from Persia to Europe is an external fact, whereas everything which concerns the system and its rules is internal. If pieces made of ivory are substituted for pieces made of wood, the change makes no difference to the system. But if the number of pieces is diminished or increased, that is a change which profoundly affects the "grammar" of the game'.[59] That is to say, linguistics can aspire to the condition of a genuine science only insofar as it respects the distinction between facts (geographical, historical, socio-cultural, etc.) that relate to its 'external' conditions of emergence and linguistic facts – properly so called – which belong to its legitimate object-domain when conceived in structural-synchronic terms. Any approach (like that of the neo-grammarians) which tends to conflate these orders of significance is thereby precluded from achieving such scientific status.

To this extent Saussure's conception of linguistic science falls square with Bachelard's critical-rationalist approach and comes out firmly opposed to any theory – such as Foucault's archaeology of knowledge – which treats the currency of 'truth' at any given time as a product of those shifting discourses or paradigms that belong to the domain of socio-historical enquiry. From his (Saussure's) point of view this could only amount to a gross confusion of realms, one that misapplies certain strictly synchronic principles (the arbitrary relation between signifier and signified and the unmotivated character of the sign) to a diachronic field of study and which moreover extrapolates wildly on this basis to a whole range of sciences where the linguistic model is of dubious relevance or value. Of course Saussure himself made some large claims for the extension of his theory to a semiological project that would 'study[] the role of signs as a part of social life', and would thus 'form part of social psychology, and hence of general psychology'. Since such a science 'does not yet exist', he concedes, 'one cannot say for certain that it will exist'. All the same, 'it has a right to exist, a place ready for it in advance', in so far as the structural-synchronic approach as applied to issues in theoretical linguistics has been able to specify its operative terms and concepts.[60] This well-known passage from the *Cours* – much cited by theorists in various disciplines during the heyday of 'classic' high structuralism – is of particular interest for suggesting an analogy between the distribution of signifying values in *la langue* and the configuration of scientific fields according to their various distinctive interests and concerns. Thus in the former case 'each of a set of synonyms like *redouter* ["to dread"], *craindre* ["to fear"], *avoir peur* ["to be afraid"] has its particular value only because they stand in contrast with one another'.[61] And in the latter case correspondingly, the scope that exists for some new theoretical endeavour (such as Saussure's projected general semiology) can be thought of as opened up 'in advance' by its potential yield in relation to other (existing) scientific disciplines. After all, 'if *redouter* did not exist, its content would be shared out among its competitors', just as (it is implied) the object-domain of this semiology-to-come has up to now been shared out – and prevented from attaining scientific autonomy – by the lack of adequate conceptual resources whereby to define and delimit that domain. All of which might be taken to suggest the idea of 'knowledge' at any given time as consisting – very much as Foucault conceives it – in those various transient configurations of 'discourse' that happen to prevail from one *episteme* to the next.

However it is sufficiently clear from Saussure's remarks elsewhere in the *Cours* that he rejects any such paradigm-relativist conception of scientific knowledge and regards it as a wholly unjustified conflation of the 'internal' (i.e., structural-synchronic) and 'external' (diachronic or historico-cultural) modes of enquiry. Thus to the question: 'Why is it that semiology is not yet recognized as an autonomous science with its own object of study?' Saussure somewhat testily responds that 'here we go round in a circle', trapped by inadequate notions of 'language' and a fuzzy grasp of what constitutes the object of semiological enquiry. 'On the one hand', he writes, 'nothing is more appropriate than the study of languages to bring out the nature of the semiological problem. But to formulate the problem suitably, it would be necessary to study what a language is in itself; whereas hitherto a language has usually been considered as a function of something else, from other points of view.'[62] Here again there is a close affinity with Bachelard's stress on the normative distinction between history of science as a discipline that studies the conditions of emergence for scientific theories and philosophy of science as an epistemo-critical discipline concerned with establishing the point of transition from inadequate (metaphorical, image-based or anthropomorphic) thinking to adequately theorized scientific knowledge. This distinction works out as closely equivalent to that proposed by the logical empiricists when they required that issues regarding the socio-historical 'context of discovery' not be confused with issues regarding the properly scientific 'context of justification'. Hence – as I have said – Bachelard's conception of 'epistemological breaks' as occurring at just those crucial stages in the passage from one to another paradigm where science overcomes the obstacles to progress that result from its lingering attachment to 'naive' or loosely analogical modes of thought.

On the other hand it is equally important to note that Bachelard, like Saussure, is very far from dismissing diachronic approaches as 'unscientific' or irrelevant to the purposes of an adequately conceptualized philosophy of science. In Saussure's case the point is best made with respect to his early *Mémoire sur le système primitif des voyelles dans les langues indo-européennes* (published at the age of 21) where, as Harris remarks, 'the word *système* already appears in the title'.[63] The main problem that Saussure addressed here – one that had long preoccupied comparative philologists – was how to reconstruct the vowel-system of a pre-literate ancestor language for which no records survived on the basis of later (recorded) languages presumed to have descended from it. More specifically, the problem concerned the vowel *a* and the claim that this 'single' vowel must in fact have had two quite distinct pronunciations or phonetic roles in primitive Indo-European since only thus could one explain those later developments. 'Saussure's contribution', Harris writes,

> [w]as to establish the fact that even postulating two different varieties of *a* still did not provide a satisfactory solution to the problem; and he postulated that in addition the language must have had a third sound, a mystery sound which was in certain respects like a vowel, but in certain respects like a consonant. Saussure could not say exactly what this mystery sound sounded like, because he thought that none of the modern European languages had a sound like it. But he claimed that it was possible to describe the mystery sound in a purely abstract way, by specifying its formal properties. These included its distinctiveness from other vowels and consonants, its capacity to stand alone as a syllable, and its capacity to combine syllabically with vowels. This made it, in Indo-European terms,

neither a consonant nor a vowel, and Saussure decided to call it a 'sonant coefficient'.[64]

As Harris further notes, this mode of inference to the best (most rational) explanation on hypothetico-deductive grounds is one that has also characterized various signal episodes in the history of the physical sciences. Thus, for instance, it comes into play when astronomers predict the existence of a 'new' (as yet unobserved) planet from perturbations in the orbit of neighbouring bodies, or when subatomic physicists postulate some 'new' particle from its effect on other particles in a cloud-chamber or cyclotron.[65] That is to say, Saussure's argument here is a striking example of scientific method not only in so far as it prefigures his later emphasis on the need to treat language in a 'formal', 'systematic' or 'purely abstract' way, but also insofar as it adopts the kind of reasoning that had long been applied – often with conspicuous success – in the natural sciences. As concerns Saussure's conjecture, its truth was borne out a half-century later 'with the decipherment of cuneiform Hittite, an Indo-European language which was found to have a phoneme with exactly the properties Saussure had specified for the mystery sound of primitive Indo-European'.[66]

Harris sees this – justifiably enough – as a vindication fully on a par with what astronomers produce when they gain access to more powerful radio-telescopes, or what physicists obtain with the advent of electron microscopes with ever-greater powers of resolution. At the same time it cautions us against too readily accepting the idea that Saussure's thought underwent a 'radical' transformation between the early period of the *Mémoire* and the period of his lectures at Geneva. What emerges very clearly, in Harris's words, 'is Saussure's early insistence that the correct solution, however counterintuitive it might seem and however unprecedented, was to be found by treating the "sound" as defined in relation to a system'.[67] But of course that 'correct solution' was applied to a problem in comparative philology, that is, a problem which arose from the field of historical-developmental research and which could only be resolved in terms appropriate to that field. So it is not so much the case that a truly 'scientific' study of language requires a clean break between the kinds of issue that preoccupied the nineteenth-century philologists and the kinds of issue that Saussure opened up through his structural-synchronic 'revolution'. Rather it is the case – here as with Bachelard's philosophy of science – that the two approaches can indeed be combined to the benefit of both just so long as one maintains a firm sense of their distinctive methods, priorities and conceptual resources. Imre Lakatos made this point, paraphrasing Kant, when he remarked that 'history of science without philosophy of science is blind', while 'philosophy of science without history of science is empty'.[68] To which he might have added that mixing them up without regard to those basic differences of aim is the surest way to create all manner of epistemological confusion.

V

So there is reason to conclude that Saussure and Bachelard are united in maintaining a construal of scientific theory change which insists on a careful separation of realms and which thus comes out sharply opposed to wholesale contextualist doctrines like those advanced by Foucault, Kuhn, Rorty and the 'strong' sociologists of knowledge. Where such thinking goes wrong – in Saussure's oft-stated view – is through the twofold error of illicitly importing synchronic concepts and categories into the diachronic study of language, and illicitly transposing diachronic data, methods or assumptions into the domain of structural linguistics. With Bachelard the emphasis typically falls on those confusions that result from eliding the distinction between pre- (or proto-) scientific stages of thought and the advent of a scientific theory, properly so called, which has reached the point of adequate conceptualization. This is *not* of course to say – in his case any more than Saussure's – that historical concerns are relegated to a merely second-order or subsidiary status. Indeed one distinctive feature of Bachelard's work as compared with mainstream anglophone philosophy of science is the prominence it gives to episodes and developments in the 'context of discovery', even while insisting that interests of this sort, though perfectly legitimate on their own terms, not be allowed to obtrude upon issues in the 'context of justification'. For Saussure likewise – as any reader of the *Cours* will know – there is absolutely no question of diachronic studies being somehow rendered obsolete or 'pre-scientific' through the advent of a structural-synchronic approach whose claim is to place linguistics on a properly scientific footing. Thus it contains at least as much discussion of a broadly diachronic, developmental or historical-comparative nature as discussion relating to the structure of *la langue* and its distinctive properties or attributes. However, as in Bachelard's case, the overriding methodological imperative is to keep these concerns each within its own, theoretically specified domain and thereby prevent them from engendering all manner of hybrid or pseudo-scientific theories and conjectures.

I have suggested that this is just what happened – and with just such unfortunate results – when Saussure's proposal for a general semiology based on the principles of structural linguistics was taken up and applied to areas of study (like the natural sciences) far beyond its specific remit. That remit – to repeat – was conceived by Saussure as involving semiology's eventual assumption of its role as 'part of social psychology, and hence of general psychology'. At this stage of as-yet-unachieved but preordained emergence 'the laws which semiology will discover will be laws applicable in linguistics, and linguistics will thus be assigned to a clearly defined place in the field of human knowledge'.[69] Yet just as linguistics can attain this role only on condition of accepting its place within a larger semiological science, so likewise that science must itself be subject to certain 'clearly defined' disciplinary limits, namely those which assign it a legitimate place within the social sciences and psychology. Thus Saussure is very far from envisaging a stage – as proclaimed by Foucault and by others with dubious Saussurean warrant – when its claims would extend (in principle at least) to every area of the natural as well as the social or human sciences. Much the same applies to Foucault's usage of the term 'epistemological break', a usage that clearly derives (*via* Canguilhem) from Bachelard's account of scientific theory change but which undergoes a notable loss of precision along with its massively extended scope as a covering term for all manner of deep-laid yet ill-defined shifts in the historico-discursive 'order of things'.

As I have said, this may well have resulted in part from the reaction provoked by Althusser's ill-starred attempt to reformulate the terms of a Marxist 'theoretical practice' under the joint aegis of Saussurean structural linguistics and Bachelardian philosophy of science. If that project failed then it did so for reasons which again had to do with the misapplication of structural-synchronic concepts to an area of discourse where the claims of diachrony (of history, agency or purposive intent) could scarcely be denied without engendering all sorts of endemic and – on its own terms – strictly irresolvable dilemmas. Saussure makes this point with maximal emphasis when he declares that 'any notion of bringing together facts of such disparate nature would be mere fantasy, [since] in the diachronic perspective one is dealing with phenomena which have no connection with linguistic systems, even though the systems are affected by them'.[70] If one catches a distant rumble here it is the sound of whole theories collapsing, among them the Foucauldian archaeology of scientific knowledge and – in a different, though related, context – those paradigm-relativist approaches (such as Kuhn's) which likewise involve a failure to observe that cardinal distinction. What results in both cases is a radically holistic or contextualist theory wherein the truth-value of any given statement is somehow (impossibly) decided by the relationship it bears to the entire existing body of beliefs-held-true during this or that period of scientific thought. Michael Devitt – writing from a realist viewpoint – has described this chapter of developments as one that places the linguistic cart very firmly before the scientific horse.[71] That is to say, it involves the strange idea that certain highly contestable theories of meaning or discursive representation should be taken as possessing stronger epistemic warrant than the kinds of causal-realist approach *via* inference to the best explanation which provide the only adequate (i.e., non-miraculist) account of how science has achieved its various advances to date.[72]

It is among the great ironies of recent intellectual history that Saussure's meticulous specification of the scope and limits of his project should since have given way to a movement of thought so markedly at odds with his own clearly stated aims and priorities. I shall now – in Chapter 4 – take a closer look at some of those developments in literary/cultural theory that have adopted an anti-realist or a 'strong' social-constructivist line, along with some ideas for an alternative approach that would offer a more adequate means to discriminate various kinds or genres of discourse and representation.

NOTES

1   Ferdinand de Saussure, *Course in General Linguistics* [1922], trans. Roy Harris (London: Duckworth, 1983); also *Cours de linguistique générale* (critical edition), ed. Tullio de Mauro; trans. Louis-Jean Calvet (Paris: Payot, 1972).

2   Rudolf Carnap, *The Logical Structure of the World and Pseudoproblems in Philosophy*, trans. R. George (Berkeley and Los Angeles: University of California Press, 1967) and *Meaning and Necessity* (Chicago: University of Chicago Press, 1959); Alfred Tarski, *Logic, Semantics and Metamathematics*, trans. J.H. Woodger (Oxford: Oxford University Press, 1956); A.J. Ayer (ed.), *Logical Positivism* (New York: Free Press, 1959).

3   See Gottlob Frege, 'On Sense and Reference', in *Translations from the Philosophical Writings of Gottlob Frege*, eds. P. Geach and M. Black (Oxford: Blackwell, 1952), pp. 56–78; Bertrand Russell, 'On Denoting', *Mind* 14 (1905), pp. 479–93 and *Logic and Knowledge*, ed. R. Marsh (London: Allen & Unwin, 1956).

4   See for instance Roland Barthes, *Elements of Semiology*, trans A. Lavers and C. Smith (New York: Hill & Wang, 1967) and *Mythologies*, trans. A. Lavers (London: Paladin, 1973); Peter Caws, *Structuralism: The Art of the Intelligible* (Atlantic Highlands, NJ: Humanities Press, 1988); Jonathan Culler, *Structuralist Poetics: Structuralism, Linguistics, and the Study of Literature* (London: Routledge & Kegan Paul, 1975); François Dosse, *History of Structuralism*, vol. 1, *The Rising Sign, 1945–1966* and vol. 2, *The Sign Sets, 1957–Present* (Minneapolis: University of Minnesota Press, 1997); Jacques Ehrmann (ed.), *Structuralism* (New York: Anchor-Doubleday, 1970); Terence Hawkes, *Structuralism and Semiotics* (London: Methuen, 1977); Jacques Lacan, *Ecrits: A Selection*, trans. A. Sheridan-Smith (London: Tavistock, 1977); Claude Lévi-Strauss, *Structural Anthropology*, trans. C. Jacobson and B.G. Schoepf (Harmondsworth: Penguin, 1977); R. Macksey and E. Donato (eds.), *The Structuralist Controversy: The Languages of Criticism and the Sciences of Man* (Baltimore, MD: Johns Hopkins University Press, 1970); Thomas Pavel, *The Feud of Language: A History of Structuralist Thought* (Oxford: Blackwell, 1990); Philip Pettit, *The Concept of Structuralism: A Critical Analysis* (Dublin: Gill & Macmillan, 1975); David Robey (ed.), *Structuralism: An Introduction* (Oxford: Oxford University Press, 1973).

5   See Note 4, above; also Fredric Jameson, *The Prison-House of Language* (Princeton, NJ: Princeton University Press, 1972) and David Lodge, *The Modes of Modern Writing: Metaphor, Metonymy and the Typology of Modern Literature* (London: Longman, 1977).

6   Louis Althusser, *For Marx*, trans. Ben Brewster (London: New Left Books, 1969); also Louis Althusser and Etienne Balibar, *Reading Capital*, trans. Ben Brewster (New Left Books, 1970).

7   See especially Ted Benton, *The Rise and Fall of Structural Marxism* (London: New Left Books, 1984) and Gregory Elliott, *Althusser: The Detour of Theory* (London: Verso, 1987).

8   See for instance – from a range of viewpoints – Derek Attridge, Geoff Bennington and Robert Young (eds.), *Post-Structuralism and the Question of History* (Cambridge: Cambridge University Press, 1987); Roland Barthes, *S/Z*, trans. Richard Miller (London: Jonathan Cape, 1975); Catherine Belsey, *Critical Practice* (London: Methuen, 1980); Josué V. Harari (ed.), *Textual Strategies: Perspectives in Post-Structuralist Criticism* (London: Methuen, 1980); Richard Harland, *Superstructuralism: The Philosophy of Structuralism and Post-Structuralism* (London: Methuen, 1987); Robert Young (ed.), *Untying the Text: A Post-Structuralist Reader* (London: Routledge & Kegan Paul, 1981).

9   See especially Roland Barthes, *Image Music Text*, trans. Stephen Heath (London: Fontana, 1977).

10 Michel Foucault, *Language, Counter-Memory, Practice*, ed. Donald F. Bouchard (Oxford: Blackwell, 1977).

11 See especially Barthes, *Image Music Text*.

12 Foucault, *Discipline and Punish*, trans. Alan Sheridan (London: Allen Lane, 1977).

13 Lacan, *Ecrits*; also E. Roudinesco, *Jacques Lacan and Co: A History of Psychoanalysis in France, 1925–1985* (Chicago: University of Chicago Press, 1990).

14 Roger Smith, *The Fontana History of the Human Sciences* (London: Fontana, 1997), pp. 732–4. See also Karen Horney, *Feminine Psychology* (New York: W.W. Norton, 1967); N.G. Hale, *The Rise and Crisis of Psychoanalysis in the United States: Freud and the Americans, 1917–1985* (New York: Oxford University Press, 1995); H.S. Hughes, *Sea Change: The Migration of Social Thought, 1930–1965* (New York: Harper & Row, 1975); Edith Kurzweil, *The Freudians: A Comparative Perspective* (New Haven: Yale University Press, 1989).

15 Jean Starobinski, *Les mots sous les mots* (Paris: Gallimard, 1971).

16 See Note 2, above; also Hans Reichenbach, *Experience and Prediction* (Chicago: University of Chicago Press, 1938).

17 W.V. Quine, 'Two Dogmas of Empiricism', in *From a Logical Point of View*, 2nd edn (Cambridge, MA: Harvard University Press, 1961), pp. 20–46.

18 See Sandra G. Harding (ed.), *Can Theories Be Refuted? Essays on the Duhem–Quine Thesis* (Dordrecht: D. Reidel, 1976).

19 Perry Anderson, *In the Tracks of Historical Materialism* (London: New Left Books, 1983).

20 W.V. Quine, *Ontological Relativity and Other Essays* (New York: Columbia University Press, 1969).

21 Thomas S. Kuhn, *The Structure of Scientific Revolutions*, 2nd edn (Chicago: University of Chicago Press, 1970).

22 Michel Foucault, *The Order of Things: An Archaeology of the Human Sciences*, trans. Alan Sheridan-Smith (London: Tavistock, 1970) and *The Archaeology of Knowledge*, trans. Sheridan-Smith (Tavistock, 1972).

23 See for instance Paul Horwich (ed.), *The World Changes: Thomas Kuhn and the Nature of Science* (Cambridge, MA: MIT Press, 1993).

24 Richard Rorty, *Objectivity, Relativism, and Truth* (Cambridge: Cambridge University Press, 1991), p. 81.

25 Ibid., p. 81.

26 On the other hand, as David Holdcroft remarks, 'it is arguable that he [Saussure] went further and maintained that there are no language-independent concepts, thus turning the position of the *Port Royale Grammar* on its head' (David Holdcroft, *Saussure: Signs, System and Arbitrariness* [Cambridge: Cambridge University Press, 1991], p. 166 n.). One way of describing the transition from structuralism to post-structuralism is in terms of this unresolved tension in Saussure's thought between a rationalist approach premised on the basically Cartesian appeal to 'clear and distinct ideas' and a full-scale semiological doctrine committed to the thesis that all our operative concepts and categories are dependent upon (or 'constructed by') particular languages or signifying systems. For further discussion, see O. Ducrot, *Le structuralisme en linguistique* (Paris: Seuil, 1968) and Harland, *Superstructuralism*.

27 Saussure, *Course in General Linguistics*, p. 82.

28 Ibid., p. 81.

29 Ibid., p. 82.

30 Rorty, *Objectivity, Relativism, and Truth*.

31 See for instance Christopher Norris, *Minding the Gap: Epistemology and Philosophy of Science in the Two Traditions* (Amherst, MA: University of Massachusetts Press, 2000).

32 Hans Aarsleff, *The Study of Language in England, 1760–1860* (Princeton, NJ: Princeton University Press, 1967).

33 Saussure, *Course in General Linguistics*, p. 79.

34 Ibid., p. 160.

35 Ibid., p. 160.

36 Ibid., p. 131.

37 Ibid., p. 119.

38 Ibid., p. 119.
39 Roy Harris, *Language, Saussure and Wittgenstein: How to Play Games with Words* (London: Routledge, 1988), p. 126.
40 Quine, 'Two Dogmas of Empiricism'.
41 See Note 7, above; also E.P. Thompson, 'The Poverty of Theory', in *The Poverty of Theory and Other Essays* (London: Merlin, 1978).
42 See for instance Norris, *Minding the Gap*; also *New Idols of the Cave: On the Limits of Anti-Realism* (Manchester: Manchester University Press, 1997) and *Resources of Realism: Prospects for 'Post-Analytic' Philosophy* (London: Macmillan, 1997).
43 Rorty, *Objectivity, Relativism, and Truth*.
44 Saussure, *Course in General Linguistics*, p. 79.
45 Ibid., p. 79; italics in the original.
46 See Gary Gutting, *Michel Foucault's Archaeology of Scientific Knowledge* (Cambridge: Cambridge University Press, 1989).
47 Foucault, *The Order of Things*.
48 Saussure, *Course in General Linguistics*, p. 16.
49 Ibid., p. 130.
50 Donald Davidson, 'On the Very Idea of a Conceptual Scheme', in *Inquiries into Truth and Interpretation* (Oxford: Clarendon Press, 1984), pp. 183–98. See also *Language, Thought and Reality: Selected Writings of Benjamin Lee Whorf*, ed. J.B. Carroll (Cambridge, MA; MIT Press, 1956).
51 Hartry Field, 'Theory Change and the Indeterminacy of Reference', *Philosophy* 70 (1973), pp. 462–81; 'Quine and the Correspondence Theory', *Philosophical Review* 83 (1974), pp. 200–28; 'Conventionalism and Instrumentalism in Semantics', *Noûs* 9 (1975), pp. 375–405.
52 Gaston Bachelard, *La formation de l'esprit scientifique* (Paris: Corti, 1938); *Le rationalisme appliqué* (Paris: Presses Universitaires de France, 1949); *Le materialisme rationnel* (Paris: Presses Universitaires de France, 1953); *The Philosophy of No: A Philosophy of the New Scientific Mind* (New York: Orion Press, 1968); *The Poetics of Reverie*, trans. Daniel Russell (Boston: Beacon Press, 1971); Georges Canguilhem, *Etudes d'histoire et de philosophie des sciences* (Paris: Vrin, 1968); *La connaissance de la vie*, 2nd edn (Paris: Vrin, 1969); *On the Normal and the Pathological* (Dordrecht: D. Reidel, 1978); *Ideology and Rationality in the History of the Life Sciences*, trans. A. Goldhammer (Cambridge, MA: MIT Press, 1988); also G. Lafrance (ed.), *Gaston Bachelard* (Ottawa: University of Ottawa Press, 1987); Dominqiue Lecourt, *Marxism and Epistemology: Bachelard, Canguilhem, Foucault* (London: New Left Books, 1975); Mary Tiles, *Bachelard: Science and Objectivity* (Cambridge: Cambridge University Press, 1984).
53 Canguilhem, *La connaissance de la vie*, pp. 64–5.
54 Bachelard, *La formation de l'esprit scientifique*, p. 81. The passage is cited in Jacques Derrida's essay 'White Mythology: Metaphor in the Text of Philosophy' (Derrida, *Margins of Philosophy*, trans. Alan Bass [Chicago: University of Chicago Press, 1982], pp. 207–71 [224]). I should mention that this is by far the most detailed, philosophically astute, and wide-ranging treatment to be found in recent discussions of the topic, whether those belonging to the broadly 'analytic' (Anglo-American) or the 'continental' (mainland-European) traditions of thought. Above all it is explicit in rejecting the Nietzschean idea – much canvassed by 'literary' deconstructionists and strong-descriptivists like Rorty – that scientific concepts are *nothing more* than a species of sublimated metaphor, or that science amounts to just a kind of 'white mythology', a discourse that has lost the courage of its own metaphorical intuitions or perceptions. (For the most influential statement of this view, see Rorty, 'Philosophy as a Kind of Writing: An Essay on Derrida', in *Consequences of Pragmatism* [Brighton: Harvester, 1982], pp. 90–109.) Thus 'there is also a *concept of metaphor*: it too has a history, yields knowledge, demands from the epistemologist construction, rectification, critical rules of

importation and exportation' (Derrida, 'White Mythology', p. 224).

No doubt one has to make allowance for Derrida's mixed-mode style of discourse or his use of an oblique ('free indirect') means of presentation when citing a source-text – here that of Bachelard – whose arguments he wishes to deploy strategically without perhaps fully endorsing them. All the same – as I have argued at length elsewhere – it is wrong to assume that Derrida is rejecting Bachelard's distinction between the realm of intuitive or pre-scientific metaphorical 'reverie' and the realm of elaborated scientific concepts where values of truth and falsehood come into play (Norris, *New Idols of the Cave*). Indeed this distinction is everywhere presupposed in Derrida's account of the history of philosophy's dealings with the problematic topos of metaphor, from Aristotle to Nietzsche, Bachelard and Canguilhem. For it would otherwise be impossible to explain how scientific knowledge could ever advance 'from an inefficient tropic-concept that is poorly constructed, to an operative tropic-concept that is more refined and more powerful in a given field and at a determined phase of the scientific process' ('White Mythology', p. 264).

55 For further discussion, see Stathis Psillos, *Scientific Realism: How Science Tracks Truth* (London: Routledge, 1999).

56 See for instance Barry Barnes, *About Science* (Oxford: Blackwell, 1985); David Bloor, *Knowledge and Social Imagery* (London: Routledge & Kegan Paul, 1976); Harry Collins, *Changing Order: Replication and Induction in Scientific Practice* (Chicago: University of Chicago Press, 1985).

57 See Reichenbach, *Experience and Prediction*.

58 Saussure, *Course in General Linguistics*, p. 23.

59 Ibid., p. 23.

60 Ibid., pp. 15–16.

61 Ibid., p. 114

62 Ibid., p. 16.

63 Harris, *Language, Saussure and Wittgenstein*, p. 39.

64 Ibid., pp. 39–40.

65 J.L. Aronson, 'Testing for Convergent Realism', *British Journal for the Philosophy of Science* 40 (1989), pp. 255–60; Gilbert Harman, 'Inference to the Best Explanation', *Philosophical Review* 74 (1965), pp. 88–95; Peter Lipton, *Inference to the Best Explanation* (London: Routledge, 1993).

66 Harris, *Language, Saussure and Wittgenstein*, p. 40.

67 Ibid., p. 40.

68 Imre Lakatos, *Philosophical Papers*, vol. 1: *The Methodology of Scientific Research Programmes* (Cambridge: Cambridge University Press, 1972), p. 102.

69 Saussure, *Course in General Linguistics*, pp. 15–16.

70 Ibid., p. 85.

71 Michael Devitt, *Realism and Truth*, 2nd edn (Oxford: Blackwell, 1986); Devitt and Kim Sterelny, *Language and Reality: An Introduction to the Philosophy of Language* (Oxford: Blackwell, 1987).

72 See especially Richard Boyd, 'The Current Status of Scientific Realism', in Jarrett Leplin (ed.), *Scientific Realism* (Berkeley and Los Angeles: University of California Press, 1984), pp. 41–82; also Hilary Putnam, *Mind, Language and Reality* (Cambridge: Cambridge University Press, 1975). The following passage is representative of Putnam's early (causal-realist) approach to issues of meaning, reference, and truth.

As language develops, the causal and noncausal links between bits of language and aspects of the world become more complex and more various. To look for any one uniform link between word or thought and object of word or thought is to look for the occult; but to see our evolving and expanding notion of reference as just a proliferating family is to miss the essence of the relation between language and reality. The essence of the relation is that language and thought do asymptotically correspond to reality, to some extent at least. A theory of reference is a theory of the correspondence in question. (Putnam, *Mind, Language, Reality*, p. 290)

In his later (post-1980) work Putnam has moved away from this position under pressure from a range of counter-arguments which he now regards as posing insuperable problems for any such 'metaphysical'-realist line of thought. His first stop was a theory of 'internal' (or framework-relative) realism which allowed statements to possess a determinate truth-value but only in so far as that value was assigned with reference to some particular range of accepted criteria, investigative interests, disciplinary standards, etc. (see especially Hilary Putnam, *Reason, Truth and History* [Cambridge: Cambridge University Press, 1981]). Since then he has put forward a number of compromise proposals for conserving some plausible notion of truth and thus avoiding the nemesis of cultural relativism while also acknowledging the impossibility (as he sees it) of maintaining any stronger, i.e., objectivist or framework-transcendent realist conception (Hilary Putnam, *The Many Faces of Realism* [La Salle: Open Court, 1987]; *Realism With a Human Face* [Cambridge, MA: Harvard University Press, 1990]; *Renewing Philosophy* [Cambridge, MA: Harvard University Press, 1992]). What is chiefly of interest in the present context is the fact that Putnam's long-haul retreat from causal realism has been prompted in large part by the same kinds of argument – holistic, contextualist, paradigm-relativist – that can also be seen to have influenced the reception-history of Saussurean linguistics. That is to say, it has resulted (in my view at least) from an over-readiness to concede the force of objections which take for granted the idea that truth cannot possibly transcend the limits of some given language-game, discourse, paradigm or conceptual scheme. For a full-length study of Putnam's work that argues this case in detail, see Christopher Norris, *Hilary Putnam: Realism, Reason and the Uses of Uncertainty* (Manchester: Manchester University Press, 2002).

4

Translation to Tralfamadore:
Images of Science in Literary Theory

During the first half of the twentieth century there was a prevalent way of thinking about the academic disciplines – the natural, social and human sciences – which assigned them each to their appointed place on a 'hard-to-soft' scale of methodological rigour. This idea had its source in logical positivism and in the 'unity of science' movement which was basically a programme for ranking those disciplines in a descending order of priority.[1] Thus physics was taken as the paradigm case of a 'hard' discipline with clearly specified criteria for what should count as a valid empirical observation and an adequate (logically rigorous) mode of reasoning on the scientific evidence. Of course there were some large differences of view about the kind of logical reasoning involved – as between inductivists and those who espoused a covering-law or hypothetico-deductive approach – and also about the content and status of empirical truth-claims. These differences were later to emerge more sharply and produce what amounted to a crisis or breakdown of the logical-positivist programme in its original, doctrinally confident form. Thus a main plank in that programme – the verification principle – was shown to fall foul of its own requirement that meaningful statements must be *either* empirically verifiable *or* self-evidently true in virtue of their logical form.[2] Since the principle satisfied neither criterion it clearly stood in need of revision and no such revision proved adequate despite the best efforts of rearguard defenders like A.J. Ayer. All the same this approach retained sufficient of its early promise to persuade most philosophers that there were good grounds for the conception of science – and physics in particular – as exhibiting a definite (if sometimes uneven) progress toward truth at the end of enquiry. For could there be any serious doubt, aside from such sceptical qualms, that physics had achieved a whole range of impressive advances which could only be explained on the assumption that its methods and procedures were reliably conducive to a better understanding of physical phenomena on every scale, from the subatomic structure of matter to the laws of celestial mechanics?

Next on the scale were chemistry and biology, thought of as rightfully aspiring to this physics-led conception of what science ought to be, but as not yet having achieved an equivalent stage of empirical and conceptual precision.[3] That is to say, these disciplines at present had to do with the kinds of complex (i.e., molecular) structure which still resisted treatment in terms of fundamental physics. Moreover this criterion was taken to apply right the way down from the more scientifically oriented branches of the social sciences (such as economics and behavioural psychology), through disciplines like sociology and history that could claim some degree of methodological rigour, to others – among them ethics, aesthetics and literary criticism – which altogether lacked such validating standards and were hence considered strictly off-bounds from a scientific viewpoint. These were not so much 'disciplines' – still less 'sciences' – but rather just a means for expressing various kinds of emotive or subjective response which perhaps had their place in the broader range of fit topics for civilized discourse but could never hope to emulate the physical sciences. Thus literary critics were deluding themselves if they thought to come up with some 'theory' of literature that would place their enterprise on a firm methodological footing.

This picture perhaps needs complicating a little if we are to understand just how much things have changed over the past half-century of 'science and literature' debate. For one thing, the positivists did make allowance for a kind of special-case promotion scheme whereby disciplines could improve their grade through an effort to incorporate the methods and standards of (what else?) the natural sciences. Thus for instance psychology, anthropology, sociology and linguistics had the chance to improve themselves – to achieve scientific status – by adopting an empirical approach and avoiding the appeal to such 'unverifiable' notions as meaning, intention or value. Economics could best continue on its path toward scientific respectability by pursuing a quantitative method which likewise – so far as possible – excluded all questions of agency and purpose. Even ethics might aspire to something like the condition of a science just so long as it acknowledged the 'emotive' character of moral judgements (that is, their lack of any ultimate validating standard) and could hence be treated as a branch of behavioural psychology.[4] What this amounted to, in short, was a further set of intra-disciplinary distinctions which ranked such approaches high insofar as they accepted a physical-science-based criterion of methodological rigour, and low insofar as they clung to some notion that theirs was a discourse irreducibly concerned with the meaning or significance of human cultural activity. In fact this whole issue goes much further back to nineteenth-century debates about the role of hermeneutic understanding – that is, prototypically, the kind of understanding involved in the reading of biblical or literary texts – *vis-à-vis* the methodology of the natural sciences.[5] Thus logical positivism can perhaps best be seen as a programmatic drive to reassert the pre-eminence of scientific method, or its own conception thereof, over any approach that claims equal standing for the different, hermeneutically oriented methods and procedures of the human sciences.

Literary critics varied widely in their response to this challenge. Some – like I.A. Richards – took what amounted to a line of least resistance, endorsed the 'emotivist' (i.e., non-cognitivist) conception of literary meaning and value, then proceeding to treat them as subject-matter for behavioural psychology, albeit with room for certain normative standards of more-or-less adequate reader-response.[6] Others – in the broadly 'hermeneutic' line of descent – protested that this was an absurdly reductive mode of approach which ignored the essential difference between the kinds of empirically based methodology appropriate to the natural sciences and the kinds of intrinsically meaningful experience that characterized the humanistic disciplines.[7] One way of writing the history of twentieth-century literary criticism and theory would be in terms of this debate between those who took science – or at least some conception of science – as their methodological lodestar and those who flatly rejected any such idea. Not that Richards had many followers in his attempt to make terms with logical positivism and the 'unity of science' project. Indeed, that project was itself fairly short-lived – at least in its original, strong form – since it soon came under attack from various quarters, not least from philosophers like W.V. Quine who challenged its most basic conceptual premises, and also (as we have seen) from critics of the verification principle who pointed out that this doctrine failed to meet its own strict requirement for distinguishing valid or meaningful from meaningless or downright nonsensical statements.[8] Besides, there were developments in subatomic (quantum) physics which coincided with the rise of logical positivism and indeed, on some early accounts, found in it their fittest philosophical expression yet which turned out to create large difficulties for its more confident claims.[9] In mathematics likewise, the new century witnessed a number of highly problematic results – such as Russell's demonstration of the set-theoretical paradoxes and Gödel's incompleteness theorem – which undermined David Hilbert's optimistic pronouncement that all the really important mathematical problems would be resolved within a few decades.[10] At any rate the 'unity of science' programme has been viewed with increasing scepticism not only by cultural theorists and sociologists of knowledge who take strong exception to its hegemonic aims but also by philosophers anxious to redeem a more nuanced, less doctrinaire and overweening conception of scientific method.[11]

II

These are arguably some of the reasons why debates about science and literature during the second half of the twentieth century shifted onto different ground, with literary critics on the whole less defensive about the status or credentials of their discipline and philosophers of science less inclined to ride the high horse of a single, presumptively superior scientific method. Still there were some marked differences of view as to whether literary criticism (or theory) might properly aspire to *its own* kind of 'scientific' rigour, that is to say, toward a general methodology that would place criticism on firm conceptual foundations and avoid any recourse to merely subjective or 'appreciative' modes of response. Among its chief advocates were those who adopted a structuralist approach deriving from the linguistic theory of Ferdinand de Saussure, one that could usefully be extended – so they claimed – to the analysis of narrative structures in fiction or various kinds of poetic device such as metaphor and metonymy.[12] At the outset this approach was mostly subject to attack by literary critics of a more traditional 'interpretative' bent who viewed it as yet another alien intrusion of scientific (or pseudo-scientific) method. Later – from the mid-1970s on – it attracted the hostility of post-structuralists (and then postmodernists) who claimed to have passed through and beyond this brief infatuation with an idea of science which even most scientists would no longer recognize as possessing the least credibility. That is to say, structuralism was a dream of method which presumed the possibility of objective knowledge, of the literary theorist – like the old-style scientist – adopting a standpoint outside and above those various texts (or physical phenomena) which constituted his or her field of enquiry.[13]

This turn to post-structuralism was nowhere more dramatically announced than in the later work of Roland Barthes who started out as an avatar of structuralist method as applied to narrative theory, poetics and the analysis of popular culture but who then took to denouncing that whole enterprise as the merest of false ('scientistic') delusions. Henceforth – he proclaimed – there could be no appeal to this once powerfully seductive idea of literary theory as a discipline with its own special standards of methodological rigour.[14] For was not 'theory' itself a kind of writing – or a textual practice – that should aim to *transform* the object of analysis (whether literary text or cultural icon), rather than aspire to such an old-fashioned 'positivist' conception of scientific method? What structuralism had failed to recognize was the sheer *impossibility* of drawing a line between the first-order language of fiction or poetry and the higher-level ('metalinguistic') discourse of literary theory. And if this betrayed an overly zealous attempt to emulate science at its own game then perhaps post-structuralism also offered a means of pursuing the argument into areas of discourse – such as the natural sciences – whose privileged epistemological status could thus be revealed as nothing more than a product of linguistic, discursive or narrative representation.[15]

Meanwhile, altogether elsewhere, philosophers like Quine had likewise challenged the logical-positivist distinction between observation statements that could be verified (or falsified) by a straightforward appeal to empirical data and supposedly self-evident 'truths of reason' whose validity was purely a matter of their logical form.[16] On the contrary, he argued: no statement can be held true 'come what may' since truth-values are holistically distributed across the entire 'web' or 'fabric' of beliefs at any given time. Which is also to say that no theory stands or falls on the outcome of a single observation – or 'crucial experiment' – since every such procedure involves a whole range of auxiliary hypotheses, all of them potentially open to challenge or revision. So if conflicts arise then there is always the option of conserving some cherished theoretical belief by citing the possibility of observational error, perceptual distortion, the limits of precise measurement, and so on. Conversely, one can always save any discrepant (theoretically anomalous) empirical result by making suitable adjustments elsewhere in the web, whether with regard to some deeply entrenched physical theory or even – at the limit – to some logical 'law of thought' which had hitherto been conceived as absolutely immune from revision.

Thus theories are 'underdetermined' by the best evidence to hand and that evidence is itself 'theory-laden' in so far as it is taken as offering support for one or other candidate hypothesis. That is to say, what scientists 'perceive' or 'observe' when performing a crucial experiment is *not* just an incoming barrage of raw, uninterpreted physical stimuli but a certain kind of phenomenon – such as the gravitationally induced motion of a pendulum, or the process of combustion as involving the uptake of oxygen, or the earth's diurnal rotation around the sun – which always involves some particular theoretical frame of reference.[17] This was also Thomas Kuhn's chief point in his book *The Structure of Scientific Revolutions*, a text that has exerted enormous influence on work in the philosophy, history and sociology of science over the past half-century, not least among cultural and literary theorists with an interest in such matters.[18] For Kuhn, in brief, the history of science should be seen as a series of 'paradigm changes' whereby one dominant frame of reference gives way to another, most often as a result of accumulated problems with the old way of thinking which eventually lead to its breakdown and replacement by another (at the time) 'revolutionary' paradigm. Where this approach goes against more traditional, realist ideas of scientific truth and progress is in its claim that such different paradigms are strictly 'incommensurable', that is, that they cannot be compared or evaluated in point of empirical adequacy or theoretical-explanatory power. Thus, where Aristotle's cosmology led him to perceive a swinging stone as an instance of matter seeking out its proper place in the sublunary order of the elements, Galileo perceived an instance of pendular (gravity-induced) motion. Where Joseph Priestley observed combustion as a process involving the emission of 'phlogiston' – and a corresponding decrease in the quantity of 'dephlogistated air' – Lavoisier observed combustion as a process that required the presence and uptake of oxygen. And where astronomers wedded to the old (Ptolemaic–Aristotelian) model of the geocentric cosmos perceived what they took to be the sun rising in the east at dawn, Copernicus, Galileo and their followers perceived what they took to be ocular proof of the earth's heliocentric rotation, despite and against the evidence of 'common-sense' perception.

Hence Kuhn's challenge to the realists and progressivists: how can we possibly rank such theories on a common scale of approximation to scientific truth if they involve such massively divergent (incommensurable) paradigms, worldviews or basic ideas of what counts as a valid observation? Rather we should learn to accept the idea that scientists on either side of a major paradigm change should be thought of as inhabiting 'different worlds', worlds that contain a whole range of different objects, constituent properties, causal powers, standards of 'adequate' (scientifically acceptable) description or explanation, and so forth. There has been much debate – and some vacillation on Kuhn's part – as to just how literally this claim should be taken, or whether it can best, most charitably be interpreted as asserting that observers perceive things in very different ways even though, in some ultimate (ontological) sense, the things they perceive can be held invariant across such radical differences of view.[19] However it is clear that approaches of this sort – along with Quine's root-and-branch attack on the programme of logical empiricism – have marked what amounts to a drastic change in the way that at least some philosophers of science conceive the relation between truth, knowledge, and the currency of scientific discourse at any given time.

So far I have merely offered an outline sketch of how this change might connect with certain developments in late twentieth-century literary theory. Among them – to repeat – is the shift from a structuralist 'science' of the literary text to a post-structuralist conception of theory as itself another kind of textual practice, one that *constructs* or *transforms* its putative 'object' of study, rather than delivering a knowledge of that object which aspires to some kind of scientific (or metalinguistic) status. Above all there has been a growing counter-movement which opposes the top-down or hard-to-soft conception of the physical *vis-à-vis* the social or human sciences in the name of a textualist or 'strong' constructivist approach which rejects such distinctions as merely a product of deep-grained ideological prejudice. This in turn goes along with developments in cultural theory and the sociology of knowledge that likewise take it as their chief aim to question 'naive' (objectivist or realist) ideas of scientific truth and method.[20] One consequence was the renewed outbreak of hostilities between scientists or those charged to promote the 'public understanding of science' and thinkers from the mainly humanistic disciplines who sought nothing more – on their own account – than to open up a space for wider discussion of its social and ethical bearings.[21] In what follows I shall offer a brief retrospective survey of the so-called 'science wars' and will then – in Section IV – attempt to predict some possible future turns in the debate about science and literary theory.

III

I should say straight off that 'science wars' is just the kind of headline-grabbing journalistic tag that tends to get attached to certain periodic flare-ups of otherwise fairly routine professional, academic or inter-disciplinary rivalry. There was a similar episode some forty years ago – the 'two cultures' debate – when the novelist, government mandarin and pro-science advocate C.P. Snow locked horns with the literary critic F.R. Leavis. That controversy was sparked by the latter's fiercely partisan claim that the term 'culture', in its primary significance, referred to those qualities of imaginative insight, moral intelligence and discriminating judgement that could only be nurtured through the right kind of literary education.[22] Snow saw this as just a narrow-minded, bigoted defence of elitist cultural values that masked a profound ignorance of science and a Luddite rejection of its vast potential for improving the material conditions of human existence.

All the same the latest round of hostilities differs from that previous episode in the extent to which it has polarized opinion and in the questions it raises with respect to basic issues of scientific truth and method. What has drawn the wrath of some scientists – especially those involved in campaigns to enhance the public image of science – is the kind of claim which they find typically advanced by cultural theorists and 'strong' sociologists of knowledge. In its most extreme form this argument goes that 'truth' is a social or linguistic construct, that 'knowledge' is merely what passes as such according to some dominant ideological consensus, and that science is itself just one more discourse (or range of discourses) subserving the interests of established 'hegemonic' power.[23] It is clear enough how such ideas might claim support from a post-Kuhnian conception of science which stresses the paradigm-relative character of theories and observation statements, or again from a Quinean holistic approach that would find room for all kinds of pragmatic 'adjustment' so as to conserve some prevalent theory against empirical disconfirmation or protect some striking empirical result from theoretical challenge. This despite Kuhn's later insistence that his arguments should *not* be taken as lending support to any form of cultural relativism, and Quine's yet more emphatic denial that philosophy – let alone sociology or cultural history – could ever come up with adequate reasons for doubting the kinds of knowledge provided by physics and the natural sciences.[24]

There are several reasons why literary theory has found itself very often at the centre of these disputes. One is the fact that literary theorists have for some time now been engaged in a two-way exchange of ideas with people in just those disciplines – that is, cultural studies, the sociology of knowledge and related fields – which are currently the main focus of hostility for upholders of science as a rational and truth-seeking enterprise. Thus post-structuralist ideas about language, discourse and representation are frequently adduced by sociologists and cultural theorists who find such ideas very much to their purpose when challenging the 'naive' scientific belief that truth is a matter of straightforward correspondence between statements (or theories) and real-world, physically existent objects and properties.[25] There is likewise a strong elective affinity between the more extreme kinds of anti-realist or social-constructivist approach to the history of science and those recently emergent forms of sceptical historiography – based on the analysis of poetic structures or modes of rhetorical emplotment – which tend to assimilate historical to fictive forms of narrative discourse.[26] This idea has also gained credence from the kind of 'genealogical' approach adopted by Michel Foucault, that is to say, the argument (with its chief source in Nietzsche) that 'objective' history is the merest of chimeras, a refuge for weak-willed chroniclers who fail to recognize that *all* history is a 'history of the present', one that reinterprets the 'truth' of past events in keeping with some current revisionist agenda.[27] And to the extent that 'postmodernism' has a bearing on these issues – as distinct from its usage as a catch-all term for whatever takes the fancy of postmodern cultural commentators – it amounts to a form of generalized scepticism with regard to scientific truth and progress. Thus – in Jean-François Lyotard's much-quoted phrase – postmodernism enjoins an outlook of downright 'incredulity' toward any meta-narrative account that would purport to validate the claims of science from a standpoint attached to the delusive idea of truth at the end of enquiry.[28]

As I have said, these are notions that have all exerted great influence – and in turn been considerably influenced by – developments in present-day literary theory. It is therefore perhaps understandable that scientists and philosophers of science who wish to defend the values of truth, objectivity, and progress should concentrate their fire not only on the claims of 'strong' sociologists and cultural constructivists but also on the way that literary theory has moved from its erstwhile, fairly marginal position among the humanistic disciplines to become a major source of ideas and analogues in various fields of study.[29] This is not just a matter of literary critics with strong inter-disciplinary interests straying into regions of special (scientific) expertise where formerly they might have feared to tread, or at any rate have trodden with somewhat more caution and deference. Rather it is often perceived as a hostile take-over bid by ill-informed, arrogant types in humanities departments who want to cut science down to size by treating its methods, principles and truth-claims as so many cultural constructions or – following Foucault – as products of the epistemic will-to-power that hides behind a rhetoric of disinterested, truth-seeking enquiry. This perception has no doubt been sharpened by the desperate competition for research funding that is so much a feature of present-day academic life. Of particular relevance here was the threatened withdrawal of US Congressional support for large-scale projects like the super-colliding particle accelerator that require huge investment for programmes with no obvious short-term practical or economic pay-off.[30] In this context it is perhaps scarcely surprising that scientists should look with suspicion – or downright hostility – on claims to demote scientific knowledge to the status of so many 'discourses' whose authority derives from nothing more than their current (or bygone) high prestige among those with the power to allocate material resources.

All the same it is tempting to make too much of these high-profile controversies and ignore the extent to which literary critics can address or incorporate scientific themes without provoking such sharp territorial disputes. One particularly striking example – from what now seems a long way back – is William Empson's *Seven Types of Ambiguity* (1930), whose closing chapter offers some brilliantly perceptive ideas about the relation between conceptual issues in the new physics and the question of how far poetic meaning is objectively 'there' in the words on the page or how far it depends upon the reader's active participant response.[31] This was a time – the 'heroic' period of Cambridge theoretical physics – when no one (least of all a Cambridge-based literary critic like Empson with strong scientific and mathematical interests) would have seen such ventures as any kind of threat to the interests and values of scientific enquiry. And it is still the case – media polemics aside – that literary criticism can get along with science in a spirit of constructive interdisciplinary exchange without provoking such outbreaks of hostility. Thus the 'science wars' have nothing to do with the kinds of comparativist study that involve, say, a reading of certain nineteenth-century poems or novels in connection with the emergence of electromagnetic-field theories, or again, the reading of certain modernist (early twentieth-century) texts in light of relativity theory or with reference to Heisenberg's uncertainty principle and other quantum-physical concepts.[32] Such approaches do not so much challenge the authority of science as accept that authority and put it to work for their own interpretative purposes.

The same can be said of some recent literary ventures into the field of chaos theory, that is, the branch of mathematics and physics concerned with certain highly complex phenomena whose evolving patterns seem entirely random or at any rate beyond our utmost powers of rational prediction.[33] Such phenomena involve what is often described as an 'extreme sensitivity to initial conditions', or the idea that – to take the best-known example – a butterfly flapping its wings in Peru might set in train a sequence of meteorological events that results in a hurricane striking Florida.[34] Chaos theory has enjoyed quite a vogue among literary theorists just lately and, as usual, has been put to quite a range of uses, some more persuasive and scientifically better-informed than others. Thus it has figured in a mainly metaphoric role as a means of explaining why certain literary 'characters' (like Shakespeare's Cleopatra) not only exert a disruptive force on people and events around them but act also as 'strange attractors' – another term borrowed from chaos theory – or as focal points where that force attains maximum intensity.[35] Elsewhere it has been deployed as a handy source of arguments against old-style 'organicist' conceptions of literary form, now conceived as maintaining their precarious ideals of unity, closure, structural integrity and so on, only by ignoring the unruly elements – the symptoms of 'chaotic' disruption – that cannot be contained by any such formalist approach.[36] Some of these analogies are less than convincing insofar as they interpret chaos theory as concerned only with the emergence of chaos from order, and not with the countervailing process by which an initial state of (apparent) disorder at length gives rise to patterns or forms which display all manner of intricate internal symmetry.[37] However my point is that work of this kind represents not so much a threat or a challenge to the scientific claims in questions but rather an attempt – with whatever degree of success – to assimilate those claims and put them to use in a different field of study.

Still there is no denying the fact that some literary and cultural theorists do have a more ambitious agenda, one that would aspire to command the high ground of interdisciplinary relations, and hence to invert the physics-led ranking order that characterized the old 'unity of science' programme. As I have mentioned already, one form that this agenda takes is the strong-sociological argument that scientific 'truths' are constructed, rather than discovered, and that the dominant consensus at any given time is determined by the interaction of various (no doubt highly complex) cultural, social, political and ideological factors. Of course there is no reason – on the face of it – why literary theory should be credited or blamed for playing a role in this attempted reversal of scientific *vis-à-vis* sociological priorities. After all, time was (and not so long ago: during the 1940s and 1950s especially) when literary critics were themselves engaged in a similar kind of defensive operation to head off the perceived threat of an approach that would treat poems or novels as so many documents for socio-cultural-historical study, rather than as texts that required a reading responsive to their own, distinctively literary qualities and value.[38] But the situation has changed since then through the advent of 'theory' as a kind of all catch-all discipline (some would say, anti-discipline) which derives very largely from post-structuralist ideas about language, discourse and representation, and which in principle acknowledges no limit to its scope for application in other fields.

Most often this aligns it with various forms of anti-realist or cultural-relativist thinking, as might be expected when a theory is carried over from literary texts (where 'realism' has to do with the *illusion* of descriptive verisimilitude) to fields – like that of physical science – where realism entails a commitment to the truth-value of statements or their correspondence to the way things stand in reality. So it is not hard to see why the 'science wars' broke out with renewed vigour during a period – the late 1990s – when 'theory' was expanding its horizons to encompass a whole range of disciplines outside and beyond the literary or fictive domain. This quarrel came to a head with the publication of a spoof article by the physicist Alan Sokal ('Transgressing the Boundaries: Toward a Transformational Hermeneutics of Quantum Gravity') which appeared in the journal *Social Text*, having (presumably) gone through the usual process of editorial and peer-group review. At about the same time there appeared another piece by Sokal in the academic house-mag *Lingua Franca* which revealed that the article was a hoax and the editors and reviewers – if any – just a bunch of incompetent frauds.[39] The essay was nothing more than a mish-mash of quotations from various cultural theorists, postmodernists, post-structuralists, 'strong' sociologists, feminists and other purveyors of the latest theoretical wisdom, interspersed with passages of his own invention which followed much the same line. Its aim was to debunk these fashionable notions and to show how lax were the prevailing standards among those in the 'science studies' camp – literary theorists included – who typically exploited vague analogies with space–time relativity, quantum mechanics, undecidability, chaos theory and the rest. What the spoof article sought to bring home – at least on Sokal's own submission – was the folly of supposing that 'left' political interests could possibly be advanced by adopting a know-nothing radical rhetoric that cut away the very grounds of rationality, progress and truth.

Thus Sokal made a point of asserting his own leftist credentials – among them the fact that he had taught physics in Nicaragua – and expressed some embarrassment at finding himself in the company of right-wing ideologues who welcomed his hoax as a timely boost to their programme for diverting educational resources away from such inherently suspect activities. After all, what purpose could there be in criticizing present socio-economic structures, or in questioning received ideas of historical truth, or even in challenging dominant conceptions of scientific method if that criticism came from a position which treated *every* truth-claim – its own (presumably) included – as a product of ideological vested interests? This is Sokal's main grouse against the sociologists of science who work on a methodological 'principle of parity', that is, on the premise that their kind of approach applies not only to failed theories (those that might seem to invite explanation on extra-scientific or ideological grounds) but also to successful theories which have so far managed to avoid empirical or predictive falsification.[40] What it amounts to, in practice, is a flat rejection of the 'old' logical-empiricist idea that philosophy and history of science could get along perfectly well by distinguishing the scientific 'context of justification' from the socio-historico-cultural 'context of discovery'.[41] Where the former had to do with standards of empirical adequacy, predictive warrant, causal-explanatory power and so forth, the latter was concerned with 'background' interests which might range all the way from psycho-biographical factors to religious belief or class affiliation, conceived as relevant from a 'life-and-times' viewpoint but as quite beside the point when it came to issues of scientific truth or falsehood. However that distinction counts for nothing with the strong sociologists of knowledge. On their account it is the merest of 'Whiggish' (progressivist) illusions which leads us to think that some theories – those that we currently accept – stand in no need of sociological explanation while others that have fallen by the scientific wayside are fair game for such treatment. Rather we should apply the principle of parity – or equal esteem – and take it that *every* theory is a product of ideological or socio-cultural conditioning.

Thus for instance – to cite one prominent example – it is mere prejudice to suppose that Robert Boyle got it right about vacuum phenomena because he carried out lots of carefully constructed, albeit imperfect, observational experiments designed to demonstrate the existence of such phenomena, whereas Thomas Hobbes got it wrong because he denied their very possibility on the basis of a strong doctrinal and ideological *parti pris*.[42] That is to say, Hobbes was in the grip of a prejudice which resulted from his experience of the English Civil War, and his belief that a vacuum – in nature as in politics – must surely be unthinkable since it could only produce a destructive and tumultuous conflict of opposed forces. Hence Hobbes's plenist conviction, that is, his harking-back to the old scholastic idea that 'nature abhors a vacuum' and that power must be exerted at every point in the physical cosmos – as likewise in the body politic – so as to avoid this disastrous consequence. On the standard view Boyle was a good scientist because he held out against such 'extraneous' motivating interests and based his theory on the verdict of informed observers who shared his respect for empirical evidence or for the replicability of certain well-attested experimental results under controlled laboratory conditions. However, as I have said, that distinction goes completely by the board if one accepts the strong-sociological thesis. On this view Boyle's approach was no less ideologically motivated for the fact that it endorsed the values of empirical warrant and of 'rational' consensus among a certain class-fraction of suitably qualified observers who could muster the resources for conducting such experiments under given economic and socio-political conditions.

Thus where Hobbes spoke for the old conception of power as vested in a sovereign authority which alone possessed the means to enforce obedience and ensure civil peace Boyle spoke for a newly emergent ideology – that of the post-1688 constitutional settlement – which stressed the importance of attaining agreement on matters of 'straightforward' empirical observation. And where Hobbes (according to the usual account) fell into scientific error by allowing his scholastic metaphysical convictions to distort his scientific views, Boyle (on the sociological account) must be seen as a thinker no less in thrall to ideological interests, albeit subtly disguised by their appeal to the sheer self-evidence of perceptual warrant as reliably vouched by a community of well-qualified rational observers. What distinguished their two positions was not the superior scientific status of Boyle's theory — its respect for the evidence, disciplined methodology and openness to empirical falsification — but rather its greater degree of success in reflecting the new consensus and recruiting support from those engaged in that same enterprise. Moreover this point has not been grasped by subsequent mainstream historians and philosophers of science who are strongly disposed to accept the standard view and thereby confirm the reputation of Boyle as among the great pioneering figures of modern scientific method. In so doing they are complicit with a certain prevalent ideology which fails to recognize its own deep investment in a narrative of scientific progress and truth, one that can only be sustained — so it is argued — by ignoring crucial evidence from the socio-historical 'context of discovery'.

I have discussed this particular case at some length because it relates closely to developments in recent cultural theory. Thus, for instance, the 'strong'-sociological approach may appear strictly even-handed as between disputants like Hobbes and Boyle, seeking nothing more than to apply its across-the-board 'principle of parity' and rescue Hobbes from his condescending treatment at the hands of mainstream scientific historians. However this approach has an inbuilt methodological bias of its own, namely its acceptance of the Hobbesian (and also the Foucault-derived) idea that scientific truth-claims are always and everywhere bound up with the exercise of socio-political power, since what *counts* as 'truth' (or 'knowledge') at any given time is itself decided by a certain conjuncture of ideological interests.[43] This in turn goes along with the post-structuralist conception of 'reality' as itself a linguistic or discursive construct, that is to say, a kind of reality-*effect* brought about — once again — by prevalent, culturally encoded norms of meaning and representation. Postmodernism effectively conjoins these claims through its outlook of extreme epistemological scepticism, its nominalist refusal to credit the existence of anything 'outside' or 'beyond' the play of multiple discourses or language-games, and what Lyotard calls its 'incredulity toward meta-narratives', for example, the meta-narrative (progressivist) account of scientific knowledge as presuming some limit-point, regulative notion of truth at the end of enquiry.[44]

Of course I am not suggesting — absurdly — that this challenge to the normative concepts and values of 'old-style' scientific realism has its chief source in the thinking of certain influential literary theorists. On the contrary, it has emerged across a wide range of disciplines, among them the social sciences, cultural criticism, historiography and even (as we have seen) certain currents of thought within present-day philosophy of science. All the same it is a challenge that consorts very readily with the kind of linguistic-constructivist approach that has tended to exercise a strong appeal for literary theorists since it gives them room to extend their favoured strategies of reading to texts — historical and scientific texts included — that would normally be thought of as lying beyond their disciplinary scope or competence. In other words, their involvement in the 'science wars' is not (or not only) the result of a crude guilt-by-association technique, or a desire – on the part of scattershot polemicists like Sokal – to discredit any discourse that questions received ideas of scientific method and truth. Rather this involvement reflects the fact that literary theory has developed over the past three decades in close alliance with just those sorts of anti-realist, constructivist and historical-revisionist argument that would relativize questions of knowledge and truth to issues of cultural or socio-political power. Such is at any rate the widespread perception among promoters of the 'public under-standing of science' – some of them better informed than Sokal with regard to the developments in question – who tend to assume that 'literary theory' is just another code-word for various concerted attempts to undermine the status of the physical sciences.[45]

Hence the approving, at times almost rapturous response to Sokal's hoax among those who were glad to see 'deconstructionists' exposed for their weak grasp of special relativity and quantum physics, or postmodernists for their uncomprehending treatment of fractals and chaos theory, or feminists for mounting their arguments about gender-difference on a misconceived contrast between the kinds of knowledge applicable to solid and fluid mechanics. What these enthusiasts failed to note – perhaps understandably – was the extent to which Sokal himself invited criticism by conflating such a range of target positions, some no doubt evincing a high degree of scientific ignorance, but others adopted by thinkers (Jacques Derrida among them) whose philosophic acumen and, besides that, whose grasp of the scientific issues is of a quite different order. Thus when Derrida alludes to mathematical proofs such as Gödel's undecidability theorem or to problematic issues in the philosophy of geometry he does so with a clear and explicit grasp not only of their pertinence to his own deconstructive project but also of the formal reasoning behind them and their implications for the disciplines concerned.[46] In short, this latest outbreak of the 'science wars' has resulted in a further stoking-up of old hostilities and a widespread failure – on the 'pro-science' side – to recognize the varied levels and standards of debate that have characterized the typecast opposition.

IV

I must now get around to the riskier business of predicting the likely course of this debate in decades to come, and suggesting how literary theorists might contribute to a better, less hostile or sharply polarized climate of exchange. One promising sign is the growth of interest in alternative approaches to the realism issue, that is to say, approaches that eschew the post-structuralist/postmodernist position of extreme epistemological scepticism and adopt a more nuanced, philosophically informed outlook which allows for the variety of possible 'fits' between text and world.

Thus some literary theorists have suggested that the best way forward is through an application of 'possible worlds' logic, or by ranging texts on a comparative scale of proximity to or remoteness from our particular, historically actualized, presently existing world.[47] (See also Chapter 5 for further discussion in a range of different contexts.) This idea was first developed by modal logicians who sought to expand the resources of classical (truth-functional) logic by incorporating the notions of *necessity* and *possibility*.[48] So – for instance – there are 'worlds' that resemble our own except in respect of some few fairly minor, inconsequential details, but where events will otherwise have followed their actual (this-worldly) course. Such worlds are maximally 'compossible' with ours in the sense that they involve no significant counterfactual departure from the way that things stand in actuality or the way that history has turned out up to now. Then there are worlds in which (say) Julius Caesar *did not* cross the Rubicon, or where Khrushchev and Kennedy between them *failed* to avert nuclear catastrophe, and where the subsequent course of events took a drastically different turn. Still such worlds are compossible with ours to the extent that they require no suspension of the laws of nature or no adjustment to the basic physical constants that determine what may or may not be the case according to our best scientific knowledge. At the furthest extreme would be worlds that differed in respect of even those basic constants, that is, where Newton's inverse-square law of gravitational attraction was replaced by an inverse-cube law, or where atomic bonding either did not occur or occurred in such a way as not to permit the emergence of organic and sentient life-forms. Indeed the only worlds that are strictly ruled out, on this modal account, are those that involve some logical contradiction or a change to such 'trans-world' necessary truths as those of mathematics and the formal sciences. Thus there is no possible world where it is true that '$2+2=5$', or where it is false that '$2+2=4$', or where both statements are true (or false). Nor is there one in which triangles have four sides, or where two contradictory propositions both hold true, or where bachelors are not unmarried men. For these are truths which hold good necessarily (that is to say, across all possible worlds), and which could not be negated – rendered false – by any different turn in the course of contingent events or any stretch of counterfactual supposition.

What this approach gives us – so its advocates claim – is a subtle, discriminate and logically powerful means of distinguishing the various kinds and degrees of possible departure from the truth-conditions that apply in our actual world. Thus it serves very usefully to explicate the logic of counterfactual-conditional statements, that is, to clarify just what kinds of non-existent situation we are talking about when we refer to the way things *might have* gone had Caesar not crossed the Rubicon, or if history had taken a different course with respect to any number of consequential actions or events.[49] Nor will this seem such a wildly speculative mode of reasoning if one considers how far historical explanations standardly rely on counterfactual-conditional arguments of the type: event x (say the Second World War) would not have occurred were it not for episodes y and z (say, the punitive conditions imposed on Germany by the Treaty of Versailles and the breakdown of democratic institutions in the Weimar Republic). Thus one clear advantage of the 'possible-worlds' approach as applied to issues in historiography is that it manages to avoid the post-structuralist or the wholesale 'textualist' conflation of historical with fictive modes of narrative discourse. Moreover it provides an alternative to the post-modernist idea that scientific truth-claims can only have to do with those language-games or forms of representation that define what shall count as 'truth' or 'knowledge' at any given time. In this way the approach gives substance to a wide range of counterfactual-supporting causal explanations, such as 'this match would not have ignited were it not for the flammable property of phosphorus, the local presence of oxygen atoms, the friction generated by striking it against the matchbox, the fact that it had not been previously plunged in water', and so forth.[50] These are known as *ceteris paribus* clauses – 'other things being equal' – which again gives a hold for causal explanations involving the claim that if certain antecedent conditions such as those listed above had *not* been satisfied then a certain event (like the match's igniting) would not in fact have occurred. So one result of this turn toward modal logic in its 'possible-worlds' formulation has been to sharpen the focus of debate about scientific realism and to clarify those issues about truth, knowledge and representation which have so pre-occupied sceptically inclined philosophers and literary theorists.

Not that philosophers are by any means agreed on the question of how such talk should be interpreted, that is to say, the ontological question concerning whether those worlds should be thought of as 'existing' only in a realm of counterfactual conjecture or whether they possess a stronger claim to reality. The most extreme position here is that adopted by David Lewis who rejects the former option as a kind of face-saving compromise deal and who makes the case that *every* possible world (every way that things might conceivably have turned out) is just as real as our 'actual' world, even though we cannot have epistemic access to worlds that have branched off from ours and whose denizens (our own branched-off selves included) are likewise debarred from having epistemic access to the world that we actually inhabit.[51] Thus, for Lewis, the term 'actual' can best be understood by analogy with terms like 'here', 'now', 'today', or the first-person singular and plural pronouns 'I' and 'we', that is, as an *indexical* or *deictic* term whose reference can be grasped only in relation to its time, place and specific context of enunciation. So when we say – commonsensically enough – that ours is the only *actual* world and that all those others are non-actual then we are right in so far as 'actuality' is construed in terms of our own epistemic standpoint and our knowledge of this-worldly events, objects, laws of nature, physical constants and so on. However we are wrong – so Lewis stoutly maintains – if we confuse the actuality issue with the realism issue, or the fact of our happening to live in just one of those multitudinous possible worlds with the idea that this particular world is unique in being *real* rather than fictive, hypothetical, 'merely' possible or whatever. Rather there are worlds – an infinity of them – wherein every possibility is realized, that is, everything that *could* be the case without transgressing the necessary truths of logic or mathematics. These worlds are strictly speaking just as 'real' as our own, despite the inclination of most philosophers to treat Lewis's claim as a piece of wild metaphysical extravagance, and to interpret the possible-worlds idiom as a handy device for clarifying certain otherwise obscure modal-logical distinctions.

What has all this to do with literary theory and its relationship to issues in science and philosophy of science? One indication is the way that possible-worlds logic has been taken up by a number of prominent literary theorists who see it as a means of advancing beyond the typically post-structuralist idea that language, discourse or representation go all the way down and hence that there is no distinguishing between historical and fictive narratives, or scientific and non-scientific texts, as concerns their purported correspondence – or lack of it – to a domain of real-world (extra-textual) objects and events.[52] Here it is worth noting that Lewis's 'realist' conception of possible worlds is one that would scarcely appeal to most philosophers of science who count themselves realists in the relevant sense, that is to say, with regard to the privileged status of this-world existent structures, causal laws, physical constants and so forth. Indeed Lewis's far-out version of modal realism could well provide a happy hunting-ground for literary theorists keen to subvert both the hegemonic discourse of scientific reason and the idea that fiction is a deviant kind of discourse, one that involves a departure from the norms of scientifically certified realism, reference and truth. As it happens they would be getting Lewis quite wrong about this since he insists very firmly on maintaining the distinction between absolute (trans-world necessary) truths such as those of mathematics and logic, objective (this-world operative) laws like those of the physical sciences, and contingent matters of fact which nonetheless hold good for our actual world, as distinct from any fictive or imaginary counterpart worlds.

However my chief point is that literary theorists – or the more philosophically informed among them – have started to deploy these ideas as a basis not only for distinguishing fictive from other (e.g., historical and scientific) kinds of text but also for drawing generic distinctions between various modes of fictive discourse. After all, these latter span a vast range from social-documentary 'realism', or novels that incorporate large amounts of historical 'background' material, to fictions that exploit the further reaches of counterfactual possibility, speculative science or sheer fantasy projection. Elsewhere the different *genres* may coexist within a single text, as with certain novels (like E.L. Doctorow's *Ragtime* or Kurt Vonnegut's *Slaughterhouse Five*) that switch – sometimes disconcertingly – from a discourse that includes reference to various 'real-world' characters and events to a science-fiction world which, in Vonnegut's case, involves the main character's teletransportation to the planet Tralfamador. (See also Chapter 6 for a more detailed treatment of these issues concerning the ontology of fictive, hypothetical and other non-actual worlds.) 'Postmodernist' is the label most often attached to such works, suggesting as it does a casual disregard for old-fashioned notions of narrative coherence or generic propriety. More useful, however, is Linda Hutcheon's term 'postmodern historiographic metafiction', which catches precisely the kinds of dislocating shift – and also, as I have argued, the kinds of transition from one to another possible world – that characterize texts such as these.[53]

Other theorists have offered suggestions along broadly similar lines, not always with explicit reference to modal logic but mostly with a view to finding some alternative, more nuanced approach to the realism/anti-realism issue. It is also worth noting – in the present context – that this approach offers a promising way beyond the old 'two cultures' debate that started out with Matthew Arnold's sombre reflections on the function of poetry in an age of advancing scientific reason, continued (as we have seen) through I.A. Richards's engagement with the doctrines of logical positivism, and thereafter pursued its melancholy course from Snow versus Leavis to the Sokal affair. For that debate was premised on the stark dichotomy between, on the one hand, a narrowly positivist conception of scientific truth and, on the other, an embattled defence of 'literary' meaning and value that very often ran close to an irrationalist creed or a flat rejection of science as possessing any claim to authentic human significance. Leavis typically expressed this idea at its most extreme when he contrasted the 'creative exploratory' use of language as exemplified pre eminently by Shakespeare and by novelists like D.H. Lawrence – with the 'technologico-Benthamite' drive to suppress creativity and reduce language to a dead level of routine functional exchange.[54] Nor were the prospects for dialogue much improved when post-structuralism entered the scene, involving as it did the odd combination of a geared-up technical vocabulary – derived from Saussurean linguistics, Lacanian psychoanalysis, Althusserian Marxism and other sources – with a strong resistance to any kind of theory (structuralism included) that emulated science in its drive for system and method, or its desire to place limits on the open-ended 'freeplay' of textual signification.[55] Indeed it has been argued that 'radical' theorizing of this sort went along very well with the emergence of a new managerial ethos – in the universities especially – which likewise conjoined the administrative functions of ever-increasing bureaucratic surveillance and control with a consumerist rhetoric of 'choice', 'freedom', and 'open access'.[56] At any rate it is fair to conclude that the science/literature or 'two cultures' debate has taken many turns over the past century and – until recently – showed little sign of progress or mutual accommodation.

Any prediction as to how far things will change over the next decade or so is of course conjectural at best. I have offered one positive suggestion in this regard, namely the evidence that some literary theorists are taking more interest in branches of philosophy which point a way beyond those deadlocked disputes that issued in the latest round of 'science wars'. I should mention also, as an ironic footnote to the Sokal affair, that these have been wars where the combatants are strangely prone to switch sides, or where it is often hard to say which party is chiefly responsible for putting about some presumed piece of modish nonsense. Thus Sokal's spoof article contains not only an assortment of quotes from postmodernists, post-structuralists, 'strong' sociologists, cultural relativists and so forth, but also a number of passages by eminent quantum physicists – such as Niels Bohr and Werner Heisenberg – who standardly count among the pioneering figures of the revolution in early twentieth-century science.[57] His purpose in citing these passages, so far as one can tell, is that they show how the

paradoxes of quantum theory – at least on the 'orthodox' (Copenhagen) interpretation – have been exploited to merely opportunist effect by people who do
not have an adequate grasp of the physics or mathematics involved. However
what is more apt to strike the reader, especially with regard to Bohr's pronouncements, is the extent to which this interpretation of quantum theory is
itself shot through with conceptual confusions and often has resort to an
obscurantist rhetoric which lends itself readily to postmodern talk of science as
having renounced all claims to truth, objectivity or progress. Such talk finds
welcome 'scientific' support in Heisenberg's orthodox insistence that the
uncertainty relations were intrinsic to the quantum domain, rather than
resulting from our limited powers of observation/measurement, and in Bohr's
likewise orthodox idea that the paradoxes of quantum physics (wave/particle
dualism, superposition, remote particle 'entanglement', etc.) were not such as
could ever – in principle – be accorded a realist interpretation.[58] From here, it is
no great distance to Lyotard's confident claim that science should henceforth
concern itself *not* with old-fashioned normative criteria such as truth, empirical
warrant or theoretical adequacy, but rather with cutting-edge 'postmodern'
notions such as chaos, paralogism, undecidability, observer-interference and the
limits of precise measurement.[59] And this claim is then projected back onto the
history of previous ('classical') physics so as to suggest – in Kuhnian fashion –
that indeed there *never was* a time when science could possibly have lived up to
its own delusions of epistemological grandeur or its own preferred 'meta-
narrative' ideals of progress and truth at the end of enquiry.

This is not the place for a detailed rehearsal of the argument for an alternative
approach to quantum physics that would – as argued by its leading proponent,
David Bohm – resolve the above-mentioned problems by providing a credible
realist ontology and by placing those problems firmly on the side of the limits to
our present knowledge or powers of observation.[60] More relevant here is the
general point: that with the passing of post-structuralism and postmodernism as
high points of 'radical' doctrine there is now a good prospect that the 'two
cultures' will achieve some workable *modus vivendi*. Not that one would wish for
the kind of settlement that involves nothing more than a mutual compact to
keep off each others' turf, or the kind of compromise deal by which I.A. Richards
consigned poetry to a realm of 'emotive' pseudo-statement, so as not to fall foul
of the strictures laid down by logical positivism.[61] On the contrary: there is
always room for a degree of productive friction, especially in areas like these
where debate has to do with crucial issues concerning the scope and limits of
attainable knowledge. However there is no reason why literary theorists with an
adequate grounding in the history and philosophy of science should not enter
such debates with a fair claim to serious (scientific and philosophical) attention.

After all, it is among the more striking features of quantum physics since the
1920s that it has involved a great many speculative thought-experiments, that is
to say, test procedures in the 'laboratory of the mind' which cannot (or at one
time could not) be conducted in physical reality yet are none the less taken as
supporting – or refuting – certain well-formed theoretical conjectures.[62] These

started out with the famous series of debates between Einstein and Bohr with respect to quantum uncertainty, debates in which Bohr maintained the 'completeness' of orthodox quantum mechanics (along with its strictly irresolvable paradoxes), while Einstein argued – in a realist spirit – that the orthodox account *must* be incomplete (and the paradoxes therefore resolvable) since it manifestly failed to meet the requirements of any adequate, that is, realist and causal-explanatory physical theory.[63] Since then physicists of a speculative mind – John Wheeler and David Deutsch among them – have proposed a whole range of (at times) extravagantly counter-intuitive ideas about the implications of quantum mechanics for our understanding of the physical world. Thus Wheeler cites the evidence of delayed-choice experiments on a laboratory scale, or instances where a momentary switch in the orientation of a measurement-apparatus appears retroactively to decide what shall 'already' have happened to the particle up until that moment.[64] In which case – he reasons – this phenomenon of retroactive, observer-induced causation must surely extend to any arbitrary space–time distance, thus entailing that astronomers' momentary choice of radio-telescope setting can 'decide' the occurrence or the non-occurrence of astrophysical events some billions of light years away. In short, quantum physics gives us to think that there is nothing absurd about 'back-to-the-future' science-fiction scenarios which involve such (on the face of it) impossible ideas as that of travelling backwards in time and altering the shape of things to come, including – presumably – the sequence of events leading up to one's own conception. At least that would seem to be the upshot envisaged in Wheeler's speculative extrapolation from the quantum to the macrophysical domain.

Deutsch is a proponent of the 'many-worlds' theory of quantum mechanics according to which there is only one solution to the measurement problem, that is, the problem of explaining just how – and at just what point on the micro- to macrophysical scale the state of quantum superposition or wave/particle dualism 'collapses' into a determinate state producing those various well-defined objects that make up our everyday physical world.[65] That solution requires us to conceive that *every possible* outcome is realized, and that ours – the world that we each of us momentarily inhabit – is just one of the vast (non-denumerable) multiplicity that coexist with our own and are equally 'real' despite our not having epistemic access to them except through certain shadowy quantum 'interference' effects that cannot be explained on any rival account. Thus the quantum 'multiverse', as Deutsch thinks of it, includes worlds in which you – the reader – have already split off into multiple divergent histories or selves, one of whom ('you') is still reading these words while others have lost interest, turned to a different chapter, succumbed to a fatal heart-attack or been vaporized by a meteor impact. Moreover it contains not only the world where Deutsch managed to finish writing his book but others where he likewise lost interest or suffered some life-transformative event that prevented its completion. This idea goes back to the seventeenth century and Leibniz's idea that the actual world is just one – as it happens, the best possible – among the many which God might have created and which can still be adduced by way of explaining the difference between necessary (trans-world valid) truths such as those of mathematics and logic and contingent (this-world applicable) truths such as those of history and the empirical sciences. In other words it is a legacy of the rationalist tradition where epistemological issues of truth and knowledge were most often approached through metaphysical debates or ontological questions concerning the ultimate nature of reality.[66]

There is an obvious resemblance between Deutsch's many-worlds interpretation of quantum theory and David Lewis's far-out variety of modal realism, that is, his claim – as summarized above – that subjunctive-conditional or counterfactual-supporting modes of causal explanation cannot be made good unless by supposing the reality of those worlds over which their statements range. Deutsch does not have much time for philosophers, taking the view that 'philosophical' questions are merely questions for which (as yet) science provides no answers but which – in so far as they are *bona fide* questions – will eventually find a scientific answer or at least an adequate formulation in physical terms. Thus he does make room for a brief mention of Lewis but only by way of token acknowledgement that even philosophers may sometimes stumble on the right answer for the wrong reasons. However, these debates at the speculative cutting edge of physics very often have as much to do with philosophical as with strictly scientific concerns. Thus when Einstein put forward his thought-experimental case *contra* Bohr for the 'incompleteness' of the orthodox quantum theory – and the need for an alternative (classical or realist) account – they each brought to bear a whole range of conflicting philosophical concepts and premises which led them to assign radically divergent interpretations to the same empirical data. Indeed one could instance many such examples from the history of physics, like Galileo's famous thought-experimental proof (as against Aristotle's cosmological theory) that bodies of differing weight were subject to the same rate of acceleration in a state of gravitationally induced free fall, rather than the heavier body accelerating faster on account of its seeking out its proper place in the fixed order of the elements.[67] Imagine, he invited us, two such bodies, a cannon-ball and a musket-ball, securely fastened together and released from a certain height. On Aristotle's theory the cannon-ball would accelerate more rapidly than the musket-ball, but the combined weight of the two objects would of course be greater than that of the cannon-ball alone, thus requiring that the composite object would accelerate more quickly than the cannon-ball alone and hence produce a strictly impossible (i.e., contradictory) outcome, given their physically inseparable state. Moreover this proof was established *before* Galileo carried out his tests at the Leaning Tower of Pisa, tests that provided striking empirical confirmation of Galileo's theory versus that of Aristotle, but whose outcome was effectively settled in advance by that same thought-experimental procedure.

My point in all this is that science very often makes progress through an appeal to unrealized though physically conceivable situations which serve as a test-case – a 'laboratory of the mind' – whereby to corroborate certain well-formed hypotheses and to falsify others. Again, such experiments depend crucially on the kinds of modal distinction that have lately preoccupied philosophers of logic and some literary theorists, that is, that between trans-world necessary (mathematical and logical) truths, truths of science that hold for all worlds congruent with ours in the relevant (physical) respects, and matters of contingent (might-have-been-otherwise) fact such as those pertaining to the course of historical events. Also there are fictive 'possible worlds' that may be shown to involve some licensed departure from the sorts of constraint that define what should count as a valid thought-experimental proof in the physical sci-ences, or from the kinds of historical-explanatory account which very often rely on a kindred process of hypothetical, counterfactual or subjunctive-conditional reasoning.[68] Indeed one could mount a case against highly fanciful scientific theories such as those of Wheeler and Deutsch precisely on the grounds that they fail to distinguish with adequate precision between the various orders of real-world, physically conceivable, hypothetical, conjectural, and purely fictive possibility. Thus Deutsch's multiverse theory may be held philosophically untenable as well as being shown to contravene the conservation-laws and other basic, or strictly indispensable precepts of physics. Philosophical considerations have a central role in such debates, whatever Deutsch's natural desire to convince us that his theory stands or falls on its purely scientific merits or its unique capacity to encompass and explain the quantum observational data. Moreover, they have emerged most clearly to view whenever science has entered a period of Kuhnian 'pre-revolutionary' crisis, or whenever existing (relatively stable) bodies of knowledge encountered some powerful challenge, for example, a whole series of anomalous empirical results or the discovery of a hitherto concealed contra-diction at their theoretical heart. In other words science has always proceeded through a kind of mutual interrogative exchange with philosophy of science, even though that exchange has sometimes been marked by a degree of mistrust or hostility on the scientists' side.

V

I have suggested – perhaps more controversially – that literary theorists have their own part to play by helping to specify what properly belongs to the realm of fictive possibility as opposed to the domain of scientific theory or historical explanation. After all, they have developed an impressive range of descriptive-analytical techniques – starting out with Aristotle's *Poetics* and developed by latter-day formalist and structuralist schools – for explaining where precisely the difference lies between these different orders of discourse. Thus, for instance, literary theorists are well placed to examine the kinds of complex generic and narrative device that allow, say, a film like *Sliding Doors* or a novel like Italo Calvino's *If On a Winter's Night a Traveller* to exploit certain suggestive analogies with the many-worlds theory of quantum physics while nonetheless signalling their fictive status through the way that characters stray across worlds or experience 'the same' event under different circumstances. These observations might well be sharpened by a close comparison with the quantum-multiverse theory as expounded by Deutsch and a consequent refinement in their grasp of those various fictive operators — shifts of viewpoint, multiple perspectives, chronological flashbacks, proleptic devices, intersecting lifelines and so forth — which characterize genres of this type. Yet literary theorists might also want to claim that the presence of such devices in other (e.g., scientific or historical) texts implies a blurring of genre distinctions — a veering across from the causal-explanatory to the fictive or speculative domain — which should at least give pause when assessing those texts on their own purported terms of reference.

In this chapter I have offered two main suggestions — one quite specific, the other more general — as to how the 'science and literature' debate might evolve over the next few decades. The first had to do with the realism issue, the waning of post-structuralist and kindred forms of hard-line anti-realist doctrine, and the emergent interest — among literary theorists — in modal (or possible-worlds) conceptions that allow for a far more nuanced and philosophically adequate approach. The second, closely connected with this, was the claim that we are now (at last) moving beyond the kind of polarized 'two cultures' thinking which led at best to I.A. Richards's negotiated truce with logical positivism, and at worst to the attitude of downright hostility manifested on the one hand by Leavis's diatribes against Snow and on the other by various, newly emboldened science warriors in the wake of the Sokal affair. A further reason for optimism is that literary theorists are nowadays less prone than they were during the period of high postmodernist fashion to issue the kinds of sweeping pronouncement — about the obsolescence of 'truth', the illusion of 'progress', the culture-relative character of scientific 'knowledge', etc. — which served only to provoke further antagonism. One significant factor here is the improved level of scientific grasp among non-specialists brought about by the plethora of first-rate books on aspects of relativity, quantum physics, chaos theory, molecular biology and so on, serving as they do to raise the general standard of debate and expose such pronouncements as highly partial or simply fallacious. Another is the somewhat belated perception that cultural relativism is a two-edged sword, useful if one wishes to resist authoritarian values and promote those of tolerance, diversity and cultural difference, but not so useful — indeed a downright liability — if one wishes to support this case with evidence or rational argument.

Thus there is not much point in arguing that certain versions of historical 'truth' have been based on a distorted or ideological (mis)reading of the evidence if that assertion then has to be qualified by conceding that *all* historical truth-claims are culture-relative or socially constructed.[69] At its most benign this position comes down to the idea that rhetorical (or narrative) persuasiveness is the best we can hope for, along with the desire to 'maximize dissensus' — in Lyotard's phrase — rather than seek some 'rational' consensus that brusquely overrides such differences of view.[70] At its worst the argument lends itself to right-wing revisionist readings of history — Holocaust denial among them — which comport well enough with the sceptical idea that historical 'truth' is always a product of interpretation or selective hindsight.[71] It seems to me, on the current evidence, that literary theorists have begun to wake up to the problems that result when their favoured modes of rhetorical or textual exegesis are applied to other disciplines where truth-values have a crucial role. Philosophy of science is the subject-domain where these issues are posed most sharply, whether on the side of a realist conception that conceives truth in terms of correspondence with the way things stand in physical (language-independent) reality, or on the side of a discourse-relativist conception that finds no room for such 'naively' objectivist ideas. It is encouraging that recent literary theory has shown more awareness of this issue and a greater willingness to take stock of arguments – like those summarized above – which cast doubt on some of its previous, more strongly expansionist claims. In Chapter 5 I shall return to the topic of possible worlds and seek to clarify both its philosophical sources and its bearing on these issues in literary theory.

NOTES

1   A.J. Ayer (ed.), *Logical Positivism* (New York: Free Press, 1959); Oswald Hanfling (ed.), *Essential Readings in Logical Positivism* (Oxford: Blackwell, 1981).

2   See for instance various contributors to G.H.R. Parkinson (ed.), *The Theory of Meaning* (Oxford: Oxford University Press, 1968).

3   Mario Bunge (ed.), *The Methodological Unity of Science* (Dordrecht: D. Reidel, 1973); Rudolf Carnap (ed.), *The Unity of Science* (Bristol: Thoemmes Press, 1995); Robert L. Causey (ed.), *Unity of Science* (Dordrecht: D. Reidel, 1977).

4   See especially Charles L. Stevenson, *Language and Ethics* (New Haven: Yale University Press, 1944).

5   Hans-Georg Gadamer, *Truth and Method*, trans. John Cumming and Garrett Barden (London: Sheed & Ward, 1979); Kurt Müller-Vollmer (ed.), *The Hermeneutics Reader* (New York: Continuum, 1985); Friedrich Schleiermacher, *Hermeneutics*, ed. Heinz Kimmerle, trans. James Duke and Jack Forstman (Missoula, MO: Scholars Press, 1977).

6   I.A. Richards, *Science and Poetry* (London: Kegan Paul, 1926); *Principles of Literary Criticism* (London: Kegan Paul, 1924).

7   See for instance F.R. Leavis, *Valuation in Criticism and Other Essays*, ed. G. Singh (Cambridge: Cambridge University Press, 1986) and Leavis (ed.), *A Selection from Scrutiny*, 2 vols. (Cambridge: Cambridge University Press, 1968).

8   See Note 1, above; also W.V. Quine, 'Two Dogmas of Empiricism', in *From a Logical Point of View*, 2nd edn (Cambridge, MA: Harvard University Press, 1961), pp. 20–46.

9   See especially Max Jammer, *The Philosophy of Quantum Physics* (New York: Wiley, 1974); Christopher Norris, *Quantum Theory and the Flight from Realism: Philosophical Responses to Quantum Mechanics* (London: Routledge, 2000); Karl Popper, *Quantum Theory and the Schism in Physics* (London: Hutchinson, 1982).

10   Michael Detlefson (ed.), *Proof and Knowledge in Mathematics* (London: Routledge, 1992); Kurt Gödel, *On Formally Undecidable Propositions of Principia Mathematica and Related Systems*, trans. B. Meltzer (New York: Basic Books, 1962); Hilary Putnam, *Mathematics, Matter and Method* (Cambridge: Cambridge University Press, 1975).

11   See for instance Joseph Margolis, *Science Without Unity: Reconciling the Human and Natural Sciences* (Oxford: Blackwell, 1987).

12   Ferdinand de Saussure, *Course in General Linguistics*, trans. Roy Harris (London: Duckworth, 1983); also Roland Barthes, *Image, Music, Text*, ed. and trans. Stephen Heath (London: Fontana 1977); Jonathan Culler, *Structuralist Poetics* (London: Routledge & Kegan Paul, 1975); Terence Hawkes, *Structuralism and Semiotics* (London:

Methuen 1977); Roman Jakobson, *Language in Literature*, ed. K. Pomorska and S. Rudy (Cambridge, MA.: Harvard University Press, 1987); Michael Lane (ed.), *Structuralism: A Reader* (London: Cape, 1970); David Lodge, *The Modes of Modern Writing: Metaphor, Metonymy, and the Typology of Modern Literature* (London: Edward Arnold, 1977).

13 Josué V. Harari (ed.), *Textual Strategies: Perspectives in Post-Structuralist Criticism* (London: Methuen, 1980); Richard Harland, *Superstructuralism: The Philosophy of Structuralism and Post-Structuralism* (London: Routledge, 1987); Robert Young (ed.), *Untying the Text: A Post-Structuralist Reader* (London: Routledge & Kegan Paul, 1981).

14 See for instance Roland Barthes, *S/Z*, trans. Richard Miller (London: Jonathan Cape, 1975) and *Image, Music, Text*.

15 For two quite distinctive but related developments of this line of thought, see Michael Foucault, *The Order of Things: An Archaeology of the Human Sciences* (London: Tavistock, 1970) and Jean-François Lyotard, *The Postmodern Condition: A Report on Knowledge*, trans. Geoff Bennington and Brian Massumi (Manchester: Manchester University Press, 1984).

16 See Note 8, above; also – for a good recent commentary – Alex Orenstein, *Quine* (Chesham: Acumen, 2002).

17 This argument received its earliest formulation (three years before Kuhn's better-known treatment) in Norwood Russell Hanson, *Patterns of Discovery: An Inquiry into the Conceptual Foundations of Science* (Cambridge: Cambridge University Press, 1958).

18 Thomas S. Kuhn, *The Structure of Scientific Revolutions*, 2nd edn (Chicago: University of Chicago Press, 1970).

19 See Paul Horwich (ed.), *World Changes: Thomas Kuhn and the Nature of Science* (Cambridge, MA: MIT Press, 1993; Paul Hoyningen-Huehne, *Reconstructing Scientific Revolutions: Thomas S. Kuhn's Philosophy of Science*, trans. A. Levine (Chicago: University of Chicago Press, 1993).

20 See for instance Barry Barnes, *About Science* (Oxford: Blackwell, 1985); David Bloor, *Knowledge and Social Imagery* (London: Routledge & Kegan Paul, 1976); Harry Collins, *Changing Order: Replication and Induction in Scientific Practice* (London: Sage, 1985); Steve Woolgar, *Science: The Very Idea* (London: Tavistock, 1988).

21 Harry Collins and Trevor Pinch, *The Golem: What Everyone Should Know About Science*, 2nd edn (Cambridge: Cambridge University Press, 1998).

22 F.R. Leavis, *Two Cultures? The Significance of C.P. Snow* (London: Chatto & Windus, 1962); C.P. Snow, *The Two Cultures, And a Second Look* (Cambridge: Cambridge University Press, 1963).

23 For further discussion see entries under Note 20, above; also Steve Fuller, *Philosophy of Science and its Discontents* (Boulder, CO: Westview Press, 1989); Karin D. Knorr-Cetina, *The Manufacture of Knowledge: An Essay on the Constructivist and Contextual Nature of Knowledge* (Oxford: Pergamon Press, 1981); Bruno Latour and Steve Woolgar, *Laboratory Life: The Social Construction of Scientific Facts* (London: Sage, 1979).

24 Thomas S. Kuhn, *The Essential Tension: Selected Studies in Scientific Tradition and Change* (Chicago: University of Chicago Press, 1977); W.V. Quine, *Pursuit of Truth* (Cambridge, MA: Harvard University Press, 1990).

25 Andrew Ross, *Strange Weather: Culture, Science and Technology in the Age of Limits* (London: Verso, 1991); Joseph A. Rouse, *Knowledge and Power: Toward a Political Philosophy of Science* (Ithaca, NY: Cornell University Press, 1987).

26 Hayden White, *Metahistory: The Historical Imagination in Nineteenth-Century Europe* (Baltimore: Johns Hopkins University Press, 1973) and *The Content of the Form: Narrative Discourse and Historical Representation* (Baltimore: Johns Hopkins University Press, 1977).

27 Michel Foucault, *Language, Counter-Memory, Practice: Selected Essays and Interviews*, trans. D.F. Bouchard and Sherry Simon (Oxford: Blackwell, 1977) and *Power-Knowledge:*

Selected Interviews and Other Writings, ed. Colin Gordon (Hassocks: Harvester Press, 1980).

28 See Lyotard, *The Postmodern Condition*; also George Robertson et al. (eds.), *Futurenatural: Nature, Science, Culture* (London: Routledge, 1996).

29 See for instance Paul R. Gross, Norman Levitt and Martin Lewis (eds), *The Flight from Science and Reason* (New York: New York Academy of Sciences, 1996).

30 Jay A. Labinger and Harry Collins (eds.), *The One Culture? A Conversation about Science* (Chicago: University of Chicago Press, 2001); Steven Weinberg, *Facing Up: Science and its Cultural Adversaries* (Cambridge, MA: Harvard University Press, 2001).

31 William Empson, *Seven Types of Ambiguity*, 3rd edn, revised (London: Chatto & Windus, 1953).

32 N. Kathcrine Hayles, *The Cosmic Web: Scientific Field Metaphors and Literary Strategies in the Twentieth Century* (Ithaca, NY: Cornell University Press, 1984), Valcric D. Green-herg, *Transgressive Readings: The Texts of Franz Kafka and Max Planck* (Ann Arbor: University of Michigan Press, 1990).

33 See for instance N. Katherine Hayles, *Chaos Bound: Orderly Disorder in Contemporary Literature and Science* (Ithaca, NY: Cornell University Press, 1990); Hayles (ed.), *Chaos and Order: Complex Dynamics in Literature and Science* (Chicago: University of Chicago Press, 1991).

34 James Gleick, *Chaos: Making a New Science* (New York: Viking, 1987).

35 See Harriet Hawkins, *Strange Attractors: Literature, Culture, and Chaos Theory* (New York: Prentice-Hall, 1995); also Colin Sparrow, *The Lorenz Equations: Bifurcations, Chaos, and Strange Attractors* (New York: Springer Verlag, 1982).

36 Hayles (ed.), *Chaos and Order*.

37 For a more detailed discussion, see John H. Holland, *Emergence: From Chaos to Order* (Reading, MA: Addison-Wesley, 1998) and M Mitchell Waldrop, *Complexity: The Emerging Science at the Edge of Order and Chaos* (London: Penguin, 1994).

38 See Note 7, above.

39 These two articles are reprinted, along with other related material, in Alan Sokal and Jean Bricmont, *Intellectual Impostures: Postmodern Philosophers' Abuse of Science* (London: Profile Books, 1998). See also Christopher Norris, 'Sexed Equations and Vexed Physicists: The "Two Cultures" Revisited', in *Deconstruction and the Unfinished Project of Modernity* (London: Athlone Press, 2000), pp. 175–200.

40 See Notes 20, 21 and 23, above.

41 On 'context of discovery' and 'context of justification', see especially Hans Reichenbach, *Experience and Prediction: An Analysis of the Foundations and the Structure of Knowledge* (Chicago: University of Chicago Press, 1938).

42 Steven Shapin and Simon Schaffer, *Leviathan and the Air-Pump: Hobbes, Boyle, and the Experimental Life* (Princeton, N.J.: Princeton University Press, 1985); also Christopher Norris, 'Why Strong Sociologists Abhor a Vacuum: Shapin and Schaffer on the Boyle/Hobbes Controversy', in *Against Relativism: Philosophy of Science, Deconstruction, and Critical Theory* (Oxford: Blackwell, 1997), pp. 265–94.

43 See Note 27, above.

44 Lyotard, *The Postmodern Condition*.

45 See Notes 29 and 30, above.

46 Jacques Derrida, *Edmund Husserl's 'Origin of Geometry': An Introduction*, trans. John P. Leavey (Pittsburgh: Duquesne University Press, 1978); *Dissemination*, trans. Barbara Johnson (London: Athlone Press, 1982); *Margins of Philosophy*, trans. Alan Bass (Chicago: University of Chicago Press, 1982); also Christopher Norris, 'Structure and Genesis in Scientific Theory: Husserl, Bachelard, Derrida', 'Supplementarity and Deviant Logics: Derrida *contra* Quine', and 'Excluded Middles: Quantum Theory and the Logic of Deconstruction', in *Minding the Gap: Epistemology and Philosophy of Science in*

the Two Traditions (Amherst, MA: University of Massachusetts Press, 2000), pp. 100–24, 125–47, 148–71.

47 Thomas A. Pavel, *Fictional Worlds* (Cambridge, MA: Harvard University Press, 1986); Ruth A. Ronen, *Possible Worlds in Literary Theory* (Cambridge: Cambridge University Press, 1994).

48 On modal logic and 'possible worlds', see especially Raymond Bradley and Norman Swartz, *Possible Worlds: An Introduction to Logic and its Philosophy* (Oxford: Blackwell, 1979); Jaakko Hintikka, *Models for Modalities: Selected Essays* (Dordrecht: D. Reidel, 1969); G.E. Hughes and M.J. Cresswell, *A New Introduction to Modal Logic* (London: Routledge, 1996); Michael J. Loux (ed.), *The Possible and the Actual: Readings in the Metaphysics of Modality* (Ithaca, NY: Cornell University Press, 1979).

49 Geoffrey Hawthorn, *Plausible Worlds: Possibility and Understanding in History and the Social Sciences* (Cambridge: Cambridge University Press, 1991).

50 J.L. Mackie, *The Cement of the Universe: A Study of Causation* (Oxford: Clarendon Press, 1980).

51 David Lewis, *On the Plurality of Worlds* (Oxford: Blackwell, 1986); also Charles S. Chihara, *The Worlds of Possibility: Modal Realism and the Semantics of Modal Logic* (Oxford: Clarendon Press, 2001).

52 See Note 47, above.

53 See for instance Linda Hutcheon, *A Poetics of Postmodernism: History, Theory, Fiction* (London: Routledge, 1988); Brian McHale, *Postmodernist Fiction* (London: Methuen, 1987); Patricia Waugh, *Metafiction: The Theory and Practice of Self-Conscious Fiction* (London: Methuen, 1984).

54 F.R. Leavis, *Nor Shall My Sword: Discourses on Pluralism, Compassion and Social Hope* (London: Chatto & Windus, 1972); *Thought, Words and Creativity: Art and Thought in Lawrence* (London: Chatto & Windus, 1976).

55 See Note 13, above; also Rosalind Coward and John Ellis, *Language and Materialism: Developments in Semiology and the Theory of the Subject* (London: Routledge & Kegan Paul, 1977).

56 Gary Day, *Re-Reading Leavis: Culture and Literary Criticism* (London: Macmillan, 1996).

57 See Note 39, above.

58 See entries under Note 9, above; also – for a range of views on this topic – Evandro Agazzi (ed.), *Realism and Quantum Physics* (Amsterdam: Rodopi, 1997); David Bohm, *Causality and Chance in Modern Physics* (London: Routledge & Kegan Paul, 1957); James T. Cushing, *Quantum Mechanics: Historical Contingency and the Copenhagen Interpretation* (Chicago: University of Chicago Press, 1994); Arthur Fine, *The Shaky Game: Einstein, Realism, and Quantum Theory* (Chicago: University of Chicago Press, 1986); John Honner, *The Description of Nature: Niels Bohr and the Philosophy of Quantum Physics* (Oxford: Clarendon Press, 1987); Michael Redhead, *Incompleteness, Nonlocality and Realism: A Prolegomenon to the Philosophy of Quantum Mechanics* (Oxford: Clarendon Press, 1987).

59 Lyotard, *The Postmodern Condition*.

60 See entries under Notes 9 and 58, above; also David Z. Albert, *Quantum Mechanics and Experience* (Cambridge, MA: Harvard University Press, 1993); David Bohm and Basil J. Hiley, *The Undivided Universe: An Ontological Interpretation of Quantum Theory* (London: Routledge, 1993); Peter Holland, *The Quantum Theory of Motion: An Account of the de Broglie-Bohm Causal Interpretation of Quantum Mechanics* (Cambridge: Cambridge University Press, 1993).

61 See Note 6, above.

62 See especially James Robert Brown, *The Laboratory of the Mind: Thought Experiments in the Natural Sciences* (London: Routledge, 1991) and *Smoke and Mirrors: How Science Reflects Reality* (London: Routledge, 1994); also Roy Sorensen, *Thought Experiments* (London: Oxford University Press, 1992).

63 For these debates between Einstein and Bohr, together with their various later reper-cussions, see J.A. Wheeler and W.H. Zurek (eds.), *Quantum Theory and Measurement* (Princeton, NJ: Princeton University Press, 1983); also Fine, *The Shaky Game*, Redhead, *Incompleteness, Nonlocality and Realism* and Tim Maudlin, *Quantum Non-Locality and Relativity: Metaphysical Intimations of Modern Science* (Oxford: Blackwell, 1993).

64 See Wheeler and Zurek (eds.), *Quantum Theory and Measurement*; also P.H. Everard, 'The EPR Paradox: Roots and Ramifications', in W. Schommers (ed.), *Quantum Theory and Pictures of Reality: Foundations, Interpretations, and New Aspects* (Berlin: Springer Verlag, 1989), pp. 48–88 and F. Selleri, 'Wave-Particle Duality: Recent Proposals for the Detection of Empty Waves', ibid., pp. 279–332.

65 David Deutsch, *The Fabric of Reality* (London: Penguin, 1997); also Bryce S. DeWitt and Neill Graham (eds.), *The Many-Worlds Interpretation of Quantum Mechanics* (Princeton, NJ: Princeton University Press, 1973).

66 For further discussion, see Norris, *Quantum Theory and the Flight from Realism*, pp. 106–64.

67 On thought-experiments in science, see entries under Note 62, above.

68 See Notes 47, 48 and 49, above.

69 See especially Keith Jenkins, *Re-Thinking History* (London: Routledge, 1991), Jenkins (ed.), *The Postmodern History Reader* (London: Routledge, 1997); also Frank Ankersmit and Hans Kellner (eds.), *A New Philosophy of History* (London: Reaktion, 1995) and – from a different but related theoretical standpoint – Derek Attridge, Geoff Bennington and Robert Young (eds.), *Post-Structuralism and the Question of History* (Cambridge: Cambridge University Press, 1987). For some spirited arguments against this post-modern-sceptical approach see Richard J. Evans, *In Defence of History* (London: Granta Books, 1997) and Joyce Appleby, Lynn Hunt and Margaret Jacob, *Telling the Truth About History* (New York: Norton, 1994).

70 See Jean-François Lyotard, *The Differend: Phrases in Dispute*, trans. Georges van den Abbeele (Manchester: Manchester University Press, 1988).

71 Richard J. Evans, *Telling Lies About Hitler: The Holocaust, History and the David Irving Trial* (London: Verso, 2002).

5

Will the Real Saul Kripke Please Stand Up?
Fiction, Philosophy and Possible Worlds

I

In Rebecca Goldstein's novel *The Mind–Body Problem*[1] we are introduced briefly to a character named 'Saul Kripke' who shares a certain range of characteristics with the actual Saul Kripke, that is to say, the US (Princeton-based) philosopher whose book *Naming and Necessity* has had a large influence on recent debates in philosophical semantics and modal logic.[2] Still he does turn up at an academics' social gathering in Princeton (and otherwise plays no part in the action) so the reader is naturally led to assume that this is indeed Saul Kripke the philosopher, brought in just to add a bit of local colour and a joky allusion for those in the know. Meanwhile, there is another, more central character who bears a marked resemblance to the real-world Kripke in various salient respects but who happens to be a philosophically inclined mathematician and is called Noam Himmel. As concerns the latter we glean quite a bit in the way of knowledge by description, that is, the sort of knowledge that typically accrues through picking up this or that range of specifying features. These include not only his intellectual proclivities but also some pretty unpleasant character traits. As concerns the former ('Saul Kripke' by name) we have much less to go on beyond the mere fact of his being thus identified for philosophically clued-up readers and his presence in a likewise clued-up novel that makes great play with questions of naming and personal identity.[3]

It is a nice conceit and one that, besides, throws an interesting light on Kripke's ideas about sense, reference and truth. Those ideas have lately been taken up by philosophically minded literary theorists who find them useful for thinking about fictive 'possible worlds' and the ways in which modal logic (i.e., the logic of possibility and necessity) might help to resolve certain longstanding problems with the notion of fictive reference.[4] Much has been said on this topic by philosophers in the mainstream analytic tradition, starting out with Bertrand Russell's classic essay 'On Denoting' where he raised the question as to how any definite truth-value ('true' or 'false') could be assigned to sentences containing some 'empty' or non-referring expression, such as: 'The present King of France is bald'.[5] On the face of it this sentence is neither true nor false since in the absence of any referent – France being a republic – it asserts no proposition that could bear such a value, any more than does the sentence: 'The present King of France is not bald'. Russell's solution took the form of his celebrated 'theory of descriptions' whereby the sentence was conceptually unpacked – or subjected to further analysis – so as to reveal the logical structure of its underlying pre-suppositions. In this case the analysis ran (and here I paraphrase Russell): 'There exists one and only one entity such that that entity is the present King of France and is bald'. Then of course the sentence comes out false insofar as it asserts an unwarranted existence claim. Thus for any Russellian 'definite description' – one that purports to pick out some unique individual – there is always the implicit rider: 'and what is more, X exists'. Still this leaves a problem about fictive referents such as 'Sherlock Holmes' since clearly it is true – in some sense of 'true' – to say of Holmes that he lived in Baker Street rather than Tottenham Court Road, or that he solved the mystery of the Hound of the Baskervilles rather than the puzzle of Who Killed Roger Ackroyd. The theory of descriptions works well enough with identity statements like 'Scott is the author of *Waverley*', which may come as news to some since although the two terms – 'Scott' and 'the author of *Waverley*' – make reference to the same individual they do so under different descriptions and the statement can hence be informative for anyone who happens not to have known that fact. However it does little to resolve the problem about Sherlock Holmes or the issue concerning that peculiar realm of fictive persons, objects and events where assertions about them would seem to have a definite truth-value even though they refer to historically non-existent entities.

To be sure, this was not the kind of problem that Russell had chiefly in view, since his theory set out to clarify the logical status of properly referring expressions, rather than to tackle questions with regard to the ontology of fictive worlds. Still, as we shall see, it is one that loomed large in his early thinking and which the theory of descriptions effectively shelved for want of any adequate alternative approach. Frege might seem to offer some assistance here since he allows that fictive statements – such as 'Odysseus stepped ashore at Ithaca' – are perfectly intelligible despite our presumed knowledge that the name 'Odysseus' refers to no real historical individual.[6] Hence Frege's cardinal distinction between 'sense and 'reference', where the sense of a term (*Sinn*) is given by some associated range of attributes, features, imputed characteristics and so forth, while its reference (*Bedeutung*) is the object or person uniquely specified by that term. So we may say that the name 'Odysseus' has sense but not reference, or that the cluster of attributes attached to it – those that we have acquired through a reading of Homer or other relevant sources – fails to pick out any such historical personage. In which case it is possible (as with the Holmes example) to be right or wrong in making statements about him but only in so far as those statements are construed as involving a fictive suspension of disbelief or a willingness to grant 'poetic licence' when assessing their truth-value. Thus the problem of fictive reference can be seen to disappear on condition that we take Frege's point and not make the mistake of supposing that statements in poems or novels have reference to anything beyond the imaginary 'worlds' to which such statements apply.

Such has been the usual line of approach among philosophers in the 'analytic' line of descent from Russell and Frege, albeit with minor variations along way. Thus speech-act theorists (John Searle among them) prefer to make the point by saying that fictive utterances involve a departure from the norms of everyday or 'ordinary' usage, one that is conventionally understood by any competent reader of novels or poems and which effectively lifts the standard conditions for good-faith, veridical statements.[7] However this argument is open to various objections, not least that mounted by Jacques Derrida when he demonstrates the sheer impossibility of fixing criteria for what should count as a 'normal' (sincerely meant or contextually warranted) sample of the kind.[8] Besides, it falls far short of explaining how readers manage to negotiate their way through the various speech-act modalities – factual, fictive, quasi-referential, counterfactual-conditional and so forth – which are all to be found in even the most traditional 'realist' forms of novelistic discourse, let alone in postmodernist narratives or what Linda Hutcheon has aptly described as 'pseudo-historiographic metafictions'.[9] That is to say, these mainstream analytical approaches will be apt to strike most literary theorists as simply not up to the task, or as failing to meet the most basic requirements for a theory that would offer some adequate account of what goes on when competent readers engage with a fictional text. Least of all will they incline to take it on trust from Searle that any problems with the notion of fictive reference – or with the distinction between 'ordinary' and fictive speech-acts – are much better dealt with by those, like himself, whose philosophical acumen enables them to see straight through the kinds of textualist sophistry indulged in by 'literary' charlatans like Derrida. For if one thing emerges very clearly from the otherwise bewildering cross-purpose sequence of exchanges between Derrida and Searle it is the latter's obdurate failure to grasp how a deconstructive reading might in fact be more faithful or responsive to the subtleties of Austin's text than an orthodox reading which perforce has to ignore so much of what Austin himself has to say about the complications of 'ordinary' speech-act usage.[10]

Of course there is the standard post-structuralist line that language (or 'discourse') goes all the way down, that 'reality' is itself a discursive (that is to say, fictive) construct, and hence that these problems just do not arise unless one buys into a wholly outmoded – 'metaphysical' – notion of truth.[11] Such was at any rate the radical *doxa* among literary theorists twenty years back and one that lives on among some 'post-analytic' philosophers (notably Richard Rorty) for whom 'truth' is whatever counts as such according to the best, most creative or inventive modes of linguistic redescription.[12] It has also taken a hold in some quarters of 'postmodern' historiography where theorists routinely dismiss the idea of objective truth-values that obtain quite apart from their modes of narrative emplotment or rhetorical construction.[13] However this approach very quickly runs up against a range of counter-arguments, not least the fact that it lies wide open to exploitation by right-wing 'revisionist' historians who would seek to refashion the narrative record in accordance with their own ideological agenda.[14] The issue becomes most highly charged when it arises in the context of Holocaust denial and the danger – as some would maintain – that postmodernist or 'strong'-textualist ideas about the discursive construction of historical events can easily provide a convenient cover (or a veneer of academic respectability) for claims that might otherwise be roundly refuted by a straightforward appeal to the mass of supporting evidence and by recourse to the best, most reliable methods of documentary scholarship.[15] However it is also a potential source of anxiety for those (among them post-colonial critics and theorists) who seek to 'rewrite' history from the standpoint of those – the oppressed or marginalized others – whose voices have hitherto been written out of the received historical narrative. For there is not much point in producing such revisionist histories unless they are taken to convict earlier scholars (e.g., the Western 'orientalists' whom Edward Said has so vigorously taken to task) of perpetrating various well-documented sins of scholarly commission and omission.[16]

That is to say, any project of this sort must ultimately depend upon certain quite traditional standards of truth, evidence, disciplined enquiry and valid inferential warrant. In Said's case – as in much post-colonial historiography – those standards are inescapably implied whenever it is matter of taxing some hitherto dominant discourse with the twin charges of *suppressio veri* and *suggestio falsi* (suppressing truth and implying falsehood), most often in order to reinforce various racial or ethnic stereotypes.[17] Hence the marked shift of emphasis in his work from a strong-textualist approach (much influenced by Foucault) whose aim is to challenge such discourses by offering a more powerful, rhetorically effective mode of narration to an approach – like that adopted in *Culture and Imperialism* – which accepts that any claim to contest or discredit received (ideological) beliefs must involve a commitment to the truth of its own and the untruth of opposing narratives.[18] Moreover, this change goes along with his acceptance that certain 'enlightenment' values – among them those of truth, critique and emancipation from various forms of unthinking prejudice are not just products of a certain phase in the development of European culture (one deeply complicit with the discourse of Western orientalism) but, on the contrary, are values held in common by all politically progressive movements of thought. Thus Said has come around to a position that repudiates a good deal of the *soi-disant* 'radical' theorizing that marked the heyday of 1980s post-structuralism and which continues to surface on occasion in the otherwise rather jaded and theoretically exhausted discourse of postmodernism.[19] Hence perhaps the kindred shift of emphasis among recent literary theorists who have raised serious doubts about the pan-textualist levelling of different types, genres or modalities of discourse and proposed a more discriminate treatment of issues concerning truth and reference. For some, like Linda Hutcheon, this involves looking closely at the complex imbrication of factual, fictive and far-out 'possible-worlds' scenarios to be found in works such as Thomas Pynchon's *Gravity's Rainbow*, E.L. Doctorow's *Ragtime*, or – most strikingly – Kurt Vonnegut's *Slaughterhouse Five*.[20] For others it requires an approach more aware of certain ontological as distinct from purely epistemological questions, that is to say, questions having to do with the mode of existence of fictive objects, persons and events rather than their modes of linguistic or narrative representation.[21]

II

These issues were much discussed by philosophers of the late nineteenth century – among them Franz Brentano and Alexius Meinong – whose influence on the early Russell has lately received a good deal of attention.[22] In particular they played a decisive role when he came to formulate the theory of descriptions as a means of avoiding unwanted ontological commitments, for example, Brentano's idea of 'inexistent' (fictive or imaginary) objects as none the less subsisting and possessing their distinctive features in a realm of purely mental phenomena. Thus, according to Brentano, such entities were 'real' in so far as they entered into acts of thought – or object-directed modes of consciousness – which could have no content were it not for their belonging to this realm of 'intentional inexistence'. In short, 'the term "mental phenomena" applies to presentations as well as to all the phenomena which are based upon presentations ... This act of presentation forms the foundation not merely of the act of judging but also of desiring and every other mental act. Nothing can be judged, desired, hoped or feared unless one has a presentation of that thing'.[23] Meinong pushed this doctrine yet further with his argument that certain imaginary objects (such as 'the golden mountain') or logically impossible since self-contradictory ideas (such as that of 'a round square') should likewise be taken as objects of thought with their own distinct properties or attributes. It was largely in reaction to claims like these – involving what he came to think of as a wildly extravagant and profligate ontology – that Russell underwent his famous conversion from idealist metaphysics to conceptual analysis in the logico-semantic mode.[24] Yet they continued to exercise the minds of philosophers in the 'other', that is, continental or mainland-European tradition, chief among them Edmund Husserl whose project of phenomenological enquiry took careful, detailed, and rigorous account of just such a diverse range of intentional (including fictive and imaginary) objects.[25] Moreover, these interests are still very much to the fore in Derrida's early writings on Husserl where he often engages with issues in the realm of fictive ontology or concerning the 'ideality' of the literary work.[26]

What is particularly striking about recent research in the area of modal logic is that it raises many of the same issues in a more 'analytic' yet closely connected way.[27] Also it offers a valuable bridge between philosophy of language as practised in the mainstream anglophone tradition and the kinds of debate that have characterized literary theory over the past two decades.[28] In what follows I shall set out some of the basic arguments (starting with Kripke's 'new' theory of reference) and then consider their wider implications not only for literary theory but also for our thinking about history and other disciplines. More specifically (in Section IV) I shall offer some reflections – no doubt from the standpoint of an erstwhile literary theorist now turned philosopher – on their relevance to current debates about new historicism, cultural materialism, and 'post-Marxist' approaches to critical theory. For it has struck me, catching up with these debates after ten or so years of relative quarantine, that there are still large problems with the basic issue as to just what is 'historical' about readings in the textualist mode that treat 'reality' as a narrative, discursive, or – in some sense – fictive construct. This is not, I should emphasize, a piece of disciplinary one-upmanship designed (like any number of similar assertions from Plato on down) to stake the claim for philosophy as a truth-telling discourse implacably opposed to the specious attractions of literature, fiction or rhetoric. Rather it is intended to point literary theorists toward certain philosophical resources that might provide a more useful and productive means of addressing these issues than the kinds of sharply polarized realist versus anti-realist position that have tended to predominate in recent bouts of polemical exchange. What is needed, I think, is a firmer grip on those various kinds of factual, counterfactual, hypothetical and fictive statement that cannot be straightforwardly separated out into various well-defined types or genres of discourse but which still give a hold for some useful analysis and clarification. Modal logic – or the logic of 'possible worlds' – is the area of philosophy concerned with precisely such issues so it seems a promising line of approach for any literary theorist wishing to come at them from a different angle.

On Kripke's account reference is fixed by an inaugural 'baptism' or act of naming – for example, 'this is *gold*', 'this is *water*', 'these are *atoms* or *electrons*', 'that creature is a *tiger*', 'let us call him *Saul Kripke*', and so forth – which thereafter hold firm and pick out just that item, individual, or natural kind despite any subsequent changes in our knowledge concerning them.[29] Thus we know a lot more about *gold* and *water* than was known when people (even experts at the time) defined the one as 'a yellow, ductile metal that resists certain corrosive agents, dissolves only in *aqua regia* (concentrated hydrochloric and nitric acids) and so on', and the other as 'that normally liquid, transparent substance that falls as rain, fills up lakes, freezes into ice or evaporates into steam at certain temperatures, and possesses certain useful cleansing attributes'. Thus, for instance, we have nowadays learned to identify *gold* as 'the metallic element with atomic number 79', and *water* as 'just that substance that in its pure form possesses the molecular constitution H_2O'. Still we are referring to the same sorts of stuff – *gold* and *water* – as people once referred to when they had not the least idea about subatomic or molecular structures. Their usage of these terms was 'truth-tracking' or 'sensitive to future discovery' in so far as it picked out a certain kind of referent, albeit somewhat unreliably, so that iron pyrites ('fool's gold') was often mistaken for the real thing through the habit of mistaking surface appearances for knowledge of real (kind-constitutive) essence.[30] Likewise in the case of proper names such as *Aristotle* and *Saul Kripke* we might discover all sorts of hitherto unknown facts which made us think quite differently about those same individuals without thereby severing the link – the causal 'chain' of transmission – that refers back to the person thus named.

Kripke's main purpose in proposing his 'new' theory of reference was to get over certain problems with the standard descriptivist account descending from Frege and Russell.[31] On this view referents (objects, kinds or persons) are picked out through an associated cluster of descriptive attributes which serve to define – and hence to identify – the particular item concerned. Thus, for instance, the name 'Aristotle' applies to just that historical individual who was a student of Plato, who tutored Alexander the Great, and who wrote a great number of texts including the *Metaphysics*, the *Poetics*, the *Nicomachean Ethics* and so on. Or again: if we refer to 'Saul Kripke' then the particular individual whom we have in mind is the philosopher who teaches at Princeton, who has authored various books and articles, and who (along with Hilary Putnam) was responsible for developing the 'new' theory of reference. But in that case what should we make of the standing (albeit remote) possibility that we might turn out to have been massively in error about Aristotle or Kripke since they did not – as it happens – do any of those things or write any of the texts attributed to them? (Perhaps it was some kind of large-scale scholarly fraud or just an instance of straightforward mistaken identity through lack of sound factual data.) On the descriptivist theory this would place us in the awkward, indeed quite absurd situation of having to conclude that 'Aristotle was not Aristotle' or 'Saul Kripke is not Saul Kripke'. For it follows from adopting that theory – as Goldstein's novel makes amusingly clear – that persons *just are* whomsoever they are taken to be according to our best current knowledge or range of identifying criteria. So if we are wrong (misinformed or systematically deceived) then the persons concerned *just are not* the persons picked out by those particular names. Or, again, should it prove to be the case that Marlowe, Bacon or somebody else wrote the plays and poems standardly attributed to Shakespeare then – knowing so little about him aside from his having (as we thought) been the author of *Hamlet*, *King Lear* and so on – we should have to say 'Shakespeare was not Shakespeare'. What leads to this surely paradoxical and counter-intuitive upshot is the failure of descriptivist theories to provide any means of fixing reference except by recourse to our state of knowledge (or grasp of the relevant identifying features) at some given time.

Hence Kripke's alternative proposal: that in the case of individuals such as Aristotle identity is fixed at the moment of conception and any reference to them thereafter conserved through a causal chain of transmission whereby their name sticks (i.e., continues to designate just those same individuals) despite the most drastic shifts or upheavals in our state of knowledge concerning them. Moreover, this approach has far-reaching metaphysical as well as logico-semantic implications. For it entails that there once existed a person – Aristotle *ipse* – whose identity was wholly unaffected by the various contingent events, actions, writing projects, philosophical involvements, and so forth, which might never have occurred in some alternative 'possible world' where Aristotle's life and career took a radically divergent course. So likewise, Saul Kripke would still have been the self-same individual had he grown up under altogether different circumstances, never become a professional philosopher, or perhaps stuck to the Frege–Russell descriptivist theory and thereby departed so far from his actual (this-world) philosophic track that he no longer answered to any description connected with the name 'Saul Kripke' by fellow-members of his academic community. Thus rather than having to say that in this possible world Kripke would not be Kripke we can say – more sensibly – that his identity was fixed at the moment of conception as a matter of trans-world necessary truth and hence that his name picks out the same individual whatever the range of thought-experimental variations that we might devise by way of inventing alternative lives and careers.

As we saw in Chapter 4, this idea of 'possible worlds' has its source in modal logic, that is, the branch of logic concerned with matters of necessity and possibility.[32] One of Kripke's chief claims is that modal logic provides some powerful argumentative resources for dealing with issues in other fields such as philosophical semantics, epistemology, metaphysics and philosophy of science. Thus it explains how certain scientific discoveries (e.g., that gold has the atomic number 79 or water the molecular constitution H_2O) give us knowledge of *a posteriori* necessary truths about the world, that is to say, truths that are not *a priori* or self-evident to reason yet which nonetheless obtain as a matter of necessity if the world is indeed as described by our best current theories. This claim has been developed in more detail through some ingenious thought-experiments by Hilary Putnam involving the hypothesis of a duplicate planet (Twin-Earth) where there looks to be plenty of water around – much to the delight of space-travellers from Earth – but where in fact that liquid has the chemical formula XYZ.[33] So if the Earthians take it for water (for the kind of stuff which they know from back home and which possesses the molecular structure H_2O) then quite simply they are wrong about this and misapplying a term whose reference is fixed by its picking out one rather than the other natural kind.

Putnam goes some highly inventive ways around in making the basic point, that is, that no list of descriptive criteria could ever suffice – in such circumstances – to distinguish genuine from non-genuine samples of a natural kind, or to determine the truth-value of statements such as 'this is water'. Rather their truth-value is decided by whether or not the sample in question actually possesses the unique identifying feature (i.e., its molecular structure) which distinguishes Earth *water* from the Twin-Earth stuff that looks just the same, fills up lakes, falls as rain, has cleansing properties, boils and freezes at the same temperatures and so on. Thus if it is true (as we suppose) that 'water – H_2O' in virtue of its very nature or chemical constitution – and hence as a matter of *a posteriori* necessity – then the space-travelling Earthians have surely been deceived by surface appearances. In the same way descriptivists get it wrong when they argue (after Frege) that 'sense determines reference', or adopt the Russellian theory of descriptions according to which referents are picked out through some associated range or cluster of descriptive attributes. For once again what this entails, in the Twin-Earth case, is the standing possibility of someone's being driven to conclude – against reason – that 'water is not water'. Just as Kripke is necessarily Kripke *ipse* across all worlds wherein he was conceived but where his life branched off in some perhaps sharply divergent directions so water is water (= H_2O) in any world physically congruent with ours as concerns that particular reference-fixing feature, whatever its differences in other contingent respects.

Hence Kripke's claim that the approach to these issues *via* modal logic has decisive implications for our thinking about other, more broadly metaphysical questions. For instance, it promises to resolve a longstanding problem about personal identity, that is, the problem as to just which components of a person's physical constitution, psychological make-up or distinctive life-history should be taken as essential to who they are – to their being *just that* person – and which should be treated as contingent features that have no bearing on the issue. Thus, according to Kripke, what is essential to Julius Caesar's having been the individual he was (and likewise essential to our picking him out correctly) is the fact of his having been conceived by certain parents at a certain moment in time. Thereafter his life might have taken any number of different turns, so that (for instance) he might *not* have crossed the Rubicon and thus – it is fair to conjecture – altered the entire course of history. Historians often deploy such modes of counterfactual-hypothetical thought with a view to explaining just why things happened as they did, in contrast to how they would predictably (or plausibly) have turned out as a consequence of this or that antecedent change in the order of events.[34]

They are also deployed by philosophers of science who take it that valid causal explanations must be counterfactual-supporting, that is, offer strong reason to conclude that had certain physical conditions not obtained or certain causally relevant factors not been present then such and such (the observed outcome) would itself not have occurred.[35] Thus if a match repeatedly failed to ignite despite containing phosphorus and despite being struck against an abrasive surface with sufficient force to generate the required degree of friction-induced heat but in an atmosphere depleted of oxygen then we should be justified in citing oxygen uptake as a causal factor in combustion. What this involves – in modal-logical terms – is an argument from various specified conditions applying to a subset of 'possible worlds', that is, those that are physically congruent with ours insofar as they contain the same kinds of substance, properties, causal powers and so on, but which differ from the normal run of things in one crucial (explanatorily relevant) respect. Hence, as I have said, Kripke's claim with regard to the existence of *a posteriori* necessary truths – like those concerning subatomic or molecular structure – which are found out through empirical investigation yet which hold necessarily in every world belonging to the same (physically specified) subset. Hence also his claim that there exists, beyond that, a much larger class of logically possible worlds wherein we might envisage any range of alternative structures, properties, physical constants, laws of nature and so forth, subject only to the strict (universal or trans-world) requirement that these should involve no conflict with the necessary truths of logic or mathematics. For any world that flouted this baseline requirement would entail the acceptance of downright contradictory propositions or of statements – such as '2+2=5' or 'there exists a prime number between 5 and 7' – which cannot be rationally entertained by any legitimate or plausible stretch of counterfactual conceiving.

III

In short, Kripke's approach to these issues is one that purports to derive some far-reaching metaphysical as well as logico-semantic lessons from the analysis of modal locutions taken as ranging over various (actual or possible) worlds. His arguments have been roundly challenged by those – among them Noam Chomsky – who reject the idea that any such purely logical project of enquiry could be thought to establish substantive truths about the way things stand (or must once have stood) with respect to real-world objects, properties or human individuals.[36] Thus, according to Chomsky, 'doubtless there is an intuitive difference between the judgement that Nixon would be the same person if he had not been elected President of the USA in 1968, while he would not be the same person if he were not a person at all (say, if he were a silicon-based replica)'.[37] However this has to do with the fact that 'Nixon' is a proper name and hence functions in a way quite distinct from other referring expressions, that is, through its directly and uniquely denominating *just that* specific individual without any further ('metaphysical') implications about personhood, identity-conditions and so forth. In which case, 'if we abstract away from the perspective of natural language, which has no pure names in the logician's sense, then intuitions collapse: Nixon would be a different entity, I suppose, if his hair were combed differently'.[38] Jaakko Hintikka takes a similar line – in his essay 'The Emperor's New Intuitions' – where he rejects the idea that intuitive judgements with regard to certain sorts of modal-logical locution might be thought to carry such a weight of metaphysical significance.[39] For this is to stray far beyond the limits of what can be conclusively proved or established on the basis of adopting this or that system of logico-semantic inference. Hintikka is himself a modal logician and very far from sharing the Quinean outlook of downright scepticism in this regard.[40] Still he thinks it wrong – an abuse of such reasoning – to draw substantive realist implications from a branch of philosophy whose proper remit is the analysis of certain distinctive modal locutions and their place within our wider range of communally sanctioned language-games or forms of intelligible discourse. Thus Hintikka inclines more toward a Wittgensteinian position when it comes to the question of what 'realism' means as a matter of linguistic as distinct from epistemological or (much less) ontological commitment.[41] That is to say, he shares Chomsky's scepticism with regard to the idea that considerations from modal logic might somehow serve as a useful or reliable guide to what must necessarily be the case in respect of those objective truths about the world that decide the truth-value of our various statements, theories, or hypotheses concerning it.

Nevertheless such objections may be held to miss the point of Kripke's argument: namely, that there do exist important distinctions between matters of contingent, *a priori* and *a posteriori* necessary truth, and moreover that these provide a basis for explicating certain crucial facts about the individuation of kinds, properties and persons. So far as Chomsky is concerned this disagreement results from his adoption of a strictly internalist approach to linguistics and cognitive psychology, one that on principle eschews any recourse to external (i.e., causal, contextual or environmental) modes of reference-fixing.[42] That is to say, those disciplines can only achieve the status of genuine sciences if they exclude such 'extraneous' (pragmatic) considerations and delimit their field to the study of innately specified cognitive-linguistic structures. Otherwise they will lose sight of their chief objective, that is, the development of a theory of language and mind that defines just what it is about human beings that equips them to produce such a range of sentences and to exhibit such a range of cognitive achievements beyond anything remotely explainable in terms of environmental stimuli or unmediated causal inputs. Hence Chomsky's two chief arguments – from 'creativity' and 'poverty of the stimulus' – against any version of the externalist case for viewing our native linguistic competence as a product of various complex interactions between mind, reality and social factors in the acquisition of concepts and meanings. These arguments reflect his deep antipathy – on ethico-political as well as theoretical grounds – to the sorts of crudely reductive behaviourist approach (typified by B.F. Skinner) that would find no room for such innate cognitive and rational capacities of mind.[43] They are also deployed, and for similar reasons, against Quine's radically empiricist programme of 'naturalized epistemology'.[44] However – as Tyler Burge among others has argued – it is wrong to suppose that semantic externalism of the Kripke/Putnam variety places any such inherent restriction on the scope and extent of human creative-intellectual powers.[45] Indeed it is Kripke's main point in distinguishing the class of *a posteriori* necessary truths that they have to be discovered through a process of empirical enquiry even though, once established, they obtain necessarily (across all possible worlds) for some specific individual, object or property thereof. So there is no reason to conclude, with Chomsky, that the externalist theory of reference-fixing involves the kind of sharply diminished role for our native intellectual endowment that results from adopting other, more doctrinaire (e.g., behaviourist) versions of the causal thesis.

Burge makes the case – convincingly, I think – that one can have *both* externalism in Kripke's sense *and* the chief components of Chomsky's theory (nativism, individualism, universalism), along with a well-defined role for social factors in the acquisition of concepts and meaning, without any degree of conceptual strain. After all, 'the kind of thought that one thinks is not supervenient on the physical make-up of one's body, specified in isolation from its relations to the environment. Thought kinds are individuated in a way that depends on relations one bears to kinds in one's physical environment. On this view individual psychology is not purely individualistic'.[46] And again, with regard to the social or communal dimension of reference-fixing: 'the individuation of our concepts and meanings is sometimes dependent on the activity of others from whom we learn our words and on whom we depend for access to the referents of our words'.[47] In which case – to repeat – there is nothing in the Kripkean externalist theory that need be taken as inimical to Chomsky's innatist-individualist approach. Rather, their conjunction (along with an allowance for social factors in the process of reference fixing) is the best means to explain how speakers can reliably acquire and manifest not only a knowledge of language – as specified in Chomsky's somewhat restrictive terms – but also a cognitively adequate grasp of real-world objects, properties and kinds. In short, this non-exclusivist approach 'grounds the view that individual psychology and the study of the semantics of idiolects are not wholly independent of assumptions of interaction among individuals'.[48] Moreover, since such interaction requires that speakers 'stand corrected' from time to time with regard to their concepts and meanings, then it must require also that the reference of terms – despite this element of social arbitration – cannot be wholly independent of external factors that serve to individuate those same concepts and meanings.

Chomsky's objections to semantic externalism (and likewise to Kripkean applications of modal logic) can therefore be met on terms that involve no compromise to his main commitments in philosophy of mind and language. This is an important point – as Burge makes clear – since if it were indeed the case that externalism came directly into conflict with the tenets of Chomskian rationalism then we should once again be stuck with the dilemma that has plagued philosophy for the past three centuries and more. That is to say, the choice would again fall out between an empiricist doctrine devoid of rational or normative orientation and a rationalist doctrine lacking any kind of empirical content. Such was the problem that Kant inherited and sought to resolve in some notoriously obscure passages of the first critique where he explains how sensuous intuitions are 'brought under' concepts of understanding through a faculty of judgement that itself depends on the workings of 'imagination'. This latter is described as 'a blind but indispensable function of the soul, without which we should have no knowledge whatsoever, but of which we are scarcely ever conscious'.[49] One motive for the so-called 'linguistic turn' in post-1920 philosophy was the desire to have done with such epistemological quandaries and provide a more adequate, conceptually rigorous basis for discussing issues of meaning, reference and truth. At its most extreme – as in Quine's programme of 'naturalized epistemology' – this reaction went so far as to admit only a behaviourist (stimulus–response) approach to the study of human knowledge-acquisition along with the most basic of logical resources, that is, those of the first-order quantified predicate calculus.[50]

Thus Quine saw nothing but a lapse into bad old 'metaphysical' ways of thought in the idea that modal logic might provide an answer to substantive philosophical problems. Rather – in his view – it created a whole new set of problems by introducing recalcitrant notions (like those of necessity and possibility) which resisted any such austerely reductionist treatment.[51] That is to say, it left one in the awkward position of having to claim that, since '9 is necessarily greater than 7' therefore 'the number of planets is necessarily greater than 7').[52] For it is clearly not a matter of *logical* necessity that the solar system should contain more than seven planets, even though it is a logically necessary truth that 9 > 7 and – at least for the sake of argument – an astronomical fact that there exist 9 planets in the solar system. Thus the impossibility of quantifying into modal contexts struck Quine as a decisive reason for regarding such talk as a regrettable throwback to quaintly scholastic habits of thought. However it should be clear enough from what I have said about Kripke's cardinal distinction between *a priori* and *a posteriori* modes of logical necessity that Quine's objections miss the mark when applied to the modal-realist theory of meaning, reference and truth. What they fail to acknowledge is the crucial distinction between truths (like those of mathematics and logic) which obtain necessarily across the entire range of possible worlds and truths (like those of the physical sciences) which obtain necessarily for every world that is congruent with ours in the relevant, that is, physically specifiable respects.

Of course this argument is incapable of yielding substantive results or advances in knowledge beyond the various scientifically established facts – such as 'water = H_2O' or 'gold is the metallic element with atomic number 79' – which offer a range of sample statements whereby to back up its case. Nor can it tell us anything new about real-world (historically existent) individuals such as Aristotle or Julius Caesar, aside from the fact that whenever we purport to discuss them our statements have a truth-value that is determined by their referring to just those unique individuals, rather than their reference somehow being fixed (as per the Frege/Russell descriptivist theory) by our current best state of knowledge. Still this is an important result, philosophically speaking, if it manages to explain how physicists can still be talking about the same kinds of thing (e.g., 'atoms' or 'electrons') after so many episodes of radical theory change, or how scholars can still be discussing the same individuals despite any past or future revisions to our knowledge of their lives and works. For one thing, as concerns philosophy of science, it provides a viable alternative to the Kuhnian paradigm-relativist idea that our entire ontological scheme undergoes a drastic transformation with every such shift of descriptive criteria.[53] This leads to a doctrine of radical incommensurability across or between paradigms, that is, to the claim that they cannot be compared one with another in point of empirical content, descriptive accuracy or causal-explanatory power. In which case there is no making sense of the idea that science has hitherto exhibited a pattern of progressive approximation to truth through the criticism of false (empirically and/or conceptually inadequate) theories and the production of better, more empirically well-founded or conceptually refined alternative accounts. Yet this goes so much against the common-sense grain – not to mention the sheer self-evidence of progress in numerous fields of applied scientific research – as to constitute something like a classic *reductio ad absurdum* of the paradigm-relativist argument.

What Kripke's approach holds out is a means of avoiding this pyrrhic upshot by explaining how fixity of reference can be conserved even in cases (like that of 'electron') where a term was first introduced to denote whatever it was that caused some, as yet unexplained, phenomenon and thereafter underwent a whole series of radical redefinitions.[54] Thus it gets over the chief problem with descriptivist accounts, namely their commitment to the strongly counter-intuitive view that when physicists like Thomson, Rutherford and Bohr talked about 'electrons' they were talking about such utterly different notional entities that their theories cannot be ranked or assessed with reference to any shared criteria of truth or evidential warrant. For Kripke, on the other hand, there is simply no need to entertain such sceptical conclusions if one accepts that theories are 'truth-tracking' or 'sensitive to future discovery', and hence that the reference of a term like 'electron' is never exhausted by its descriptive usage at some given stage in the process of enquiry. Rather it is fixed to begin with through an act of ostensive definition ('this is *gold*', 'this is *water*', '*electrons* are the cause of that remote luminescent effect', etc.) and then subject to various forms of more elaborate, for example, microstructural specification. In which case the modal-realist theory of reference offers a highly plausible alternative to Quine's twin theses of the radical underdetermination of theory by evidence and the theory-laden character of observation statements, as well as an answer – on logical grounds – to Kuhn's yet more extravagant conjecture that 'the world changes' for scientists working before and after some episode of radical paradigm change. What speaks strongly in its favour is (1) the manifest failure of such theories to account for our knowledge of the growth of scientific knowledge, and (2) the impossibility of conceiving how such progress could ever have come about were it not for the fact – as Putnam says – that 'terms in a mature scientific theory typically refer' and that 'laws of a mature scientific theory are typically approximately true'.[55] On the Kripkean – unlike the descriptivist – account these claims have a force of rational self-evidence grounded not only in certain modal-logical considerations but also in a wide range of case studies from the history and philosophy of science.

This line of argument is further strengthened by Putnam's idea of the 'linguistic division of labour', or the way in which acts of reference can go through – pick out the right kinds of object – despite the fact that individual speakers may very often lack an adequately informed conceptual-descriptive grasp of just what it is they are talking about.[56] Thus people can successfully refer to 'gold' without knowing its atomic number, or 'water' without knowing its molecular constitution, or 'Aristotle' while remaining largely ignorant of who the man was or what he wrote, just so long as there are other, more expert types around who could provide the relevant information if needed. For there would otherwise be a large problem with the causal theory of reference, namely the fact that speakers *can and do* manage to talk about all sorts of things – and secure a good measure of communicative uptake – despite their not being favourably placed with regard to the causal 'chain' of transmission or their lack of any such expert knowledge. As Burge puts it:

> Sometimes, even in cases where the individual's substantive *knowledge in explicating* features of the referent is vague, incomplete, or riddled with false belief, the reference is as determinate as anyone else's. The reference of an individual's word is not always dependent on what the individual knows or can specify about the referent. When the individual defers to others, it is not in all cases to sharpen or fix the reference, but to sharpen the individual's explicative knowledge of a referent that is already fixed.

Our and the individual's own attitudes toward the specification of the reference often makes this clear.[57]

Thus reference is fixed through a process of empirical knowledge-acquisition which also involves certain social factors (*via* the community-wide sharing of cognitive-linguistic resources) along with the existence of *a posteriori* necessary truths concerning the objects or properties in question. After all (Burge again), 'even where the individual has epistemic access to the examples independently of others (for example, where he perceives instances directly), others may have superior knowledge of the examples'[58]. In such cases, 'the individual's deference may be cognitively appropriate', since those others – relative experts in the field – 'have put together relevant cognitive materials in a way that provides standards for understanding the individual's words and concepts'.[59] All of which lends further support both to Putnam's idea of the 'linguistic division of labour' and to Kripke's claim for the causal theory as our best (least problematical) account of how reference is conserved across theory change or how speakers can pick out identical referents despite large divergences of background knowledge or conceptual grasp.

Nevertheless it is clear that the above sorts of argument (i.e., those adducing the corrective influence of expert knowledge) are such as must involve some modification to the causal theory in its basic Kripkean form. Thus they require that the theory should incorporate at least certain elements of the older descriptivist account, among them the fact that speakers may achieve an improved (scientifically informed) understanding of a term like 'electron' which henceforth produces a change in their referential usage of the term, that is, their operative knowledge of the item concerned and its range of identifying properties. So likewise with a name such as 'Aristotle' and the fact that any extra information acquired – say, through our reading the latest scholarship – will impinge upon the process of reference-transmission to a point where it may quite radically affect our grasp of what counts as a truth-apt statement about Aristotle *ipse*. There has been much debate in the recent literature as to whether it is really a question of deciding between these two (descriptivist and causal) accounts, or whether – as seems more likely – we should think of them rather as complementary approaches that both have a strong claim to capture certain of our standing linguistic intuitions.[60] Thus the causal theory would best explain how to avoid the sorts of problem that arise on a pure-bred descriptivist account ('gold is not gold', 'Aristotle was not Aristotle', etc.) while the descriptivist theory would best explain how to make sufficient allowance for the corrective input of expert knowledge and the reference-modifying role of newly acquired scientific or other information.

Such – to repeat – is Rebecca Goldstein's ingenious point in *The Mind–Body Problem* when she attaches the name 'Saul Kripke' to a character who shares nothing of his known life-history, academic career, philosophical interests and so on, and attributes them instead to another, differently named individual who (on the strict descriptivist account) would have to be identified as none other than the real-world Saul Kripke. That the joke works so well in fictive terms is no reason to conclude that these are just the sorts of issue that preoccupy philosophers when least engaged with matters of a serious, real-world import. Indeed, it is one of Kripke's leading claims that an approach *via* modal logic promises not only to revive interest in metaphysical questions but also to show how they bear upon crucial topics in epistemology, philosophy of science and a range of other disciplines where issues of truth are bound up with issues of sense and reference. At any rate he (like Putnam) has managed to raise this claim through a range of highly inventive and resourceful thought-experimental techniques which are none the less cogent for lending themselves to such fictive treatment. Moreover, as I have said, there are signs that literary critics are turning in a similar direction – that is, toward the idiom of 'possible worlds' as a guide to ontological issues in the theory of fictive reference – by way of a promising alternative to post structuralist approaches or postmodernist ideas with regard to the textual (discursively constructed) character of 'truth' and 'reality'. (Nelson Goodman, in his book *Ways of Worldmaking*, pushes just as far along this path from a starting point within the mainstream analytic tradition.[61]) What modal logic most usefully provides is a range of resources for generic classification, that is to say, for distinguishing the various kinds and degrees of departure from the norms of 'this-world' veridical statement exhibited by various forms of fictive discourse.[62]

IV

All the same it is important – from a realist viewpoint – to keep a firm hold on the different criteria that apply when using the resources of modal logic on the one hand to address philosophical questions about (e.g.) the role of counterfactual reasoning in causal or historical explanations, and on the other as a means of pursuing enquiry into realms of fictive or speculative thought. Failing that, the approach is apt to produce all sorts of excess ontological baggage or extravagant metaphysical claims that offer no help with matters of this-world conceptual or explanatory grasp.

Thus, for instance, the philosopher David Lewis has pushed his realist interpretation of possible-worlds talk to the point where such crucial distinctions can longer get any grip.[63] Thus, according to Lewis, we have to bite the bullet and treat all those worlds as really existing and requiring that we treat them as ontologically on a par with our own, albeit – he concedes – in a realm of possibility unactualized in the world that we ourselves inhabit. So there is a world in which Caesar *did not* cross the Rubicon, in which Aristotle *did not* study with Plato, tutor Alexander, write the *Metaphysics* and so on, and where *gold* and *water* – not to mention *electrons* – possess some different physical structure or charge characteristic. These worlds are indeed just as 'real' as our own but epistemically inaccessible to us on account of our inhabiting just one among the sheer multiplicity that coexist along the endless proliferating branch-lines of might-have-been. Thus 'actual', for Lewis, is best construed as a deictic or token-reflexive term – like 'I', 'you', 'here', 'now' or 'yesterday' – which involves some strictly irreducible reference to the person who utters it in this or that particular spatio-temporal location. That is to say, the truth-value of statements containing them is defined over just that world to which the utterer belongs or within which the order of contingent events has followed just that particular course. However – he argues – we should not confuse the *real* with the *actual* since the former must be taken to include every conceivable (logically possible) world whatever the scale or degree of its departure from the way things actually stand. To treat possible-worlds talk as just a handy technical device – a *façon de parler* which translates what we mean by everyday locutions like 'might have been' – is for Lewis nothing more than a philosophic cop-out, or an *'ersatz'* version of the modal claim which fails to justify its usual range of applications, for example, in the case of counterfactual-supporting statements. Such statements would lack all explanatory force were they not taken as involving a commitment to the real existence of every such world and a consequent willingness to expand our ontology far beyond the narrowly parochial limits of a this-world (actualist) metaphysic. The only sorts of world that are *a priori* ruled out are those that assign an identical truth-value to some pair of logically inconsistent propositions or which contravene some established truth of mathematics. For such truths possess an order of trans-world necessity that admits of no possible exception, unlike (say) the elementary laws of physics, which might just conceivably involve different values and constants in a world maximally remote from our own on the scale of physical resemblance.

The case of mathematics is crucial for Lewis since it provides him with an answer to sceptics (or common-sense realists) who ask what reason we could possibly have for believing in the 'reality' of all those worlds to which we lack any means of epistemic or perceptual access. After all, the same applies to abstract objects like numbers, sets and classes, objects whose reality transcends or eludes any kind of epistemic contact, yet which are taken to offer some purchase for our various computations and proof-procedures.[64] Thus, according to Lewis, 'it's too bad for epistemologists if mathematics in its present form baffles them, but it would be hubris to take that as any reason to reform mathematics ... Our knowledge of mathematics is ever so much more secure than our knowledge of the epistemology that seeks to cast doubt on mathematics'.[65] And again: 'causal accounts of knowledge are all very well in their place, but if they are put forward as general theories, then mathematics refutes them'.[66] In which case why should philosophers balk at accepting the reality of possible worlds which likewise cannot be known or accessed by any means at our perceptual-epistemic disposal but which none the less play a crucial role in our reasoning on various counterfactual matters? Therefore – it seems – we should follow Lewis, eschew any form of *ersatz* or compromise solution, and embrace a full-blooded version of modal realism that finds no room for epistemic constraints on the range of equally real (though non-actual) candidate worlds.

This argument has struck many philosophers as going far beyond the bounds of credibility and even as amounting to a kind of unintended *reductio ad absurdum* of fully fledged modal realism. I have summarized it here mainly in order to stress the difference between Lewis's and Kripke's approach to these issues, since for Kripke the usefulness of modal logic has to do with its capacity to clarify certain basic distinctions between the orders of contingent, *a priori* and *a posteriori* necessary truth. To be sure, these distinctions are no less important for Lewis, although they are drawn so as to promote the kind of argument on *a priori* grounds that would take mathematics as its privileged instance of objective knowledge, and thus – as we have seen – open the way for a massively inflated realist ontology with only the most tenuous purchase on matters of this-world epistemic or causal-explanatory grasp. By the same token he tends to downplay the constraints imposed by Kripke's conception of *a posteriori* necessity, that is, the requirement that modal logic should earn its keep – scientifically speaking – by explaining how it is (in Putnam's words) that 'terms in a mature scientific theory typically refer' and that 'laws of a mature scientific theory are typically approximately true'. But there is not much use in adopting a modal-realist approach if it does not provide some adequate (scientifically acceptable) account of how knowledge accrues with respect to real-world operative physical laws, structures, causal powers and so on And that account had better keep a close eye on the cardinal Kripkean distinction between truths of this sort – necessary truths that are none the less grounded in discoverable facts about the structure of physical reality – and necessary truths whose trans-world validity renders them entirely void of such empirical content.

This is not to deny Lewis's commitment to a thoroughly realist approach as regards those various objects and properties of the 'actual' world that concern the physical sciences as we know them, or those historical events and personages that concern the historian when not embarked upon some exercise in counterfactual reasoning. Nor is there anything in the least objectionable – again from a realist angle – about his appeal to mathematics as a paradigm instance of objective (trans-world necessary) truth. Where the problem arises is with Lewis's way of sinking ontological distinctions so that realism with respect to mathematical and other kinds of abstract object is thought to provide the basis for a doctrine of wholesale modal realism with respect to the existence (as distinct from the counterfactual-supporting utility) of alternative possible worlds. For it is just Kripke's point – strongly borne out by the various examples cited above – that how the laws of nature are discovered to lie in our own or any other such physically constituted world is a matter of *a posteriori* necessity rather than of merely contingent fact or *a priori* truth. Thus there is simply no arguing on *a priori* grounds for any thesis with regard to the reality of worlds that differ from our own in this or that detail of their physical structure or the various alternative courses of event that make up their history to date. Such a notion invites the twofold charge of flouting certain basic modal distinctions and of over-extending its 'realist' claims to the point where they lack any kind of substantive (e.g., causal-explanatory) content. It seems to me that Kripke's intuitions are right on the main points at issue even though the causal theory of reference needs to incorporate certain elements of the 'old' descriptivist theory if those intuitions are to carry the weight that Kripke places upon them.

This all gives a new slant on the problem of fictive reference and one that should provide literary theorists with more useful and productive ideas to work with than those old, often rather sterile debates that typified approaches in the Frege–Russell tradition. What they shared – and what a philosopher like Searle still takes for granted – is the idea that there must be some basic difference between, on the one hand, language in its usual role as a means of veridical or good-faith (truthful) communicative utterance and, on the other, those various 'deviant' uses of language that include fictive statements or speech-acts that are quoted, cited, uttered by characters in a novel, and so forth.[67] It would, I think, be wrong to claim that Derrida's deconstructive reading of Austin (along with his response to Searle) had simply put paid to the prospects of maintaining any such distinction.[68] Certainly he shows that it does not hold up in anything like Searle's version, that is, as a clear-cut classificatory means of parcelling speech-acts – or entire genres of discourse – into one or other of these two supposedly exclusive categories. Indeed (as I have argued at length in Chapter 1) Derrida most adroitly turns the tables on Searle by showing just how vague and imprecise are the latter's claims to be speaking up for the virtues of 'logical' precision and clarity as against his (Derrida's) retreat into woolly-minded mystification.[69] Still his point is not at all to turn the tables on philosophy *vis-à-vis* literary criticism, history *vis-à-vis* fiction, or – in the Austinian context – instances of good-faith performative utterance *vis-à-vis* 'deviant' samples of the kind. Rather what Derrida shows to convincing effect is the fact that these distinctions come nowhere near explaining how difficult it is to unravel the order of priority in the case of any given utterance, whether factual or fictive, 'constative' or 'performative', or straightforwardly 'used' in some appropriate context as distinct from 'mentioned' (i.e., taken 'out of context') for illustrative purposes. What he *does not* for one moment suggest is that truth-values drop out altogether or – like Rorty – that everything is a matter of suasive or (in this sense) purely 'performative' utterance. Indeed he insists (most emphatically so in his second-round response to Searle) that deconstruction can proceed only on the basis of a rigorous logic that undoubtedly *complicates* these issues about truth, intention, meaning and reference but in no sense writes them off as old hat.[70]

Perhaps the chief relevance of all this for literary and cultural theorists will have to do with its bearing on issues of historical interpretation and on the kinds of debate that have recently swirled around movements like new historicism and cultural materialism, not to mention those varieties of Marxist (or 'post-Marxist') thought which continue to stake out their own distinctive agendas.[71] For if there is one question that unites them across some otherwise sharp differences of view it is the question as to just how far – and in what precise sense – literary texts can be taken as yielding a knowledge of historical events that is not just the product of some regnant ideology, whether this be located in their original 'context of production' or their present-day 'context of reception'. Beyond that, there is the debate between those who regard literary (and perhaps all other, including historical) texts as so many forms of fictive or rhetorical representation and those who would make a stronger – realist – claim for their historically informative or truth-telling aspect. Some twenty years ago when these debates first surfaced the dividing-line was drawn, roughly speaking, between post-structuralists, Foucauldians and nascent postmodernists on the one hand and on the other a range of positions that owned some allegiance – whether Marxist or cultural-materialist – to the idea of critical practice as aimed toward knowledge of the various ideological determinants involved in the process of literary production.[72]. That this latter kind of talk will most likely have a quaint, even somewhat absurd ring for theorists of the younger generation is no doubt a sign of how interests have moved on and how the relevant issues are nowadays framed in terms that more or less explicitly endorse the former way of thinking.

Still it is far from clear that those issues have yet been resolved, least of all as regards the marked tension between new historicist claims to *get things right* in certain scholarly, documentary and historical respects and their acceptance of the Foucault-derived idea that all history is 'history of the present' and all knowledge a product of ever-shifting discursive representations. Indeed this tension is nowhere more apparent than in Foucault's veering back and forth between a detailed and meticulous 'archaeology' of the social and human sciences based on extensive archival research and a commitment to the Nietzschean 'genealogical' view that truth is just a figment of the epistemic will-to-power hiding behind a rhetoric of pure, disinterested scholarly enquiry.[73] Moreover, as I have said, it continues to haunt those varieties of post-colonial criticism and theory that espouse a strong-revisionist (or textualist) approach to the issue of historical 'truth' yet would plainly lack any motivating purpose or argumentative force were it not for their claim to expose the sundry suppressions, distortions and ideological blind spots that can be shown to have typified various modes of colonialist discourse.[74] The same applies to feminist critiques which stress the 'performative' element of gender-role ascription, that is, its discursively constructed character, and hence the capacity of subjects to challenge or subvert received stereotypes by adopting a likewise strong-revisionist stance with regard to both the 'truth' of their own gender-identity and the documentary record of hitherto existing attitudes, values and beliefs.[75] Here again there is a problem in reconciling any such approach with the claim to expose how those stereotypes have functioned to impose certain clearly marked limits on the range of permissible gender-roles under certain material or socio-historical (as well as 'discursive') conditions and in keeping with certain dominant modes of ideological enforcement. That is to say, if one takes the postmodernist line that questions of truth have now given way to issues of 'performativity' then whatever one's arguments may stand to gain in terms of suasive or rhetorical power will always be offset by their consequent lack of any adequate historical and critical purchase.[76]

To this extent the old debates around 'post-structuralism and the question of history' – to cite the title of a once much-discussed anthology – have not so much been settled as allowed to rumble on slightly out of earshot.[77] Thus there might be some benefit for literary critics in looking beyond the rather self-enclosed sphere of recent theoretical exchange and taking stock of those developments in modal or possible-worlds logic that have raised such issues in a more philosophically nuanced way. At the same time – and this will be my chief topic in Chapter 6 – philosophers might do well to reflect on what literary critics and theorists have had to say about the role of metaphor and figural language in their own (the philosophers') canonical texts. For despite the exorbitant claims to this effect put forward by some deconstructionists with dubious warrant from Derrida there is a good deal of evidence, especially (as I show) in Wittgenstein's later writings, that philosophy has yet to make peaceable terms in what Plato was already calling its 'ancient quarrel' with literature.

NOTES

1   Rebecca Goldstein, *The Mind–Body Problem* (New York: Penguin, 1983).

2   Saul Kripke, *Naming and Necessity* (Oxford: Blackwell, 1980).

3   I am grateful to Dan Fitzpatrick and Charles Pigden for correcting me on a couple of details when I mentioned Goldstein's novel in response to somebody on PHILOS-L who was looking for good texts to discuss in a class on philosophy and fiction. It seems that 'Saul Kripke' (the character thus named) was given his walk-on role just in order to block the possibility of a libel suit over Noam Himmel's (supposedly) Kripke-like and somewhat disreputable character traits. Moreover (so it is said) the lawyer who came up with this saving device had a background in philosophy of language and took the line that Kripke would be hard-put to sue since, on his own submission, 'Saul Kripke' uniquely or rigidly designates that and no other individual across all the possible (including fictive) worlds containing any personage thus named. From which it followed – again on his anti-descriptivist account – that no set of traits attaching to the character 'Noam Himmel' could possibly be taken as picking out the real-world Kripke, however striking the purported resemblance. Actually my informants differed as to whether the lawyer was consulted by Kripke with a view to bringing the libel suit but advised him against on these grounds, or was approached by the author/publisher for legal guidance and advised them to include the walk-on part so as to head off the threat. Whichever way, the point was well made.

4   See for instance Peter Lamarque and Stein Haugom Olsen, *Truth, Fiction, and Literature: A Philosophical Perspective* (Oxford: Clarendon Press, 1994); Thomas Pavel, *Fictional Worlds* (Cambridge, MA: Harvard University Press, 1986); Ruth A. Ronen, *Possible Worlds in Literary Theory* (Cambridge: Cambridge University Press, 1994).

5   Bertrand Russell, 'On Denoting', *Mind* 14 (1905), pp. 479–93.

6   Gottlob Frege, 'On Sense and Reference', in Peter Geach and Max Black (eds), *Translations from the Philosophical Writings of Gottlob Frege* (Oxford: Blackwell, 1952), pp. 56–78.

7   John Searle, *Speech Acts: An Essay in the Philosophy of Language* (Cambridge: Cambridge University Press, 1969); see also Gregory Currie, *The Nature of Fiction* (Cambridge Cambridge University Press, 1990).

8   Jacques Derrida, 'Signature Event Context', *Glyph* 1 (1977), pp. 172–97. See also Christopher Norris, 'Supplementarity and Deviant Logics', in *Minding the Gap: Epistemology and Philosophy of Science in the Two Traditions* (Amherst, MA: University of Massachusetts Press, 2000), pp. 125–47.

9   Linda Hutcheon, *A Poetics of Postmodernism: History, Theory, and Fiction* (London: Routledge, 1988).

10   J.L. Austin, *How to Do Things with Words* (Oxford: Oxford University Press, 1963).

11   See for instance Antony Easthope, *British Post-Structuralism: Since 1968* (London: Routledge, 1988); Josué V. Harari (ed.), *Textual Strategies: Perspectives in Post-Structuralist Criticism* (London: Methuen, 1980); Richard Harland, *Superstructuralism: The Philosophy of Structuralism and Post-Structuralism* (London: Methuen, 1987); Robert Young (ed.) *Untying the Text: A Post-Structuralist Reader* (London: Routledge, 1981).

12   Richard Rorty, *Consequences of Pragmatism* (Brighton: Harvester, 1982) and *Objectivity, Relativism, and Truth* (Cambridge: Cambridge University Press, 1991).

13   Derek Attridge, Geoff Bennington and Robert Young (eds.), *Post-Structuralism and the Question of History* (Cambridge: Cambridge University Press, 1987); Keith Jenkins, *Re-Thinking History* (London: Routledge, 1991); Jenkins (ed.) *The Postmodern History Reader* (Routledge, 1997); Hayden White, *Tropics of Discourse* (Baltimore, MD: Johns Hopkins University Press, 1978) and *The Content of the Form: Narrative Discourse and Historical Representation* (Johns Hopkins, 1987).

14   For further discussion see Norris, 'Postmodernizing History: Right-Wing Revisionism and the Uses of Theory', in Jenkins (ed.), *The Postmodern History Reader*, pp. 89–102; *Truth and the Ethics of Criticism* (Manchester: Manchester University Press, 1994); *Reclaiming Truth: Contribution to a Critique of Cultural Relativism* (London: Lawrence & Wishart, 1996); also Perry Anderson, *A Zone of Engagement* (London: Verso, 1992); Joyce Appleby, Lynn Hunt and Margaret Jacob, *Telling the Truth About History* (New York: Norton, 1994); Richard J. Evans, *In Defence of History* (Cambridge: Granta, 1997); Alex Callinicos, *Theories and Narratives: Reflections on the Philosophy of History* (Cambridge: Polity Press, 1995).

15   See various entries under Note 14; also Peter Baldwin, *Reworking the Past: Hitler, the Holocaust, and the Historians' Debate* (Boston: Beacon Press, 1990); Saul Friedlander (ed.), *Probing the Limits of Representation: Nazism and the 'Final Solution'* (Cambridge, MA: Harvard University Press, 1992); Geoffrey H. Hartman, *Holocaust Remembrance: The Shapes of Memory* (Oxford: Oxford University Press, 1994); Dominick LaCapra, *History and Memory after Auschwitz* (Ithaca, NY: Cornell University Press, 1998); Berel Lang (ed.), *Writing and the Holocaust* (New York: Holmes & Meier, 1988); James E. Young, *Writing and Rewriting the Holocaust: Narrative and the Consequences of Interpretation* (Bloomington: Indiana University Press, 1988).

16   Edward W. Said, *Orientalism* (London: Routledge & Kegan Paul, 1978).

17   See also Said, *Covering Islam: How the Media and the Experts Determine How We See the Rest of the World* (London: Routledge & Kegan Paul, 1981).

18   Said, *Culture and Imperialism* (London: Chatto & Windus, 1993).

19   See Notes 11 and 13, above.

20   Hutcheon, *A Poetics of Postmodernism*.

21   Brian McHale, *Postmodernist Fiction* (London: Methuen, 1987).

22   See especially Peter Hylton, *Russell, Idealism, and the Emergence of Analytic Philosophy* (Oxford: Clarendon Press, 1990); also Franz Brentano, *Psychology from an Empirical Standpoint* (London: Routledge & Kegan Paul, 1874); Roderick M. Chisholm, *Brentano and Meinong Studies* (Amsterdam: Rodopi, 1982); J.N. Findlay, *Meinong's Theory of Objects and Values* (Oxford: Oxford University Press, 1963).

23   Brentano, *Psychology from an Empirical Standpoint*, p. 79.

24   See Hylton, *Russell, Idealism, and the Emergence of Analytic Philosophy*.

25   See for instance Edmund Husserl, *Logical Investigations*, trans. J.N. Findlay (London: Routledge & Kegan Paul, 1970).

26   Jacques Derrida, *Speech and Phenomena and Other Essays on Husserl's Theory of Signs*, trans. David B. Allison (Evanston, IL: Northwestern University Press, 1973); *Writing and*

Difference, trans. Alan Bass (London: Routledge & Kegan Paul, 1978); *Le Problème de la genèse dans la philosophie de Husserl* (Paris: Presses Universitaires de France, 1990).

27 See entries at Note 32, below.

28 See Note 4, above.

29 Kripke, *Naming and Necessity*; also Stephen Schwartz (ed.), *Naming, Necessity and Natural Kinds* (Ithaca, NY: Cornell University Press, 1977).

30 Hilary Putnam, *Mind, Language and Reality* (Cambridge: Cambridge University Press, 1975); also Gregory McCulloch, *The Mind and its World* (London: Routledge, 1995) and Christopher Norris, *Hilary Putnam: Realism, Reason, and the Uses of Uncertainty* (Manchester: Manchester University Press, 2002).

31 See Notes 5 and 6, above.

32 See Raymond Bradley and Norman Swartz, *Possible Worlds: An Introduction to Logic and its Philosophy* (Oxford: Blackwell, 1979); Jerome S. Bruner, *Actual Minds, Possible Worlds* (Cambridge, MA: Harvard University Press, 1986); Charles S. Chihara, *The Worlds of Possibility: Modal Realism and the Semantics of Modal Logic* (Oxford: Clarendon Press, 2001); Rod Gierle, *Modal Logics and Philosophy* (Teddington: Acumen, 2000) and *Possible Worlds* (Teddington: Acumen, 2002); G. Hughes and M. Cresswell, *A New Introduction to Modal Logic* (London: Routledge, 1996); L. Linsky (ed.), *Reference and Modality* (Oxford: Oxford University Press, 1971); M. Loux (ed.), *The Possible and the Actual: Readings in the Metaphysics of Modality* (Ithaca, NY; Cornell University Press, 1979).

33 Putnam, *Mind, Language and Reality*.

34 See especially Geoffrey Hawthorn, *Plausible Worlds: Possibility and Understanding in History and the Social Sciences* (Cambridge: Cambridge University Press, 1991).

35 See for instance J.L. Mackie, *The Cement of the Universe* (Oxford: Clarendon Press, 1974); Ernest Sosa (ed.), *Causation and Conditionals* (Oxford: Oxford University Press, 1975); Wesley C. Salmon, *Scientific Explanation and the Causal Structure of the World* (Princeton, NJ: Princeton University Press, 1984); M. Tooley, *Causation: A Realist Approach* (Oxford: Blackwell, 1988).

36 Noam Chomsky, *New Horizons in the Study of Language and Mind* (Cambridge: Cambridge University Press, 2000). For some relevant commentary see also James McGilvray, *Chomsky: Language, Mind, and Politics* (Cambridge: Polity Press, 1999) and Alexander George (ed.), *Reflections on Chomsky* (Oxford: Blackwell, 1989).

37 Chomsky, *New Horizons*, pp. 41–2.

38 Ibid., p. 42.

39 Jaakko Hintikka, 'The Emperor's New Intuitions', *Journal of Philosophy* 96 (1999), pp. 127–47.

40 See Jaakko Hintikka, *Models for Modalities: Selected Essays* (Dordrecht: D. Reidel, 1969); also the various essays by Quine and others in Linsky (ed.), *Reference and Modality*.

41 See for instance Jaakko Hintikka, *Logic, Language-Games and Information: Kantian Themes in the Philosophy of Logic* (Oxford: Clarendon Press, 1973); also Merrill B. Hintikka and Jaakko Hintikka, *Investigating Wittgenstein* (Oxford: Blackwell, 1986).

42 See especially Noam Chomsky, *Cartesian Linguistics* (New York: Harper & Row, 1966); *Language and Mind* (New York: Harcourt, Brace, Jovanovich, 1972); *Knowledge of Language: Its Nature, Origin, and Use* (New York: Praeger, 1986); *Language and Thought* (London: Moyer Bell, 1993); 'Language and Nature', *Mind* 104 (1995), pp. 1–61.

43 See Noam Chomsky, 'A Review of B.F. Skinner's *Verbal Behavior*', *Language* 35 (1959), pp. 126–58; also B.F. Skinner, *Verbal Behavior* (Englewood Cliffs, NJ: Prentice-Hall, 1957).

44 Noam Chomsky, 'Quine's Empirical Assumptions', *Synthèse* 19 (1968), pp. 53–68; W.V. Quine, *Ontological Relativity and Other Essays* (New York: Columbia University Press, 1969).

45 See Tyler Burge, 'Individualism and the Mental', *Midwest Studies in Philosophy* 4 (1979),

pp. 73–121 and 'Individualism and Psychology', *Philosophical Review* 95 (1986), pp. 3–45.

46   Tyler Burge, 'Wherein is Language Social?', in George (ed.), *Reflections on Chomsky*, pp. 175–91 (178).

47   Ibid., p. 187.

48   Ibid., p. 187.

49   Immanuel Kant, *Critique of Pure Reason*, trans. N. Kemp Smith (London: Macmillan, 1964), p. 112.

50   See especially Quine, *Ontological Relativity and Other Essays* .

51   W.V. Quine, 'Reference and Modality', in Linsky (ed.), *Reference and Modality*, pp. 17–34; also – for counter-arguments to Quine on these issues in modal logic – Ruth Barcan Marcus, *Modalities: Philosophical Essays* (New York: Oxford University Press, 1993).

52   Quine, 'Reference and Modality', pp. 20–1.

53   Thomas S. Kuhn, *The Structure of Scientific Revolutions*, 2nd edn (Chicago: University of Chicago Press, 1970); Quine, 'Two Dogmas of Empiricism', in *From a Logical Point of View*, 2nd edn (Cambridge, MA: Harvard University Press, 1961), pp. 20–46.

54   See Putnam, *Mind, Language and Reality*; also *Representation and Reality* (Cambridge, MA: MIT Press, 1988).

55   Putnam, *Mind, Language and Reality*, p. 290.

56   Putnam, *Representation and Reality*.

57   Burge, 'Wherein is Language Social?', p. 180.

58   Ibid., p. 186.

59   Ibid., p. 186.

60   See for instance Gareth Evans, *The Varieties of Reference*, ed. J. McDowell (Oxford: Clarendon Press, 1982); also Gregory McCulloch, *The Game of the Name: Introducing Language, Logic and Mind* (Oxford: Clarendon Press, 1989) and Schwartz (ed.), *Naming, Necessity and Natural Kinds*.

61   Nelson Goodman, *Ways of Worldmaking* (Indianapolis: Hackett Publishing Co., 1978); also Goodman's responses to his critics in Peter J. McCormick (ed.), *Starmaking: Realism, Anti-Realism, and Irrealism* (Cambridge, MA: M.I.T. Press, 1996).

62   Ronen, *Possible Worlds in Literary Theory*.

63   David Lewis, *The Plurality of Worlds* (Oxford: Blackwell, 1986).

64   See especially Paul Benacerraf, 'What Numbers Could Not Be', in Paul Benacerraf and Hilary Putnam (eds.), *The Philosophy of Mathematics: Selected Essays*, 2nd edn (Cambridge: Cambridge University Press, 1983), pp. 272–94); also W.D. Hart (ed.), *The Philosophy of Mathematics* (Oxford: Oxford University Press, 1996).

65   Lewis, *The Plurality of Worlds*, p. 109.

66   Ibid., p. 109.

67   J.L. Austin, *How To Do Things with Words*; also Searle, *Speech Acts: An Essay in the Philosophy of Language* and 'Reiterating the Differences: A Reply to Derrida', *Glyph* 1 (1977), pp. 198–208.

68   Derrida, 'Signature Event Context'; also 'Limited Inc abc', in Gerald Graff (ed.), *Limited Inc* (Evanston, IL: Northwestern University Press, 1989), pp. 29–110.

69   Norris, 'Supplementarity and Deviant Logics'; also 'Derrida on Rousseau: Deconstruction as Philosophy of Logic', in Christopher Norris and David Roden (eds.), *Jacques Derrida*, 4 vols (London: Sage, 2003), vol. 2, pp. 70–124.

70   Derrida, 'Afterword: toward an ethic of discussion', in Graff (ed.), *Limited Inc*, pp. 111–60.

71   See for instance John Brannigan, *New Historicism and Cultural Materialism* (Basingstoke: Macmillan, 1998); Claire Colebrook, *New Literary Histories: New Historicism and Contemporary Criticism* (Manchester: Manchester University Press, 1997); Jeremy Hawthorn, *Cunning Passages: New Historicism, Cultural Materialism, and Marxism in Contemporary Literary Debate* (London: Arnold, 1996); Kiernan Ryan (ed.), *New Historicism and*

Cultural Materialism: A Reader (London: Arnold, 1996); Stuart Sim (ed.), *Post-Marxism: A Reader* (Edinburgh: Edinburgh University Press, 1998); H. Aram Veeser (ed.), *The New Historicism* (New York: Routledge, 1989); Veeser (ed.), *The New Historicism Reader* (New York: Routledge, 1994).

72   See for instance Catherine Belsey, *Critical Practice* (London: Methuen 1981); Tony Bennett, *Outside Literature* (London: Routledge, 1990); Rosalind Coward and John Ellis, *Language and Materialism: Developments in Semiology and the Theory of the Subject* (London: Routledge & Kegan Paul, 1977); Terry Eagleton, *Criticism and Ideology* (London: New Left Books, 1976); John Frow, *Marxism and Literary Theory* (Cambridge, MA: Harvard University Press, 1986); Raman Selden, *Criticism and Objectivity* (London: Allen & Unwin, 1984); David Silverman and Brian Torode, *The Material Word: Some Theories of Language and its Limits* (London: Routledge & Kegan Paul, 1980).

73   Cf. Michel Foucault, *Discipline and Punish: The Birth of the Prison*, trans. Alan Sheridan (Harmondsworth: Penguin, 1979); *Madness and Civilization: A History of Insanity in the Age of Reason*, trans. Richard Howard (London: Routledge, 1989); *Language, Counter-Memory, Practice: Selected Essays and Interviews*, trans. and ed. D.F. Bouchard and S. Simon (Oxford: Blackwell, 1977).

74   For a range of views on these and related issues, see Bill Ashcroft, Gareth Griffiths and Helen Tiffin, *The Empire Writes Back: Theory and Practice in Post-Colonial Literatures* (London: Routledge, 1989); Bill Ashcroft, Gareth Griffiths and Helen Tiffin (eds.), *The Post-Colonial Studies Reader* (London: Routledge, 1995); Peter Childs and Patrick Williams, *An Introduction to Post-Colonial Theory* (London: Harvester-Wheatsheaf, 1997); Patrick Williams and Laura Chrisman (eds.), *Colonial Discourse and Post-Colonial Theory: A Reader* (London: Harvester-Wheatsheaf, 1993).

75   See especially Judith Butler, *Gender Trouble: Feminism and the Subversion of Identity* (New York: Routledge, 1990) and *Bodies that Matter: On the Discursive Limits of 'Sex'* (Routledge, 1993).

76   Jean-François Lyotard, *The Postmodern Condition: A Report on Knowledge*, trans. Geoff Bennington and Brian Massumi (Manchester: Manchester University Press, 1984).

77   Attridge, Bennington and Young (eds.), *Post-Structuralism and the Question of History*.

6

Extraordinary Language:
Why Wittgenstein Didn't Like Shakespeare

I

Shakespeare's Falstaff, so we are told in the play and as Dr Johnson heartily agreed, was not just witty himself but also the cause that great wit was in other men.[1] To this extent Falstaff differed strikingly from the philosopher Ludwig Wittgenstein whose writings and recorded remarks, while often (not always) acutely perceptive in themselves, have tended to have the opposite effect – to induce a curious literal-mindedness and absence of creative or independent thought – in his many disciples and exegetes. This would be a fact of no significance whatever were it not for Wittgenstein's notorious remarks to the effect that Shakespeare had been vastly over-rated and that his reputation was most likely a product of received opinion acting on the depraved taste for extreme novelties of style and verbal technique. At the same time Wittgenstein was naggingly aware that he stood pretty much alone in this opinion and that there might just be something about Shakespeare that he had not quite managed to grasp.

This mixture of confident heterodox judgement and occasional self-misgiving comes out very clearly in the following passage from *Culture and Value* where his comments are all the more revealing for their impromptu and – so far as he could possibly have known – their not-for-publication character. 'It is remarkable', he writes,

> [h]ow hard we find it to believe something that we do not see the truth of for ourselves. When, for instance, I hear the expression of admiration for Shakespeare by distinguished men in the course of several centuries, I can never rid myself of the suspicion that praising him has been the conventional thing to do; though I have to tell myself that this is not how it is. It takes the authority of a Milton really to convince me. I take it for granted that he was incorruptible. – But I don't of course mean by this that I don't believe an enormous amount of praise to have been, and still to be, lavished on Shakespeare without understanding and for the wrong reasons by a thousand professors of literature.[2]

The most striking thing about this passage is its veering about between a tone of superior contempt for the purveyors of hand-me-down critical opinion and a deference to just the kind of authority – Milton's – as to place him (Wittgenstein) on the side of the angels even if he remains personally unconvinced. At any rate his comments on Shakespeare are worth some attention in so far as they seem to touch closely upon matters that conjured a complex, overdetermined and at times distinctly prickly mode of response. What I propose to do is talk about Wittgenstein's philosophy of language (despite his reiterated claim to be offering no such thing); about his mainly negative yet often highly ambivalent evaluation of Shakespeare; about what other Wittgenstein-influenced philosophers have had to say on the topic of Shakespearean poetry and drama; and also – following from this – about the nature of perceptive intelligence or 'wit' as applied to, or as manifest in, certain ways of talking and thinking. In a general sense my interest here has to do with the 'ancient quarrel' between philosophy and literature which Plato was among the first to engage and that has lately flared up with renewed force in various institutional contexts, including those of 'analytic' versus 'continental' philosophy, the latter very often equated with literary theory and its upstart philosophical pretensions. However I would hope that the focus on Shakespeare and on Wittgenstein's comments in this regard will help to sharpen the relevant issues and avoid just adding a further chapter to that history of mostly cross-purpose hostile exchange.

For Shakespeare has presented a peculiar challenge to philosophy, a challenge that is all the more troublesome if one takes the late-Wittgensteinian view that everything most important for human existence is (or ought to be) fully expressible in the sorts of 'language-game' normally played in our everyday communal discourse or cultural life-forms.[3] It is hard to square this ordinary-language reading of Wittgenstein with the kinds of *extra*ordinary language that are everywhere to be found in Shakespeare's plays and which have often taxed understanding to the limit, as witness the unending interpretative travails of critics and textual editors alike. Faced with such problems, one cannot get far by simply declaring: 'this language-game is played', and thus ruling out any further attempt to explicate the sense (or decide between textual variants) on the all-purpose Wittgensteinian principle: 'don't ask for the meaning, ask for the use'.[4] Nor is it very helpful to advise, again after Wittgenstein, that philosophy 'leaves everything as it is', and that literary critics can best comply in their own field of endeavour by permitting the text to speak for itself and holding their creative-revisionary impulses properly in check. There is just too much going in Shakespearean English for that kind of counsel to have much force or to persuade exegetes – whether editors, textual scholars or interpreters – to apply such a strictly self-denying ordinance. For they could not make a start in understanding what these texts are all about except by ignoring that injunction and allowing that linguistic creativity may always exceed whatever limits are laid down by the warrant of received or customary usage.

At one time, not so long after Shakespeare's, this tendency to flights of sheer linguistic exuberance – of ambiguity, wordplay, paradox, multiplied metaphor and so forth – was very often deplored by earnest-minded critics who viewed it as a sad liability and a sign that the poet's powers of invention were unfortunately not matched by powers of linguistic self-discipline and a due sense of dramatic decorum.[5] Thus Dr Johnson famously lamented that Shakespeare was all too prone to such flights and unable to restrain his genius within the bounds of linguistic good taste. At issue here – as so often in eighteenth-century discussions of language – is the question how best to establish (or enforce) a proper relationship between signifier and signified or word and world such that ideally there would be no room for ambiguities of reference or semantic scope.[6] A 'quibble' to Shakespeare, Johnson opined, 'is what luminous vapours are to the traveller; he follows it at all adventures, it is sure to lead him out of his way ... It has some malignant power over his mind, and its fascinations are irresistible ... A quibble was to him the fatal *Cleopatra* for which he lost the world, and was content to lose it'.[7] Or again, to likewise censorious effect:

> Not that always where the language is intricate the thought is subtle, or the image always great where the line is bulky; the equality of words to things is very often neglected, and trivial sentiments and vulgar ideas disappoint the attention, to which they are recommended by sonorous epithets and swelling figures.[8]

All of which stands in marked contrast to Johnson's intense admiration for Shakespeare and his impatience with those – especially upholders of the classical virtues represented by French dramatists like Corneille and Racine – who were apt to mount a similar charge against Shakespeare's lack of linguistic restraint along with his blatant disregard for the Aristotelian unities of time and place. No doubt there is a strong element of national and cultural chauvinism here, a desire to assert the superiority of Shakespeare's native genius as compared with the frigid perfections of that classical style. All the same Johnson is keen to assert his disapproval of Shakespeare's frequent running to the opposite extreme, that is, toward a style of profligate linguistic licence which threatens not only the principles of literary decorum but also those of the English language as a medium of well-conducted communicative discourse and, beyond that, the very bases of social, civil and political order.

We should recall that Johnson was writing at a time when the English Civil War was still very much in the forefront of collective memory, and when issues of linguistic and cultural propriety were felt to have a direct, even urgent bearing on issues of wider socio-political concern. Thus Johnson's conviction (like Wittgenstein's after him) of the harm that can easily result when language 'goes on holiday' – when it yields to extravagant flights of metaphor or self-indulgent wordplay – goes along with his sense that Shakespeare's plays were somehow symptomatic of the looming crisis of religious and secular authority that would soon give rise to that catastrophic outcome.[9] There is a kindred tone about his commentaries on Donne and other early to mid seventeenth-century poets whose 'metaphysical' or 'conceited' style Johnson deplores as a matter of taste and considered critical judgement even while conveying a strong, at times almost elegiac sense of just how much has been lost in the passage to his own

more restrained and decorous age.[10] What chiefly comes across in these writings
– above all in his *Preface to Shakespeare* – is the need to maintain a due 'proportion' or 'equality' between words and things, words and ideas, or language
and its sundry practical (e.g., referential and social-communicative) purposes.
What may also strike the reader who approaches them with Wittgenstein's
antipathy to Shakespeare in mind is the way that certain sorts of linguistic
creativity – certain modes of departure from the norms of communal or
'ordinary' usage – can exert a decidedly unsettling effect on philosophers or even
on literary critics whom one might expect to hold such language in the highest
esteem.

Thus, for Wittgenstein, philosophers typically go wrong – mistake their
proper calling and fall into various kinds of nonsense-generating error – if they
seek to offer more than the therapeutic benefit of bringing us to see, through a
shrewd choice of examples, just how and where we are habitually led astray by
our profligate way with words. In short, philosophy 'leaves everything as it is'
since everything is perfectly in order with our everyday, communal language-
games and cultural life-forms just so long as they are not taken over and subjected to the kinds of 'metaphysical' distortion that characterize much philosophical discourse. What is left is the less glamorous but also less intelligence-
bewitching business of patiently assembling those needful reminders and
thereby – in Stanley Cavell's words – helping to lead philosophy 'back, *via* the
community, home'.[11] Dr Johnson seems to strike a similar note when he writes,
in the *Preface to Shakespeare*, that 'he who has mazed his imagination in following
the phantoms which other writers raise up before him, may here be cured of his
delirious ecstasies by reading human sentiments in human language'.[12] To this
extent Shakespeare is clearly meant to stand as an exemplar of English common-
sense wisdom and native-intuitive genius, as against the dangers of an over-
heated imagination or – Johnson's chief target elsewhere – an overly prescriptive
and obsessional concern with abstract principles and theories. On the other hand,
he is just as apt to set Shakespeare up as a cautionary instance of verbal creativity
run wild, or of what goes wrong with literature in its social or communal role
when that kind of genius oversteps the limits of reason, moderation or accepted
good taste.

II

I think that we can best get a handle on all this – in Wittgenstein's as in Dr
Johnson's case – by considering also what the latter has to say with regard to the
business of textual scholarship, and especially the problems (the well-nigh
insuperable problems, as Johnson describes them) of editing Shakespeare. The
editor's task has this much in common with the philosopher's according to
Wittgenstein: that there is no room here for displays of ingenuity, for speculative ventures, system-building theory or anything that smacks of intellectual
or expressive self-promotion on their part. Thus Johnson declares himself

downright opposed to the sorts of highly conjectural and, to that extent, inventive or creative editing that would gladly sacrifice the humdrum virtues of disciplined scholarly method to the challenge and rewards of ingenious textual emendation. Such indulgence must lead to an 'unhappy state', one in which 'danger is hid under pleasure'. And yet, 'the allurements of emendation are scarcely resistible', since 'conjecture has all the joy and all the pride of invention, and he who has once started a happy change is too much delighted to consider what objections may rise against it'.[13] His own practice as editor of Shakespeare – one by no means averse to offering just such far-fetched conjectures when given the chance by some especially obscure or textually corrupt passage – is evidence enough of Johnson's ambivalent feelings in this regard. Indeed, his description of the editor's role as set about with all manner of 'allurements' and temptations cannot but recall what Johnson says about Shakespeare and the 'luminous vapours', 'malignant powers' or 'fatal Cleopatra' of Shakespearean wordplay. For in truth – as he is sometimes willing to concede – there is no more possibility of the editor's avoiding such conjectural licence when confronted with such passages than there is of Shakespeare's having somehow achieved his best, most inspired dramatic and poetic effects without going in for the kinds of highly complex verbal figuration that tend to create exegetical problems and hence call forth both the critic's and the editor's powers of creative re-imagining.

It is here – in the attempt to reconcile these sharply conflicting critical priorities – that Johnson's editorial travails have a bearing on Wittgenstein's failure (or refusal) to see what it was that people so admired about Shakespeare. For if one thing is clear both in Wittgenstein's writings and their subsequent reception-history it is the similar conflict that exists between a therapeutic will to coax thinking down from the heights of 'metaphysical' temptation where language is all too prone to spin free in giddy gyrations of its own inventing and the countervailing impulse to devise all manner of extravagant conjectures, thought-experiments, sceptical scenarios and so forth, whereby to test that programme to its limits and beyond. Thus there is an unresolved tension between, on the one hand, Wittgenstein's professed desire to 'give philosophy peace' through the saving ministrations of ordinary language and the cultural life-forms wherein such language is at home and, on the other, his constant, well-nigh obsessional raising of just the sorts of problem that the therapy is expressly intended to cure. Chief among them are the problems abut rule following, 'private language', other minds and the existence of an external world, all of which Wittgenstein purports to show up as products of a deeply disordered philosophical mind set – or as resulting from the mere 'bewitchment of our intelligence by means of language' – but all of which he treats with such vigour, tenacity and inventiveness in putting the adversary (sceptical) case as to cast real doubt on his statements of curative intent. What I think best explains this curious ambivalence on Wittgenstein's part is also what explains Dr Johnson's veering about between opposed valuations of Shakespearean language and likewise of the editor's hard-put role when confronted with its proneness to 'go on holiday' – or indulge all manner of rhetorical or figural excess – and hence lose touch with customary usage. In both cases there is a strong sense that the communitarian or 'ordinary-language' approach is one that undergoes considerable strain once exposed not only to Shakespeare's stylistic proclivities but also to the kinds of inventiveness displayed by even the most everyday, routine, or casual instances of verbal exchange.

That is to say, *all* language requires interpretation beyond what is envisaged by the doctrine of meaning-as-use, or the idea that any utterance will make good sense if understood according to its own implicit norms of intelligibility, these latter equated with the values and beliefs of some given communal or cultural tradition. In its orthodox form this doctrine can acquire a remarkable, almost talismanic power to stifle thought and produce the kind of reflex, conformist response that declares – in effect – 'this is our (or their) language-game so critics had better keep off'. Its impact has been greatest in the social sciences and cultural theory where one regularly comes across the argument that in order to criticize a custom, belief, institution or social practice one must first have *understood* it with the same sense of inward acceptance and involvement as those for whom it constitutes a veritable way of life. So one could only have missed the point – or adopted an uncomprehending externalist view – if one presumed to take issue with some item of faith (say in witchcraft or Azande magic or the Christian doctrine of atonement) that happened not to fit with one's own ideas of rational belief.[14] After all, did not Wittgenstein draw this lesson from his own early effort, in the *Tractatus Logico-Philosophicus*, to devise a purely truth-functional language that would find room for just those statements which could be verified (or falsified) according to the strictest requirements of logic and empirical science?[15] Was it not the main purpose of his subsequent 'therapeutic' writings to wean us away from this narrow conception of language, truth and logic by reminding us just how many and varied are the language-games or cultural forms of life whereby human beings make sense of the world and their place in it?

Such has at least been the usual understanding of the mid-career 'turn' in Wittgenstein's thought. It was the turn clean away from an atomistic theory of language premised on the doctrines of logical positivism to a wiser, more tolerant and pluralist acceptance that no single language-game – least of all that one – could ever lay claim to an adjudicative standpoint *vis-à-vis* those other kinds of communally sanctioned and (by their own interpretative lights) perfectly legitimate modes of thought and expression. Commentators have of course differed on the question of whether or just how far the *Tractatus* should be seen as already, in its last few paragraphs, marking a break with the precepts of old-style Russellian logical atomism.[16] For those paragraphs famously contain some passages which suggest that Wittgenstein's main purpose in apparently adopting that approach was to point beyond it to regions of enquiry – ethics, aesthetics, religious belief – any talk of which would be counted strictly meaningless (or emptily 'metaphysical') by verificationist criteria, but which nonetheless concerned matters of the deepest human and spiritual import. Hence his various cryptic suggestions: that the *Tractatus* should be treated as a ladder and kicked away as no longer of use when one has reached the top; that certain truths may perhaps be *shown* but not *stated* through language since they belong to a realm altogether beyond that of propositional sense or logical form; and that 'the limits of my language are the limits of my world' in so far as language can state everything that is empirically the case with respect to the world as I know it and yet leave room – on this understanding – for whatever exceeds or transcends the bounds of verifiable knowledge. In which case, seemingly, the best way forward (and that taken by the later Wittgenstein) is to give up the whole idea that there exists any means of assessing or contrasting languages in point of truth, logical rigour or accuracy of representation. Rather those values will be viewed as 'internal' to this or that particular language, and therefore as exerting no legitimate claim to criticize forms or expressions of belief which fail to accord with their own culture-specific criteria. So it is – in short – that those cryptic closing passages in Wittgenstein's *Tractatus* have often been read as a kind of coded rehearsal for the pluralist theory of language-games, life-forms and meaning-as-use that emerged into full view in later texts like the *Philosophical Investigations*.

My point is that Wittgenstein's attitude to Shakespeare may well have been connected   like Johnson's more complex, appreciative, yet highly ambivalent response – with a keen sense of the anarchic potential in language when released from the constraints of a due regard for the proprieties of communal usage. Moreover, as emerges in Johnson's remarks on the problems of textual editing, this desire to place a curb on the wilder, more licentious extremes of Shakespearean wordplay can sometimes go along with a certain forcefulness in the methods used to contain it. Thus (to repeat): 'where any passage appeared inextricably perplexed, I have endeavoured to discover how it may be recalled to sense with least violence'. Indeed, the very effort to moderate that 'violence' – to bring Shakespeare's language back within the bounds of civilized intelligibility while nonetheless respecting its creative power – is such as to require a kind of self-imposed sobriety and even a willed effort of repression on the editor's part. That is, it involves a resolute check upon the twin temptations of an overly indulgent approach to Shakespearean wordplay and an overly zealous attachment to the virtues of rational or decorous restraint. Moreover, this amounts to a choice (or a precarious balancing act) between violence toward what Johnson himself regards as the chief characteristic of Shakespeare's native genius – his capacity for flights of creative invention beyond the furthest reach of classical dictate or plain-prose editorial redaction – and violence toward the norms laid down by a decent regard for just those estimable values. So it is that Johnson can write of the editor's task, in a plaintive and indeed near-tragic tone, that this calling if practised with a due sense of its many and varied requirements 'demands more than humanity possesses', so that 'he who exercises it with most praise has very frequent need of indulgence'. In which case, now rather testily, 'let us be told no more of the dull duty of an editor', even if – or just because – that duty entails a readiness to stress the prosaic virtues when confronted with

Shakespeare's more extreme passages of multiplied metaphor and other such forms of linguistic promiscuity.[17]

Thus Johnson is torn between a high and a low estimation of the editor's role: low in the sense that he had better keep his inventive faculties on a tight rein and not fall in too readily with the poet's extravagant verbal ways, but high in so far as the business of producing some acceptable conjecture, emendation or interpretive hypothesis may 'demand more than humanity possesses'. Hence the account of how his dutiful trawl through previous editions of Shakespeare encountered 'on every page Wit struggling with its own sophistry, and Learning confused by the multiplicity of its views'.[18] Nor can this comedy (or tragedy) of errors really be found so surprising, given that 'in his [i.e., the editor's or critic's] art there is no system, no principal and axiomatical truth that regulates subordinate positions'.[19] So one can see why Johnson the editor of Shakespeare – like Johnson the lexicographer – was prone to such wildly fluctuating estimates of his own role, its extreme demands in the way of self-abnegating rigour and yet (as he sometimes uneasily admits) the rewards that derive from its exercise as a kind of surrogate creativity. Just as lexicographer Johnson – the 'harmless drudge' – came up with all manner of idiosyncratic (not to say maverick or quirky) definitions, so editor Johnson found occasional room for just the kinds of inventive or 'conceited' idea that he elsewhere deplored with such vehemence whether in previous editors or (strangely enough) in Shakespeare himself. My point, to repeat, is that the appeal to 'ordinary language' – whether in Johnson's sturdily common-sense or Wittgenstein's therapeutic mode – is one that inevitably runs into trouble as soon as it encounters the creativity (i.e., the non-ordinariness) that is manifest not only in Shakespearean English but also in a good deal of what passes for everyday communicative discourse. Thus both have to register the awkward fact that language – their own language included – just will not settle down to a decent regard for the proprieties of good stylistic form or communally sanctioned usage.

In Johnson this produces a chronic oscillation between one set of values (those of eighteenth-century classical decorum and restraint) and another – those connected with pre-Civil-War 'wit', 'sophistry' or suchlike linguistic licence – which he is prone to judge harshly on ideological as well as on literary grounds, but which can nonetheless be seen to exert a constant seductive pull on his imagination. In Wittgenstein it shows up as a mixture of bafflement at Shakespeare's high reputation, suspicion of those who go along with the received view, refusal to accept that his (rather than theirs) just might be the aberrant or defective response, and yet – somehow co-existing with this – the uneasy sense that perhaps he, Wittgenstein, is failing to grasp something extraordinary and quite beyond the reach of commonplace aesthetic, literary and ethical standards of judgement. Thus 'it may be that the essential thing with Shakespeare is his ease and authority and that you just have to accept him as he is if you are going to be able to admire him properly, in the way you accept nature, a piece of scenery for example, just as it is'. In which case, he continues, 'my *failure* to understand him could then be explained by my inability to read him *easily*, as one views a splendid piece of scenery'.[20] That is to say – although Wittgenstein nowhere, to my knowledge, uses the term – Shakespeare is 'sublime' in just the sense that has come down from Longinus, through German and English Romanticism, to present-day cultural theorists and philosopher–critics.[21] In short, it connotes whatever is taken to surpass the powers of rational explanation, to transcend the utmost capacities of art as a product of cultivated skill or human contrivance, and hence to represent (very much as Wittgenstein conceives it) a force of nature that expresses itself through the answering force of creative genius. Thus, to similar effect: 'people stare at him [Shakespeare] in wonderment, almost as at a spectacular natural phenomenon. They do not have the feeling that this brings them into contact with a great *human being*. Rather with a phenomenon'.[22] Here again we can recognize something of Johnson's ambivalent feelings in this regard, mistrustful as he is of such talk – since it conjures up just the kinds of politically or religiously motivated 'enthusiasm' that had played a large role in the upheavals of recent British history – yet anxious to defend Shakespeare's claims and, *ipso facto*, those of unruly genius against the French neo-classical stress on order and decorous restraint. What unites them also is an attitude of principled respect for the wisdom and authority of 'ordinary language' coupled with a strong countervailing sense that in truth this cannot get one very far in accounting for the kinds of creativity that characterize language not only in exceptional cases like that of Shakespeare but also in its everyday communicative uses and contexts.

Wittgenstein seems to be partly acknowledging and partly fending off this (to him) problematical idea when he says that Shakespeare's similes are bad 'in the ordinary sense', but that maybe we should treat them as wholly *sui generis*, or as simply not subject to received notions of communal acceptability. 'So if they are all the same good – and I don't know whether they are or not – they must be a law in themselves. Perhaps, e.g. their ring gives them plausibility and truth.'[23] However it is not at all clear how this concession might square with the *echt*-Wittgensteinian doctrine that words or expressions are intelligible only in the context of some given language-game or cultural life-form. Of course one might argue – as exegetes often do when confronted with this sort of objection – that the language-games or life-forms in question are sufficiently plural, varied and open-ended to accommodate any amount of expressive innovation just so long as it arises from some more-or-less novel or inventive combination thereof. However this response is plainly inadequate – just a shuffling evasion of the issue – since it fails to explain as a matter of principle how any such juggling of pre-existent speech forms or idioms could possibly produce the sorts of creativity that the objector has in mind. Wittgenstein's curious remarks about Shakespeare show that he is fully aware of such problems with the notion of meaning-as-use. In fact one might suggest that he seeks to head off that challenge by adopting a special-case argument whereby Shakespeare becomes in effect the exception that proves the rule, or the writer whose genius, however suspect its nature, had best be acknowledged so as to avoid any more threatening implications. What sharpens this threat is the way that such a fall-back notion of linguistic exceptionalism is apt to lose credence – or look very much like a strategy of last resort – as soon as one considers how very *extra*ordinary are the kinds of inventiveness routinely displayed by speakers and interpreters of 'ordinary language' when they encounter some hitherto unmet-with situation or context of utterance. Wittgenstein may think to get around the problem by suggesting (or decreeing) that we think of Shakespeare as utterly *sui generis*, as a force – maybe a freak – of nature whose productions we can safely admire though only on condition that we cordon them off from those other sorts of context where language enjoys no such licence to 'go on holiday'. However this leaves him hard put to explain how we could possibly make the least sense of those passages where Shakespeare is at his most Shakespearean, where his language (to recall Johnson's complaint) appears most 'inextricably perplexed', since 'the equality of words to things is very often neglected'.

Wittgenstein never goes so far in his negative judgements but does very clearly imply that there is something about this language that puts it beyond the pale of communal intelligibility. Hence the odd passage in *Culture and Value* where he declares himself 'deeply suspicious of most of Shakespeare's admirers', and goes on to say: 'the misfortune is, I believe, that he stands by himself, at least in the culture of the west, so that one can only place him by placing him wrongly'. For this reason 'I could only stare in wonder at Shakespeare; never do anything with him'. And again, in the most deeply ambivalent and powerfully suggestive of all these remarks: 'I do not believe that Shakespeare can be set alongside any other poet. Was he perhaps a *creator of language* rather than a poet?'[24] His idea, it seems, is that any form of critical-evaluative 'placing' will have to make sense or carry conviction by the lights of some particular language-game, life-form or shared set of communal standards, in which case – quite simply – it cannot be done since Shakespeare occupies a space so remote from all such agreed-upon criteria of judgement as to render them inevitably otiose or wide of the mark. Thus, to similar effect, 'if Shakespeare is great, his greatness is displayed only in the whole "corpus" of his plays, which create their "own" language and world'.[25] And again:

> His pieces give me the impression of enormous 'sketches' rather than paintings; as though they had been 'dashed off' by someone who can permit himself 'anything', so to speak. And I can understand how someone can admire that and call it 'supreme' art, but I don't like it. – So if anyone stands in front of these pieces speechless, I can understand him; but anyone who admires them as one admires, say, Beethoven, seems to me to misunderstand Shakespeare.[26]

Here again one finds Wittgenstein playing the familiar Johnsonian card of associating Shakespeare's nonpareil 'greatness' with the stark impossibility of 'placing' him *vis-à-vis* other writers or artists, even – strange to say – a composer like Beethoven whom one might have expected to occupy a similar, that is, strictly *sui generis* niche. For Wittgenstein's point, as I take it, is that such 'admiration' is wholly misapplied to Shakespeare since his plays defy compar-isons of any kind but is perfectly in order as concerns (say) the Beethoven late quartets or piano sonatas since here the judgement can claim to be advanced on safer, more-established since communally warranted grounds.

This strikes me as a pretty dubious line of argument in both respects, that is, in so far as it under estimates the extent to which careful, intelligent and perceptive reading can define what is most distinctive about Shakespeare's language while also – by way of this ill-chosen contrast – exaggerating the extent to which Beethoven's music falls in with received or customary modes of response. However what I wish to bring out here is the way that these suppo-sedly anomalous features of Shakespearean English constitute a challenge or a sharp provocation to everything that Wittgenstein had come to think about the communally shared or warranted nature of meaning, value and belief. When he professes to have no problem with anyone who 'stands in front of these pieces speechless', but only with the herd of talkative admirers, one cannot but recall that celebrated passage at the end of the *Tractatus* in which Wittgenstein counsels, 'whereof we cannot speak, thereof we must be silent'.[27] It also brings to mind his cardinal distinction between 'saying' and 'showing', intended – so the commentators mostly opine – as a means to make sense of all those earlier propositions whose purport would otherwise be placed in question (or rendered downright nonsensical) by this Zen-like conclusion. I shall later have more to say about the long-running debate as to how we should best interpret that passage along with the others leading up to it, or – speaking bluntly – as to whether the *Tractatus* is nonsense in very large part or nonsense through and through.[28] For the moment my point is that Wittgenstein's remarks about Shakespeare might well be construed as pointing in the same direction, that is, toward a realm of the strictly ineffable where the admirers' talk would show up as nothing more than a string of pretentious and vacuous pseudo-propositions. That is to say, the absurdity of thinking to evaluate Shakespeare – to rank him somewhere on a common scale with other writers, no matter how high on that scale – would be much like the absurdity of thinking to elucidate those earlier passages of the *Tractatus* which appeared to make sense in propositional or logical terms but which then turned out (if we are to take his retrospective word for it) as having been 'nonsense' all along. Except that, of course, they were a *special* kind of nonsense designed with the longer-range therapeutic purpose of leading us through and beyond the illusion that they had ever made sense to begin with.

III

So this is one way of taking Wittgenstein's cryptic remarks about Shakespeare: that silence (or speechlessness) is the only fitting response when faced with an *oeuvre* that so completely overwhelms one's powers of articulate discriminative judgement. All the same it is hard to conceive that an interpretation along such lines was really what he had in mind, given both the negative tenor of those remarks – whatever their nuances of detail – and the plentiful evidence that Wittgenstein regarded our constant proneness to 'bewitchment by language' as a chief source of philosophical error and confusion. Thus when he says that Shakespeare's 'similes' (i.e., metaphors and other kinds of figural language) should be thought of as bad 'in the ordinary sense', it is evading the issue – or adopting a line of least resistance – if one resorts to the special-case/genius clause and assumes that Shakespeare has earned exemption since, according to Wittgenstein, those 'ordinary' standards simply do not apply in this instance. Rather, one should take the word 'ordinary' in a normative sense more akin to its usage elsewhere in his later work, namely as as applying to those language-games or modes of expression that accord with our proper, communally warranted 'forms of life' as distinct from those others – 'metaphysical' excrescences among them – that enjoy no such warrant.

At this stage it is tempting to draw comparisons with Johnson's largely pejorative usage of the term 'metaphysical' in connection with that strain of overly ingenious or 'conceited' poetry that characterized the early seventeenth century and which, to his mind, carried an ominous pre-echo of looming civil strife. If the metaphors of Donne – like those of Shakespeare – were 'far-fetched' and very often 'not worth the carriage', then this objection was raised on much the same grounds of linguistic and communal propriety as Wittgenstein's complaint about the proneness of philosophic language to spin free in metaphysical gyrations of its own perverse inventing.[29] Of course this is not to claim (absurdly) that Johnson and Wittgenstein make common cause through their adverse deployment of the term 'metaphysical', a term whose sheer variety of senses – philosophical and literary – is such as to preclude any argument along these lines. What it does bring out, suggestively at least, is their convergence on a certain idea of language and its relation to the interests of communal stability through a public sphere of shared communicative grasp. Thus it is not so far-fetched to draw the analogy with Johnson when Wittgenstein speaks of his therapeutic aim as that of 'bringing philosophy peace' by talking it down from the heights of metaphysical abstraction and leading it back to a sense of its place within the range of 'ordinary' languages and life-forms. If such peace is to be had – both thinkers believe – then it can come about only through a sensible acceptance that the 'limits of my language' are indeed 'the limits of my world', and moreover that those limits had best be defined in terms of communal warrant.

Hence Wittgenstein's quietist injunction that philosophy should 'leave everything as it is', that is to say, content itself with simply assembling reminders of the various ways that our forms of utterance can go right or wrong – possess or fail to possess such warrant – in the sundry contexts of everyday or specialized linguistic exchange. Only by adopting this scaled-down descriptivist approach, rather than indulging its chronic penchant for revisionist schemes in the old metaphysical or new analytic (i.e., Frege–Russell) mode, can philosophy achieve that wished-for state of deliverance from all its inherited woes.[30] Hence also, in Johnson, the frequent complaint that Shakespeare despite his pre-eminent genius is nonetheless gravely at fault for imposing such a well-nigh intolerable burden on editors and exegetes through his willingness to indulge all manner of ill-judged 'metaphysical' conceits. What gives the comparison added point is the fact that they both very clearly associate Shakespeare's proclivities in this regard with his likewise deplorable lack of standards when it comes to apportioning credit or blame among his *dramatis personae*, or distributing rewards and punishments in line with a due sense of moral worth. Thus Johnson's criticisms of Shakespeare on linguistic/stylistic grounds are closely bound up with his (to us) somewhat skewed or off-the-point judgements, like his finding the last act of *King Lear* – especially the death of Cordelia – so offensive in its utter lack of regard for just desert that he could scarcely bring himself to read it over again. As with the dramatist's 'conceited' style, so with his handling of plot and character: in both cases there is a gross disproportion or a failure to respect what Johnson – like most of his contemporaries – deemed morally and socially fitting. If 'trivial sentiments and vulgar ideas disappoint the attention, to which they are recommended by sonorous epithets and swelling figures' then just as frequently our sense of propriety is outraged by the grisly fate of virtuous characters and the comparative ease with which Shakespeare's villains very often seem to meet their end.[31] To Johnson's way of thinking – as likewise to Wittgenstein's – the corruption of thought not only starts out from the corruption of language but finds its most striking and symptomatic instances in certain kinds of linguistic pathology.

So one can see why Wittgenstein found it deeply puzzling that Shakespeare was so much admired by so many otherwise intelligent and thoughtful people. Most often the response to this presumed eccentricity on Wittgenstein's part has been to turn the puzzlement around and wonder what it was that got in the way of his appreciating Shakespeare to the full. He recorded no opinion about Falstaff, so far as I know. However, one may guess from the published remarks that Wittgenstein's dislike of Shakespeare had something to do with that contagious quality – 'wit', conceit, verbal exuberance, language 'going on holiday' – that has struck many critics (from Maurice Morgann to William Empson) as a source of Falstaff's dramatic appeal and his power to deflect the sorts of stern moral judgement that his character and actions would otherwise seem to invite.[32] What Empson says elsewhere about the character of Hamlet by way of defence against the critical fashion for debunking or cynical treatments would also (and perhaps more fittingly) apply in this case: that the question whether you can 'put up' with Falstaff is a question 'within hail of the more painful question whether you can put up with yourself and the race of man'.[33] His quarry here was John Dover Wilson, who had come out against this appreciative view of Falstaff as a complex character whose roguish or 'blow-the-gaff' charm went along with moments of genuine pathos, a certain impulsive generosity of spirit, and – above all – an enduring appeal to our sense of shared humanity. Thus Empson declared himself totally at odds with Dover Wilson's idea of Falstaff as merely a stock character type, a lineal descendant of the Vice figure in mediaeval morality plays whose function is to tempt young Prince Hal and who is then cast aside without the least regret when Hal becomes the Ideal King.[34] So we are deluded – in the grip of some Romantic (or Renaissance) fallacy – if we consider Falstaff in terms of a fully fledged dramatic 'character' possessing any kind of inner life or any qualities beyond those laid down by the routine requirements of the genre. Rather he is a plot-function or a bundle of vices whose role is merely to be discarded – banished from the king's presence – as divine providence runs its course. On the contrary, Empson replies:

> The idea is not simply that Falstaff is debauched and tricky, though that in itself made him give Hal experience, and hardly any price was too high to pay for getting a good ruler, but that he had the breadth of mind and of social understanding which the Magnanimous Man needs to acquire. This is very unmedieval, seems a lower-class rather than an upper-class line of thought and is, of course, militantly anti-Puritan, as we can assume the groundlings tended to be, and Falstaff can be regarded as a parody of it rather than a coarse acceptance of it by Shakespeare, but surely it is obviously present; indeed I imagine that previous critics have thought it too obvious to be worth writing down – there was no need to, till Dover Wilson began preaching at us about his Medieval Vice and Ideal King.[35]

My point in all this is that responses to Shakespeare have often divided over issues that are jointly linguistic and ethical, that is to say, which involve a valuation (positive or negative) of Shakespearean language conceived as a register of moral intuitions or judgements.

What lends special interest to Empson's defence of Falstaff against Dover Wilson's strictures is the fact that Empson, in his earlier work, was a close reader of unparalleled brilliance and acuity whose later essays turned toward aspects of authorial biography or character psychology but who approached these distinctly unfashionable topics with the same zest for detailed analysis and subtle exegesis of meanings and motives.[36] Thus the main point of Empson's pro-Falstaff case is that we get Shakespeare wrong – fail to recognize how complex are his language and dramatic psychology alike – if we take the Dover Wilson line and assume that whatever is 'there' in the play must have its source in some stock repertoire of character types or some range of inherited figures and tropes. The same issue came up in Empson's exchange with the critic Rosamund Tuve who objected on scholarly (but also, he thought, on religious–ideological) grounds to passages in his book *Seven Types of Ambiguity* which claimed to discover all manner of heterodox meanings or implications in the language of avowedly Christian poets like Donne and George Herbert.[37] Here again Empson's rejoinder took the form – as with his riposte to Dover Wilson – of asserting not only the scope for creativity in language but also the values of Renaissance humanism against what he saw as the denial of those values in the name of a critical doctrine which placed sharp limits on the reader's (as well as the poet's) freedom of intellectual conscience.[38] This is the connection – otherwise hard to perceive – between Empson's *Seven Types*, where the sheer multiplicity of meanings teased out by close verbal analysis tends to obscure any interest in matters of authorial intention or character psychology, and the later work where Empson declares himself firmly in favour of these approaches and just as firmly opposed to the orthodox New Critical veto on them.[39] What it amounts to, in short, is an outlook of sturdy common-sense rationalism as regards the virtues of logico-semantic analysis joined to a likewise high valuation of the meanings and motives that typically inspire the most complex and rewarding instances of human linguistic-communicative grasp.

Thus Empson has absolutely no patience with those 'bother-headed' theoretical critics who produce all sorts of ingenious argument for counting a poet's intentions unknowable or thinking it naive – just a remnant of quaint old Romantic-humanist beliefs – to raise questions about 'character' in fiction or drama. His defence of Falstaff is a challenge not only to certain fashionable trends in literary theory but also to what he saw as a lately resurgent 'neo Christian' ethos with palpable designs on the reader. Hence the many books and essays of his last two decades where Empson does battle with scholars, critics and editors whose 'pious' misreadings of various authors – Donne, Herbert, Marvell, Fielding, Coleridge and Joyce among others – he seeks to rebut through a shrewd combination of textual close reading with broader, cultural-historical and psycho-biographical approaches.[40] Hence also my extended detour *via* Empson in the context of discussing Wittgenstein's curious response (or lack of responsiveness) to Shakespeare. For it strikes me that one of the things Wittgenstein found so unsettling or offensive in Shakespeare was just what Empson so greatly admired in Falstaff. That is, it had to do with the powerful dramatic effect that comes of a character's combining such a range of contradictory attributes – comedy with pathos, generosity with low-mindedness, verbal exuberance (or talking for victory) with fear of the rejection that finally drives him into tragic isolation and death – and doing so, moreover, in ways that connect with our common humanity or our shared sense of how closely this touches on the human predicament at large. After all, as Empson briskly remarks in one of those offhand yet resonant passages that tend to leave academic commentators somewhat at a loss, 'the object of life ... is not to understand things, but to maintain one's defences and equilibrium and live as well as one can; it is not only maiden aunts who are placed like this'.[41]

Here it is worth noting his response to Dr Johnson's reflections on Falstaff, since what Empson likes about these – in contrast to Dover Wilson's placidly orthodox line of attack – is the typical Johnsonian capacity to see all around a complex character or situation and not let his own prejudices get too much in the way. Thus Johnson may 'officially' loathe everything that Falstaff stands for, yet still find room for a sympathetic impulse or a sense of opposing considerations which derive very largely from aspects of his own experience. The relevant passage from Empson needs quoting at length since it serves to bring out both the nexus of affinities between Falstaff, Johnson and Empson and – in sharp contrast to that – some possible reasons for Wittgenstein's dislike of Shakespeare. Thus:

[The] interior of Falstaff, rather hard to get at for most of us, is also sharply lit up by some remarks of Dr. Johnson; and one could wish that Dover Wilson, who is rightly fond of pointing out that later critics have not had the firm good sense of Johnson, had profited by his master here. It is not surprising that Johnson speaks with confidence about this sort of life, because he had observed it; he could say without absurdity that he regretted not having met Falstaff. Also he himself was a man of startling appearance; a pugnaciously and robustly amusing talker, who regularly conquered but never won anything that mattered, a hero of taverns, fretted by remorse (which Falstaff makes great play with if nothing more), starved of love, unwilling to be alone. He has several comments such as that 'a man feels in himself the pain of deformity'; 'however, like this merry knight, he may make a sport of it among those whom it is his interest to please'. If we compare this with the struggle of Dover Wilson to prove that Falstaff was a Medieval Vice, with no interior at all, surely the truth of Johnson stands out like a rock.[42]

What stands out here in a similarly rock-like way is a basic assumption in all Empson's work, and one that he found all too seldom displayed by the 'Eng-Lit' professionals who had managed – through doctrines like W.K. Wimsatt's 'Intentional Fallacy' – to cut literature off from the sources of shared human understanding and turn it into a specialized preserve to which they alone could claim access.[43] Briefly put, it is the continuity principle which holds that literary language has much in common with the language of everyday communicative utterance, even if raised to a higher expressive power and therefore responding more readily to the kind of close-focused verbal analysis deployed to such remarkable effect in *Seven Types of Ambiguity*. Along with this goes the equally unfashionable claim that what literature does best – and what criticism should do also if it is to be of any use – is put us in touch with modes of experience that likewise appeal to a wider sense of collective human involvement, even if presented through more extreme (since imaginatively more compelling) situations or predicaments.

Such was already Empson's firmly held belief in *Seven Types*, as shown by the following paragraph where he moves straight across, without any too sharp or painful sense of incongruity, from a passage of hard-pressed logico-semantic exegesis to a register of broadly sympathetic concern with the conflicts and antinomies of human existence. Thus 'when a contradiction is stated with an air of conviction', he writes,

[i]t may be meant to be resolved in either of two ways, corresponding to thought and feeling, corresponding to knowing and not knowing one's way about the matter in hand. Grammatical machinery may be assumed which would make the contradiction into two statements; thus 'p and $-p$' may mean: 'If $a=a_1$, then p; if $a=a_2$, then $-p$'. If a_1 and a_2 are very different from one another, so that the two statements are fitted together with

ingenuity, then I should put the statement into an earlier type; if a_1 and a_2 are very like one another, so that the contradiction expresses both the need for and the difficulty of separating them, then I should regard the statement as an ambiguity of the seventh type corresponding to thought and knowing one's way about the matter in hand. But such contradictions are often used, as it were, by analogy from this, when the speaker does not know what a_1 and a_2 are; he satisfies two opposite impulses and, as a sort of apology, admits that they contradict, but claims that they are like the soluble contradictions, and can safely be indulged ... One might think that contradictions of this second sort must always be foolish, and even if they say anything to one who understands them can quite as justifiably say the opposite to one who does not. But, indeed, human life is so much a matter of juggling with contradictory impulses (Christian-worldly, sociable-independent, and suchlike) that one is accustomed to thinking people are probably sensible if they follow first one, then the other, of two such courses; any inconsistency that it seems possible to act upon shows that they are in possession of the right number of principles, and have a fair claim to humanity.[44]

This may remind us of Empson's remarks about Johnson in the essay on Falstaff, and the way he treats Johnson's conflicting responses – torn between a strong sense of revulsion at Falstaff's gross moral faults and a barely repressed sense of sympathetic fellow-feeling – as evidence likewise that he (Johnson) is 'in possession of the right number of principles', and therefore has 'a fair claim to humanity'. What also comes across very clearly is Empson's commitment to the continuity principle in its various forms. These include the belief that literary language (even at its most complex or sharply paradoxical) is continuous with so-called 'ordinary' language; that the deepest-laid conflicts of human existence are continuous with some of our more commonplace social problems, and that the sorts of logico-semantic analysis brought to bear by philosophers like Russell – an obvious influence here – have a genuine bearing on the sorts of dilemma, and their real or imaginary means of resolution, that often arise in the course of our everyday lives.[45]

Above it brings out the close relationship in Empson's thought between a willingness to acknowledge the full extent of human linguistic creativity and a willingness, like Johnson's, to make large allowance for modes of conduct or expression that require a good deal of sympathetic working out if they are to seem in the least degree 'sensible' or open to rational interpretation. This is why Empson is so keen to commit every one of the 'fallacies' held up for condemnation by orthodox exponents of the New Criticism such as Wimsatt, namely the appeals to authorial intention, to biography, to historical or cultural context, and – above all – to prose paraphrase as a means of unpacking the complexities of poetic language.[46] In each case what he is out to defend is that same continuity principle which refuses to treat poetry as a realm apart, that is, a realm of self-enclosed and self-validating 'paradox', 'irony' or even 'ambiguity' if the latter is conceived – in a manner quite contrary to Empson's practice – as requiring that a *cordon sanitaire* be drawn around that sacrosanct poetic domain.[47] My point, to repeat, is that this goes along with his sturdy belief in the capacities of human reason and in the need for those capacities to be carried across into the reading of poetry, even – or especially – where the poetry puts up maximal resistance to such treatment. Such is Empson's chief justification for the kinds of intricate verbal analysis pursued in his early work: that even if 'the object of life ... is not to understand things, but to maintain one's defences and equilibrium and live as well as one can', still it is useful to have the added confidence that comes of trying to get some rational grip on the various highly complex but not (or not always) irrational processes involved.

It is here also that we might get a grip on what makes the difference between Empson's (in every sense) appreciative readings of Shakespeare and Wittgenstein's resistance to just those aspects of Shakespearean language and dramatic ethos to which Empson responds with such subtlety, sympathy and sheer critical gusto. For Wittgenstein clearly belongs with those dissident readers – Tolstoy among them – who have professed to find Shakespeare (and Shakespeare's admirers) woefully lacking in moral seriousness.[48] As we have seen, Dr Johnson shared these misgivings up to a point, entering some well-known solemn caveats with regard to Shakespeare's deplorable weakness for wordplay and connecting this with his frequent failure to allocate blame and credit where due among his various *dramatis personae*. All the same, he can be found firing up in Shakespeare's defence against the narrowly prescriptive dogmas (of *genre*, morality and verbal decorum) that typified the thinking of French neo-classicist detractors such as Voltaire. Shakespeare then becomes the wild, untutored genius – the literary child of nature as opposed to the prisoner of stale academic convention – whose claim to pre-eminence was a major stake in subsequent Anglo-French culture wars. Yet the feeling remained, even among some of Shakespeare's strongest advocates, that at some point one needed to hold a line – a principled moral line – against the sorts of 'bewitchment by language' that might otherwise adversely affect our powers of discriminate judgement.

F.R. Leavis, for one, took Shakespeare as the paradigm of that special 'creative-exploratory' use of language that characterized English poetry at its best and whose virtue was precisely to show up the limits of other, more abstract or conventional modes.[49] This connected with Leavis's famous refusal – starting out from his rejoinder to René Wellek and sustained after that with increasing polemical force – to back up his various literary judgements with anything in the nature of a worked-out 'theory' or 'philosophy'.[50] Such demands merely showed that the critics concerned were in the grip of a deadening rationalist prejudice that closed their minds to all the vital qualities (of 'intelligence', 'maturity', a 'reverent openness before life') which Shakespeare most strikingly embodied, along with those select few poets and novelists who had approached the same level of creative-exploratory depth or imaginative power. Yet in Leavis, as in Dr Johnson, there is often a sense that moral judgements are pulling sharply against this idea of language – Shakespearean language – as somehow providing its own criteria of human-evaluative worth. Nowhere is this more apparent than his essay on 'Othello' where Leavis goes some tortuous ways around in explaining why we should not be taken in (along with naive and sentimentalizing critics like A.C. Bradley) by Othello's strain of 'noble' rhetoric, his worked-up pathos, grandiloquent gestures, tragic self-image and so forth. For there is a sense in which Leavis's Iago-like debunking of Othello – along with his attack on Bradley – can be seen as involving a complex psychological pattern of transference where nothing serves as an evaluative norm except that appeal to an *authentic* Shakespearean ('creative-exploratory') use of language against which Othello's rhetoric is somehow to be judged. Moreover it is far from clear that the appeal can sustain anything like this crucial load-bearing role. That is, Leavis offers no adequate (non-circular) terms for distinguishing between, on the one hand, the way that Othello achieves his spurious 'rhetorical' effects and, on the other, the way that Shakespeare's language supposedly works to induce strong currents of audience- or reader-identification with characters who merit such treatment. At very least there is a problem in maintaining this high-toned moral argument in the case of a poet–dramatist who famously distributed a lot of fine poetry to 'bad' characters and, if less often, managed to pull off the same odd trick in reverse.

IV

It seems to me that we are now within reach of explaining some deeper-laid aspects of Wittgenstein's aversion to Shakespeare, or – by way of these contrasts and comparisons with Dr Johnson, Empson and Leavis – giving some account of the jointly philosophical and temperamental mindset that lay behind that negative verdict. Most often the response among admirers of Shakespeare and Wittgenstein alike has been to cast around for some plausible means for accounting for his curiously off-the-point remarks. One fairly obvious factor – though not, I think, one that comes anywhere close to an adequate explanation – is Wittgenstein's having approached the plays as a non-native English speaker whose less than full command of the language, especially when faced with such extreme metaphorical and other stylistic complexities, may well have increased his sense of their alien and somehow disturbing nature. However, as I say, this does not get us very far, especially when one considers the extent to which Shakespeare had been taken up into the mainstream of German cultural tradition, and indeed the claim (maybe apocryphal) among some German scholars that his genius was better served by the classic Schlegel/Tieck translations than by the plays' original language.[51] More to the point is that combination of likely or possible factors that I have tried to bring out in this chapter so far. They include what Wittgenstein seems to have regarded as Shakespeare's verbal self-indulgence or weakness for extravagant flights of metaphor; his lack of a firm moral compass and failure (as Tolstoy likewise complained) to observe the most basic requirements of dramatic justice; and, as emerges most clearly from the contrast with Empson, the requirement on those who wish to understand (rather than just vaguely 'appreciate') Shakespeare's poetry to approach it with a willingness to stretch their mind around some large challenges to their powers of analytic or conceptual grasp.

It is here – I suggest – that we might see the relevance of Wittgenstein's mid-career break with the aims and priorities of Russellian logico-semantic analysis, along with the turn toward a pluralist conception of 'language-games' and cultural 'forms of life' which led him to regard any such logicist (or rationalist) approach as one of those chronic philosophical illusions that required therapeutic treatment. For if one thing emerges from the lengthy passage of Empson quoted above it is the role of logical analysis in any attempt to make adequate sense of the best, most rewardingly complex kinds of poetry, even if this process must be thought to go on at a level of unconscious (or preconscious) response that would rarely, if ever, be present to mind in even the most perceptive and intelligent act of reading. Empson himself makes no such claim, preferring to suggest that analysis of this sort belongs to a more specialized activity – that of reflective or theoretically inclined literary criticism – but that the process can, all the same, make a genuine and lasting contribution to our sensibility. Above all, it gives readers some assurance that there is nothing about their 'appreciation' of poetry, that is, their immediate, intuitive or deeply felt modes of response that necessarily lies beyond reach of explanation in more analytical terms. Thus, 'things temporarily or permanently inexplicable are not to be thought of as essentially different from things that can be explained in some terms that you happen to have at your disposal; nor can you have any reason to think them likely to be different unless there is a great deal about the inexplicable things that you already know'.[52] And again: 'it often happens that, for historical reasons or what not, one can no longer appreciate a thing directly by poetical knowledge, and yet can rediscover it in a more controlled form by prosaic knowledge'.[53] And there is always room for such rational assurance insofar as it provides a good working basis for getting on terms with modes of experience (whether in poetry or in life) that might otherwise seem beyond hope of better understanding.

It is fair to say, on all the evidence, that Wittgenstein took a very different view of these matters. More specifically, he differed with a thinker like Empson – as with his own erstwhile mentor Russell – over just this question regarding the role of analysis or the scope and limits of logical thought when applied to our everyday language-games, practices or cultural forms of life. Thus Wittgenstein came to reject the whole idea of language as a more or less perspicuous means of representing or 'picturing' reality, of propositions as standing in a one-to-one relationship with real-world factual states of affairs, and of logic as defining the very conditions of linguistic or conceptual intelligibility. Rather, he believed, we should learn to accept that there exist as many different ways of making sense as there exist communal norms, contexts or traditions whereby to interpret some given utterance. In which case the notion of language as aspiring to an ideal crystalline purity and of philosophy as the discipline best equipped to attain it was a chimera that Wittgenstein had once embraced – chiefly under

Russell's influence – but could now set aside as just another false picture that had held philosophers captive.

Of course there are various conflicting accounts of just how and where – at what precise point in composing the *Tractatus* – this realization first struck and persuaded him to write those famously cryptic closing passages. Their gist, to repeat, is that readers who have discerned the true (as distinct from the vulgar or exoteric) import of his book will thereby have learned to treat the entire sequence of foregoing statements as so much strictly nonsensical matter that serves to introduce a radically different perspective, one from which the logicist and verificationist projects can be seen to self-deconstruct. Interpretations have ranged from Russell's view of the *Tractatus* as a basically logical-positivist (or logical-atomist) text tricked out with some quasi-mystical passages that are best tactfully ignored to subsequent accounts which emphasized the 'saying'/'showing' distinction and its significance for those matters of ultimate human concern (ethics chief among them) which lay beyond the realm of factual or logical accountability. Most recently there has emerged a new school of thought – self-characterized as 'austere' or 'resolute' – according to which we should take Wittgenstein very much at his word and construe the greater part of the *Tractatus* as nonsense all the way down, so to speak, or as finally resisting any attempt to render at least some few of those statements meaningful or valid on their own terms. To this way of thinking we simply 'chicken out' or shy away from Wittgenstein's deepest though most problematical and heterodox insights if we adopt some alternative line of less resistance.[34]

I shall return to this curious debate later on and not pursue it here save to remark – with my central topic in mind – that it brings out the strain of asceticism or self-renunciation that runs so strongly through Wittgenstein's thought, and which also leaves its imprint on his more devoted exegetes. Hence the quasi-monastic rhetoric of 'austerity' and the idea of a 'resolute' facing-up to what is seen, by these latest commentators, as a challenge that sorts the sheep from the goats – or, more aptly, the lions from the sheep – amongst interpreters of the *Tractatus*. Renunciation is a theme that resounds in so many of Wittgenstein's aphorisms, images, metaphors, recollections and passages of self-analysis, not to mention the episodes and character traits recollected by friends, students and biographers, that one might ask whether this perhaps had something to do with his attitude of stern disapproval toward Shakespeare. What makes the conjecture more plausible is the fact that it ties in suggestively with the various other contrasts and comparisons that I have offered up to now. Perhaps most significant in this regard is the Tolstoy connection, since Wittgenstein himself acknowledged the depth of that influence and indeed – as biographers have often noted – kept a copy of Tolstoy's book *The Gospel in Brief* with him throughout his months in the trenches during the First World War.[35] It is not, I think, stretching the evidence too far to suggest that the Christian-ascetic imperative or the ethos of self-denial that Tolstoy preached in his final years – the renunciation of his wealth, social status and all such worldly goods – played a role in Wittgenstein's kindred desire to have done with whatever might obstruct or deflect his quest for self-knowledge or salvation. Nor can it be counted merely a coincidence that he came to share something of Tolstoy's hostile attitude toward Shakespeare, based as that attitude was – in both instances – on a sense that Shakespeare's exuberant inventiveness went along with a cavalier lack of respect for generic or structural constraints and, worse still, a blatant disregard for the requirements of moral justice.

In Tolstoy's case the conversion experience also meant renouncing what he now deemed the elitist satisfactions of literary authorship for the sake of a closer, more authentic bond with the Russian peasantry in whom he located the sole hope for spiritual regeneration.[56] Wittgenstein's seems to have involved – among other things – a similar desire for the good of the soul rather than perfection of the intellect and a giving up of the Russellian idea that logical clarity might be more important than the sources of wisdom enshrined in ordinary language or everyday practices. For both, this turn toward widely shared as opposed to expert or specialized ways of thought can be seen to have gone along with a deep mistrust of any language – like Shakespeare's – that required a stretch of interpretative grasp beyond what might plausibly be taken to fall within the scope of such communal sense-making norms. And for both it entailed an effort of willed renunciation or a sternly self-denying ordinance which led them to single out Shakespeare as the poet whose particular kind of genius – his ability to conjure so powerful an effect while flouting such a range of received linguistic, generic and moral codes – was at once the main source of his seductive appeal and the chief reason for resisting it. Here it is worth recalling George Orwell's essay 'Lear, Tolstoy and the Fool', where he speculates that one possible motive for Tolstoy's antipathy to Shakespeare and, more specifically, his choice of *King Lear* as a prime exhibit was Tolstoy's awareness that he, like Lear, had renounced everything and perhaps – galling to reflect – gained nothing in return.[57] More than that: Tolstoy's motives for this far from self-effacing, indeed highly public gesture of renunciation might well be interpreted, again like Lear's, as the product of an overweening desire for displays of love and devotion on the part of his admirers rather than a genuine will to have done with all such worldly attachments.

There is ample evidence in Wittgenstein's writings, not to mention various details of his life recorded by friends and colleagues, that he shared Tolstoy's need to project a self-image of extreme, almost saintly asceticism.[58] Moreover, this desire often took the form of devaluing his own work – or dismissing his achievements to date – as merely a distraction from other, more significant (and, for that reason, philosophically intractable) concerns. It is also very striking that the great majority of exegetes and biographers have tended to endorse that self-image and to base their understanding of the work as well as the life on a quasi-secularized variant of the spiritual conversion narrative that has its prototype in Augustine's *Confessions*, also one of Wittgenstein's most cherished books. What they are not so willing to contemplate is the idea that this might be open to a reading more like Orwell's diagnosis of the Tolstoy case, that is to say, a more robustly critical approach that would raise the sorts of question about

Wittgenstein's motives and psychological promptings that are usually (and tactfully) elided by the orthodox commentators. Of course there is the probable objection – often well-founded – that any such psycho-biographical approach to distinctively philosophical issues must be seen as a gross confusion of realms and a failure to respect the most basic standards of intellectual propriety. However the charge does not have so much force when applied in this context since Wittgenstein himself made a cardinal point of rejecting what he saw as the false distinction between life and work, and insisting that philosophy could be no more than a trivial offering of pseudo-solutions to pseudo-problems if divorced from matters of real-life practical, moral and spiritual concern.

This point has been so much emphasized by Wittgenstein's commentators that it leaves them little room for objecting to other, more heterodox readings of the life–work relationship. Thus on the one hand biographers such as Ray Monk tend to construct their narratives around an image of Wittgenstein as one who lived his philosophical doubts, perplexities and crises to the point where life and work became strictly inseparable.[59] On the other there has arisen a school of exegesis – as characterized briefly above – which interprets Wittgenstein's philosophical visions and revisions as stages in an intellectual odyssey devoted to uncovering the various sources of human, all-too-human self-deception or metaphysical 'bewitchment by language'. In Monk's way of telling it the life acquires even greater iconic or exemplary force through the contrast with Russell to whom he devoted another biographical study and who tends to come off, in comparison, as a clever but philosophically shallow and (by the same token) morally dubious or downright disreputable character.[60] Thus Russell is presented as a kind of anti-Wittgenstein, not only on account of his finding fault with Wittgenstein's later views but also insofar as he (Russell) is taken to embody the kind of ultra-specialized philosophical thinking that loses itself in arid technicalities at the expense of authentically human ethical concern. This idea is reinforced by the exegetes, especially those of a 'austere' or 'resolute' mind, who likewise equate the intellectual rigour and philosophical cogency of Wittgenstein's thinking with his strength of moral character as evidenced by that same ascetic or renunciatory drive.[61]

Hence the odd notion – odd from any but an *echt*-Wittgensteinian viewpoint – that philosophical wisdom should be taken to consist in a stern repudiation of whatever might encourage the tendency of language or speculative thought to find a certain pleasure, solace or creative stimulus in modes of expression that depart from the norms of received or communal usage. Hence also, I would suggest, the striking kinship between Wittgenstein's failure to recognize in his own work the very sickness that it claimed to diagnose yet to which, ironically, it bore symptomatic witness, and Tolstoy's frustrated quest for spiritual redemption by renouncing worldly fame along with the seductive enticements of literature. What gives this comparison added force is the constant awareness, in Wittgenstein's later writing, that most probably the cure would not work, that the same old problems would continue to arise, and – most painfully of all – that his own contributions, if at last they found a receptive readership, were likelier than not to generate yet more futile controversy. Nor can it be said that these fears were misplaced, given the full-scale academic industry that has developed around topics from late Wittgenstein, among them the endlessly proliferating debates about 'private language' and 'following a rule'.[62] After all, his own puzzled and puzzling remarks on these topics are themselves scarcely evidence of Wittgenstein's success in laying to rest the various ills to which philosophy had fallen prey. Rather, when he and his followers insist on the integral character of life and work – or on the artificial nature of those problems that result from allowing philosophy to lose touch with contexts of everyday human experience – one is tempted to turn this argument around and remark on the extent to which Wittgenstein's philosophical perplexities seem to have had their source in his failure to resolve certain issues (not least that of 'other minds') that impinged on his personal life. It is hard to read very far into Monk's biography without gaining the distinct impression that Wittgenstein *ipse* was constantly assailed by just the kinds of deep-laid fear, anxiety and sceptical doubt that his writings purported to remedy.

This is why I have suggested that Orwell's remarks about Tolstoy are just as relevant in Wittgenstein's case. That is, he may likewise have been periodically subject to that especially sharp and complex form of *ressentiment* that comes of a thwarted asceticism, or the knowledge that one's most strenuous efforts of renunciation have failed in their purpose and indeed turned out to have had just the opposite of their proper or intended effect. At least this would go some way toward explaining Wittgenstein's curiously mixed response to Shakespeare, on the one hand his downright distaste for the poet's undisciplined language – for the proneness to become, as Winston Churchill remarked of a fellow politician, 'intoxicated by the exuberance of his own verbosity' – and on the other his acknowledgement of Shakespeare's genius as strictly *sui generis*, like a force of nature, not to be judged by commonplace standards of linguistic or dramatic decorum. At the same time it might help to account for Wittgenstein's equally ambivalent sense that Shakespeare's (to his mind) gross derelictions of moral propriety – his seeming indifference to just desert and willingness to inflict the most hideous torments on innocent or virtuous characters – must somehow be regarded as beyond the reach of commonplace ethical criteria. One result of recent Wittgenstein scholarship has been to bring out the extent of his reading in, or at any rate his acquaintance with, those developments in post-Kantian German thought (especially Schopenhauer) which viewed philosophy as aspiring to the condition of literature or art, and which thus raised the notion of creative genius to a high point of philosophical doctrine.[63] Yet these commentaries have also drawn attention to the countervailing impulse in his thought – very much a matter of personal and intellectual temperament – that rejected any such claim on his own behalf and treated it with clear mistrust when applied to philosophy in general. So there is something both singularly apt and pointedly ironic about the subtitle of Monk's biography, 'The Duty of Genius'. What it catches is the sharp conflict of values, both in Wittgenstein's work and its reception-history, between a sense of his having something so important and original to say – at least as regards the scope and limits of philosophy – that the term 'genius' would not be misapplied and a sense that, after all, the main purpose of that work is to cure philosophers of entertaining such absurdly grandiose delusions. It is this constant veering about between high and low valuations of philosophy – and of his own contribution to it – that can be traced throughout Wittgenstein's writings, early and late, and through the various attempts by his exegetes to explain how that work can be both a means of deliverance from all such delusions and yet (for the very same reason) a philosophical achievement of the highest, most impressive and unprecedented order.

V

These contradictions emerge at full blast in the unusually self-revealing remarks assembled in the volume *Culture and Value* where Wittgenstein is clearly not writing for publication – if indeed he ever did – and where he comes closest to broaching the kinds of issue raised by these recent commentators. Thus, for instance, 'one's style of writing may be unoriginal in form – like mine – and yet one's words may be well chosen; or, on the other hand, one may have a style that's original in *form*, one that is freshly grown from deep inside oneself'.[64] What comes through here is Wittgenstein's lingering attachment to a notion of genius with its main source in Goethe's organicist thinking and the tradition of German Romanticism, along with his sense – partly but not entirely regretful – of somehow falling short in just that regard. Another passage is even more revealing insofar as it shows Wittgenstein connecting his awareness (whether justified or not) of this falling-short with his idea of Jewish artists and thinkers – himself included – as belonging to the second rank of merely 'talented' rather than first-rate creative or original minds. 'Amongst Jews', he writes,

'[g]enius' is found only in the holy man. Even the greatest of Jewish thinkers is no more than talented. (Myself for instance.) ... I think there is some truth in my idea that I really only think reproductively. I don't believe I have ever *invented* a line of thinking. I have always taken one over from someone else. I have simply straightaway seized on it with enthusiasm for my work of clarification. That is how Bolzmann, Hertz, Schopenhauer, Frege, Russell, Kraus, Loos, Weininger, Spengler, Sraffa have influenced me ... What I *invent* are new similes.[65]

This passage would bear a good deal of commentary, not least with respect to the extraordinary mixture of diverse sources and the presence among them of a thinker like Otto Weininger who seems to have exerted a powerful influence on Wittgenstein's ambivalent, not to say conflictual or even self-excoriating attitude toward his own Jewishness. Indeed, the idea of a distinction between 'genius' and 'talent' that runs along racial (more specifically: along Aryan versus Jewish) lines is one that goes back, *via* Weininger to Schopenhauer and which

had its main source in the tradition of German Romantic or counter-Enlight-
enment thought.[66] Thus it tended most often to work out as a set of closely
related binary oppositions between, on the one hand, values such as spontaneity,
originality, intuitive insight or the rule-breaking prerogative of natural genius
and, on the other, prosaic virtues such as reason, logic, common-sense wisdom
and the well-regulated conduct of thought through a language that avoids any
kind of metaphoric or rhetorical excess. Along with this went the notion that
genius was very much a matter of *genius loci*, of rootedness in the soil of an
authentic native culture, whereas talent and those various lesser attributes were
typically at home amongst more cosmopolitan or deracinated thinkers and
artists.

As scarcely needs saying, such ideas later gave rise to some of the most vicious
and barbaric racist ideologies, including the strain of Austro-German anti-
semitism that was gathering force as Wittgenstein penned these thoughts. So it
is highly revealing of the conflicts and tensions present in his thinking at the
time when he writes, in *Culture and Value*, that 'I believe my originality (if that
is the right word) is an originality belonging to the soil rather than to the seed',
and that perhaps – by way of explaining his talent (rather than genius) for
philosophy – 'I have no seed of my own'.[67] I shall not here enter into the debate
surrounding Wittgenstein's guilt-ridden attitude toward his own sexuality and
its relation to his likewise tortured sense of Jewishness as a marker of alien
cultural and intellectual character.[68] All the same it is worth noting the curious
distinction that Wittgenstein draws between 'soil' and 'seed', evoking as it does
the same organicist rhetoric of growth and development, yet devaluing just that
aspect of it – the notion of genius as nourished by the 'soil' of a rich native
tradition – which figured most prominently in the discourse of those (like
Heidegger) who took it wholeheartedly on board.[69] What the seed metaphor
brings to mind is a kindred though crucially different discourse, that is to say,
the Goethe-influenced idea of human self-knowledge and self-discovery as in
certain respects analogous to forms and processes of natural growth. It is clear
enough from passages elsewhere in his writing that this Goethean strain of the
organicist idea – one consonant with liberal values of *Bildung*, autonomy and
personal development – was far closer to what Wittgenstein had in mind than
any Heideggerian notion of the highest good as consisting in the subjugation of
individual will to the summons of epochal (or national) destiny. Yet it is also
clear that the two sorts of metaphor cannot be so sharply distinguished as to
bring him out in firm opposition to the kind of thinking that had managed to
exploit that strain of national aestheticism and which took its most virulent
form in a doctrine of cultural-linguistic (and ultimately racial) supremacy.

Hence the ambivalence in Wittgenstein's language when it comes to this
complex of issues around genius *vis-à-vis* mere 'talent' and the question –
ideologically charged at the best of times – of just how genius might relate to
the inherited values or characteristics of some given national culture. Now it
might seem perverse to connect all this with Wittgenstein's unresponsiveness to
Shakespeare, or perhaps – as I have suggested – his acute responsiveness to

certain aspects of the plays and their iconic standing which struck a discordant note. However the connection may appear less strained if one considers both the extent of German cultural investment in Shakespeare's reception-history and its entwinement with notions of national character or identity to which Wittgenstein stood at an oblique, even painfully skewed or dislocating angle. At any rate there were clearly large issues involved in his grudging yet somehow compelled acceptance of Shakespeare's genius – whatever his objections to it on linguistic, moral and aesthetic grounds – and the idea that his own merely 'talented' work fell short of any such achievement. Perhaps the most revealing passages are those where Wittgenstein takes Mendelssohn as an example of the fact that Jewish artists may exhibit great gifts of ingenuity, inventiveness, superficial brilliance, technical command or other such cultivated gifts but manifestly lack the depth of character to produce works of genius. Thus Mendelssohn stands – along with Wittgenstein – as a figure emblematic of the merely 'reproductive' talent, rather than the truly 'productive' artist or thinker whose work transcends all received or conventional standards of evaluative judgement. If Mendelssohn is 'the most untragic of composers' and 'wrote no music that is hard to understand', then these defects must be put down – so Wittgenstein thinks – to his lacking the artistic mastery and strength of moral as well as creative will that can only be achieved through communion with 'man's primitive drives'.[70]

It is hard not to hear echoes of Wagner's infamous reflections on the topic of 'Judaism in Music', together with his viciously pointed portrayal of Beckmesser, in *Die Meistersinger*, as the embodiment of just those un-German strains of rootless cosmopolitan 'talent' which later became the very stuff of Nazi cultural propaganda.[71] Beyond that, Wittgenstein's language here picks up on a strain of anti-intellectual rhetoric that has its proximate source in Nietzsche's reworking of Schopenhauerian themes and its upshot in various latter-day creeds of a deeply reactionary, often racist cast. What makes the musical connection *via* Mendelssohn yet more telling – especially when set against the complex of attitudes that Wittgenstein displays toward Shakespeare – is the fact that analogies between music and philosophy (or his own way of doing philosophy) occur quite often in Wittgenstein's writing and are clearly intended to bear some weight of significance. Moreover, they touch upon just that nexus of themes – genius, talent, literary style, metaphor, 'composition' as what he laboured to perfect yet found sadly wanting in his own work – which we have seen to constitute a central preoccupation, early and late. For instance, he typically draws the comparison between grasping a sentence (or proposition) as something more than just the sum of its constituent lexical or grammatical parts and understanding a musical theme (or motif) as something more than just hearing one note after another. Thus: 'we speak of understanding a sentence in the sense in which it can be replaced by another which says the same; but also in the sense in which it cannot be replaced by any other. (Any more than one musical theme can be replaced by another.) In the one case the thought in the sentence is common to different sentences; in the other, something that is expressed only by these words in these positions.'[72] That is to say, if we want to get a feel for how language actually communicates – rather than how it can be decomposed through a false (e.g., Russellian or early-Wittgenstein) logical-atomist approach – than we might do best to think of it by analogy with musical phrasing, melodic contour, harmonic progression and so forth. For we shall then not so easily be tempted to suppose that understanding begins and ends with the capacity to analyse language into its various component parts and then reassemble or reconstitute those parts into meaningful chunks of discourse. Just as the 'sense' of a musical theme transcends or eludes any such process of analysis, so likewise the sense of this or that term in a meaningful proposition must be thought of as irreducibly context-dependent. And just as the significance of any such theme cannot be grasped except by way of its role within some larger pattern of harmonic, rhythmic, tonal or structural development so likewise propositions make sense – and acquire whatever truth-value they possess – only through their counting as meaningful within some shared language-game or cultural 'form of life'.

It is here that Wittgenstein most notably parts company with Frege, Russell and other thinkers for whom the context principle extended only so far as the isolated sentence, statement or proposition since to take it further or adopt a more radical version of meaning-holism would involve giving up any claim to clarify (or rectify) the logical structure of language. Such, after all, was Quine's decisive move in his 1957 essay 'Two Dogmas of Empiricism' which claimed to deconstruct the very foundations of mainstream analytic philosophy as practised up to then, and which is generally taken – along with the discovery of Wittgenstein's later work – to have signalled the end of that project in its confidently orthodox form.[73] And from the context principle thus conceived it is no great distance to all those problematical issues – of truth, meaning, reference, intentionality, rule following, private language and so forth – that have generated such a mass of secondary literature despite Wittgenstein's therapeutic aim to 'give philosophy peace' by putting an end to such futile debate. It seems to me that his remarks about Shakespeare are highly relevant in this regard, and likewise his various musical analogies and metaphors, although not in quite the way that Wittgenstein intended. What they bring out most clearly is the tension that exists between his idea of philosophy as a discourse that 'works' by allaying its own sceptical doubts and metaphysical quandaries – that is, by recalling philosophers to the good sense embodied in ordinary language – and the way that Wittgenstein's writing itself gives rise to yet more extreme and hyperbolic versions of them. This in turn has to do with the odd combination in his work of a deep mistrust of those confusions that result when language 'goes on holiday' – when it becomes embroiled in metaphorical excesses, wayward figurations or idiosyncrasies of style – with a marked proneness to just such forms of linguistic self-indulgence. For it is the sheer inventiveness of Wittgenstein's thought and his singular talent (not to say genius) for hitting on apt similes and metaphors in order to make his point that have often succeeded, against his better wisdom, in setting off debates like those around the private-language issue and the rule-following 'paradox'.

Thus the upshot of all his endeavours, so far from giving philosophy peace, has been to provoke new, more ingenious and worrisome kinds of philosophical perplexity. And this irony is further sharpened by the fact that the only Wittgenstein-approved 'solution' is a recourse to the communitarian idea that 'agreement in judgement' amongst some group of like-minded and duly accredited subjects is the furthest one can get toward answerable standards of truth, knowledge or correctness. Hence what Kripke construes as Wittgenstein's 'sceptical solution' to his own 'sceptical paradox', namely the proposal that we give up searching for grounds of objective, verification-transcendent or non practice-relative truth and acknowledge – as finally we must – that communal warrant is all we have and is enough for all practical (including all legitimate philosophic) purposes.[74] Yet even Kripke is apt, on occasion, to express himself dissatisfied with Wittgenstein's answer and bewildered, even affronted by the 'incredible', 'bizarre' and downright 'absurd' character of the sceptical problem that gave rise to it. So likewise with many participants in the academic mini-industry that has grown up around the topic of rule following, torn as they often are between a sense that this whole debate is wildly off the track and a sense that there must be something very special about the 'Kripkensteinian' dilemma that requires a response *on its own sceptical terms*, rather than a straight solution along alternative (realist) lines.[75] Indeed, as I have argued elsewhere, Kripke's most remarkable achievement is having managed so successfully to swing this debate that the 'sceptical solution' – or a more or less qualified version of it – has come to be accepted as the default position while any such alternative is often regarded as missing the point in some naive or patently question-begging way.[76]

This skewing of the issue has much to do with Wittgenstein's extraordinary (not to say perverse) gift for introducing all kinds of highly infectious sceptical doubt under cover of a claim to do just the opposite, that is, to 'let the fly out of the fly-bottle' or cure philosophy of its various misconceived problems and dilemmas. Moreover, this gift is in turn very closely related to some of the most distinctive aspects of Wittgenstein's literary style, among them aspects which invite comparison with Shakespeare but also – in a sense more difficult to define – with the kinds of music that seem to have exerted the most powerful (whether positive or negative) effect on his aesthetic sensibility. Here we should recall his famous cryptic pronouncement in the *Tractatus* that 'ethics and aesthetics are one and the same' in so far as they both involve the appeal to a dimension of meaning or significance that can best be termed 'transcendental'. That is, they are both concerned with an order of insight that takes us beyond the realm of the sayable (whatever can be adequately expressed in the form of factual statements or logical propositions) to a realm of truths that can only be shown or manifested through some altogether different, oblique or perhaps metaphorical mode of presentation. So it is by no means detracting from the depth or significance of Wittgenstein's thought to put the case that some of the most significant passages in his work depend crucially on certain characteristic turns of language or style. On the other hand this was clearly not something that Wittgenstein found it altogether easy to accept, given his suspicion of the harm that language is always liable to do when released from the constraints of 'public', that is, communally sanctioned intelligibility. So there is a constant two-way tug – in Wittgenstein as in his commentators – between the wish to respect those ordinary-language constraints and the sense that if philosophy is to offer a fresh perspective on well-worn problems or to find a new path over ground that has long since been trodden into ruts of sterile and deadlocked debate then it will need to exhibit a high degree of linguistic and conceptual inventiveness.

VI

Amongst the exegetes there is one division that cuts deeper than most, namely that between those who take Wittgenstein pretty much at his word as regards his therapeutic claim to talk philosophy down from the heights of linguistic-metaphysical delusion and those who are more inclined to pursue his meta-phoric, fictive, thought-experimental, or likewise speculative leads. The former group is pretty much co-extensive with Wittgenstein's mainstream following in British and US philosophy departments, though with certain notable exceptions – such as Stanley Cavell – who adopt a basically therapeutic (i.e., problem-dissolving) approach but who also permit themselves a more hermeneutically adventurous line of thought.[77] The latter group includes a number of thinkers who refuse to take sides in the typecast 'analytic' versus 'continental' quarrel and for whom it is a basic precept that philosophical style cannot be divorced from philosophical argument or conceptual content. Thus they tend to be responsive – albeit in varying degrees – to Jacques Derrida's claim that philosophical texts invite and require the kind of detailed, close-focused and rhetorically sophisti-cated reading that has more often been the province of literary criticism. Henry Staten's *Wittgenstein and Derrida* goes furthest in this deconstructive direction while Newton Garver and Seung-Chong Lee rather confuse the issue of priority by entitling their book *Derrida and Wittgenstein* but take a more conservative view that acknowledges the sheer inventiveness and brilliance of Derrida's work but in the end plumps firmly for a Wittgensteinian emphasis on the saving virtues of ordinary language and common-sense/intuitive wisdom.[78] Still it would be wrong to present this as just another round in the old analytic/continental feud since Staten's approach – his treatment of Wittgenstein as a highly inventive and stylistically challenging writer – itself has a major source in the work of O.K. Bouwsma, whose writings strongly resist classification in any such ready-made terms.[79] Thus Bouwsma's attention was focused very much on mainstream 'analytic' problems (especially issues in philosophy of mind and epistemology) while nonetheless paying the closest regard to precisely that 'other', creative-exploratory dimension of Wittgenstein's language.

My point, to repeat, is that these complex patterns of response amongst philosophers writing about or influenced by Wittgenstein can be traced back to

tensions and complexities within his own project. Probably the thinker who has
managed to keep them most keenly and productively in play is Stanley Cavell
throughout his four decades of intensive yet brooding and often inconclusive
reflection on a range of themes such as scepticism, private language, other
minds, intentionality and Cartesian dualism.[80] What gives Cavell's work its
particular relevance here is his striving to hold a hard-won balance between
appreciation of Wittgenstein's therapeutic aim – his genuine desire to 'give
philosophy peace' – and a sense that these problems cannot be resolved once and
for all by any amount of philosophical counselling since they are problems that
arise in manifold contexts of real-life human experience, rather than issues of a
strictly (or narrowly) philosophical concern. Moreover, some of Cavell's most
striking work in this vein has been conducted through a reading of texts from
outside the received (academic) philosophical canon, whether by 'borderline' or
trans-generic thinkers like Thoreau and Emerson or again – more directly to the
point here – by poets and dramatists, Shakespeare chief among them. Thus for
instance his way of broaching the issue of other minds, or the related Wittgensteinian *topos* of private language, is to look at how such questions might
have a bearing on the predicament of tragic figures like Othello, King Lear or
Coriolanus. These characters are subject to a kind of extreme and self-destructive
sceptical doubt that impels them to seek indubitable evidence of other people's
feelings – of their fidelity, devotion, undivided loyalty, unqualified respect and
so forth – where such evidence cannot be had, as distinct from those always-
fallible signs of trust, recognition or acknowledgement that constitute the basis
of any lasting or viable human relationship.[81]

This in turn leads back to those issues about truth, meaning, intention and
speech-act fidelity that Cavell addressed in his early book *Must We Mean What
We Say?*, and which he saw as arising not only in the context of Austinian and
late-Wittgensteinian philosophy of language but also with regard to the special
kinds of challenge posed by developments in modern literature, music and art.
However what I wish to emphasize here is the central role of Shakespeare in
Cavell's interpretation of Wittgenstein, extending as it does both to matters of
character psychology – of self-knowledge, mutual understanding, the failures
and achievements of reciprocal love or trust – and to matters of linguistic-
communicative grasp which very often (as in the case of *Othello*) link directly to
the play's thematic and dramatic content. For it is precisely the standing possibility of failure, of miscommunication or cross-purpose understanding that
haunts Wittgenstein's later thought as it does Shakespeare's characters – especially his tragic protagonists – when their lives and relationships begin to
fracture. Hence perhaps Wittgenstein's attitude to Shakespeare and, in particular, toward the poet's fondness for multiplied metaphors and flights of figural
language, taken to embody not merely a stylistic defect but also, his comments
often imply, a grave moral as well as poetic and dramatic fault. Yet one also finds
Wittgenstein declaring that 'philosophy ought really to be written only as a
poetic composition', and wondering whether, in that case, he was 'thereby revealing
[him]self as someone who cannot quite do what he would like to be able to

do'.[82] There is the same ambivalence about his remarks on the function of 'similes' in philosophic discourse, that is, his recognition that metaphor, analogy and other such figural devices play a crucial – indeed indispensable – role in the thinking of philosophers (himself included), yet also his reluctance to concede that fact except by way of grudging acceptance or avowal of his own failure to achieve a more adequate mode of articulation. Thus when Wittgenstein remarks that 'what I *invent* are new similes' his claim is clearly meant as a limiting judgement or a sad reflection on his 'talent' rather than his 'genius' for philosophical thought.[83] In fact it comes at the end of a passage (cited above) in which he denies that Jewish thinkers ('holy men' apart) are capable of rising from talent to genius, confesses that 'I really only think reproductively', and owns to never having truly 'invented a line of thinking'.[84]

So there is, to say the least, a certain tension between Wittgenstein's idea of philosophy as properly aspiring to the status of 'poetic composition' and his refusal to accept that the gift of coming up with some new and revealing metaphorical insight might itself count as a first-rate contribution to philosophy, or a 'productive' as distinct from merely 'reproductive' exercise of philosophic thought. This tension is ratcheted up by the fact that – as most commentators would agree – so much of Wittgenstein's thinking is conducted through just those kinds of analogical reasoning and often highly 'inventive' transference between diverse topic-domains that he seems to regard as at best merely 'talented' and at worst a positive threat to the interests of plain and perspicuous expression. Hence his frequent laments to the effect that his are just bad, second-rate or in some way misleading metaphors, that they fall far short of what the finest poets (or even the finest philosophers) have been able to achieve, and that insofar as 'philosophy ought really to be written only as poetic composition' this must be taken to reveal Wittgenstein as 'someone who cannot do what he would like to be able to do'. Thus he often seems to be torn both ways between a sense of having somehow missed his vocation through writing philosophy rather than poetry – or the kind of poetry that would meet his own high standards of judgement – and a sense that his efforts in philosophy are compromised (prevented from attaining the wished-for clarity and intellectual strength) through the same admixture of poetic language that constitutes their very hallmark. Such is the case when Wittgenstein says, in one of his most striking and 'poetically' resonant phrases, that 'a picture held us captive', and that 'we could not get outside it, for it lay in our language and language seemed to repeat it to us inexorably'.[85] No doubt what he has most directly in mind is the picture-theory of meaning – the idea of veridical propositions or statements as latching onto factual states of affairs through a kind of quasi-geometrical projective correspondence – that had so captivated Wittgenstein's thinking (to all appearances at least) in the *Tractatus Logico-Philosophicus*. However, despite all his efforts to break the hold of that picture in his later work, still it was the habit of thinking in pictures – in similes and load-bearing images or metaphors – that continued to leave a deep and indelible imprint. Indeed, the very force with which Wittgenstein rejected that earlier way of thinking was such as to create a whole range of contrasted metaphors – for example, those relating to maps, mazes, landscapes, urban topographies, highways and byways, geological strata, rivers, river-beds and so forth – all of which are clearly meant to convey the open-ended multiplicity of human communicative purposes and contexts, but each of which (as emerges very clearly from the secondary literature) can at times exert a captivating force of its own.

So it is scarcely surprising that Wittgenstein displayed such a deep mistrust of figural language (and Shakespeare's language in particular), even though – or just because – he recognized the depth, extent and ubiquitous nature of its role in his own writings, early and late. There is a similar ambivalence about his attitude toward music, representing on the one hand a kind of unattainable ideal to which language can and should aspire, yet on the other standing as emblematic of everything that Wittgenstein thought inimical to the practice of properly disciplined philosophic thought. Thus when he writes that 'my style is like bad musical composition' what he seems to have in mind is the disjointed, aphoristic and non-developmental character of his work, that is, the way that it typically works through a montage-like bringing together of contrasted yet suggestively associated themes and ideas, rather than through any rigorously consequent process of argumentation.[86] This way of writing is so integral to Wittgenstein's later thought that it seems distinctly odd – or downright perverse – for him to treat it not merely as a defect of style but as a deep-laid fault of intellectual and moral character with its nearest analogue in certain kinds of literature and music. However the reasons for his low self-estimate may appear more plainly if one considers his likewise ambivalent feelings about the high German cultural tradition from Classicism to Romanticism and, beyond that, to the modernist developments of his own formative period in early twentieth-century Vienna. What then emerges is his deep attachment to the values of that same tradition but also a sharp division of loyalties between his principled regard for its earlier, more classical (i.e., formally articulate and emotionally restrained) ethos and a stronger yet hard-to-acknowledge love of its later, more wayward and idiosyncratic manifestations.

In this connection it is worth noting that Wittgenstein more than once named Schumann as the composer with whom he felt the closest intellectual and temperamental affinity. Thus 'I often wonder whether my cultural ideal is a new one, i.e., contemporary, or whether it comes from the time of Schumann. At least it strikes me as a continuation of that ideal, though not the continuation that actually followed then. That is to say, the second half of the nineteenth century has been left out'.[87] This is a curious statement for several reasons, among them the fact that Schumann was the most protean, volatile and non-'classical' of German Romantic composers. At any rate that description applies very much to those works for solo piano – like *Carnaval* – which capture the ethos of German Romanticism (more specifically: the spirit of heightened self-consciousness and intensely ironic self-reflection) which found its most typical literary expression in the writings of E.T.A. Hoffmann and its closest philosophical equivalent in those of post-Kantian Romantic ironists like Tieck, Novalis and the Schlegel brothers.[88] Yet there is also a strong counter-current in Wittgenstein's thinking that inclines him to regard that whole chapter of musical, literary and philosophical developments as a falling away from classical ideals and a symptom of advanced cultural decline. Hence his idea that, when judged by the highest standards, music might be said to have 'come to a full stop with Brahms', and that even in the works of Brahms one can 'begin to hear the sound of machinery'.[89] This tension in Wittgenstein's thought can be somewhat defused – if scarcely resolved – by reflecting that perhaps his admiration for Schumann had to do with that composer's extreme spontaneity and breaking free of classical constraints, as contrasted with Brahms's frequent recourse to certain formal or structural procedures of an earlier, that is, less overtly Romantic style. However this explanation really will not do since there is plenty of evidence elsewhere that what Wittgenstein most valued about the Austro-German artistic and intellectual tradition was precisely its having managed to reconcile the claims of individual expression or creative genius with a due regard for the classical virtues of discipline and self-restraint. Nor indeed should one expect otherwise, given his stress on the communal nature of all understanding and the impossibility that any language – whether verbal or (presumably) musical – could acquire such a 'private' or idiosyncratic character as to place it beyond that communal sphere without thereby giving up any claim to cultural-linguistic intelligibility.

Of course this is not to say that one can simply conflate Wittgenstein's remarks about music, tradition and aesthetic value with the kinds of concern voiced in those much-discussed passages from the *Investigations* where he raises the issue of 'private language' *vis-à-vis* the problem about what counts as cor- rectly or properly 'following a rule'.[90] While the former have to do with matters of a broadly hermeneutic or cultural-historical nature the latter must be seen – at least if we accept Kripke's interpretation – as bearing on the most fundamental problems of philosophy and as pressing the sceptical challenge to a point where it calls into question every last item of hitherto accredited knowledge. All the same these two kinds of concern are closely related, as can be seen from Witt- genstein's way of bringing them together at just those points where he is keenest to emphasize the role of communal 'agreement in judgement' as the precondi- tion for defeating – or at any rate deflecting and defusing – the sceptic's chal- lenge. That is to say, the Wittgensteinian 'sceptical solution' which takes such agreement as our last, best recourse in the face of radical doubt is one that he often expresses in terms of those deep-laid cultural, artistic and aesthetic values which mark the existence of a shared tradition with agreed-upon norms of understanding. Thus: 'you get a picture of what you may call a very high culture, e.g., German music in the last century and the century before, and what happens when this deteriorates'.[91] And again: 'the words we call expressions of aesthetic judgement play a very complicated role, but a very definite role, in what we call the culture of a period. To describe their use or to describe what you mean by a cultured taste you have to describe a culture. What belongs to a language-game is a whole culture'.[92] Passages like this lend weight to the charge that Wittgenstein has promoted an outlook of ethically and politically disabling cultural relativism, that is, an ideologically complicitous stance whereby any criticism of received practices or customary 'forms of life' would be rendered off the point or downright meaningless to members of the cultural community whose values and beliefs were thus called into question.

I have put this case myself on various occasions and consider it sufficiently borne out by much of what Wittgenstein has to say about the communal nature of belief and the imbrication of concepts such as 'certainty', 'truth' and 'knowledge' with the practices and language-games within which they play a socially agreed-upon role.[93] Indeed, I would argue that most of these problems result from his mistaken restriction of truth to the scope and limits of attainable knowledge, and of knowledge to whatever counts as 'certain' according to communally valid standards of epistemic or assertoric warrant. Hence the quite extraordinary hold exerted upon recent philosophical debate not only by the Kripkensteinian pseudo-dilemma about 'following a rule' but also by Dummettian anti-realism and by various proposed compromise solutions of a response-dispositional or kindred middle-ground, that is, epistemically constrained character.[94]

VII

That these proposals are more a part of the problem than of any adequate solution to it is again a case that I have argued at length elsewhere and will not press further in the present context.[95] What interests me here is the conflict between Wittgenstein's emphasis on communal language-games or forms of life — along with its implied devaluation of individual creativity — and that aspect of his intellectual and aesthetic temperament that clearly found room for the idea of genius, not least when driven to contrast it with the merely 'talented' or 'reproductive' nature of his own writing. This takes us to the heart of Wittgenstein's antipathy toward Shakespeare, mixed as it was with a keenly responsive yet curiously baffled sense of something going on in Shakespeare's poetry that others gave every sign of enjoying and finding profound but to which he somehow did not have access. One is reminded of a likewise curious passage in F.R. Leavis's memoir of Wittgenstein where he recounts how the philosopher had asked his opinion of William Empson's poetry, and Leavis had obliged by bringing along a copy of 'Legal Fictions', written in a strongly 'metaphysical' or 'conceited' style reminiscent of Donne.[96] Wittgenstein requested Leavis to explain what the poem was about, to which he responded — very much in the style that Empson as literary critic had done a great deal to promote — by unpacking some of its central themes and pointing out various structures of imagery and metaphor. However this failed to satisfy Wittgenstein who said that of course he understood all *that* and had wanted Leavis to go much deeper than mere *explication de texte*. He then proceeded to offer what Leavis recollects — albeit without further specification — as a highly perceptive analysis which indeed far surpassed his own effort in terms of exegetical depth and grasp. There is something rather comical about all this, especially since Leavis then goes on to upbraid Wittgenstein for his extreme rudeness and arrogance on other occasions, and moreover to record how Wittgenstein once told him to 'give up literary criticism' and devote himself to some worthier calling. What I think the episode shows – quite apart from the clash of wills between two notoriously prickly characters – is Wittgenstein's anxiety to prove himself up to the task in hand. For Empson's poetry at its best has just the kind of metaphorical complexity that Wittgenstein found so offensive – or maybe so disconcertingly elusive – in the plays of Shakespeare, and which seems to have triggered a complex response related to his own ambivalent feelings about the notion of being at home in any language, whether (in his own case) native German or adoptive English.

Those feelings come out in a variety of ways, including – as we have seen – his contradictory desire both to distance himself (or his mode of composition) from the legacy of German Romanticism, along with its cult of individual genius, and to acknowledge those elements of his own work that bore a marked affinity to it. Among them was undoubtedly Wittgenstein's attraction to the kind of aphoristic, discontinuous, non-linear and (at times) sharply paradoxical writing that had become such a hallmark of the post-Kantian idealist line of descent, especially on the 'literary' wing of that tradition epitomized by a poet– philosopher like Friedrich Schlegel.[97] Hence Wittgenstein's typical lament – actually (one is tempted to suggest) more a mixture of covert self-praise and ironic self-deprecation – that 'forcing my thoughts into an ordered sequence is a torment for me', since 'I squander an unspeakable amount of effort making an arrangement of my thoughts which may have no value at all.'[98] And again, to similar effect:

> I have written down these thoughts as *remarks*, short paragraphs, of which there is sometimes a fairly long chain about the same subject, while I sometimes make a sudden change, jumping from one topic to another. — It was my intention at first to bring all this together in a book whose form I pictured differently at different times. But the essential thing was that the thoughts should proceed from one topic to another in a natural order and without breaks.[99]

However, so he ruefully (or mock-ruefully) admits, this desire for system and method continued to defeat his best efforts and must therefore be discerned between the lines of his text by sufficiently perceptive or well-attuned readers. Such ideas were common coin among the German Romantics for whom the philosophico-poetic fragment – developed to a high point of literary art by theorists like Schlegel – became a new genre with privileged access to an order of imaginative insight unachievable by the earnest-minded system-builders. Most relevant here is the fact that these thinkers took Shakespeare as their chief inspiration for the claim that language could somehow intimate truths or communicate ideas that surpassed the utmost limits of plain-prose statement, logical form, or consecutive reasoning.[100] That Wittgenstein was strongly drawn to this idea yet deeply mistrustful of it – even (or especially) in so far as it applied to his own work – is evident enough from passages like those cited above and also, of course, from the structure and style of that work itself. Thus his failure to 'bring all this together in a book', or to give his thoughts at least a semblance of book-like cohesion, is among the most striking traits of Wittgenstein's entire *oeuvre*, whether in the Tractarian guise of numbered propositions whose seeming continuity and logical articulation is often belied by their drastically disjunctive character, or again in the later (posthumously published) texts where any sense of consecutive argument is more a matter of vaguely localized thematic 'clumping' than of any consistent overall design.

If the resultant tension is clearly perceptible in Wittgenstein's remarks about Shakespeare and other literary figures, then it is equally apparent in his various comments on the topic of music or, more precisely, of music conceived in Romantic terms as a mode of individual self-expression versus its role as a communal practice or shared cultural life-form. This emerges most strikingly in his attitude toward Mendelssohn, a composer (as we have seen) whose creative and intellectual temperament Wittgenstein considered to be much like his own in certain, mainly negative respects. That is to say, his music was 'reproductive' rather than 'productive' and lacked the depth, originality and strength of character that marked out 'genius' from mere 'talent', or which distinguished the great line of pure-bred Austro-German musical descent from that admixture of 'Jewish' expressive elements that Wittgenstein detected (and was apt to decry) in his own philosophical writing.[101] Yet on at least one occasion his musical response was sufficiently powerful to hold this prejudice in check, since his friend Drury reports him as saying of Mendelssohn's Violin Concerto that this work was 'remarkable in being the last great concerto written for the violin', and that the second (slow) movement contained a passage that was 'one of the great moments in music'.[102] As with Shakespeare, so with Mendelssohn: it is just when Wittgenstein's responses are at their most complex or strongly over-determined that they also seem most deeply bound up with a mixed estimation of his own work and its likely effect for good or ill on those readers who may be receptive to his message. That is to say, whenever it is a question of something (call it 'genius' or 'creativity') that touches on the scope and limits – more especially, the limits – of 'ordinary language' or communal warrant then Wittgenstein tends to display the same oscillating pattern of intense self-involvement and sharp recoil from the implications of his own response. Among the reasons for this, I believe, is his partial awareness that the kind of linguistic therapy offered in his later writings can scarcely be expected to work if it relies on a power of persuasion whose chief source is a highly idiosyncratic way with words, or a singular capacity for hitting on suggestive metaphors, similes, parables and so on, in order to make his case. One need only look at the burgeoning literature devoted to the rule-following 'dilemma' and other such late-Wittgensteinian themes to realize the full irony of this predicament, or the full extent of his failure to 'give philosophy peace' by deploying such a range of supposedly problem-solving but in fact – as it turned out – endlessly problem-generating topics of thought.

Some commentators, James Conant among them, advise that we can find the most illuminating parallel in Kierkegaard's modes of indirect communication, that is, his strategies for bringing the reader around to a radically transformed understanding through 'literary' means such as multiple viewpoints, many-levelled irony, pseudonymous narration and constant unsettling shifts of authorial perspective.[103] However this comparison is perhaps too close for comfort if one wishes, like Conant, to justify Wittgenstein's approach and claim that he succeeds in putting his points across despite – or precisely in virtue of – his recourse to these various rhetorical and narrative devices. For if there is one major problem for Kierkegaard's fideist, that is, Christian, exegetes it is that of explaining just where these strategies come to an end, or of drawing a firm and principled line between the different stages of existence (aesthetic, ethical, religious) to which – supposedly – his texts can be assigned in keeping with the overall plan laid down in 'authentic', first-person statements of intent like *The Point of View for My Work as an Author*.[104] That is to say, Kierkegaard's account is one that depends on a strongly intentionalist (indeed providentialist) conception of his own authorship and which can always be called into doubt through a 'literary', that is, close and rhetorically sophisticated reading of those same texts, including *The Point of View* and even such earnest professions of faith as the *Edifying Discourses*.

No doubt any reading along these lines is one that flies absolutely in the face of Kierkegaard's original purposes, at least as he conceived them when writing an elaborately structured work like *Either/Or* and when seeking to provide a redemptive gloss that would explain his tortuously roundabout approach. Besides, he had to justify the risk involved in publishing certain parts of that work – like the 'Diary of a Seducer' – which might have just the wrong kind of appeal for those in whom the desire for aesthetic or erotic stimulation out-weighed their desire for the edifying lessons held out by his other, on the whole less attractive (or seductive) writings.[105] Yet there is a very real question as to whether we are obliged to respect Kierkegaard's intentions – his manifest or overt intentions – when they seem to be belied by so much that is brilliantly inventive and might be considered to represent Kierkegaard in a better light, not only from a 'literary' standpoint but also as concerns the moral and religious dimension of his thought. For the resisting reader may well conclude that the theology of a work like *Fear and Trembling* with its message of total, unquestioning obedience to God's commands, even when they require what must otherwise count as a downright barbaric course of action, is one that we should do best to reject as the product of a warped and repulsive religious doctrine working on a morbid and deeply disturbed (although marvellously gifted) sensibility.[106] All the more so, indeed, since Kierkegaard's idea of a 'teleological suspension of the ethical' – the need to renounce our human, all-too-human conceptions of the moral good through a leap of faith to some radically different, theologically sanctioned ground – can itself be applied to opposite effect. Thus his gloss on the Abraham/Isaac story is open to the twofold objection that it permits all manner of wicked or inhuman behaviour while inviting just the sort of revisionist approach that would reject this particular interpretative leap for the sake of another, more humanly acceptable (though to his way of thinking merely evasive or bad-faith) interpretation.

My point is that Conant's Kierkegaardian reading of Wittgenstein has this much in common with Kierkegaard's authorship: that it risks turning out too powerful or suggestive for its own intended purpose, implying as it does that Wittgenstein's texts have a similar tendency to generate responses or provoke philosophical debates that are strongly at odds with their express therapeutic intent. Hence the curious veering about between, on the one hand, his low estimation of Shakespeare's poetry on account of its far-fetched metaphors (or 'similes') and supposed lack of formal as well as moral integrity and, on the other, his appeal to something very like the Romantic sublime in order to convey what it is about Shakespeare that makes such judgements seem largely or totally irrelevant. From this point of view – to repeat – 'you just have to accept him as he is if you are going to be able to admire him properly, in the way you accept nature, a piece of scenery for example, just as it is'. Of course such notions were very much a part of that late-Romantic cultural ethos that was under attack from various modernist and *avant-garde* quarters during Wittgenstein's formative years yet which still exerted a powerful hold over those who avowedly rejected it. This intellectual climate was first and most vividly captured in Toulmin and Janik's 1971 study *Wittgenstein's Vienna*, and has since been subject to a great deal of further, more detailed historical and socio-cultural commentary.[107] Most relevant here is the clash of values that resulted from his lingering attachment to that earlier way of thought – a metaphysics most aptly summed up in the style of Schopenhauer's *The World as Will and Representation* – and his overt espousal of a modernist worldview that found no room for such residual ideas of a noumenal reality beyond phenomenal appearances that could be accessed only by way of creative or imaginative genius.

It is not hard to see how the Schopenhauerian influence comes through in the *Tractatus* with its drastic dichotomy of 'saying' and 'showing', or that which can be represented in the form of logical or factual statements and that which inherently eludes any such means of articulate expression despite having to do with matters of the utmost, for example, ethical or religious concern. In his later work this dichotomy is present as an unresolved conflict at the heart of Wittgenstein's thought concerning the scope and limits of linguistic, poetic and musical creativity. It is the conflict between a communitarian conception according to which creativity can or should be exercised only within the authenticating context of a shared cultural-linguistic 'form of life' and a different, more Romantic conception that acknowledges the claim of expressive individuality – or that which inherently surpasses the norms of acculturated meaning and value – even though this idea goes strongly against the manifest drift of Wittgenstein's later writings. I would hope to have offered sufficient evidence to make good my case that those writings were subject to a range of contradictory motives or impulses, among them – not least – his genuine desire to release philosophy from its self-imposed travails of sceptical doubt but also his proneness to deepen and multiply those same sources of perplexity. Indeed, if one were asked to define or describe what was most 'creative' about Wittgenstein's later thought then one would surely have to place the main emphasis on its power to create fresh problems, novel dilemmas, and – as with the rule-following debate – new and ingenious means to develop far-out sceptical hypotheses.

It seems to me that Cavell gets it pretty much right when he compares Wittgenstein's with Shakespeare's way of raising these issues and suggests that the comparison comes closest in the case of tragic figures – like Lear and Othello – for whom the philosophical problem about 'other minds' takes on a far deeper and humanly destructive dimension.[108] Thus Cavell sees more clearly than the majority of Wittgenstein's mainstream, that is, analytically minded exegetes that the issues raised by his later work have an aspect that can best (or can only) be conveyed by way of certain broadly 'existential' themes such as solitude, non-communication, failure of trust, crisis of belief and unassuageable desire for the kind of security in personal relationship that cannot be had because the very effort to achieve it leads to a form of reactive scepticism with potentially dire consequences. That is to say, Cavell's Wittgenstein has a depth and complexity of human motivation notably absent from the flattened-out, technical and often rather arid debates that result when these themes undergo the process of conversion into analytic talk about 'private language', 'other minds', 'first-person epistemic access' and so forth. On the other hand Cavell is so strongly persuaded by Wittgenstein's therapeutic claims – by the notion that his work actually achieves that purpose, rather than striving (and perhaps failing) to achieve it – that he tends to play down just those aspects of Wittgenstein's thought that most call for interpretation in existential rather than 'purely' philosophical terms. In short, philosophers who take him at his word when he professes to cure them of all their self-induced dilemmas are thereby apt to find themselves in thrall to a whole new range of 'problems from Wittgenstein' – like that about following a rule – which often have an even more compulsive, not to say obsessive-neurotic character.

VIII

I have put the case elsewhere that these are best regarded as pseudo-dilemmas whose tenacious grip on the discourse of present-day analytical philosophy is symptomatic of the long drawn-out crisis that has afflicted it ever since Quine's attack on the two last 'dogmas' of old-style logical empiricism.[109] Hence the quite extraordinary power and fascination that Wittgenstein's writings have managed to exert over the half-century since his later texts were first translated and edited. What makes this whole chapter of developments yet more intriguing from a cultural-diagnostic viewpoint is the fact – borne out by some of his own melancholy reflections – that Wittgenstein himself very clearly foresaw the most probable effect of those writings, that is to say, the likelihood of their generating yet more futile debate on a range of problems which he hoped to have resolved, or at least shown up as philosophically misconceived. Along with this, I suggest, went an intermittent sense of the conflict between his therapeutic aim – premised as it was on the appeal to 'ordinary language' as a source of redemptive common-sense wisdom – and his remarkable gift for the inventive deployment of metaphors, images and similes whose persuasive force very often bore an inverse relation to their problem-solving (or problem   -dissolving) power. So there is reason to suppose that some complex transference mechanisms might be in play when Wittgenstein expresses his dislike of Shakespeare on distinctly kindred grounds, that is, on account of Shakespeare's precocious style, the way that his language so exuberantly 'goes on holiday', and the connection between this verbal self-indulgence and the lax moral standards that supposedly characterize his dramatic distribution of weal and woe. At the same time this disapproval is mixed with a keen awareness, on Wittgenstein's part, of the crucial role that such 'literary' devices must be seen to play in his own most persuasive and characteristic work, and hence a nagging sense of what that work has in common with the kinds of language that he wishes to place beyond the pale of philosophical or everyday acceptability. As I have said, this puts Wittgenstein directly in line with a long tradition of critical responses – from Dr Johnson down – that have seen fit to acknowledge Shakespeare's pre-eminent status in certain respects (most of all as regards his extraordinary powers of linguistic inventiveness) but have nonetheless hedged that estimate around with various caveats and qualifications which strangely have to do with just the same imputed qualities.

In recent years it has become almost de rigueur for 'continentally' influenced philosophers – or literary theorists with an eye to what Plato was already calling the 'ancient quarrel' between philosophy and poetry – to remark the extent of philosophy's reliance on metaphors, similes and figures of thought that cannot be excluded from its discourse since they constitute some of its most basic (indeed strictly indispensable) resources.[110] One way to classify readings of Wittgenstein is to range them on a scale with respect to their acceptance or non-acceptance of this fact, or again – amongst those who broadly accept it   with respect to the conclusions they are apt to draw concerning its implications for philosophy in general and Wittgenstein's thinking in particular. If the rejectionist group is pretty much co-extensive with the mainstream analytic approach then those who accept the claim by and large must still be recognized as falling into two quite distinct and, at times, even hostile camps. On the one hand are proponents of the moderate view that figural language indeed has its place in philosophy but that this should be seen as natural enough and not as creating any kind of conceptual or methodological problem.[111] After all – as Wittgenstein does well to remind us – philosophical language is deeply intertwined with the languages of our everyday communicative life-world, including those various metaphors, images and other such expressive devices by which we make sense of ourselves and the world. On the other are ranged deconstructionists like Paul de Man or, more ambivalently, Jacques Derrida who do perceive a genuine problem in the fact that so many philosophers of otherwise diverse persuasion – from Plato to Descartes, Leibniz, Locke, Kant, Frege and beyond – have striven to achieve the impossible by envisaging a language made fit for purpose (i.e., for the purpose of perspicuous logical or scientific thought) by expunging all such metaphoric residues.[112]

As I have said, this dichotomy is reflected in the difference between commentators on Wittgenstein who take him to have settled the deconstructive 'problem' before it even gets off the ground and others – call them 'textualists' – who emphasize the figural complexity of his later work and the extent to which it puts obstacles in the way of any such placidly self-assured, conformist or fideist approach. On the latter reading it is plausible to think that Wittgenstein himself had a shrewd premonition of the sorts of tangle that his exegetes would most likely get into if they pursued his metaphors with the same attentiveness and sensitivity to verbal nuance that literary critics had brought to their study of Shakespeare. After all, a good many of the well-known passages where Wittgenstein counsels philosophers to leave off their high metaphysical/metaphoric gyrations can be seen to derive their persuasive force from his telling deployment of metaphors like that of showing the fly a way out of the fly-bottle or returning from the slippery surfaces of abstract speculation to the 'rough ground' of our everyday practices and language-games. Nor is it hard to show that some of these metaphors have further, perhaps unwanted or (by him) unnoticed implications that tend to undermine or considerably complicate their overt, intended sense. Such is the case, for instance, when Wittgenstein offers the analogy of a river by way of suggesting how certain deeply held beliefs within a given cultural community can be taken as true, unrevisable or immune from challenge even though they possess that privileged role only by community-relative standards of judgement.[113] Thus the river may well be periodically disturbed by surface swirls and eddies, or by turbulent currents and counter-currents at a middling depth, but will nonetheless pursue its course undeflected over long periods of time since that course is determined by the river-bed and by enduring features of the physical terrain through which it flows. In the same way, Wittgenstein suggests, there are firmly entrenched items of belief – or of knowledge, for all practical purposes – which hold good throughout many short-term fluctuations and thereby constitute those 'hinge propositions' upon which our other, more changeable beliefs must be taken to depend. Yet of course this metaphor does nothing to turn back the charge of cultural relativism often brought against Wittgenstein by realists or objectivists (in fields ranging from epistemology and philosophy of science to ethics, sociology and history) who point to his notion of truth as internal to this or that language-game or cultural form of life. For it takes only the slightest pressure on his fluvial analogy to show that what is in question is not so much a clear-cut or principled contrast between knowledge and opinion, or truth and communal 'agreement in judgement', but rather a kind of scalar conception whereby such agreement is the furthest one can get toward 'knowledge' and 'truth'.

This particular type of metaphor involving notions of forward movement or directional orientation is one that runs deep in Wittgenstein's later thought and which has come to exert a singular, almost talismanic power over many of his present-day exegetes. It is especially rife among contributors to the rule-following debate who often home in on Wittgenstein's remarks about the fallacy of supposing that standards of correctness in arithmetic, logic and other such formal operations must involve a 'super-rigid rail' conception of objectivity and truth whereby those standards should be thought of not only as applying to all our past and present calculations but also as stretching out to encompass any future operations of the same sort.[114] Hence the purported 'sceptical paradox': that we cannot know for sure whether or not we have applied those standards consistently from one reckoning to the next, or whether (conceivably) our notion of what constitutes 'the same' operation has not undergone some radical transformation entirely unbeknownst to us. Hence also the Kripkensteinian 'sceptical solution' whereby that dilemma is supposedly resolved – but in truth simply posed in a more anodyne, less overtly threatening form – through the appeal to communal warrant as our last, best defence against radical scepticism. My point is that this whole debate has been skewed by the false choice that Wittgenstein's metaphor contrives to present, that is, the choice between truth conceived as a matter of our somehow knowing in advance (or clearly picturing) the correct answers to a limitless range of arithmetical or logical problems, and truth or correctness as *nothing more* than what happens to count as such according to the norms of acknowledged best judgement or accredited expertise. Thus the 'super-rigid rail' image, like the river simile, purports to bring philosophy back to its senses by providing a suitably scaled-down, that is, de-sublimated conception of truth while in fact it succeeds merely in redefining – or effectively defining away – the distinction between knowledge and belief that alone provides an adequate working basis for epistemological enquiry. So we now have a large secondary literature putting the case for some alternative approach (like those advanced by response-dispositionalists or back-to-Kant thinkers like McDowell) that would offer a viable compromise solution, one disabused of the 'super-rigid', that is, objectivist conception of knowledge and truth, yet still preserving – or so it is claimed – a decent measure of mind- or language-independence.[115]

Here again I must refer the reader to previously published work where I argue that these solutions fail through an over-willingness to meet anti-realists on terms of the latters' skilfully contrived or shrewdly pre-emptive choosing.[116] Hence the constant tendency to yield vital ground by adopting a middle-way or fall-back stance which makes room for truth just so long as it is conceived as epistemically constrained or as not, in any strong sense, verification-transcendent. This tendency is most visible in a thinker like Crispin Wright who wishes to avoid any direct endorsement of fully fledged Dummettian anti-realism whilst sufficiently impressed by what he takes to be the force of such arguments – along with the rule-following considerations – to expend great ingenuity in devising a

range of plausible alternatives at various points on the scale.[117] Amongst his
favoured candidates are 'superassertibility' and 'cognitive command', both of
which notions (the latter especially) are so framed as to strengthen the justificatory requirements beyond those entailed by Dummett's criteria of warranted
assertibility yet neither of which goes so far as to accommodate any idea of truth
as objective, recognition-transcendent or epistemically unconstrained. There can
be little doubt that Wright's endeavours in this regard have been prompted very
largely by his close engagement with Wittgenstein's thinking and, in particular,
his effort to salvage a workable conception of truth in mathematics, logic and
the formal sciences from Wittgenstein's remarks on those topics.[118] It is here –
as likewise in McDowell's protracted efforts to square his revisionist reading of
Kant with a de-fanged version of Wittgenstein's rule-following paradox and
thereby produce a kind of scaled-down 'realism' proof against sceptical attack –
that recent philosophy has been most subject to the spell cast by that 'super-
rigid rail' metaphor and its powerfully inhibiting effect on any stronger, less
qualified or compromised statement of the realist-objectivist case.

As so often, it is Wittgenstein himself who provides the aptest description of
what is going on – albeit in a different context and to different intended effect –
when he remarks that 'a picture held us captive', and moreover that 'we could
not get outside it, for it lay in our language and language seemed to repeat it to
us inexorably'.[119] This passage strikes me as a perfect example of what commentators typically have in mind when they allude to the 'poetic' quality of
Wittgenstein's writing, or when they place him in the company of other great
'literary' stylists, essayists and aphorists. Any attempt to explain its powerful
evocative charge would have to include the mixture of ironic self-deprecation
carried by the 'us' and 'we' (since Wittgenstein is reflecting on his own erstwhile
and maybe his continuing liability to that captive state) with the strong hint of
superior insight that comes of his having at last won through to a clear-eyed,
undeluded knowledge of just what it was that so persistently held him in thrall.
Also there is the strange double-take effect that results from his putting this
tendency down to the mischievous, illusion-working effects of language while
nevertheless appealing to language as our last, best hope of deliverance from such
linguistically generated errors. Of course it will be said that this is merely to
ignore Wittgenstein's cardinal distinction between 'ordinary language' (or
customary usage) as the sole means of guidance in these matters and the kinds of
hyper-cultivated, artificial language that philosophers typically indulge and
thereby create all manner of needless problems and false dilemmas. However, as
we have seen, it is far from easy to hold the line between these two sorts of
language or to distinguish the picture that once held Wittgenstein captive from
the various alternative or substitute pictures – even those that he explicitly
rejects, like the 'super-rigid rail' metaphor – which come to the fore in his later
work. No doubt his chief purpose is to steer readers firmly away from the
mistaken Tractarian idea (as he now sees it) that language could ever hook up
with the world through a direct correspondence or homology between veridical
statements and factual states of affairs, a relationship conceived (metaphorically

again) on the model of projective geometry. Yet it is possible for minds to be held captive by rejected as well as by accepted ideas, or for routes of enquiry to be closed off by a fixed determination to avoid at all costs the kinds of error which are taken to result from adopting some presumptively naive, discredited, or picture-bound mode of thought.

Such is the case with Wittgenstein's later thought where a good many of the governing images and metaphors are those that express his reactive desire to break altogether with his previous conception of language, logic and truth. More precisely: what he now rejected outright was the logical atomist and verificationist approach that had struck most early readers, Russell among them, as the central and defining feature of Wittgenstein's *Tractatus*, but should rather be thought of – or so it seems in light of his cryptic final remarks – as having already been left behind in the process of composing that text. Such is at any rate the lesson derived by the majority of commentators since, and pressed to an extreme by those 'new Wittgensteinians' who read it as a full-scale exercise in auto-deconstruction, a self-destroying artefact whose every proposition nonsensically strives to 'say' what can only be 'shown', or to articulate in the form of verifiable or logical statements what can only be conveyed obliquely through the inevitable failure to achieve that purpose. Where the commentators err, it seems to me, is in giving too much credit to Wittgenstein's preferred retrospective account of his own intentions when composing the *Tractatus*, and also in blurring the crucial line – crucial for philosophers if not necessarily for those of a more 'literary' or hermeneutic bent – between textual exegesis and critical assessment of the issues raised. There is no doubt that Wittgenstein himself came to view it very much as an exercise of the type proposed by these tough-minded new readers, that is, as a work that self-deconstructs to the point of rendering itself – or the greater proportion of its own statements – either deeply problematic or downright nonsensical. Most likely he arrived at this negative conclusion in the course of writing or when striving to set his disjointed thoughts in some kind of logical order, a task – as we know from his remarks elsewhere – that Wittgenstein found extremely difficult. So the exegetes are justified in claiming that he must have been irked by the response of those (Russell and Moore chief among them) who took the *Tractatus* as a logical positivist or logical-atomist manifesto, and who therefore inclined to treat its final, self-demolishing paragraphs either in tactful silence or with frank expressions of somewhat irritated bafflement.

However this does not mean that they are likewise justified in claiming that Wittgenstein was so much in charge of his project from the start – so perfectly clear-sighted with regard to its outcome and (presumed) esoteric gist – that we should take his later comments at face value and join him in deploring the obtuseness of those who failed to get the point. Nor is it to say that we are somehow obliged to accept the resultant philosophical agenda, that is, the whole set of Wittgensteinian problems about language, logic and representation (including the issue about nonsense and whether it comes in kinds or degrees) as necessarily binding on anyone who *has* got the point and interpreted

Wittgenstein aright. The first error lies in supposing that authorial hindsight or first-person retrospective statements of intent are always reliable in such matters, that is, when it comes to the detailed business of reading a text like the *Tractatus* with a view to various aspects of its argument, its conceptual or logical structure, and (for the purposes of intellectual history) its compositional provenance. The comparison with Kierkegaard is highly instructive here since it underlines the fact that, in Wittgenstein's case also, the 'point of view for my work as an author' is not so much a source of indisputable authority with regard to that work as one further, no doubt very often highly revealing but always questionable source of interpretative insight.[120] This connects with the second error, namely the idea that Wittgenstein's (supposed) demolition job on all those foregoing statements is such as to create a more generalized or non-case-specific problem about nonsense which requires an answer *on approved Wittgensteinian terms* if philosophers are to carry on addressing these topics with any hope of success. After all, on any reasonable view of the matter there is not just one sort of nonsense – complete and utter nonsense, so to speak – but a number of different sorts that competent language users are able to pick out with a fair degree of confidence. These range all the way from sheer gibberish, through cases of semantically absurd, though syntactically well-formed, utterance, to statements or larger stretches of discourse where the failure to sustain any sensible, rational or logically consistent interpretation may require a good deal of careful unpacking in order to detect the underlying fallacy or conceptual category mistake.[121]

Granted, the exegetes have reason to suppose that Wittgenstein was driven to adopt something like the 'one kind of nonsense' view by his emergent doctrine of meaning-as-use, or his strong contextualist idea that words have meaning only within some given language-game or cultural life-form, holistically construed. If this were indeed the case then no doubt it would follow, as night follows murky day, that any word or expression used aberrantly or outside the cultural-linguistic context within which alone it had a rightful (communally sanctioned) place would *ipso facto* be altogether meaningless or nonsensical. However one has only to compare, say, a reading of Lewis Carroll's 'Jabberwocky' with a recital of strictly non-signifying 'concrete poetry', or again, a grammatically well-formed but meaningless sequence like Chomsky's famous 'green ideas sleep furiously' with a string of haphazardly concatenated lexical items in order to see that this argument just cannot work. In which case the tough-minded exegetes must be wrong when they assert – supposedly with good Wittgensteinian warrant – that nonsense does not come in various kinds or degrees but should rather be taken as an all-or-nothing or a one-size-fits-all linguistic phenomenon. Moreover, if they are wrong about this then the issue is placed squarely back within the realm of first-order or substantive philosophical debate. That is to say, it is removed from that ambivalent border zone where one is hard put to know whether they are discussing such first-order questions with particular reference to Wittgenstein or discussing exegetical problems from Wittgenstein with reference to just those questions.

My point – to repeat – is that much of the secondary literature finds itself stranded, knowingly or not, on this disputed terrain between philosophy and textual exegesis, or between the philosophically salient interest of achieving rational consensus over well-defined issues of language, truth and logic and the interests of achieving a better, more faithful or adequate account of what Wittgenstein had in mind. The resultant confusion is most clearly visible in debates like those around the *topoi* of rule following and nonsense where the interpreters seem both obsessed with this issue of priority (i.e., whether they are concerned to get things right *stricto sensu* or to get things right in accordance with Wittgenstein) yet strangely unable or unwilling to declare firmly on either side. It strikes me that their ambivalence has sources deep within Wittgenstein's work, early and late, and that the tension is conveyed most powerfully at just those points where the claims of philosophy come up against the claims of literature or literary criticism. This stems from the uneasy co-presence in that work of a call for certain kinds of interpretative insight that go far beyond the scope and limits of pure-bred conceptual analysis with a contrary sense of the risks courted by any giving way to the seductive temptation of metaphor, analogy or other such rhetorical devices. It might seem absurd – a flagrant example of just that overly 'literary' approach – to have piled such a vast weight of significance on the fact that Wittgenstein had problems in appreciating Shakespeare, or that something about Shakespeare's language (along with other, e.g., moral and character-related aspects of his plays) triggered an adverse even though, at times, a hard-put admiring response. However I would hope that my argument has gained plausibility through the range of complex and over-determining factors that can be seen to have crowded in upon Wittgenstein's encounter with a mode of linguistic creativity so hard to reconcile with certain of his own deeply held philosophical beliefs. Indeed I would suggest that his remarks about Shakespeare, mere *obiter dicta* though they are, give an insight into certain problematical dimensions of Wittgenstein's thinking and its later reception-history that is not to be had through more orthodox, hermeneutically cautious or downright fideist approaches.

No doubt it is the case that some literary theorists have tended to press so far in this direction – with the Nietzschean and quasi-deconstructive claim that 'all concepts are metaphors', 'all "truths" just a species of fiction', 'all philosophy a sub-genre of literature' and so forth – as to lose sight of Derrida's cardinal point: that those who think simply to 'turn the page' on philosophy are sure to end up 'philosophising badly'.[122] At the same time, as I have emphasized in this and previous chapters, philosophers may also have something to learn from those other, more intelligent and critically perceptive kinds of textual close reading to which literary theorists – 'deconstructionists' among them – have brought a high point of technical refinement and sophistication. In particular, their way of approaching the topic of metaphor and its role in certain 'non-literary' forms of discourse, philosophy included, might well throw a sharp and revealing light not only on the problems confronted by Wittgenstein and his faithful exegetes but also on the 'ancient quarrel' between philosophy and literary theory upon which Plato first remarked and which still rumbles on in various academic quarters. Having previously come at the issue from both sides and sometimes approached it – as I now think – in spirit of overly partisan zeal on one side or the other I would hope that this book has so far managed to strike a more ecumenical stance without yielding ground to those anodyne strains of inter-disciplinary thought whose effect, very often, is to point up the truth of Der-rida's cautionary statement.

In Chapter 7 there is a shift of focus toward one of the most basic issues in philosophy of mind, metaphysics and ethics, namely that of free-will versus determinism or – as it tends to work out nowadays – the claims of human autonomy, agency or decision-making power as opposed to the claims of a scientific worldview that would seem to leave no room for such outmoded 'folk-psychological' notions. In fact this is not such a drastic shift since the linguistic turn has left its mark here also, to the point where philosophical ideas about language – along with ideas from other quarters such as theoretical linguistics and cognitive science – are taken to hold decisive (albeit often sharply con-flicting) implications for any adequate treatment of the issue. I shall therefore put the case, very much in keeping with previous chapters, that some of these conflicts might best be resolved – or at any rate more revealingly approached – through a greater openness on the part of analytic philosophers to developments in the 'other', continental or mainland-European line of descent. Chief among them is the debate between phenomenology and structuralism that has posed this question with particular force in the context of post-1960 French philo-sophy, and which received its most intensive critical treatment in Derrida's early and formative encounter with Husserl.[123] My aim here is partly negative in seeking to emphasize the inherent limits of certain linguistically oriented modes of thought on both sides of the analytic/continental rift, that is, in some forms of hard-line conceptual or logico-semantic analysis as well as in structuralist approaches that adopt an overly doctrinaire version of Saussure's methodological paradigm. However I also make the positive case that analytic philosophers might engage more productively with the free-will/determinism issue by reflecting on those limits and what they suggest concerning the expressive potential of language in relation to the human capacity for choice – for the exercise of responsible freedom – under various kinds of constraint.

That is to say, linguistic creativity can be manifested only on condition that the speaker is subject to certain language-constitutive rules in the absence of which they would be wholly unable to produce or interpret the endless variety of speech-acts that make up the run of everyday social-communicative discourse. So likewise, human agents can manifest their powers of deliberative thought and conduct only against a background of restrictions – whether physical, psycho-logical or circumstantial – on what they are able or placed do to in any given context. 'Continental' thinkers have typically raised such questions in a more paradoxical or sharply dramatized way, as with Sartre's existentialist writings (philosophy and fiction) or Derrida's later, Kierkegaardian musings on the idea of genuine ethical choice as involving a strictly unprecedented leap of faith beyond every existing standard of decent, socially acceptable or even morally permissible behaviour. I shall enter some caveats with regard to what I see as the distorting emphasis on extreme situations – or the tendency to treat them as a benchmark for ethical authenticity in general – which has often given rise to this exaggerated notion of freedom as an all-or-nothing matter, and a consequent failure to make due allowance for the range of factors that must always, in practice, place limits on the extent of human autonomy and choice. All the same it offers a needful antidote to that strain of Wittgensteinian linguistic 'therapy' that has exerted such a dormitive influence on present-day ethical or meta-ethical discourse, not least with respect to the topic of rule following. Besides – as I shall argue in this closing chapter – there is always an appeal open to those landmark early-Derrida texts, especially his essays on the problem of structure and genesis in Husserl, which constitute a rigorous yet also a highly creative thinking it through of these core questions in metaphysics and philosophy of mind.

NOTES

1 Samuel Johnson, 'Notes on Henry IV' in *Rasselas, Poems, and Selected Prose*, ed. Bertrand H. Bronson (San Francisco: Rinehart, 1971), p. 72; also Shakespeare, *Henry IV, Part Two*, 1.2.10.

2 Ludwig Wittgenstein, *Culture and Value*, 2nd edn; ed. G.H. von Wright; trans. Peter Winch (Oxford: Blackwell, 1980), p. 48e.

3 Ludwig Wittgenstein, *Philosophical Investigations*, trans. G.E.M. Anscombe (Oxford: Blackwell, 1953) and *On Certainty*, ed. and trans. Anscombe and G.H. von Wright (Blackwell, 1969).

4 See Wittgenstein, *Philosophical Investigations*.

5 See especially Maurice Charney (ed.), '*Bad' Shakespeare: Revaluations of the Shakespeare Canon* (Madison, NJ: Fairleigh Dickinson University Press, 1988).

6 Samuel Johnson, 'Preface to the Plays of William Shakespeare', in *Dr Johnson on Shakespeare*, ed. W.K. Wimsatt (Harmondsworth: Penguin, 1969), pp. 57–98.

7 Ibid., p. 68.

8 Ibid., pp. 67–8.

9 For further discussion see Derek Attridge, *Peculiar Language: Literary Language from the Renaissance to Joyce* (London: Routledge, 1988).

10 Samuel Johnson, *The Lives of the Most Eminent English Poets: With Critical Observations on their Works*, ed. Roger Lonsdale; 4 vols (Oxford: Oxford University Press, 2006).

11 Stanley Cavell, *Must We Mean What We Say?* (New York: Oxford University Press, 1969), p. 94.

12 Johnson, 'Preface to the Plays of William Shakespeare', p. 61.

13 Ibid., p. 96.

14 See especially Peter Winch, *The Idea of a Social Science and its Relation to Philosophy* (London: Routledge & Kegan Paul, 1958) and *Trying to Make Sense* (Oxford: Blackwell, 1987).

15 Wittgenstein, *Tractatus Logico-Philosophicus*, trans. D.F. Pears and B.F. McGuiness (London: Routledge & Kegan Paul, 1961).

16 See especially Alice Crary and Rupert Read (eds.), *The New Wittgenstein* (London: Routledge, 2000).

17 Johnson, 'Preface to the Plays of William Shakespeare', p. 84.

18 Ibid., p. 95.
19 Ibid., pp. 95–6.
20 Wittgenstein, *Culture and Value*, p. 49e.
21 See especially Terry Eagleton, *The Ideology of the Aesthetic* (Oxford: Blackwell, 1989); Paul de Man, *Aesthetic Ideology*, ed. Andrzej Warminski (Minneapolis: University of Minnesota Press, 1996); Longinus, *On the Sublime*, trans. W.H. Fyfe; rev. Donald Russell (Cambridge, MA: Harvard University Press, 1995); Philippe Lacoue-Labarthe and Jean-Luc Nancy, *The Literary Absolute: The Theory of Literature in German Romanticism*, trans. Philip Barnard and Cheryl Lester (Albany: State University of New York Press, 1988); Thomas Weiskel, *The Romantic Sublime: Studies in the Structure and Psychology of Transcendence* (Baltimore, MD: Johns Hopkins University Press, 1976).
22 Wittgenstein, *Culture and Value*, p. 85e.
23 Ibid., p. 49e.
24 Ibid., p. 84e.
25 Ibid., p. 83e.
26 Ibid., p. 83e.
27 Wittgenstein, *Tractatus*, Proposition 7.
28 See Note 16, above; also Cora Diamond, *The Realistic Spirit: Wittgenstein, Philosophy and the Mind* (Cambridge, MA: MIT Press, 1995). According to Diamond, 'for Wittgenstein there is no kind of nonsense which is nonsense on account of what the terms composing it mean – there is as it were no positive nonsense', and moreover '[this] view of nonsense . . . was consistently held to by Wittgenstein throughout his writings, from the period before the *Tractatus* was written and onwards' (ibid., pp. 106–7).
29 Johnson, *Lives of the Most Eminent English Poets*.
30 See especially Gottlob Frege, 'On Sense and Reference', in M. Black and P.T. Geach (eds.), *Translations from the Philosophical Writings of Gottlob Frege* (Oxford: Blackwell, 1952), pp. 56–78 and Bertrand Russell, 'On Denoting', in *Logic and Knowledge* (London: Allen & Unwin, 1930), pp. 41–56.
31 Johnson, 'Preface to the Plays of William Shakespeare'.
32 See especially William Empson, 'Falstaff', in *Essays on Shakespeare*, ed. David B. Pirie (Cambridge: Cambridge University Press, 1986), pp. 29–78.
33 Empson, 'Hamlet', in *Essays on Shakespeare*, pp. 79–136 (118).
34 See John Dover Wilson, *The Fortunes of Falstaff* (Cambridge: Cambridge University Press, 1943); also Wilson (ed.), Shakespeare, *Henry IV, Parts I and II* (Cambridge: Cambridge University Press, 1946).
35 Empson, 'Falstaff', p. 57.
36 See especially Empson, *Seven Types of Ambiguity*, 2nd edn (London: Chatto & Windus, 1953); *Using Biography* (London: Chatto & Windus, 1984); *Argufying: Essays on Literature and Culture*, ed. John Haffenden (London: Chatto & Windus, 1987).
37 Empson, *Seven Types of Ambiguity*; also Rosamund Tuve, 'On Herbert's "The Sacrifice" ', *Kenyon Review* 12(1) (1950), pp. 51–75.
38 Empson, 'Communication: George Herbert and Miss Tuve', *The Kenyon Review* 12(4) (1950), pp. 735–8.
39 See especially Empson, *Using Biography*.
40 Ibid; also Empson, *Argufying*.
41 Empson, *Seven Types of Ambiguity*, p. 247.
42 Empson, 'Falstaff', p. 65.
43 For full-dress examples of the anti-intentionalist approach, see Cleanth Brooks, *The Well Wrought Urn: Studies in the Structure of Poetry* (New York: Harcourt Brace, 1947) and W.K. Wimsatt, *The Verbal Icon: Studies in the Meaning of Poetry* (Lexington, KY: University of Kentucky Press, 1954). For Empson's vigorous rebuttals of the doctrine, see *Argufying*, especially Section I, 'Literary Interpretation: the Language Machine', pp. 67–

189; also – by way of counter-riposte – John Crowe Ransom, 'Mr. Empson's Muddles', *Southern Review* 4 (1938–39), pp. 322–39.

44 Empson, *Seven Types of Ambiguity*, p. 197.

45 See Note 30, above.

46 See Notes 36 and 43, above.

47 See especially Brooks, *The Well Wrought Urn* and Wimsatt, *The Verbal Icon*.

48 Leo Tolstoy, *What is Art?*, trans. Aylmer Maude (New York: Macmillan, 1960).

49 F.R. Leavis, 'Diabolic Intellect and the Noble Hero: Or the Sentimentalist's Othello', in *The Common Pursuit* (London: Chatto & Windus, 1952), pp. 136–59. See also Christopher Norris, 'Post-Structuralist Shakespeare: Text and Ideology', in *Deconstruction and the Interests of Theory* (London: Pinter, 1988), pp. 109–25.

50 F.R. Leavis, 'Literary Criticism and Philosophy: A Reply', in *The Importance of Scrutiny*, ed. Eric Bentley (New York: New York University Press, 1964), pp. 30–40.

51 See especially Ken Larson, 'The Classical German Shakespeare as Emblem of Germany as "Geistige Weltmacht": Validating National Power Through Cultural Prefiguration', available online at http://aurora.wells.edu/~klarson/papers/mla91.htm and 'Did Shakespeare Really Write in German Or: How the Bard Became *ein Klassiker*; Notes on the Politics of Culture' [http://aurora.wells.edu/~klarson/papers/tacclub1.htm]. For further discussion of related topics, see Terence Hawkes, *Meaning By Shakespeare* (London: Routledge, 1992).

52 Empson, *Seven Types of Ambiguity*, p. 252.

53 Ibid., p. 252.

54 Crary and Read (eds.), *The New Wittgenstein*.

55 See especially Ray Monk, *Ludwig Wittgenstein: The Duty of Genius* (London: Jonathan Cape, 1990).

56 For some illuminating commentary, see Orlando Figes, *Natasha's Dance: A Cultural History of Russia* (Harmondsworth: Penguin, 2002).

57 George Orwell, 'Lear, Tolstoy and the Fool', in *Shooting an Elephant and Other Essays* (London: Secker & Warburg, 1950), pp. 114–33.

58 See especially Monk, *Ludwig Wittgenstein*.

59 Ibid.

60 Monk, *Bertrand Russell: The Spirit of Solitude* (London: Jonathan Cape, 1996) and *Bertrand Russell: The Ghost of Madness* (Cape, 2000).

61 Crary and Read (eds.), *The New Wittgenstein*.

62 Wittgenstein, *Philosophical Investigations*, Sections 201–9; Saul Kripke, *Wittgenstein on Rules and Private Language: An Elementary Exposition* (Oxford: Blackwell, 1982); also Alexander Miller and Crispin Wright (eds.), *Rule-Following and Meaning* (Chesham: Acumen, 2002); Bob Hale and Crispin Wright (eds.), *A Companion to the Philosophy of Language* (Oxford: Blackwell, 1997), pp. 369–96.

63 For some pioneering early work in this vein, see P.M.S. Hacker, *Insight and Illusion: Wittgenstein on Philosophy and the Metaphysics of Experience* (Oxford: Oxford University Press, 1972).

64 Wittgenstein, *Culture and Value*, p. 53e.

65 Ibid., p. 19e.

66 See Hacker, *Insight and Illusion*.

67 Wittgenstein, *Culture and Value*, p. 36e.

68 See Monk, *Ludwig Wittgenstein*.

69 See especially Martin Heidegger, *Poetry, Language, Thought*, trans. Albert Hofstadter (New York: Harper & Row, 1971); also *The Question of Being*, trans. W. Kluback and J.T. Wilde (New York: Twayne, 1958) and *The Question Concerning Technology*, trans. William Lovitt (Harper & Row, 1977).

70 Wittgenstein, *Culture and Value*, pp. 1e, 23e, 37e.

71 Richard Wagner, 'Judaism in Music', trans. William Ashton Ellis; available online at http://reactor-core.org/judaism-in-music.html.

72 Wittgenstein, *Philosophical Investigations*, Section 531.

73 W.V. Quine, 'Two Dogmas of Empiricism', in *From a Logical Point of View*, 2nd edn (Cambridge, MA: Harvard University Press, 1960), pp. 20–46.

74 Kripke, *Wittgenstein on Rules and Private Language*.

75 See Note 62, above.

76 See also Christopher Norris, 'The Limits of *Whose* Language? Wittgenstein on Logic, Science and Mathematics', in *Language, Logic and Epistemology: A Modal-Realist Approach* (London: Palgrave, 2004), pp. 66–110 and 'Kripkenstein's Monsters: Anti-Realism, Scepticism, and the Rule-Following Debate', in *On Truth and Meaning: Language, Logic and the Grounds of Belief* (London: Continuum, 2006), pp. 155–202.

77 See Cavell, *Must We Mean What We Say?*; also *In Quest of the Ordinary: Lines of Skepticism and Romanticism* (Chicago: University of Chicago Press, 1994); *Philosophical Passages: Wittgenstein, Emerson, Austin, Derrida* (Oxford: Blackwell, 1994); *The Claim of Reason*, 2nd edn (Oxford: Oxford University Press, 1999); *Disowning Knowledge in Six Plays of Shakespeare*, 2nd edn (Cambridge: Cambridge University Press, 2002).

78 Henry Staten, *Wittgenstein and Derrida* (Lincoln, NB: University of Nebraska Press, 1984); Newton Garver and Seung-Chong Lee, *Derrida and Wittgenstein* (Philadelphia, PA: Temple University Press, 1995).

79 See for instance O.K. Bouwsma, *Without Proof or Evidence: Essays of O.K. Bouwsma* (Lincoln, NB: University of Nebraska Press, 1984).

80 See Note 77, above.

81 See especially Cavell, *The Claim of Reason*.

82 Wittgenstein, *Culture and Value*, p. 24e.

83 Ibid., p. 19e.

84 Ibid., pp. 18–19e.

85 Wittgenstein, *Philosophical Investigations*, Section 115.

86 Wittgenstein, *Culture and Value*, p. 39e.

87 Ibid., p. 3e.

88 For a useful selection of these texts, see David Simpson (ed.), *The Origins of Modern Critical Thought: German Aesthetics and Literary Criticism from Lessing to Hegel* (Cambridge: Cambridge University Press, 1988).

89 Cited from conversation by Rush Rhees, *Ludwig Wittgenstein: Personal Recollections* (Oxford: Blackwell, 1981), p. 127.

90 See Note 62, above.

91 Ludwig Wittgenstein, *Lectures and Conversations on Aesthetics, Psychology and Religious Belief,* ed. Cyril Barrett (Berkeley & Los Angeles: University of California Press, 1967), p. 9.

92 Ibid., p. 9.

93 See Note 62, above.

94 For further discussion, see Christopher Norris, *Truth Matters: Realism, Anti-Realism and Response-Dependence* (Edinburgh: Edinburgh University Press, 2002).

95 See Notes 76 and 94, above.

96 See F.R. Leavis, *The Critic as Anti-Philosopher: Essays and Papers*, ed. G. Singh (London: Chatto & Windus, 1982).

97 See Simpson, *Origins of Modern Critical Thought*.

98 Wittgenstein, *Culture and Value*, p. 28e.

99 Wittgenstein, *Philosophical Investigations*, p. vii.

100 See Simpson, *Origins of Modern Critical Thought*.

101 See Rees, *Ludwig Wittgenstein*.

102 Ibid., p. 126.

103 James Conant, 'Putting Two and Two Together: Kierkegaard, Wittgenstein and the

Point of View for their Work as Authors', in Timothy Tessin and Mario von der Ruhr (eds.), *Philosophy and the Grammar of Religious Belief* (Basingstoke: Macmillan, 1995), pp. 248–331.

104 Soren Kierkegaard, *The Point of View for My Work as an Author*, trans. Walter Lowrie (New York: Harper & Row, 1962).

105 Kierkegaard, *Either/Or*, vol. 1; ed. and trans. Howard V. Hong and Edna H. Hong (Princeton, NJ: Princeton University Press, 1987).

106 Kierkegaard, *Fear and Trembling*, ed. C. Stephen Evans; trans. Evans and Sylvia Walsh (Cambridge: Cambridge University Press, 2006).

107 Allan Janik and Stephen Toulmin, *Wittgenstein's Vienna* (New York: Simon & Schuster, 1973).

108 Cavell, *The Claim of Reason*.

109 See Quine, 'Two Dogmas of Empiricism'.

110 For one of the most influential (if widely misinterpreted) texts of this kind, see Jacques Derrida, 'White Mythology: Metaphor in the Text of Philosophy', in *Margins of Philosophy*, trans. Alan Bass (Chicago: University of Chicago Press, 1982), pp. 207–71; also Paul de Man, 'The Epistemology of Metaphor', in Sheldon Sacks (ed.), *On Metaphor* (Chicago: University of Chicago Press, 1979), pp. 11–28 and – reflecting my own (early) change of mind on this topic – cf. Christopher Norris, *The Deconstructive Turn: Essays in the Rhetoric of Philosophy* (London: Methuen, 1983) and *The Contest of Faculties: Philosophy and Theory after Deconstruction* (London: Methuen, 1985).

111 See for instance Bernard Harrison, 'White Mythology Revisited: Derrida and his Critics on Reason and Rhetoric', *Critical Inquiry* 25(3) (Spring 1999), pp. 505–34; Paul Ricoeur, *The Rule of Metaphor: Multi-Disciplinary Studies in the Creation of Meaning in Language*, trans. Robert Czerny with Kathleen McLaughlin and John Costello (London: Routledge & Kegan Paul, 1978).

112 See Note 110, above.

113 See especially Wittgenstein, *On Certainty*, Sections 95–9.

114 See Note 62, above; also John McDowell, 'Wittgenstein on Following a Rule', *Synthèse* 58 (1984), pp. 325–63.

115 See Note 114, above; also John McDowell, *Mind and World* (Cambridge, MA: Harvard University Press, 1994).

116 Norris, *Realism, Anti-Realism and Response-Dependence*.

117 Crispin Wright, *Truth and Objectivity* (Cambridge, MA: Harvard University Press, 1992).

118 Crispin Wright, *Wittgenstein on the Foundations of Mathematics* (London: Duckworth, 1980).

119 Wittgenstein, *Philosophical Investigations*, Section 115.

120 See Notes 103–6, above; also Christopher Norris, 'Fictions of Authority: Narrative and Viewpoint in Kierkegaard's Writing', in *The Deconstructive Turn*, pp. 85–106.

121 See Crary and Read (eds.), *The New Wittgenstein* and Wittgenstein, *Culture and Value*, p. 83e; also – for a different, more nuanced and less resolutely Wittgensteinian approach to these issues – Jean-Jacques LeCercle, *Philosophy of Nonsense: The Intuitions of Victorian Nonsense Literature* (London: Routledge, 1994).

122 Jacques Derrida, 'Structure, Sign, and Play in the Discourse of the Human Sciences', in *Writing and Difference*, trans. Alan Bass (London: Routledge & Kegan Paul, 1978), pp. 278–94 (288).

123 See especially Jacques Derrida, '"Genesis and Structure" and Phenomenology', in *Writing and Difference*, pp. 154–68 (159); also *'Speech and Phenomena' and Other Essays on Husserl's Theory of Signs*, trans. David B. Allison (Evanston, IL: Northwestern University Press, 1973).

7

Free-Will, Creativity and Structural Constraint:
Linguistics as a Guide to Metaphysics

I

The issue of free-will versus determinism is one of the deepest, longest-running and most intractable that philosophers have taken on board.[1] Probably no other has been so much discussed and with so many claims to have resolved it, or at least to have moved the discussion forward, yet with so few signs of anything that might remotely justify that claim. Indeed, one could take the view that this character of endlessly eluding resolution and provoking further (likewise problematical) re-statements of the issue is itself the very hallmark of what counts as a properly 'philosophical' debate, as distinct from one that might end up in an area of the natural or human sciences where there was some prospect of its actually being resolved. Any survey of the various answers put forward by philosophers and the various problems that have constantly risen up against them would require much more space, and far more patience on the reader's part, than I have any right to assume. Besides, it is unlikely – on all the evidence to date – that such a survey would produce anything more than a deepened sense of perplexity or a strengthened inclination to let the issue go until (if ever) there occurs some decisive advance in neurophysiology or cognitive science that might offer an escape from all these philosophically induced dilemmas.

At present, so far from offering the glimpse of a solution, those disciplines have tended rather to push it even further out of sight by posing the same old problems in a yet more acute or intractable form. Indeed their main impact has been to bring home the sheer recalcitrance of certain issues like those concerning the nature of consciousness, the existence or non-existence of purely phenomenal (subjective or qualitative) mind-states, and the question whether – as hard-line physicalists would have it – such mind-states might be reducible to brain-states in the fullness of neuro-scientific time.[2] Clearly there is a close connection between the free-will/determinism debate and this issue with regard to qualia, that is, those modes of sensory-perceptual or phenomenological experience that might seem strictly inconceivable except from a first-person privileged epistemic standpoint. Thus the upholder of free-will or moral autonomy is likely to maintain some version of the irreducibility thesis in respect of qualia – that they could never in principle be fully cashed out or explained away in physicalist terms – while the determinist about human actions, motives and beliefs will probably take the opposite view, that with the advent of a mature neuro-science this idea will be shown up as just a remnant of our old, 'folk-psychological' ways of thinking. Up to now there is little sign that either party is capable of mounting an argument that would impress the other as properly engaging the issue rather than exploiting some equivocal point or begging some crucial question. Hence the great range of thought-experimental variations on both sides of the qualia debate, with anti-reductionists appealing to fictive cases (like Frank Jackson's famous example of Mary the sensorily deprived colour-scientist[3]) which purport to show that there is always something left out of any science-based or physicalist account, while opponents seek to trump them by drawing the analogy with previous instances of successful reductions in the history of science to date, like those of heat to mean kinetic energy of molecules or of light to electro-magnetic radiation.[4] Much the same applies to the free-will/ determinism issue, since here also there is a strong impression of cross-purpose argument and mutual suspicion that the other party is failing (or refusing) to grasp what that issue is all about.

As I have said, it is far beyond the scope of this chapter to provide anything like an adequate survey of the field, let alone an alternative answer that would steer the debate in some radically new direction. Still I should hope to do more by way of constructive problem-solving than those, like Colin McGinn, who adopt a 'mysterian' view of such matters according to which we are simply incapable of resolving the problem, maybe by dint of our limited intelligence or some quirk of our cognitive apparatus.[5] Rather I want to suggest that one useful line of approach is by thinking about our capacity as language users or what is involved in the everyday, seemingly unproblematical business of talking straight ahead and – at least for the most part – managing to secure a good measure of communicative uptake. For it strikes me, after much reading around during the past two decades, that neither linguists nor philosophers of language have yet come close to explaining how it is that we are able to bring off this common-place yet quite remarkable feat. Thus they may offer all sorts of sophisticated insight into the various (e.g., the logical, syntactic, semantic, structural-semiotic or pragmatic) dimensions of language-use and yet leave it a total mystery how we can normally manage to say what we mean and mean what we say. Moreover, I think that this explanatory gap has a great deal to do with the free-will/ determinism issue since it concerns the remarkable fact – all the more so for its being so much a part of our ordinary competence as language users – of our ability somehow to string words together in a way that must (or so we are apt to believe) be conscious, deliberate or intentional yet which also seems to occur at a level of preconscious, quasi-automatic or at any rate not transparently accessible cognitive-linguistic processing. So this is my case, or a part of it: that we can best get a feel for the arguments that weigh on both sides of that issue by reflecting on the nature of linguistic creativity and what goes on in the process of everyday verbal communication. For if indeed there is strong intuitive warrant for the idea that we do (normally or properly) say what we mean in the sense of having intended to say *just that*, then there is also warrant for the contrary claim that we do not know what we were meaning to say until we have said it, or cannot be sure what our intentions were until they have achieved articulate form.

Of course this puzzle could easily be solved if it amounted to no more than the point that a lot of our linguistic parsing – especially in matters of grammar or syntax – simply *has* to go on at a preconscious level since we should otherwise be wholly incapable of fluent, impromptu and context-sensitive speech. It is precisely this salient feature of language that Chomsky sought to explain by positing a modular, that is, a specialized or dedicated language-faculty which enables speakers to construct grammatically well-formed sentences – and to recognize others that flout the norm – with such uniform speed and regularity across otherwise large differences of cultural or socio-linguistic background.[6] Thus any adequate theory would have to explain how speakers could produce a potentially infinite or open-ended range of grammatical sentences on the basis of certain recursive rules for generating just those sentences from a finite stock of basic structures and depth-to-surface (e.g., active-to-passive) syntactic transformations. According to Chomsky this provided the only adequate account of how they could exercise that basic competence – that native capacity for talking straight ahead and making grammatical sense – from one context to another, or despite their varying degrees of acquired linguistic-communicative skill. Moreover, he saw it as strengthening the case for a rationalist philosophy of mind, that is to say, an approach to cognitive psychology which totally rejected the behaviourist idea of human beings as passive receptors of sensory stimuli and instead emphasized the active, productive or creative character of human intelligence.[7] His main argument to this effect was from what Chomsky termed the 'poverty of the stimulus', or the fact that children at an early stage of psycho-cognitive development were able to deploy a wide range of grammatical constructions to which they had not been exposed in their cultural-linguistic environment. Among his chief items of evidence here was their tendency to follow the normal rules for plural or past-tense formation even in cases – like irregular plurals or non-standard past tenses – where people around them (parents and teachers) were using the 'correct', that is, irregular or rule-breaking forms.

These arguments are closely connected with Chomsky's ethico-political stress on the need for people to exercise their democratic rights, to think responsibly about matters of shared social concern, and thereby to resist the kinds of passive ideological conditioning encouraged by exposure to government propaganda or collusive mass-media disinformation.[8] Thus his rationalist approach in philosophy of mind and his transformational-generative theory of linguistic (grammatical) competence were taken to possess decisive implications for our status as moral agents with the innate capacity to think for ourselves and hold out against the pressures of 'manufactured consensus'. Along with this went the positive counterpart of his negative 'poverty of the stimulus' thesis, namely Chomsky's constant appeal to the inherent creativity of human language or the fact that it enables speakers to generate an endless multiplicity of different, novel, even (on occasion) hitherto unspoken sentences from a finite repertoire of underlying structures and stock of combinatorial elements. Here again there is a close analogy between the high estimate of human cognitive powers implicit in this conception of language and the high estimate of our native capacity for autonomous moral and socio-political engagement expressed in Chomsky's voluminous writings as a critic of US foreign and domestic policy.[9] Thus he takes it as pretty much axiomatic that a rationalist philosophy of mind – and especially of the mind as revealed or manifested in our competence as language users – conduces to (or at any rate consorts most readily with) an ethics and a politics committed to the values of truth, freedom, participant democracy and the open expression of dissident views on matters of shared public concern.

This connection was made more explicitly in Chomsky's earlier writings, and has perhaps been somewhat muted of late because his critics on the right – political opponents mostly but also some linguists of a contrary mind – were apt to deploy his political views as a stick to beat his more specialized work in the fields of linguistics and cognitive psychology.[10] However it may be that he now finds something problematic about the notion of deriving those ethico-political values from an approach that stresses the *essentially* rule-governed character of language, the modular (or 'hard-wired') nature of many high-level cognitive as well as perceptual or reflex-response mechanisms, and the claim that so much of what we normally think of as 'free', 'spontaneous' or *non*-ruled-governed speech or behaviour is in fact subject to just such formal constraints. Thus there is a marked tension between Chomsky's rationalist emphasis on the sheer resourcefulness that human minds (or brains) typically display by acquiring, using and interpreting language in accordance with those complex but strictly specifiable constraints and his emphasis on freedom – on the scope for moral, political, and intellectual autonomy – as an absolute prerequisite for any properly functioning democratic system. No doubt this tension can be somewhat reduced by invoking, as Chomsky does, the remarkable creativity of language users, here defined as their innate capacity to produce an infinite (or non-denumerable) range of well-formed grammatical utterances from a finite repertoire of deep syntactic structures and depth-to-surface transformations. Yet 'creativity' of this sort – the kind that goes along with tightly specified rules as to just *what counts* as grammatical well-formedness – is scarcely the most promising basis for any conception of 'creative' involvement in the ethical and socio-political spheres. That is to say, it can offer no substantive support for any activist-participant conception (like Chomsky's) that would hold self-styled liberal democracies – especially US type – of the present-day more fully accountable to their own professed standards of freedom, equality and justice.

Clearly issues of precise definition are of crucial importance here since conflicting or ambiguous usages of terms like 'creativity' and 'freedom' – terms with a technical as well as a broader, strongly evaluative sense – can often be a potent source of confusion. The one type of 'freedom' has to do with the language user's native (and to this extent hard-wired) competence in deriving a potentially endless variety of context-specific, pragmatically oriented sentences from the nonetheless strictly delimited range of grammatical options that make for well-formedness and hence for communicative uptake. The other has to do with open possibilities of action, commitment and properly autonomous (freely willed though responsibly exercised) agency and choice which cannot be conceived in such formal terms, least of all by the lights of a thinker like Chomsky who espouses a thoroughgoing left-libertarian – indeed an avowedly anarchist – view of what democracy might and should entail. It is here, as I have said, that thinking about issues in linguistics and philosophy of language raises questions that are often within close reach of the free-will/determinism debate, and which might even help to re-focus that debate in a useful way. Chomsky posed some of those questions – and to powerfully convincing effect – when he mounted his critique of B.F. Skinner's behaviourist account of language-acquisition and human cognitive development.[11] Thus he showed not only that this theory failed to explain how infants acquired language (*vide* his 'poverty of the stimulus' argument) and how speakers managed to achieve such feats of 'creative' language-use, but also how behaviourism served as a spurious justification for politically motivated strategies of social conditioning that viewed human subjects as passive receptors of whatever ideology happened to suit the currently most powerful arbiters of 'public opinion'. Yet if Skinner-type behaviourism marked the *ne plus ultra* of empiricist epistemology – a stance adopted (albeit with certain qualifications) by philosophers like W.V. Quine – then it is not entirely clear that its Chomskian rationalist counterpart succeeds in avoiding a determinist upshot or in carving out the requisite space for human 'creativity' and 'freedom'.[12] That is to say, there is still a problem about the analogy between those terms as applied in their technical (theoretical-linguistic or cognitive-psychological) sense and those terms as applied in the context of debate concerning the scope and limits of human freedom. Where the former defines that scope as conceivable only within certain specified formal bounds the latter requires a far more substantive, that is, an ethically and politically meaningful conception of autonomous agency and choice.

Of course there are various alternative ways of stating this distinction, most of them showing a similar tendency to raise large issues of ethics and politics by way of what can look very like a semantic or 'merely' definitional ground of dispute. Among them are the kinds of controversy that have arisen between 'negative' and 'positive' conceptions of liberty; deontological (Kantian) versus consequentialist theories of ethics; procedural (i.e., rule-based) approaches in philosophy of law, politics and the social sciences versus other, more strongly interpretivist lines of thought; and the issue in philosophy of language as regards the claims of a formalized, logico-semantic mode of analysis versus those of a more hermeneutically oriented, language-based or expressly normative conception of meaning and truth. What complicates matters yet further is the fact that in each case the latter persuasion may appear more liberal and open to the diverse range of human beliefs, values and concerns yet can easily give way to a cultural-relativist outlook that would leave no room for effective criticism of existing ethical or socio-political mores. That is, such approaches – whether communitarian, pragmatist or late-Wittgensteinian – can always be deployed in the service of a highly conformist or deeply conservative creed that equates the scope and limits of intelligible discourse with the range of communal 'language-games' or cultural 'forms of life' which between them define what properly counts as a meaningful or relevant contribution to debate.[13] In which case the interests of political justice and enlightened or progressive social critique would be far better served by the alternative (rationalist) approach that comes at these issues with an opposite set of priorities, that is, through a logico-semantic conception of language and meaning, coupled (as in Chomsky) with a truth-based account of how thinking is able to put up resistance to the blandishments of state-sponsored ideology or large-scale media disinformation. However, as I have said, the main problem here – one that has loomed large in debate since Kant – is the problem of deriving substantive ethical precepts or sources of guidance from a deontological theory whose maxims and imperatives apply at so remote a level of abstraction from our practical, everyday moral concerns.[14] What this comparison with Chomskian linguistics helps to bring out is the connection – at any rate the close analogy – between issues concerning the scope, limits and precise nature of human 'creativity' in language and issues concerning moral autonomy or the freedom to criticize and re-envisage our socio-political conditions of life.

II

I hope that this excursion through some varied philosophical terrain will have helped to clarify my central point in the opening paragraph. It had to do with the way that reflection on the rival claims of free-will versus determinism might profit from reflection on the kindred issue of linguistic intentionality, that is, the question how speakers can talk straight ahead with an (apparently) clear sense of what they wish or intend to say and yet – as may be verified through momentary introspection – without any more than a vague, approximate, tentative or always revisable grasp of how their utterance will turn out. This is the paradox nicely captured by whoever it was who is supposed to have asked 'How can I know what I mean until I see what I've said?' It is also, I suggest, the kernel of truth in Heidegger's vatic pronouncement that 'language speaks' ('*Die Sprache spricht*'), rather than – as the commonplace 'humanist' idea would have it – language serving as a strictly subordinate means of expression or an always available standing-reserve for the speaker's communicative purpose.[15] On the other hand Heidegger's claim goes along with a large amount of surplus doctrinal baggage that we might very well want to shed. This includes both his early, politically compromised idea that truth spoke only through the privileged medium of certain national languages – ancient Greek and German – and also his later, more chastened yet still (in the circumstances) highly dubious idea that we could hearken to it only by adopting a wisely passive or receptive attitude and hence, in effect, disowning any personal responsibility for certain less than creditable past utterances.[16] At very least one may hazard that some such motive may well have played a role in Heidegger's post-war *Kehre*, his much-discussed 'turn' from a language of resolutely facing-up to the call of authentic Being to a language of *Gelassenheit*, or 'letting-be'.[17]

So there is reason, on ethico-political as well as philosophic grounds, for rejecting his claims in this regard and maintaining – with warrant, after all, from the native intuition of most speakers in most contexts – that meaning what we say and intending our words to be taken in accordance with their overt (or sometimes covert) drift is intrinsically an aspect of our normal activity as language users. Moreover, it is an aspect that has received much notice from philosophers of various persuasion, be they speech-act theorists, hermeneutic thinkers, pragmatists, phenomenologists, followers of Davidson's truth-based logico-semantic approach to propositional content, Habermasian advocates of discourse-ethics, or exponents of Gricean ideas about conversational implicature.[18] What they all have in common – and can claim to share with the outlook that Heidegger dismissively terms the 'average, everyday' grasp of such matters – is the basic belief that language serves as a more-or-less reliable and well-adapted means for the communication of thoughts, attitudes and feelings between speakers and listeners. No doubt they differ widely on a great range of issues such as those concerning the order of priority between sense and reference, the claims of logical analysis versus those of 'ordinary language', or the question as to whether – and precisely how – an utterer's meaning (or expressive purport) can diverge from the norms of 'linguistic meaning' as encoded in conventional modes of speech. However these differences of emphasis will appear less significant when set against the shared baseline assumption that language can and must do a pretty good job in establishing a link between what the speaker has it in mind to say and what the recipient can (or should properly) take her as saying. Of course this way of putting it will strike many philosophers as highly simplistic and as raising a number of difficult issues – like those instanced above – which cannot be brusquely set aside by claiming the warrant of speaker's intuition or the supposed self-evidence of adequate uptake in most communicative contexts. Still it is an approach that at least has the virtue of managing to capture those same intuitions and doing so, moreover, with considerable back-up from a range of philosophic quarters.

Where it chiefly falls short is in its failure to acknowledge the force of that counter-intuition which is apt to strike speakers when talking straight ahead but also, momentarily, adopting a reflective distance from the onward flow of speech and wondering whether their expressive intent can possibly have been fully formed or present to mind before the utterance turned out to have taken *that* particular linguistic shape. For whatever one's doubts about Heidegger's '*die Sprache spricht*', or kindred (e.g., post-structuralist) ideas about the 'death of the subject' and suchlike fashionable themes, still there is a genuine sense in which language can be known to outrun or elude the conscious, deliberate, intentional grasp of the speaker at any given moment. This is one reason why early critics of the Chomskian transformational-generative theory – and also some of its defenders – spent a great deal of time discussing whether it could claim to represent certain actual, psychologically 'real' goings-on in the minds of language users or whether it should rather be viewed as an abstract representation devised for descriptive-theoretical purposes.[19] That question could always be kept on hold so long as the programme worked for those purposes and so long as the question of its 'psychological' – more exactly, its expressive or intentional – content could be thought of as one to be settled once all the evidence was in. However it became more pressing when Chomsky, along with most of his followers, set about revising his early approach wherein issues of semantics or interpretation played a strictly subordinate role *vis-à-vis* issues of syntactic structure, and instead offered various proposals for assigning semantic content at an early stage in the generative process.[20] For there was then a more obvious need to get clear about just what that content was supposed to be or what the process actually entailed. Once the project sought to find room for a semantics that would dovetail with its formalized approach to syntax then the question arose as to how this development might square with its emphasis on linguistic 'creativity' as that which enabled language users to produce an open-ended variety of well-formed sentences from a finite stock of underlying grammatical structures.

This question was posed all the more forcibly by Chomsky's continued, if lately more cautious, way of linking these issues in linguistics, cognitive psychology and philosophy of mind with matters of an ethical and socio-political import.[21] That is to say, it was less than self-evident that the kind of 'freedom' invoked by his rationalist approach – what enabled human beings to exhibit powers of linguistic creativity far beyond anything explainable in behaviourist terms – was also the kind of freedom required by his commitment to an ethics and politics of autonomy, open democratic debate, and unconstrained individual conscience. Indeed, the former might even be seen as inimical to the latter or at least in tension with it – since the Cartesian tradition invoked by Chomsky is one that places its chief emphasis on the rule-governed or logic-based character of rational thought, and which hence does little to endorse or promote those other, more freely 'creative' (including ethical and socio-political) dimensions.[22] This is not for one moment to deny that the interests of a critical-emancipatory politics are far better served by a theory of language or a cognitive science premised on a high estimate of the human capacity for rational, reflective and ethically responsible thinking than by a Skinner-type behaviourist or reflex-response theory premised on the opposite assumption. Nor is it to claim (absurdly) that a politics or ethics aimed toward expanding the scope of human creativity and freedom could possibly dispense with those resources of critical thinking that rely on the exercise of logically consistent and rationally motivated thought. Rather it is to say that a philosophy of mind with these particular rationalist antecedents cannot offer very much by way of support for a substantive conception of ethico-political freedom and responsibility.

This dilemma is all the more acute for the fact that Chomsky's evolving programme in theoretical linguistics and cognitive psychology is by far the most developed, refined and sophisticated model that we have for bringing those disciplines together and also for assessing their potential relevance to just such wider concerns. What I want to suggest is that its value lies partly in having raised these issues to a high point of visibility and also having shown how intimate yet deeply problematical is the link between language – theoretical linguistics and philosophy of language but also the straightforward, everyday business of linguistic communication – and questions regarding the scope and limits of human freedom. Thus our views on each matter are likely to divide along much the same lines and, once we take the reflective step back, to come up against much the same sorts of problem or counter-arguments. On the one hand it is well-nigh impossible for speakers *not* to have the strong intuitive conviction – at least while talking straight ahead – that they are more or less successfully saying what they mean or meaning what they say and doing so, moreover, through an exercise of choice (albeit under certain language-specific constraints) between various possible modes of expression. So likewise, it is well-nigh impossible for human agents performing or deciding on a given course of action *not* to feel that the outcome was underdetermined in advance, that there existed a significant margin of choice, and that what they did (or refrained from doing) was the upshot of autonomous or freely willed decision rather than a product of causal factors perhaps too numerous and complex for them (or anyone) fully to grasp. On the other hand just as we know, on reflection, that 'talking straight ahead' is a largely preconscious and often quite inscrutable process wherein what we say (or turn out to have said) may exceed the limits of deliberate or purposive intent, so likewise a more distanced view of our various morally significant acts may suggest that their motivating springs and sources may lie elsewhere than in the exercise of conscious, volitional agency. What typically goes on in both cases – speech-acts and modes of practically oriented conduct – is then apt to strike us as more subject to various kinds of constraint (or less within our power of deliberative choice) than we might incline or wish to suppose.

This is once again where the problem is posed most sharply with respect to Chomskian psycholinguistics, namely the question whether all those transformational-generative rules and structures should be thought of as describing what actually occurs in the minds of individual speakers or rather as heuristic devices which offer an abstract representation for specialized theoretical purposes. That is to say, the conjunction of a rationalist outlook in philosophy of mind with a strongly modularized or 'black-box' approach to issues in cognitive psychology would appear to leave little room for any other than a notional kind of 'creativity' or 'freedom'. This problem looms even larger when the case is extended to the realm of ethics and politics, where it offers – as I have said – rather dubious support for those value-commitments on account of its allegiance to a doctrine of hard-wired (innately programmed) cognitive-linguistic competence which yields at most a highly abstract or formal conception of human liberty. If the connection between these two aspects of Chomsky's thought receives less emphasis in his later writing then it may be for just that reason, along with the fact that his current approach to issues in theoretical linguistics has sought to dispense with a good deal of that earlier depth-to-surface transformational machinery.

Still anyone browsing through his huge list of works and unfamiliar with these developments might easily suppose that a title like *Government and Binding* – his name for the new syntax-parsing approach – placed that book firmly in the 'politics' category.[23]

Let me repeat – lest these remarks be misunderstood – that to raise such issues is not to impugn the significance of Chomsky's revolution (the term seems appropriate for once) in the fields of theoretical linguistics and cognitive psychology, nor to question the likewise exemplary value of his activist involvement in matters of ethical and socio-political concern. Rather, what I want to bring out is the way that a sustained and critical reflection on the scope of human linguistic creativity has an inbuilt tendency to emphasize just those deep-laid philosophic problems that have regularly surfaced in the longstanding debate about free-will versus determinism. Thus there seems to operate something like a law of inverse or diminishing returns whereby any greater degree of exactitude in the specification of linguistic-cognitive capacities goes along with an increasingly narrow conception of what counts – for theoretical purposes – as the kind and degree of 'freedom' involved. Such is the problem that Chomsky would appear to have confronted in his earlier attempt to extrapolate from one to the other domain, that is, from the fact of speakers' ability to produce an open-ended range of well-formed grammatical utterances from a finite stock of depth-structural elements to his claim for their autonomy as rational agents with the freedom and the right to decide for themselves in matters of ethico-political conscience.

Here again it needs stressing that this argument should not be confused with the various kinds of facile anti-humanist rhetoric – or premature reports concerning the 'death of the subject' – that have lately been doing the rounds among sundry Heideggerians, Foucauldians, post-structuralists, postmodernists and others.[24] That such talk most often goes along with an equally facile (and, in ethical terms, equally suspect) anti-Enlightenment bias is further reason to make clear that any problems raised with regard to Chomsky's defence of rationalist and humanist principles should be understood not as seeking to discredit those principles but rather, very much in their own spirit, as critically examining their presuppositions. What then becomes apparent is the curious fact that Foucault and others have set up a distinctly hybrid entity – 'Enlightenment humanism' – just in order the more easily to knock it down. Thus Foucault took Kant as his chief philosophical exemplar of a discourse that went on to dominate the nineteenth-century human sciences and which produced the idea of 'man' as a temporary 'fold' in the order of things, a 'strange empirical-transcendental doublet' whose epoch was now nearing its end – 'like a face drawn in sand at the ocean's edge' – with the advent of a post-humanist paradigm grounded in the turn toward language as the absolute horizon of intelligibility.[25] For Heidegger likewise, Kant stands squarely in the line of those philosophers, from Descartes to Husserl, whose thinking bore witness to the epochal swerve from a primordial language of authentic Being and truth to a discourse marked by the pre-dominance of 'metaphysical' (by which he means basically humanist and epistemological) concerns.[26] Yet there is something distinctly awry about that whole genealogy of 'Western metaphysics' which finds in Kant – or indeed, for that matter, in thinkers like Descartes and Husserl – its prime examples of this large-scale philosophic aberration. After all, Kant was at great pains in his first critique to insist, *contra* Descartes and others in the rationalist tradition, that the transcendental subject was purely the condition of possibility for knowledge and experience in general, and therefore that it served in a strictly formal or abstract place-holder role rather than affording substantive knowledge of human nature and its various attributes.

Of course this is precisely Heidegger's point: that what one finds in Descartes, Kant and Husserl – at any rate those writings of Husserl that most closely approximate the stipulative goal of a transcendental phenomenology – is a massive evasion of the central issues as these would strike any thinker not in thrall to such delusive 'metaphysical' ideas.[27] However it is simply wrong to suppose, as Heidegger does, that there exists so close or intrinsic a tie between the epistemologically oriented project of Enlightenment thought and those humanist values which he, like Foucault, calls into question. No doubt a strong case can be made for viewing the Enlightenment as a culmination of that broadly humanist (i.e., secularizing) movement of thought which first emerged among the more liberal-progressive thinkers of the Renaissance and thereafter gained ground – albeit intermittently – through the gradual separation of religious belief from state-sponsored powers of doctrinal enforcement. Moreover there are many aspects of Kant's thinking that clearly warrant the humanist description, from his critical-emancipatory injunction *sapere aude* ('have the courage to think for yourself!') to his ethical stress on the autonomy of individual conscience and his championing of cosmopolitical values such as freedom, democracy, religious tolerance and the development of better transnational relations in the interest of 'perpetual peace'.[28] So one could have no objection, in general terms, to the idea of Kant as a leading philosophical proponent of humanist precepts and values. However the claim is less convincing – or more in need of qualification – when it comes to his treatment of epistemological issues and of the transcendental subject as that which makes possible all modes of human experience, knowledge and judgement. For here, as I have said, it is a notable feature of Kant's thinking that he insists absolutely on the formal, *a priori* character of any deductions we can make in this regard and hence the mistake of supposing that they might provide psychology or the other human sciences with some kind of substantive content. Thus Heidegger and Foucault can be seen to have got Kant wrong in so far as they assume that these two (i.e., humanist and epistemo-critical) orientations of his thinking are so closely bound up as to form an indivisible whole. All of which suggests that Foucault is constructing something of a straw-man target – and that the charge might better be directed back against his own strategic misreading – when he writes that well-known passage about the Kantian image of man as a 'strange empirical-transcendental doublet' destined for oblivion with the advent of a new, post-humanist dispensation.

III

Let me draw together the main lines of argument in this chapter so far and explain what bearing I take them to have on the issue of linguistic creativity and constraint *vis-à-vis* the issue of free-will and determinism. My point about Chomsky is that a rationalist approach to linguistics and cognitive psychology is one that may align itself expressly with the former term in each pair – with the value-commitments entailed by a belief in human creativity and freedom – and yet have problems in making its case insofar as that approach itself entails a commitment to certain conceptual and methodological priorities which allow little room for those values. That is to say, his substantive theses with regard to the modularity of mind and the hard-wired (innate or 'encapsulated') nature of our shared linguistic and cognitive skills are such as might be thought not only to sit rather awkwardly with his ethico-political claims but even to place sharp limits on the scope for any genuine – other than abstract or notional   exercise of human freedom and autonomy. Of course there is a vast difference between Chomsky's naturalistic, physicalist or neurologically based way of treating these issues and the outlook of entrenched mind-body dualism that has typified most of his rationalist precursors, from Descartes down. All the same his approach has this much in common with theirs: that it involves a theory of cognitive function – of the various mental capacities that constitute our native endowment – which by no means offers unambiguous support for a voluntarist or autonomist position on matters of moral and intellectual conscience.

Hence, to repeat, the question that arises when Chomsky puts forward his rationalist (Cartesian) thesis with regard to the nature of human linguistic 'creativity' and its bearing on wider issues in ethics and philosophy of mind. For that thesis of course has as much to do with the constraints upon what can properly count as a well-formed, grammatical or intelligible sentence (i.e., with its basically rule-governed or recursively specifiable character) as with the open-ended range of such sentences that speakers may produce in this or that content of usage. To be sure, the central claim of Chomskian linguistic theory – and the heart of its challenge to Skinnerian behaviourism – was precisely its ability to explain how a finite stock of depth-grammatical structures could somehow give rise to a limitless variety of just such particular or context-specific utterances. Yet the problem remains, with regard to Chomsky's philosophical and ethico-political theses, that this kind of 'creativity' and 'freedom' must nonetheless be thought of as tightly constrained by the logical, syntactic and (ultimately) neurochemical bases of linguistic-communicative competence. Thus his challenge to Skinnerian behaviourism, however justified on these grounds, cannot offer much support to a philosophy of mind or an outlook on ethical issues that seeks to vindicate the claims of free-will and moral autonomy over those of a hard-line determinism which – as Chomsky clearly perceives – lends itself to various humanly degrading forms of socio-political indoctrination.

What emerges here, I suggest, is yet another version of the old dilemma that has dogged debates on this issue all the way from the ancient Greek philosophers, *via* Descartes and Kant, to the present-day proponents of central-state or eliminative materialism versus the advocates of an anti-reductionist, compatibilist or downright dualist theory of mind.[29] Whence the special interest of Chomskian psycholinguistics: that it poses the free-will/determinism issue with particular clarity and force owing first to its sheer degree of refinement in descriptive-explanatory terms, and second (as I have said) to its pushing that issue to a high point of visibility. Not that one needs to take this relatively technical and specialist way around in order to get an intuitive feel for the kinds of dilemma – or the philosophic problems – involved. Indeed they are likely to have struck any individual with a penchant for sometimes, momentarily reflecting on what transpires in the process of 'straightforward' speech and our relationship to it as (supposedly) conscious, deliberative language users who are apt to assume – unless things go wrong – that we are managing to mean what we say and say what we mean. Such reflection is apt to produce a countervailing sense that we *do not* in fact enjoy any such privileged, first-person access to our meanings, intentions or expressive purport at least in so far as these are conceived as pre-existing the particular utterance or speech-act in which they take shape. On the contrary: the experience of talking straight ahead – as distinct, say, from composing a written sentence where the process most often seems to involve a revision or reformulation of already verbalized thoughts – is just the kind of experience which brings that sense of our words being somehow dictated in advance, or our minds being somehow made up for us at a preconscious level beyond that of deliberative speaker's intent. Yet of course the distinction that I have drawn here – between spoken and written utterance – is one that very quickly breaks down on the fact that those already-verbalized (rough-draft) stages of articulation are such as must themselves have occurred, or come to mind as suitable stuff for reworking, in a likewise preconscious or non-deliberative way.

Let me repeat: I am not invoking some version of Heidegger's quasi-mystical *Die Sprache spricht*, nor some variant of modish post-structuralist talk about the 'death of the subject', nor again – though this comes rather closer – some idea of the conflicting intuitions we have in this regard as akin to the kinds of antinomy that Kant discussed in his first *Critique*, and which continue to haunt the discourse of present-day epistemology, ethics and philosophy of mind. My main reason for rejecting the latter view is that Kant's claim to transcend those antinomies involved a drastic shift of gear from the phenomenal realm of experience, knowledge and conceptual understanding to the noumenal realm of speculative metaphysics whose effect was (and is) to create ever more difficult and downright insoluble problems for epistemology and ethics alike.[30] On the other hand there is no answer to be had – or none that genuinely seeks to resolve rather than evade the issue – from Wittgensteinian assurances that this problem cannot arise (except amongst philosophers stricken with the plague of needless sceptical doubt) since 'everything is in order' with our language as it serves for the various expressive, informative, creative, religious, scientific and other such purposes that have a place in our communal 'forms of life'.[31] So one may doubt those followers of Wittgenstein who promote his linguistic-therapeutic approach as a cure for all our philosophical ills, especially the kinds of problem induced by the chronic misconception – as they think it – that these language-games could possibly stand in need of any further explanation or justification.

This argument has been run, with minor variations, against just about every major school of modern philosophical thought, from the Frege–Russell analytical approach and its latter-day progeny to Chomsky's transformational-generative programme in linguistics and cognitive science.[32] In each case the suggestion is – again with presumptive warrant from Wittgenstein – that we should give up all those pointless attempts to analyse the structures of logico-semantic or logico-syntactic implication that (supposedly) underlie and account for those practices. Rather we should see, once again, that to make sense of them involves nothing more – though also nothing less – than participation in the various acculturated language-games or 'forms of life' that effectively decide what counts as a meaningful utterance or a valid procedure in matters of reasoning, reckoning, causal explanation, inferential warrant and so forth. From which it follows that philosophers and theorists of language who claim to get beyond this straightforward appeal to the way we customarily talk and think – who hold out the notion of some further, deeper, more adequate explanatory or justificatory account – are thereby revealing their continued enthralment to a false conception of language, thought, and the relationship between them. More precisely: they are showing a lamentable failure to grasp that any 'rules' of grammar or formal conditions for the conduct of well-regulated thought are themselves inextricably bound up with those same language-games and life-forms that constitute their very conditions of meaningful or valid application. So when philosophers presume (after Russell and Frege) to explain or unpack what is really going on when we deploy certain kinds of uniquely referring expression, or when transformational grammarians purport to do the same for our 'surface' forms of linguistic usage, then they are plainly in need of some carefully arranged 'reminders' – Wittgenstein's term – of the sundry ways in which thought can be led astray by such deluded attempts to clarify, disambiguate or even (at worst) to revise or correct our everyday modes of discourse. Conversely, what philosophy does best – or with least risk of inflicting harm – is assemble those reminders in a manner that is perspicuous and able to show how the errors came about while itself renouncing any reform agenda beyond that of restoring philosophical discourse to a due sense of modesty *vis-à-vis* the claims of ordinary, everyday usage.

However this clearly gets us no closer to finding a way beyond the free-will/determinism quandary or the kindred issue with regard to language and linguistic creativity. True, it does something to relieve the kinds of inbuilt conceptual strain that Wittgensteinians might adduce as good reason to abandon the Frege–Russell or Chomskian approach, that is to say, the sorts of problem that typically result from a theory of mind and language premised on a highly formalized (i.e., logico-semantic or depth-syntactical) account of the processes involved. However it is far from evident that an alternative approach of the type here proposed – one that stresses the shared or communal rather than the formal or rule-governed character of language – can be shown to fare any better when it comes to the question at hand. For there is still the same problem of explaining what margin of freedom can possibly exist if one takes it that the limits of intelligibility are those set by some given range of life-forms along with the language-games in which they typically or rightfully find a place. Hence the chief objection to this whole line of thought: that it works out as an *a priori* veto on the notion that we might – at least once in a while – come to see what was ethically wrong or irrational about those life-forms, or get to know more about what gives rise to the often ambiguous or actively misleading surface forms of this or that natural language. That is to say, there is something highly con-servative or downright uncritical about this Wittgensteinian counsel of wise acquiescence in our customary ways of speaking, thinking and acting. Moreover, as I have said, it offers no glimpse of a solution to the issue concerning our linguistic creativity or – by analogy – the scope of our freedom in those other, philosophically salient and ethically crucial respects. After all, if its parameters are set in advance by what properly counts as an intelligible motive, reason, intention or justificatory ground according to the standards that happen to prevail within some given linguistic or socio-cultural community then any 'freedom' to be had is at most a freedom to abide by those norms or else simply fail to make rational or moral sense.

Here again, as with Chomskian psycholinguistics though for just the opposite reason, there emerges a curious counter-logic whereby an argument expressly adopted in the name of deliverance from certain constraints turns out to impose its own tight limits on the scope for linguistic creativity and moral autonomy. Thus Chomsky takes it that his thesis with regard to human linguistic creativity – the way in which speakers are able to produce any number of well-formed grammatical utterances from a finite stock of underlying structures – is sufficient to refute the claims of a Skinner-type behaviourist or operant-conditioning approach to linguistics, psychology and philosophy of mind. However, as we have seen, this invites the rejoinder that Chomsky's programme is no less restrictive in its ultimate implications since it merely substitutes one kind of determinism for another, that is, the constraints imposed by a rationalist (innately specified, modular and syntax-based) conception of mind for those imposed by a crudely reductionist reflex-response model. Yet if that counter-argument is advanced – following Wittgenstein – through an appeal to the variety of social and communicative contexts within which our utterances make sense and which provide their ultimate criteria of meaning or intelligibility then it is open to the charge that in truth this is just another, albeit less obvious (since socially and communally grounded) version of linguistic determinism. My point, to repeat, is that debates about language not only have a bearing on these wider issues in metaphysics, ethics and philosophy of mind but can also be seen to present them in a highly revealing and philosophically productive way.

IV

It may seem that my approach so far has taken us into some fairly specialized areas, or onto ground that is pretty remote from the business of everyday communicative utterance. To be sure, there is much about Chomskian psycholinguistics and discussions of Wittgenstein's later work – ironically enough, given his desire to 'bring philosophy peace' and put an end to all such wranglings – that would justify that impression. All the same it is, I think, a matter of widespread experience among those who occasionally pause to reflect on their own linguistic performances that there is something extraordinary – something that challenges reflection to the utmost – about our capacity to talk straight ahead and to make a good shot at expressing what we have it in mind to convey. Moreover, this is not just the kind of misplaced puzzlement or hyper-cultivated problem-mongering that, in Wittgenstein's view, always results when philosophers allow language to 'go on holiday' and cut loose from its moorings in the discourse of everyday practical affairs. Rather, it is the kind that has always been produced by reflection on the issue of free-will versus determinism – together with kindred philosophical conundrums like the mind/body (or mind/brain) relationship – and which no amount of therapeutic coaxing-down in the late-Wittgensteinian manner can really do much to assuage or dispel.

My suggestion is that these problems find a test-case in the conflicting intuitions we have about language or, more precisely, in our conjoint sense of knowing when we have managed (more or less successfully) to 'say what we mean' whilst not having known – until the utterance emerged, so speak, fully fledged – what exactly it was that we meant or intended to say. To this extent the puzzle about linguistic creativity is on all fours with the problem in philosophy of mind about consciousness and its place (if any) in a physicalist worldview, or again, the problem in ethics as to whether – if at all – that worldview can accommodate our much chipped-away-at, though stubbornly persistent, notions of human free-will and autonomy. In each case the issue falls out between those who would resolve it straightforwardly in one or the other, causal-determinist or voluntarist direction, those who would seek some viable middle-ground stance, and those – like the 'mysterians' in philosophy of mind – who consider it beyond hope of solution owing to its sheer intractability or our limited powers of intelligence.[33] What makes the linguistic-creativity problem a good place to start is the fact that it appeals to the standing intuitions of language users who can reasonably be assumed (in some yet to be determined or clarified sense) to know pretty much what they are talking about. Thus it may be a better, more secure starting point than the issue about ethics where debate so often stalls on the non-negotiable dispute between rule-based or deontological and decisionist or existentialist conceptions, or the issue in philosophy of mind where determinists and voluntarists so often give the same impression of talking straight past each other. Also it offers a fair hope of advancing beyond the mysterian idea that these questions are not for the likes of us since our powers of conceptual grasp or theoretical understanding lag so far behind whatever must be supposed to transpire at a level of intuitive or preconscious thought.[34]

Here it is worth noting that even Chomsky's more elaborately theorized accounts of depth-to-surface grammatical transformation must still be checked against the native intuitions of competent speakers whose judgement in the matter decides whether or not the analysis is right. This is not to say – far from it – that the Wittgensteinian case goes through, that customary usage or communal warrant must always have the last word, and hence that any claim to theorize the workings of language in terms unavailable to the competent native speaker should be treated as yet another symptom of inbred philosophical delusion. Rather it is to say that what goes on in this process – like what goes on in the business of creative thought or in ethical decision-making – is a complex mixture of theories, principles, causal influences, factual considerations, evaluative priorities, pragmatic adjustments to context and so forth, which cannot be fully present to mind as a matter of conscious intent yet which should figure in any attempt to explain how it was that the utterance took that particular shape or how that particular decision was arrived at. Where philosophers tend to get the emphasis wrong is by supposing that these various factors must belong squarely on one or the other side of a line that falls between free-will and determinism, autonomy and constraint, or again (in linguistic terms) between approaches that stress the creativity of language and those that stress its rule-governed or formally specifiable aspects. Hence – as I have argued elsewhere – the massive misdirection of philosophical effort and ingenuity that has gone into the Wittgenstein-influenced debate about rule following, private language and whether or not there exist adequate (other than circular or question-begging) criteria for what counts as consistently and properly following a rule.[35] For this dilemma can only get a hold through the curious willingness of many philosophers to take it as read that correctness in such matters must have to do either with some 'private' (apodictic or introspectible) state of knowledge on the subject's part or with some purely mechanical procedure devoid of normative warrant or validity.[36]

Thus it parallels those other dilemmas – for example, between broadly voluntarist and deontological (rule-based) conceptions of ethics, or expressivist and structural conceptions of language – that have likewise created such a deal of trouble in recent philosophic debate. To regard them as false or pseudo-dilemmas, while justified from a certain, that is, practical-ethical or practical-communicative viewpoint, is nonetheless wrong in so far as they express – like Kant's antinomies of pure reason – certain ways that thinking is constitutively liable to go when reflecting on matters that resist any treatment in clear-cut conceptual or analytic terms. Here again, I should not wish to be taken as recommending either a downright 'mysterian' outlook which counts them altogether too deep, complex or obscure for our limited human powers of comprehension nor a Wittgensteinian approach whereby they can supposedly be laid to rest through a dose of much-needed linguistic therapy. For there is still a deep puzzle – all the more so, indeed, once we take this turn toward language as the end point of all philosophical enquiry – as to how we might reconcile the sharply conflicting claims of a conception that asserts the primacy of language in its creative or expressive aspects and one that lays chief stress on the various ways in which our sayings are constrained by factors largely or wholly beyond our power to control. Amongst these latter must be counted the range of structural characteristics which constitute language (Saussure's *la langue*) as an object of systematic study, along with the logico-semantic apparatus that may be thought to subtend our grasp of sense and reference, and also – despite its notional allowance for the scope of human linguistic creativity – the depth-grammar of articulate thought that forms the theoretical backbone of Chomskian psycho-linguistics.[37] Moreover the constraints very likely extend to those various supra-sentential, that is, contextual, cultural or broadly pragmatic functions that some linguists and philosophers of language nowadays take as falling within their descriptive-explanatory remit. These aspects of language may seem to offer less hold for rigorous formalization and hence more scope for the kind of expressive freedom or capacity for novel modes of utterance opened up by individual responses to particular, unique speech situations. Yet that scope must be thought of as drastically reduced insofar as any useful, informative or theoretically adequate approach along these lines will involve specifying certain relevance-conditions or criteria of apt usage which place definite limits on the range of speech-acts that would make sense – or not be thought wildly off the point – in this or that enunciative context.[38]

So one result of the widespread 'linguistic turn' across various branches of philosophical thought has been to shift not only the focus of interest but also the burden of unresolved antinomies from epistemology, metaphysics and philosophy of mind, as traditionally conceived, to philosophy of language conceived as their rightful successor discipline. That is to say, they have remained very much on the agenda despite the switch of emphasis hailed by many in the mainstream analytic line of descent as a long-wished-for means of deliverance from all those problems. Hence the re-emergence, in 'linguistified' form, of the singlemost intractable and deep-laid problem of philosophy from Descartes down, namely that of explaining how consciousness and its various (genuine or supposed) attributes – amongst them freedom of will – can find any place in the naturalistic worldview that has increasingly come to characterize the thinking of scientists and philosophers alike. Hence also what I have here described as the various attempts to solve that problem by appealing to language itself as the basis of all philosophical enquiry, whether through the kinds of logico-semantic analysis pursued by thinkers in the Frege–Russell tradition or the approach of those – after Wittgenstein and J.L. Austin – who count such analysis mis-conceived since ordinary (non-philosophical) language is our best, indeed only reliable source of guidance. Austin, in his essay 'A Plea for Excuses', famously opines that philosophers would be better employed in attending to the nuances of language-use – especially those conveyed by certain adverbial qualifiers – when they debate ethical issues of free will and responsibility, rather than venturing into distant and uncharted seas of metaphysical thought.[39] Thus, for

instance, they might note the subtle distinctions drawn by defending or pro-
secuting counsels in a court of law through the deployment of words like
'accidentally', 'inadvertently', 'unwittingly', 'impulsively', 'intentionally',
'knowingly', 'deliberately' and so forth, words whose effect is clearly to imply an
increasing degree of moral accountability for the actions (or sometimes the
speech-acts) concerned.

There is no doubting the acuity of Austin's remarks and the fact that these
adverbs are capable of marking a range of pertinent distinctions with potentially
large consequences in ethical and juridical terms. Yet the question remains,
regarding this appeal to the wisdom enshrined in 'ordinary language', as to
whether one can properly accept the verdict of received or customary usage –
along with its various shades of communally sanctioned judgement – while
nonetheless taking it as evidence of the human capacity for exercising powers of
independent discriminative thought. After all, there is something odd about a
theory – whatever Austin's keenness to disown any such description – which
rests that claim on the presumptive authority of certain well-entrenched or
socially established ways of talking and thinking. At the very least it would
seem to involve a certain tension between the human capacity which those
adverbs are supposed to describe in its various, more-or-less qualified or cir-
cumscribed forms and what is implied by their treatment as veritable touch-
stones not only of correct (communally sanctioned) usage but also of sound
(morally and sometimes legally authoritative) judgement. Thus it is hard to
square the limit-point notion of moral accountability as requiring the exercise of
conscious, autonomous, freely willed, deliberative choice with the idea that our
subtlest moral reckonings – our sense of just when and of just how far that
standard applies – should best be decided on the basis of shared linguistic
intuitions. For no matter how perceptive or sharp-eared the analysis it will still
lie open to the obvious charge of raising the common currency of judgement,
along with all its possible limiting assumptions or blind spots of prejudice, into
a privileged source of wisdom in such matters. Some of Austin's more critical
commentators have been quick to note how readily the appeal to 'ordinary
language' can be used to claim common-sense warrant – even universal validity
– for idioms, expressions or turns of phrase which might otherwise be thought to
carry certain highly distinctive social and ideological inflections.[40] In the present
context what I want to suggest is that its upshot when applied to issues of an
ethico-juridical character – issues which are always closely intertwined with that
of free-will versus determinism – is to reinforce habituated modes of judgement
by steering debate safely away from the kinds of 'metaphysical' questioning that
Austin regards as a mere distraction and waste of philosophical effort.

That this approach can have decidedly conservative implications is evident
enough from a well-known passage in his essay 'A Plea for Excuses'. Thus,
according to Austin:

Our common stock of words embodies all the distinctions men have found
worth drawing, and the connexions they have found worth marking, in the

lifetimes of many generations: these surely are likely to be more numerous, more sound, since they have stood up to the long test of the survival of the fittest, and more subtle, at least in all ordinary and reasonably practical matters, than any that you or I are likely to think up in our arm-chairs of an afternoon – the most favoured alternative method.[41]

Still it would be wrong to let this passage stand as witness to Austin's conservativism in respect of matters linguistic and socio-cultural without also citing a less-known passage from a few pages later on where he lets in some crucial qualifications. 'Certainly', he writes,

[o]rdinary language has no claim to be the last word, if there is such a thing. It embodies, indeed, something better than the metaphysics of the Stone Age, namely, as was said, the inherited experience and acumen of many generations of men. But then, that acumen has been concentrated primarily upon the practical business of life. If a distinction works well for practical purposes in ordinary life (no mean feat, for even ordinary life is full of hard cases), then there is sure to be something in it, it will not mark nothing: yet this is likely enough to be not the best way of arranging things if our interests are more extensive or intellectual than the ordinary. And again, that experience has been derived only from the sources available to ordinary men throughout most of civilized history: it has not been fed from the resources of the microscope and its successors. And it must be added too, that superstition and error and fantasy of all kinds do become incorporated in ordinary language and even sometimes stand up to the survival test (only, when they do, why should we not detect it?) Certainly, then, ordinary language is not the last word: in principle it can everywhere be supplemented and improved upon and superseded. Only remember, it is the first word.[42]

These passages capture very well the tension between, on the one hand, an 'ordinary-language' approach that purports simply to dissolve philosophical problems – or (in Wittgenstein's manner) to make them appear just symptoms of pointless hyper-cultivated doubt – and on the other an approach that has also taken the linguistic turn yet not so far as to proffer a counsel of wise acquiescence in the way things stand with our acculturated language-games and forms of life. For it is precisely when our interests are 'more extensive or intellectual than the ordinary' that we are driven to philosophize about issues like that of free-will versus determinism, issues that retain their power to challenge or unsettle our placidly commonsense habits of thought despite the best efforts of Wittgensteinian therapy. What has chiefly inspired those efforts is the notion that by recasting the central problems of philosophy, so to speak, *more linguistico* they could at last be released from the sphere of futile (unending since often cross-purpose) 'metaphysical' debate and enter the realm of debate about language where at least disagreements could brought out into the open and receive an intelligible airing.

Yet it is far from clear that this has been the case if one considers how deep the disagreement runs between (say) proponents of 'ordinary language' as a cure for all our philosophical ills and others – those of a broadly Fregean–Russellian disposition – who press the claims of a more analytic (or logico-semantic) approach wherein communal habits of usage carry nothing like so strong a normative force. Thus Richard Rorty, in his Foreword to the 1967 anthology *The Linguistic Turn*, was already suggesting that these two strains of thought were so far apart on basic issues of method and priority that it made no sense to treat them as variant forms of a single enterprise.[43] Rather, we should draw the lesson that agreement is not to be had, that 'constructive' or problem-solving philosophy in the analytic mode has demonstrably failed to produce it, and hence that the best way forward is through a sensibly scaled-down pragmatist acceptance of philosophy's role as just one more voice in the 'cultural conversation of mankind'.[44] This he conjoined with the hermeneutic idea that interpretation goes 'all the way down' and the strong-descriptivist claim that changes in our language are also, inseparably, changes in our world. Yet here again, the suggested remedy turns out to pose just the same problems in a different, less overt but equally intractable form. Where they show up most strikingly is in Rorty's subscription to a pair of contradictory theses which cannot be reconciled despite the assurance – carried very largely by his easy-going, mildly ironic and unruffled style of address – that they can get into conflict only for philosophers who have not yet learned the new conversational rules of the game. One is the basically Wittgenstein-derived idea that our thoughts, theories, beliefs, principles, value-judgements and so forth, only make sense against a background or horizon of communally shared language-games and practices that define their conditions of intelligibility and which we therefore cannot question or criticize without *ipso facto* placing ourselves beyond the pale of genuine understanding. The other – flatly opposed to this – is the Jamesian-pragmatist notion of the 'will to believe', that is to say, the idea that beliefs are justified not so much (or not at all) by their measuring up to the way things stand in reality but rather by their serving to promote the interests of human psychological, social, or spiritual welfare.[45] This notion translates readily enough into Rortian neo-pragmatist (i.e., linguistified) terms as the belief that changing our language-games, idioms or preferred 'final vocabularies' is enough to bring about a commensurate change in what counts for us – and hence for all practical purposes – as 'reality' or 'truth'.

Of course this claim lies open to the charge that Bertrand Russell brought against James, namely that an outlook based on the conflation of truth with the currency of received, socially acceptable or humanly desirable belief was in effect nothing more than a doctrine of wishful thinking and one with far from beneficial effects on our everyday moral as well our philosophical habits of thought.[46] If carried right through, it would amount to a recommendation of the state of being blissfully well deceived or the conviction that if one just believed hard enough in this or that comforting item of faith then wishing could make it true. In support of his case Russell gave some striking examples of the kinds of behaviour – and motivating impulse – that might find a spurious justification in James's arguments for the will to believe. (Here one should mention also the earlier, equally spirited and probably more influential response to similar effect by W.K. Clifford.[47]) However my point is not so much to belabour this particular problem with Rorty's position, as for instance by remarking that it goes along all too readily with 'alternative' or self-help therapies that sometimes leave the uncured or relapsed patient with an extra burden of guilt for not having effected their own recovery by dint of positive thinking. Rather, it is to point out the tension that exists between, on the one hand, Rorty's Wittgensteinian idea that our meanings, beliefs, concepts, values, principles, philosophical commitments and so forth, are ultimately those – and only those – that make sense according to our shared language-games or cultural life forms and, on the other, his strong-descriptivist idea that we can always decide to 'change the conversation' (or adopt some different 'final vocabulary') and thus, for all practical purposes, change our world. Well, one or the other, it is tempting to respond, but surely not both unless at the cost of falling straight back into one of those vexing Kantian antinomies that Rorty is so keen to avoid.

Nothing – I submit – could more strikingly demonstrate the way in which the free-will/determinism problem tends to re-emerge with all the more force when philosophers claim to have left it behind or shown it up as just a figment of outmoded 'metaphysical' ways of thought. Moreover, this is only to be expected given that the widespread turn toward language, in whichever philo-sophical guise, as the putative basis of all understanding is sure to pose that problem in a particularly sharp and intractable form. For if there is one lesson that has been driven home constantly in recent analytic debate it is the fact that philosophers who have taken that turn seem destined to repeat all the same argumentative moves and run into all the same resultant dilemmas that were met with by Kant and which then gave rise to the see-saw movement between 'objective' and 'subjective' idealism amongst thinkers from Fichte, Schelling and Hegel down.[48] Nor is the irony of this situation in any way lessened through the 'rediscovery' of Kantian themes and their pertinence to current analytic (or post-analytic) debate by philosophers like John McDowell, or through appeals to Hegel on the topic of conceptual mediation by those, like Robert Brandom, who see him as a useful ally in the cause of inferential-role semantics.[49] The trouble with these ecumenical moves is not only that they give such a strong impression of re-inventing the wheel but also that they tend to re-invent it in a way that takes no account of later developments, in this case by ignoring pretty much the entire reception-history of German idealism down to the present day.[50] As a result, their proffered solutions most often take the form of a moderately nat-uralized, de-transcendentalized, semi-linguistified revisionist approach, one with distinct Wittgensteinian leanings but intended to reclaim just enough of that old idealist baggage to stave off the spectre of sceptical doubt or the equally troubling 'Kripkensteinian' appeal to communal warrant as our last, best source of assurance in such matters. However, as I have argued at length elsewhere, these 'continental' overtures typically suffer from the usual result of attempting to have the best of both worlds.[51] That is to say, they end up with just another version of the same dilemma expressed in terms that, if anything, manage to leave it yet more shrouded in philosophical perplexity.

Thus McDowell's idea of Kantianism minus the metaphysics – or minus those parts, like the noumenon/phenomenon dualism, which he thinks irredeemably beyond the pale – is more like Kantianism minus Kant, or Hamlet without the prince. For, whatever its undoubted liabilities, that aspect of his thinking is fundamental to Kant's entire project and cannot be wished away without leaving it devoid of just those distinctive resources that McDowell hopes to exploit. After all, any argument put forward as a solution to the normative impasse of old-style logical empiricism and the sceptical conclusions that some (like Kripke) have drawn from Wittgenstein's later philosophy is one that must yield substantive grounds for supposing our knowledge to result – as Kant claimed – from the mind's active yet empirically constrained processes of cognitive uptake. This in turn would depend on the jointly operative powers of 'receptivity' and 'spontaneity', a dualism which McDowell much prefers to Kant's talk of sensuous intuitions being somehow 'brought under' adequate or matching concepts since it stresses their inseparable character – the mistake of drawing an other than merely notional line between them – rather than involving his various intermediary ideas of 'judgement', 'imagination' and 'schematism' as a means of somehow (impossibly) bridging the intuition/concept gap. Yet it is not hard to see how McDowell's formulations of this case fall into exactly the same oscillating movement or the same, often tortuous attempts to dismount from what he calls the dualist 'see-saw' as have typified the course of epistemological debate from Kant right down to logical empiricism and beyond. More than that: the anti-'metaphysical' drive of McDowell's and other such recent claims to redeem what is useful while rejecting what is otiose in the German idealist tradition has the further untoward effect of lopping off precisely those alternative resources – however problematical their nature – which are thought of (in no very definite or precise way) as offering an escape route from the post-empiricist predicament. Thus it cannot fulfil the promise of heading in a different, that is, non-dualist and normatively adequate direction such as might resolve the Kripkensteinian sceptical impasse about rule-following and its equally sceptical communitarian 'solution'.[52]

V

What is lost with the turn toward a jointly linguistic and naturalistic recasting of Kantian themes is also what seemed to hold out that promise in the first place, namely their offering a point of epistemological purchase – along with a hold for normative considerations – that would remedy the shortfall in just those respects inherited by thinkers in the mainstream analytic line of descent. In other words it is very much a case of throwing the baby out with the bathwater, even if – as these thinkers rightly perceive – the water of Kantian metaphysics is too murky to be of much use for their own purposes. Thus McDowell is driven to some tortuous lengths of Chinese-box phraseology in the attempt to explain, as he puts it, that,

> [w]hat we find in Kant is precisely the picture I have been recommending: a picture in which reality is not located outside a boundary that encloses the conceptual sphere ... The fact that experience involves receptivity ensures the required constraint from outside thinking and judging. But since the deliverances of receptivity already draw on capacities that belong to spontaneity, we can coherently suppose that the constraint is rational; that is how the picture avoids the pitfall of the Given.[53]

Things become still more complicated when McDowell goes on to develop a related case with regard to ethics and his idea of how Kantian practical reason – with its strongly universalist (hence abstract and non-case-specific) claims – might yet be reconciled with a due regard for the contingent and situated character of human moral choice. Here likewise he maintains that most debate on this topic has been subject to the false and distorting belief that it must involve some ultimate, non-negotiable choice between a doctrine of unqualified free-will, autonomy or self-determination and a view of human actions or motives that would emphasize those strictly heteronomous factors – whether causal, cultural or ideological – which leave no room for meaningful ascriptions of moral agency or choice. McDowell thinks to steer a third-way course and show how we can have both an adequate (humanly acceptable) measure of freedom and a proper regard for the limits imposed by our physical, creaturely mode of existence. This is why he brings in the idea of 'second nature' as a mediating term intended to bridge the otherwise yawning gulf between a Kantian insistence on the absolute autonomy of ethical will and everything that counts against such a view from a naturalized or revisionist, that is, metaphysically scaled-down Kantian standpoint. However, the wished-for equilibrium cannot be achieved since McDowell's various formulations constantly topple over in one or the other direction, that is, toward a phrasing that conjures either the kind of 'bald naturalism' that he is keen to disavow or the notion of a totally 'unconstrained freedom' that he finds just as implausible.

Thus when Wittgenstein uses the term 'natural history' in a human life-world context he must be deploying it, McDowell surmises, to signify 'the natural history of creatures whose nature is largely second nature'. After all, 'human life, our natural way of being, is already shaped by meaning. We need not connect this natural history to nature as the realm of law any more tightly than by simply affirming our right to the notion of second nature'.[54] Already one can see how there might be certain problems looming here, problems much akin to those we encountered with McDowell's attempt to explain how Kantian 'receptivity', thought of as involving certain needful constraints from the outside world, might be reconciled with Kantian 'spontaneity', thought of as allowing sufficient scope for the exercise of active comprehension or intellectual grasp. For the idea of 'second nature', despite its obvious attractiveness for those seeking such a middle-way approach, cannot really bear the crucial weight of mediation that is here placed upon it, any more than can that other forced amalgam of disparate terms. To be sure, there is something wrong about the kind of dualist, orthodox-Kantian or anti-naturalist thinking which holds – in McDowell's words – that 'the freedom of spontaneity ought to be a kind of exemption from nature, something that permits us to elevate ourselves above it, rather than our own special way of living an animal life'.[55] That is, one can readily accept his claim that any viable interpretation of Kant that hopes to avoid this disabling upshot will have to be revisionist – or naturalized – at least to the extent of disowning whatever in Kant's doctrine of the faculties results from, or depends upon, the noumenon/phenomenon dualism. All the same it cannot go so far in that direction as to make 'second nature' a matter of communally shared and linguistically mediated meanings, customs and values without thereby losing touch altogether with the critical and normative dimension of Kantian episte-mology and ethics. For in that case 'second nature' would amount to a kind of linguistified naturalism, a falling-back on pre-existent beliefs or value-commitments which – as might well be inferred from Wittgenstein's usage of the term – scarcely leaves room for the exercise of reflective, autonomous or ethically responsible thought.

Perhaps McDowell is right when he suggests that 'if we can rethink our conception of nature so as to make room for spontaneity . . . we shall by the same token be rethinking our conception of what it takes for a position to deserve to be called "naturalism"'.[56] But then one has to ask: what remains of 'nature' once the sense of that term has been radically transformed so as to incorporate the mind's spontaneous powers, or again: what is left of 'spontaneity' once its scope and limits have been so redefined as to bring it within the compass of a gen-uinely naturalist conception? Nothing more, it would seem, than a notion of nature with curiously animist or Fichtean-idealist leanings and, on the other hand, a notion of mind wherein the only possible means of escape from a fully fledged naturalism with drastically determinist implications is the appeal to a cultural-linguistic 'second nature' which itself places sharp limits on our free-doms of thought and belief. McDowell is far from unaware of this latter pro-blem, since a good part of his work over the past twenty years has been devoted to seeking some way beyond what he clearly perceives as the normative deficit or the lack of adequate justificatory grounds entailed by any such communitarian appeal. Thus:

> If there is nothing to the normative structure within which meaning comes into view except, say, acceptances and rejections of bits of behaviour by the community at large, then how things are – how things can be said to be with a correctness that must partly consist in being faithful to the meanings one would exploit if one said they are thus and so – cannot be

independent of the community's ratifying the judgement that they are thus and so.[57]

Hence McDowell's quest for some alternative source of validity-conditions or standards of correctness in activities like rule following, that is to say, one that would avoid the pyrrhic outcome of Kripke's 'sceptical solution' to Wittgenstein's 'sceptical problem'. However, his approach works out not so much as a genuine, philosophically viable alternative but rather as an ultimately failed attempt to have it both ways on the issue of naturalism versus normativity, and of communal assent or Wittgensteinian 'agreement in judgement' versus the claims of objective, recognition-transcendent truth.

Here again, where the failure shows up most clearly is in the detailed phrasing of McDowell's argument and the way that it elides, rather than integrates or reconciles, these apparently conflicting requirements. As he puts it at one point, 'human beings mature into being at home in the space of reasons or, what comes to the same thing, living their lives in the world; we can make sense of that by noting that the language into which a human being is first initiated stands over against her as a prior embodiment of mindedness, of the possibility of an orientation to the world'.[58] But in that case, one has to ask, what becomes of the (non-absolute but humanly definitive) realm of freedom and autonomy that McDowell wishes to redeem through this appeal to the 'space of reasons'? After all, the idea that we 'mature into being at home' within that space is one that presses strongly in a naturalistic direction, toward a way of conceiving 'second nature' – through the metaphor of growth and organic development – which implies a close kinship between our physically embodied and our humanly, rationally or ethically autonomous modes of being-in-the-world. Nor is this suggestive bias significantly offset by McDowell's idea that our 'orientation' in respect of that world – our capacity for reasoned and reflective thinking about it in whatever context of enquiry – is enabled through 'the language into which a human being is first initiated', a language that furthermore 'stands over against her as a prior condition of mindedness'. For we shall then be at risk of merely exchanging one kind of determinism for another, that is, a naturalistic approach that conserves only a notional 'space' in which to locate the exercise of human reason, free-will and autonomy for a language-based approach that would likewise place tight limits on its scope. These implications seem to be mutually reinforcing when McDowell describes language – the inherited language through which we enter the space of reasons – as a 'prior embodiment of mindedness', one that 'stands over against' the initiate and offers her sole means of access to the state of fully achieved humanity. Thus 'second nature' turns out to have a meaning, contextually defined, which brings it much closer to 'bald naturalism' and/or fully fledged linguistic determinism than McDowell is willing to admit. Moreover, this falls in readily enough with common usage since when people talk about this or that belief, practice or item of behaviour as a product of 'second nature' what they mostly have in mind is a purely habitual or at any rate largely unreflective instance of the kind.

Of course it may be argued – *contra* Wittgenstein and Austin – that 'ordinary language' need not always have the last word in these matters and that certain forms of utterance that pass muster for everyday, common-sense or folk-psychological purposes may well prove inadequate or downright misleading when subject to more rigorous modes of conceptual analysis. Indeed, we have already seen Austin making just this concession with regard to the standing possibility that the way people ordinarily talk might for certain other (e.g., philosophical and maybe legal) purposes be open to correction along such lines. However it is not at all clear how McDowell might avail himself of this possibility, given his notion of 'second nature' in its linguistic-cultural aspect as that which enables our being-in-the-world as sentient, rational, reflective and responsible subjects but also – on his own submission – as that which necessarily precedes and determines the scope and limits of our freedom. Thus when it comes to the question of just how far critical thinking might challenge or subvert the beliefs and values that constitute a given cultural-linguistic 'form of life', McDowell takes a distinctly conservative view. After all, he remarks, 'even a thought that transforms a tradition must be rooted in the tradition that it transforms ... The speech that expresses it must be able to be intelligibly addressed to people squarely placed within the tradition as it stands'.[59] This is very much the standpoint adopted by hermeneutic philosophers like Gadamer – whom McDowell approvingly cites – in opposition to the claims of those, like Habermas, who would emphasize the socially liberating power of critical-reflective reason rather than its always being subject to certain communal or culture-specific limits and constraints.[60]

Thus, according to McDowell, 'understanding is placing what is understood within a horizon constituted by a tradition, and ... the first thing to say about language is that it serves as a repository of tradition'.[61] This follows straightforwardly from the fact, as he takes it, that 'a natural language, the sort of language into which human beings are first initiated, serves as ... a store of historically accumulated wisdom about what is a reason for what'.[62] In which case Gadamer must be right, just as – by the same token – followers of Wittgenstein must be right when they assert the primacy of shared language-games and communal forms of life as against the argument that this is a deeply conservative, uncritical and (at worst) ideologically complicitous line of thought. McDowell is by no means insensitive to such objections and indeed makes a point of meeting them, as when he remarks that tradition 'is subject to reflective modification by each generation that inherits it', so that 'a standing obligation to engage in critical reflection is itself a part of the inheritance'.[63] However this allowance is more than offset by his stress on the delusion of aspiring to think beyond or outside that ultimate 'horizon' of intelligibility which forms the precondition for meaningful thought, or again – to yet more constrictive effect – that 'repository' of in-place ideas, beliefs and values that constitutes the basis of a communal tradition.

This goes some way toward explaining why so much of McDowell's argument in *Mind and World* has to do with the distinction between human and non-human-animal modes of sentient experience. On the one hand he clearly sees what is wrong with the residual Cartesian strain in a good deal of present-day philosophy of mind which assumes or implies – even where it does not explicitly endorse – a dualist approach that would treat human 'mindedness' as strictly *sui generis* and not to be confused with other, more or less complex or intelligent life-forms. On the other he just as clearly wants to say that there *is* a real difference, that it goes deep, and moreover that it takes us a long way toward explaining what is still valid and relevant about Kant's philosophy once relieved of its surplus metaphysical baggage. Thus the question becomes: 'how can spontaneity permeate our lives, even to the extent of structuring those aspects of them that reflect our naturalness – those aspects of our lives that we share with ordinary animals?'[64] And again:

> We do not need to say that we have what mere animals have, non-conceptual content, and we have something else as well, since we can conceptualize that content and they cannot. Instead we can say that we have what mere animals have, perceptual sensitivity to features of our environment, but we have it in a special form. Our perceptual sensitivity to our environment is taken up into the ambit of the faculty of sponta-neity, which is what distinguishes us from them. [65]

These passages show how tight is the connection, as McDowell sees it, between the issue with regard to human *vis-à-vis* non-human-animal mentality and the Kantian issue concerning 'spontaneity' in relation to 'receptivity'. The former term should here be taken in its twofold (epistemological and ethical) role as that which ensures both the active involvement of human understanding in the deliverances of perceptual uptake and the scope for autonomy and free-will – though always subject to the dictates of practical reason – in the ethical sphere.

McDowell would most likely reject this formulation as too 'metaphysical' by half. That is to say, he would regard it as leaning too far toward an *echt* Kantian dichotomy between the realm of phenomenal cognition (where sensory appearances are 'brought under' adequate concepts) and the noumenal realm where no such requirement applies since here it is a matter of principles whose sphere of application lies altogether outside and beyond the cognitive domain. However, once again, this places him in the awkward position of maintaining a quasi-naturalized ethical outlook which cannot *quite* let go of that transcendental dimension since it seems to offer the sole means of escape from the kind of all-embracing causal-determinist philosophy of mind and nature that Kant was so anxious to avoid. Like Strawson before him, McDowell is forced back upon a compromise revisionist stance that seeks to steer a path between the twin perils of endorsing Kant's drastically dualist conception along with all its otiose 'metaphysical' commitments or rejecting that conception outright and thereby (apparently) leaving no room for any other-than-notional domain of free-will and moral autonomy.[66] Thus the reason why McDowell has so much to say about the human/non-human-animal distinction is that it maps precisely onto what he has to say about the best (indeed only intelligible) way of conceiving the relation between human 'spontaneity' and 'receptivity' as they bear upon our powers of cognitive, intellectual and ethico-evaluative judgement. Hence his remark – justifiably enough – that 'no one without a philosophical axe to grind can watch, say, a dog or a cat at play and seriously consider bringing its activities under the head of something like automatism'. All the same he feels obliged to qualify this claim in keeping with his scaled-down, moderately naturalized, but still dualist conception by observing that 'we can deny Kantian spontaneity [to animals] while leaving plenty of room for the self-movingness that is plain to the unprejudiced eye in such a scene'.[67] 'Spontaneity' is here doing all the same epistemological work that German post-Kantian idealist thinkers required of the mind in its active, indeed its world-constitutive, role and likewise all the ethical work required by upholders of fully fledged autonomy and free-will. However, as McDowell is keen to stress, it has to do so without in any way involving those other, metaphysically overcommitted aspects of Kantian thinking that cross the line of what is acceptable in present-day analytic terms. Thus the point of adopting this revisionist approach, he writes, 'is that it shows in some detail how we can acknowledge what is common between human beings and brutes, while preserving the difference that the Kantian thesis forces on us'.[68]

If the word 'brute' here jumps off the page with uncommon force (or bru-tality) then this perhaps has to do with the tension or the outright conflict that exists between McDowell's Kantian-autonomist principles and his naturalistic or – to that extent – decidedly un-Kantian inclinations. Indeed it is a version of the same unresolved conflict that surfaces constantly in Kant's attempts to distin-guish the sphere of rational autonomy and moral will from the realm of merely 'pathological' human instincts, affections and desires.[69] One can trace its aftermath right down to the dilemmas of recent epistemological debate, from logical positivism, *via* all the problems (chief among them the lack of normative criteria) with Quine's radically physicalist approach, to Richard Rorty's neo-pragmatist idea that one can be as 'realist' as one likes about the causal impact of photons on Galileo's eyeball while insisting all the same that such an outlook of bottom-line realism does nothing whatever to decide the issue – the clash of competing worldviews – between Galileo and the church authorities.[70] Thus, in Rorty's typically insouciant phrase, 'the astronomers of Padua took it [i.e., the purported ocular proof of the existence of Jupiter's moons] as merely one more anomaly which had somehow to be worked into a more or less Aristotelian cosmology, whereas Galileo's admirers took it as shattering the crystalline spheres once and for all'.[71] That is to say, even if 'the datum *itself* is utterly real . . . quite apart from the interpretation it receives', nevertheless any 'truth' with regard to those rival cosmologies can only be a matter of interpretation since surely we know – after Quine and Kuhn – that theories are always underdetermined by the best evidence to hand, that observation statements are themselves theory-laden, and hence that no raw, uninterpreted data are sufficient to resolve such a conflict either way.[72] Moreover, this dichotomy is carried across – and with equally damaging effect – to the sphere of ethical judgement where it works out, in McDowell's case, as a distinctly strained or highly problematical compromise solution. Thus it involves on the one hand a qualified naturalism (his idea of moral sentiments or conduct as 'second nature'), and on the other a likewise qualified Kantian autonomist conception, namely his appeal to the 'space of reasons' as that which sets us apart from the 'brutes' or non-human animals.

This is why McDowell cannot achieve what he hopes to achieve with Kant's assistance, that is, some means of dismounting from the 'see-saw' of contrary movements – between rationalism and empiricism, concepts and intuitions, free-will and determinism, unbridled spontaneity 'all the way out' and passive receptivity 'all the way in' – which he sees as a chief legacy of old-style logical empiricism. In fact that legacy goes much farther back and finds its singlemost extreme and complicated instance in Kant's ultimately failed attempt to explain how those dichotomies might finally be resolved or those conflicts at last laid to rest. For Kant, the answer lay in an approach to epistemological issues that somehow combined 'transcendental idealism' with 'empirical realism', and an ethics that defused the free-will/determinism problem by invoking a purely noumenal domain – that of practical reason – where the rule of cognitive understanding (that phenomenal intuitions be 'brought under' adequate concepts) simply had no application.[73] This is not the place for a detailed account of the various difficulties that Kant faced (and that his exegetes have also had to confront) in the effort to follow this project through without giving rise to yet further, more complex and vexatious dualisms.[74] Sufficient to remark that the problems bequeathed by Kantian epistemology and ethics remain very much on the current analytical agenda, and none the less so for that widespread 'linguistic turn' whose promise – in various ways – was to point a way beyond those metaphysical quandaries. Indeed most of the disputes that have lately arisen within and between the various schools of theoretical linguistics and philosophy of language can best be seen as displaced, disguised or sublimated versions of the same dilemmas which they themselves count as just a product of confused thinking.

Thus the 'turn' would appear to have brought nothing like its promised share of benefits, at least to the extent that these are equated – as by Wittgenstein and (more reservedly) Austin – with the therapeutic virtue of coaxing us down from all our misconceived philosophical anxieties. Yet it is just as clearly the case that reflection on language, and especially those aspects of it that continue to create such problems, does have a fair claim to provide a better, more perspicuous treatment of them than the old Cartesian–Kantian 'way of ideas'. Hence my suggestion: that the issue of freewill versus determinism is posed with particular clarity and force when we think about language not only as an object of more-or-less detached philosophical enquiry but also as a kind of privileged reflective and intuitive vantage point from which to achieve some insight into that otherwise thoroughly opaque and recalcitrant issue. Privileged, that is, insofar as it offers a uniquely intimate way of access to the actual experience of saying what we mean or, by analogy, of doing what we intend while also – as philosophers are nowadays keen to insist – avoiding the 'private language' fallacy by virtue of its strictly indispensable appeal to the realm of communal or public intelligibility.

VI

It seems to me that this potential in philosophy of language to clarify long-standing metaphysical issues such as that of free-will versus determinism has been squandered – or at any rate seriously under-exploited – on account of the perceived (and hence to a large extent self-confirming) rift between 'analytic' and 'continental' approaches. Thus analytic debate in the Frege–Russell line of descent has typically turned its back on anything that smacks of a phenomenological and hence, according to the verdict of thinkers from Frege to Ryle and Dummett, an indefensibly subjective or 'psychologistic' mode of thought.[75] As a result – and for want of precisely those additional resources – it has been driven into various kinds of conceptual impasse, whether that of a logico-semantic methodology devoid of any adequate normative criteria or that of a Kripkean sceptical outlook on issues of normative warrant whose sole resort is to a 'sceptical solution' along Wittgensteinian or communitarian lines.[76]

Things might very well have taken a different course had thinkers in the mainstream anglophone tradition followed up that tantalizing hint of J.L. Austin that his project of 'ordinary language' analysis could just as well be viewed as a sort of 'linguistic phenomenology'.[77] For if Austin's suggestion had been noted and developed – by himself or by others of a similar language-first but undogmatic persuasion – then there might have been no need to recount this story of alternative paths not taken or of hopeful prospects prematurely blocked. Indeed it is a fair bet that Austin's imprimatur would have done a great deal to counteract the influence of Ryle's famous *volte-face* when he renounced his earlier, well-developed interest in Husserlian phenomenology and its relevance to issues in analytic philosophy of language and declared that Husserl's entire enterprise was, after all, just a species of thinly disguised 'psychologism'.[78] My own view, as should be clear by now, is that this anti-continental bias has exerted a highly restrictive and damaging effect on anglophone philosophy over the past half-century and more. Thus it has acted as a strong disincentive against any sustained attempt – like those made by a good many thinkers in the 'other' tradition from Husserl down – to combine reflection on the nature and workings of language with reflection on the free-will/determinism issue.[79] That is to say, this tenacious post-Fregean prejudice has effectively blocked the kind of approach that would recognize the close relationship between that issue and the problem of accounting for linguistic creativity while making due allowance for the various constraints or grammatical and logico-semantic structures that define what shall count as an intelligible utterance.

Among the most salient differences here is the way that analytic debates on this topic tend to take the form of a flat disagreement or conflict of priorities between different schools of thought rather than a process of thinking-through that strives to hold both arguments together in a kind of productive tension. This latter approach has been something of a hallmark in 'continental' philosophy of mind and language, one that no doubt has its ultimate source in Kant's antinomies of pure reason and has thence come down *via* Hegel to Husserl, Merleau-Ponty and the early writings of Jacques Derrida. Thus with Derrida it takes the form of a rigorously argued immanent critique of those passages in Husserl where the phenomenological emphasis on language in its creative-expressive aspect comes up against its limit through the encounter with structuralism, and of those likewise symptomatically revealing passages in the work of structuralist thinkers – from Saussure to Lévi-Strauss – where the claims of system, method and structure come up against a strictly irreducible surplus of expressive over conventional, routine or pre-constituted meaning.[80] This is why, as Derrida says, 'a certain structuralism has always been philosophy's most spontaneous gesture', where 'structuralism' must be understood as referring not only to the recent, Saussure inspired and linguistically-oriented, movement bearing that name but also to the basic philosophical drive for conceptual understanding and mastery.[81] Both senses are present, though the former (restricted) sense most obviously, in his description of it as 'a form or function organised according to an internal legality in which elements have meaning only in the solidarity of their correlation or their opposition'.[82] Hence the fact that, no matter how refined and sophisticated, any structuralist approach in linguistics, philosophy or the human sciences will always tend strongly toward 'a reflection of the accomplished, the constituted, the *constructed*'. Hence also Derrida's claim – from a distinctly phenomenological standpoint – that 'what I can never understand, in a structure, is that by means of which it is not closed'.[83]

What emerges most strikingly here, as likewise in some of Merleau-Ponty's late essays, is a mode of thought very much on the cusp between phenomenology and structuralism, that is to say, between the rival claims of that which purportedly transcends or eludes the utmost powers of conceptual grasp and that which drives philosophers, linguists, anthropologists and others to seek just such a formal or systematized *modus operandi*. Thus Merleau-Ponty is clearly trying to find some way of accommodating both claims when he refers to 'that paradoxical operation through which, by using words of a given sense, and already available meanings, we try to follow up an *intention* which necessarily outstrips, modifies and in the last analysis stabilises the meanings of the words that translate it'.[84] There is a similar point to his wonderfully perceptive commentary on a film about Matisse which showed the painter in the last stages of completing a work, and hesitating for a moment over the final brush-stroke. At this precise juncture, Merleau-Ponty writes, 'the line was chosen in such a way as to observe, scattered out over the painting, twenty conditions which were unformulated and even informulable for anyone but Matisse, since they were only defined and imposed by the intention of executing *this painting which did not yet exist*'.[85] He can therefore be seen as raising the same issues as Derrida with regard to the aporetic relationship between genesis and structure, or the creative-expressive *vis-à-vis* the 'given' or preconstituted aspects of language and art, but as coming at these issues more from the standpoint of a phenomenologist persuaded of the pertinence of certain structuralist insights than from that of a structuralist anxious to meet the phenomenological challenge. In Derrida's case, there is every sign of his having been impressed early on by the strictly inescapable character of both projects and hence the necessity of thinking them through with the utmost conceptual precision and critical rigour so as to define more precisely those points where they generated certain deep-laid conflicts of method and priority.

Moreover – the main burden of my argument here – those conflicts are inseparably bound up with the issue between free-will and determinism, at least insofar as it is nowadays posed (like just about every erstwhile 'metaphysical' issue) in linguistic terms or as a problem whose solution is to be found, if at all, through reflection on language in one or other of its aspects. Thus it has typically been played out between proponents of a mainstream-analytic versus a 'continental' line of approach, or – on the analytic side – descriptive versus prescriptive, constative versus performative, or logico-semantic versus ordinary-language schools of thought. However, as I have said, the 'analyticals' have this much in common: that they all retain something of the Fregean hostility toward what is considered the retrograde 'continental' idea that philosophy of language still needs to take account of that other, phenomenological dimension wherein these issues continue to arise with undiminished force and persistence. Thus it is pretty much assumed that the 'linguistic turn', in whichever guise, has had the altogether beneficial effect of focusing attention on the public domain of communicable meanings, manifest intentions, speech-act implicatures and so forth, thereby cutting out the mistaken (and scepticism-inducing) appeal to some inward, 'private', and hence inaccessible realm of first-person mental goings-on. Such is famously Wittgenstein's claim in his later writings, and such – albeit on different grounds – the claim of those other, more analytically minded types (like Dummett) who seek to specify the precise conditions under which any given statement or hypothesis may count as meaningful, truth-apt or properly (i.e., verifiably) assertible.[86]

Yet, as I have argued here, both approaches give rise to some thoroughly intractable problems and dilemmas of their own, not least the Wittgensteinian puzzle about rule following which finds nothing like an adequate answer in his own (and Kripke's) last-ditch appeal to communal sanction, or 'agreement in judgement', as a putative solution. Moreover, it is hard to see what benefit accrues through Dummett's adopting what amounts to a somewhat more refined version of the old verificationist principle, that is, the idea – as he frames it – that statements can be meaningful only insofar as they pass the test for warranted assertibility according to our best available methods of formal proof or empirical investigation. For here again, as with Wittgenstein on rule following and 'private language', the result is not so much a means of deliverance from all our self-induced sceptical doubts but rather – *vide* the groaning shelves of secondary literature – a deepening sense of bewilderment as to what could possibly count as an adequate answer to the sceptic's challenge.[87] That is to say, Dummett's claim to defeat the challenge by replacing objectivist truth-talk with anti-realist talk of assertoric warrant (or 'truth' within the limits of attainable knowledge, proof or verification) is such as to leave the problem very firmly in place. For this offers the sceptic an open invitation to repeat his basic point, namely that no argument along such lines can possibly explain the obvious fact – borne out by the entire history of science and human enquiry to date – that best opinion or expert judgement can always turn out wrong. Or again: if 'truth' is re-defined as epistemically constrained, that is, as subject to the scope and limits of available proof or verification then there is simply no way to explain either the standing possibility of error or our knowledge of the growth of knowledge. Thus despite its claim to defeat the sceptic by bringing truth within the scope of actual or potential human knowability anti-realism can be seen to defeat its own object – and concede the main point at issue – by adopting this philosophical line of least resistance.

It seems to me that these two, rather striking examples of the kinds of impasse typically encountered by philosophy of language in the mainstream analytic tradition are very largely due to its fixed – even obdurate – habit of mistrust toward any approach belonging to the 'other', continental or phenomenological line of descent. A third, as we have seen, is McDowell's attempt to reclaim what he regards as the useful parts of Kant's project – its purported overcoming of the various dualisms of mind and world, concept and intuition, free-will and determinism – through an appeal to the jointly operative powers of 'spontaneity' and 'receptivity' while nonetheless refusing to have any truck with the murkier ('metaphysical', 'noumenal' or 'transcendental') aspects of Kantian thought.[88] This is not so much a case of trying to have one's cake and eat it as of trying to bake the cake without some essential ingredients and then recommending the resultant stuff as a cure-all for someone afflicted with acute vitamin deficiency. For it leaves us not only with another problematical dualism (that of 'spontaneity' and 'receptivity') which cannot be resolved simply by declaring that in truth it is no such thing, but also with a analytically domesticated version of Kant that is deprived of some crucial load-bearing structures and which hence fails to make good its own central claims, let alone rescue the analytic enterprise from its current doldrums. I have suggested that this is the long-term result of that parting of the-ways that began with Frege's mistaken rejection of Husserlian phenomenology as just a form of thinly disguised psychologism, was later reinforced by Ryle's arguments to similar effect, and then – most recently – endorsed by Dummett in the name of a programmatic turn to language as the basis of all valid reasoning on matters of truth, knowledge or epistemic warrant. In Dummett's case the bias emerges very clearly even where he goes some way toward conceding that Husserl was alert to this charge and hence that his project may not, after all, have been so deeply at odds with the Fregean requirement that logic be thought of as having to do with a realm of purely objective (i.e., non-mind-dependent) senses, concepts and truth-values.[89] Yet of course it is just the point of Husserl's entire project – and what chiefly sets it apart from the analytic enterprise – that it does seek a grounding for those various kinds of knowledge (primordial intuitions, apodictic truths, predicative judgements, prepositional contents, modes of time-consciousness, etc.) that cannot be reduced without remainder to their forms of linguistic expression or articulation.[90] And so, as might be expected, Dummett's concessions turn out to have a sharp limit: if the charge of 'psychologism' does not quite stick, then Husserl must all the same be held at fault for not having taken full measure of Frege's linguistic or logico-semantic revolution.

However the tables can be turned at this point by remarking – as I have above – that analytic philosophy has often run aground on problems that can now be seen to have resulted from its rejection of those same alternative resources which Frege, and a good many thinkers after him, decreed to be wholly beyond the pale of reputable philosophical method. That is to say, the 'linguistic turn' in its fully fledged (echt-analytic) form is such as to exclude a whole range of conceptual, critical and normative dimensions in the absence of which, quite simply, philosophical reflection must lack any adequate purchase on issues of meaning, knowledge and truth. Moreover, it can be shown that where analytic thinkers have become most aware of this deficit, so they have tended – albeit after their own style – to reintroduce certain themes and ideas of a distinctly phenomenological cast. Such is, for instance, McDowell's recourse to the synthesizing power of Kantian 'spontaneity' and 'receptivity', or again (as Derrida once somewhat mischievously pointed out) John Searle's crypto-Husserlian appeal to intentionality as the *sine qua non* of mind, consciousness and meaning.[91] However, where these 'continental' overtures stop short is at just that point where Austin likewise drew a line, that is, by accepting how his enterprise might aptly be viewed as a kind of 'linguistic phenomenology' while failing (or declining) to follow up this idea with anything more substantive by way of philosophical justification.[92] To be sure, Austin is quite clear about his claim that such justification is not to be had, or that philosophers are much better employed in turning an ear to the subtleties and nuances of 'ordinary language' than in troubling their minds with all those old, up to now unsolved and most likely insoluble problems, among them that of free-will versus determinism. Hence his approach, in 'A Plea for Excuses', *via* a detailed study of those various adverbs that imply a range of moral or legal judgements with regard to the different kinds or degrees of forethought, deliberation, conscious intent or mindedness to do this or that as opposed to cases of involuntary action, oversight, negligence, diminished responsibility and so forth.[93] However, as I have said, there is still a sense which Austin's linguistic distinctions, no matter how keenly observed, cannot really be held to have answered those questions – such as the free-will/determinism issue – that have vexed philosophers down through the history of Western 'metaphysical' thought.

No more, for that matter, can the 'linguistic turn' as canvassed by thinkers of otherwise diverse (e.g., Wittgensteinian or Fregean) persuasion be held to offer an adequate solution to the problem that arises with regard to the antinomy of language conceived on the one hand as a standing repertoire of codes, conventions or structural attributes and on the other as an expressive-creative surpassing of any such pre-existent constraints. I have shown how this antinomy is pressed to the limit in Derrida's reflections on the conflict of aims between structuralism and phenomenology, a conflict that in many ways replicates the issue between determinist and voluntarist conceptions in philosophy of mind, morals and language. My point is that the issue has been largely ignored – at any rate sidetracked or finessed – by analytic thinkers from Frege, *via* Ryle and Austin to Dummett who have supposed that any appeal beyond language to the phenomenology of human consciousness, experience or expressive intent must *ipso facto* betray a lapse into bad old 'psychologistic' habits of thought. Yet there is no reason, philosophical prejudice apart, to suppose that close study of linguistic usage could settle any issue with regard to our possession or non-possession of moral autonomy, let alone – *pace* Dummett – any issue concerning the truth or untruth (more precisely: the truth-apt status) of our various claims in respect to matters of scientific, historical or empirical-investigative warrant. What this notion amounts to is a straightforward case of putting the cart before the horse, or the strictly (etymologically) *preposterous* idea that certain more-or-less widespread ways of talking should be taken not only as useful pointers to our ways of thinking, reasoning, judging and so on, but as marking both the limit of intelligibility and – for all philosophical purposes – the sole standard of truth in such matters.[94] This is likely to be the realist's response when Dummett argues from his 'language-first' perspective to his anti-realist position, that is, that 'warranted assertibility' (rather than truth) is the most that our statements can legitimately claim since it makes no sense to suppose the existence of objective, verification-transcendent, or (to us) unknown and therefore unassertible truths. And she will then just as likely follow up by remarking that there have been in the past – and undoubtedly still are – a great many mathematical, scientific, historical and other truths that lay (or still lie) beyond the limits of attainable human knowledge yet would none the less render any statement of them true if uttered by way of hypothesis, conjecture or mere lucky guess.

This is also to say, as many realists would, that there are truth-makers (whether real-world, physical states of affairs or the abstract realia of logic, mathematics and the formal sciences) and truth-bearers – propositions or statements about them – and that the former decide the truth-value of the latter, irrespective of whether or not we are epistemically placed to know or determine that value. For anti-realists, conversely, truth must always be thought of as epistemically constrained, or subject to the scope and limits of human enquiry or cognitive endeavour.[95] Thus realists take it as blindingly obvious that there are – must be – a whole vast range of objectively true or false statements that just happen to elude our best powers of proof or falsification while anti-realists are just as firmly convinced that this claim cannot make sense since we could never be in a position to know whether or not it applied in any such case. However my main focus here is not so much on this particular (Dummett-inspired) variant of the realist/anti-realist debate but more on those closely related issues in philosophy of language that have large implications for our thinking about the free-will/determinism problem. My point is that the mainstream analytic approach – as a result, very largely, of its resolute hostility to everything in the 'other', that is, continental line of descent – has been narrowed to such a degree that it cannot find room for the kinds of philosophical insight that might otherwise result from a disciplined reflection on the actual experience of talking straight ahead and managing to express whatever it is that we have it in mind to communicate.

This applies just as much to 'ordinary language' philosophy in the Wittgensteinian or Austinian mode as to formalized, *echt*-analytic approaches in the Frege–Russell tradition that reject any appeal to commonplace usage as our last, best source of wisdom in such matters. Where the one goes wrong by uncritically endorsing what amounts to a veto on the very idea that such usage might at times be confused, unclear or even systematically misleading, the other makes the opposite mistake of pressing so far with its reformist or logical-revisionist programme as to leave little room for the intentional or expressive dimensions of everyday speech. No doubt there is a version of the 'analytic' tale where the most significant dividing line falls between those approaches that adopt a more-or-less explicitly determinist view of their subject-domain and those which place their chief emphasis on the scope for linguistic creativity or expressive freedom. On the one side would be grouped a wide range of theories, from the behaviourist notion of linguistic performance as a product of operant or reflex-response conditioning to the structuralist model of language as a system of purely differential relationships 'without positive terms', along with those strains of analytic thought that privilege the logico-semantic over the intentional-expressive aspects of language.[96] Here also one would have to include that dimension of Chomskian linguistics whereby the scope of human 'creativity' is defined in strictly formal or computational terms, that is, as a matter of the various surface structures that are taken to derive *via* the rules of transformational-generative syntax from an underlying repertoire of depth-grammatical structures.[97] Moreover, this limiting judgement would also apply to the ordinary-language approach insofar as it leans so heavily in the opposite, that is, usage-first or communitarian direction. Hence the objection that Austin's thoughts about the wisdom enshrined in our 'ordinary' habits of speech are conservative not only in the sense of conserving, that is, showing adequate respect for its various subtleties and nuances but also in the sense that they exhibit an overly tradition-bound (even, some would say, a distinctly Oxford common-room) regard for the proprieties of customary usage.[98]

What is thereby excluded – or at any rate heavily discounted – is the idea that language might inherently manifest the kind of creativity or open-ended inventiveness that goes far beyond anything accountable in formal, structural, rule-governed, contextualist or broadly pragmatic terms. Between them, these latter can fairly be claimed to describe or exhaust the entire current repertoire of linguistic philosophy as conceived within the broadly analytic tradition. Moreover, they serve to emphasize my point about its missed opportunity with regard to the issue of free-will versus determinism and the way that reflection on the nature, scope and limits of linguistic creativity might help to clarify that issue. Thus there is much to be learned from Husserl's, Merleau-Ponty's and Derrida's treatment of problems that have constantly resurfaced to vex the proponents of mainstream analytic debate and just as often been subject to the kind of response that fails to engage them at an adequate depth through its desire to steer the discussion back onto more or less familiar (i.e., analytic) ground. These have to do precisely with the question of how – by what philosophical means – we can best come to terms with the aporias of genesis and structure, freedom and necessity, or the expressive-creative *vis-à-vis* the formal dimensions of language. At the same time, there is a need for such relatively abstract considerations to be assessed in terms of what counts as an adequate or 'right' response from the standpoint of a native speaker's intuition, or again – by analogy – from the standpoint of intuitive practical judgement with regard to the various kinds and degrees of freedom exhibited by various sorts of human behaviour. This is clearly the case with Chomskian linguistics and cognitive psychology, where any candidate hypothesis (i.e., any proposed explanation of mental goings-on in transformational-generative or modular terms) cannot hold good unless it matches up with the evidence of what competent speakers and thinkers are disposed to count as a well-formed grammatical utterance or an instance of valid reasoning. And of course that requirement is even more basic to 'ordinary language' approaches – whether in philosophy of mind, epistemology, ethics, or any other branch of enquiry – which make a virtue of appealing to customary usage as opposed to the unwarranted presumptions of abstract theorizing.

VII

So it is, in Austin's famous phrase, that 'our common stock of words embodies all the distinctions men have found worth drawing, and the connexions they have found worth marking, in the lifetimes of many generations, and that these are 'more subtle, at least in all ordinary and reasonably practical matters, than any that you or I are likely to think up in our arm-chairs of an afternoon – the most favoured alternative method'.[99] All the same those armchair thinkers, 'continental' types among them, might sometimes be found to shed a fresh and revealing light not only on the subtleties of everyday speech but also on the ways in which 'ordinary language' bears witness to quite *extra*-ordinary powers of expressive and creative deployment. I have suggested that the present-day 'linguistic turn' in its various analytic manifestations has failed to engage with certain deep-laid issues, such as that of free-will versus determinism, very largely on account of its shying away from what it takes to be the overly speculative, abstract, or 'metaphysical' cast of work in the post-Kantian mainland-European line of descent. This failure is all the more regrettable since reflection on language from the range of viewpoints opened up by that 'other' tradition of thought is exceptionally well-placed to make allowance for the complex interplay of freedom and necessity – of creative innovation and structural, formal or causal constraint – which characterizes human practical agency and linguistic aptitude alike. Nowhere are these issues more acutely and productively raised than through the kinds of debate carried on in the wake of Husserlian phenomenology by thinkers like Merleau-Ponty and Derrida, that is to say, thinkers who have pursued them to a high point of reflective and critical awareness. What chiefly distinguishes their approach from the mainstream of post-Fregean analytic philosophy is not, as adherents to the latter tradition would have it, an unfortunate lack of conceptual rigour and a likewise deplorable tendency to lapse into 'psychologistic' habits of thought. Rather it is an openness to certain questions – such as those of genesis and structure or the expressive *vis-à-vis* the formal aspects of language – that cannot be simply shunted aside in the interests of intellectual hygiene as defined by this particular, highly restrictive conception of philosophy's proper remit.

Moreover, those questions are within reach of its singlemost challenging issue at least since Kant, namely the issue as to how we can wrest an adequate margin of freely willed, autonomous commitment to our various actions and beliefs (or our various ways of expressing them) from the otherwise implacably determinist order of physical or causal necessity. I have suggested here that one useful way of engaging that problem on a basis of shared human experience as well as in philosophical terms is through our grasp of what is involved in the process of talking straight ahead and (more-or-less successfully) saying what we mean whilst subject to the jointly restraining and enabling conditions of language in its twofold, that is, its formal-structural and expressive-creative aspects. However, if it is to take full advantage of the prospects thus opened up, analytic philosophy will need to extend its purview so as to accommodate a range of insights from the 'other', that is, post-Kantian mainland-European tradition of thought. For that tradition has kept open certain lines of enquiry that were blocked by the 'linguistic turn' in its hitherto predominant analytic forms, among them an openness to ways of thinking about these issues that are none the less rigorous and cogent for their not observing the strict bounds of ordinary-language custom or usage on the one hand or pure-bred logico-semantic analysis on the other. Such thinking involves an acute sense of the tension between these approaches, and of the need to keep that tension constantly in mind rather than resolve it prematurely in either direction.

This is why I have put the case that metaphysical issues like that of free-will versus determinism – issues whose solution has long eluded the best efforts of philosophy – might best be approached through our native understanding of what goes on in the process of linguistic-communicative utterance. That is, the antinomy which Kant raised to a high point of philosophical doctrine – though also, for his followers and exegetes, to a high point of philosophical bafflement – is one that can be brought more within reach of our jointly reflective and intuitive powers if we see it as analogous to the complex interplay of expressive freedom and structural constraint in even the most 'ordinary', 'everyday' speech-acts. Of course there is a sense in which we are not and cannot be fully aware of those goings-on when we talk straight ahead, get the grammar more-or-less right, and manage to communicate meanings or intentions beyond whatever might plausibly be thought of as present to mind in that process. Very often it is a case of discovering just what it was we wanted to say only after having said it, or having had some rather vague or largely inchoate expressive intent which achieved articulate (and consciously available) form only in and through the act of utterance itself. Derrida puts it well in a passage from *Of Grammatology* that should give pause to anyone who claims, as his critics frequently do, that he is offering a hermeneutic *carte blanche* or a licence to make what one will of texts which after all – as Socrates remarks in his adverse judgement of writing in Plato's *Phaedrus* – do not have the ability to answer back and correct any possible misunderstandings.[100] Thus deconstruction, according to Derrida,

> cannot consist of reproducing, by the effaced and respectful doubling of commentary, the conscious, voluntary, intentional relationship that the writer institutes in his exchanges with the history to which he belongs thanks to the element of language. This moment of doubling commentary should no doubt have its place in a critical reading. To recognize and respect all its classical exigencies is not easy and requires all the instruments of traditional criticism. Without this recognition and this respect, critical production would risk developing in any direction at all and authorize itself to say almost anything. But this indispensable guardrail has always only *protected*, it has never *opened*, a reading.[101]

This passage helps to reinforce Derrida's case that all the negative predicates often attached to writing – among them, not least, its openness to misinterpretation through removal from the sphere of self-present speaker's meaning – are in fact equally pertinent to speech since here likewise there is no guarantee of a perfect match between the *vouloir dire* of expressive purport and what transpires in the process of linguistic exchange or listener's uptake. At the same time, as it also makes clear, the appeal to intention is strictly indispensable for any understanding or interpretation of language, whether written or spoken, that would not court the charge of hermeneutic irresponsibility or mere 'textualist' gamesmanship.

That this is not just a pious pretence on Derrida's part but a claim borne out to convincing effect by his deconstructive readings of Plato, Aristotle, Rousseau, Kant, Husserl, Austin and others is a case that I have argued at length elsewhere and which – I venture to say – will find acceptance among readers who have taken the trouble to engage those readings at anything like their own level of detailed analytic rigour.[102] My point here is that it catches precisely the nature of that interplay between expressive freedom and structural-linguistic constraint that Derrida locates at the heart of philosophy in the wake of Husserlian phenomenology and the challenge to that project represented by the then newly emergent structuralist 'sciences of man'. Moreover, its significance extends beyond that particular episode in the history of recent French thought to encompass some of the most basic issues of epistemology, ethics and philosophy of mind. That is to say, it connects in an especially revealing and intimate way with the issue of free-will versus determinism, or the question as to how this

classical antinomy might be approached through a mode of thinking more alert
to its metaphysical dimension than anything within the analytic or 'ordinary-
language' lines of descent but also more responsive to the actual experience of
how these claims might conceivably be reconciled in and through the act of
creative-expressive utterance. It is in this sense, to repeat, that Derrida can
remark how 'a certain structuralism has always been philosophy's most spontaneous gesture' while none the less maintaining that 'what I can never
understand, in a structure, is that by means of which it is not closed'.[103]

It seems to me that the debate between phenomenology and structuralism in
the narrower, that is, post-1960 and chiefly French philosophical context is
always within reach of those larger, perennial questions concerning the scope and
limits of human freedom and responsibility. Thus, for instance, it bears crucially
on the dilemmas faced by liberal defenders of free speech when confronted – as so
often nowadays – with a conflict between the case for allowing a freedom to
express any range of (sometimes illiberal) doctrines or articles of faith and the
case for restricting such 'abuses' of that principle in the interests of (what else?)
greater freedom of thought and expression. Not that philosophers are likely to
come up with a solution to those problems – any more than a solution to the
free-will/determinism issue in its classic 'metaphysical' form – through some
advance in the powers of conceptual analysis or some speculative insight beyond
anything attained during the past two millennia of concentrated effort. All the
same, if it is wrong to adopt such an overly confident, even hubristic outlook
then it is just as wrong to conclude from the history of failed attempts so far that
the problem is downright insoluble or – like those of a 'mysterian' persuasion
with regard to the equally intractable problem of consciousness – that it is now
and forever beyond reach of our limited creaturely intelligence.[104] What is
needed, especially in this context, is that quality of open-minded and creative
willingness to challenge received ways of thought that has typified a good deal of
work in the recent 'continental' tradition but has so far been conspicuous mainly
by its absence in the mainstream analytic line of descent. Here again one might
suggest (with Derrida's texts chiefly in view) that the best remedy is a greater
attentiveness to just those aspects of language – its own language included –
that tend to go unnoticed in most analytic philosophy, whether through an
overly narrow conception of the analytic enterprise itself or through a tendency
to take the regulative notion of 'ordinary' usage as a given, self-evident ground
of appeal. This is nowhere more evident than in orthodox readings of the later
Wittgenstein that often single out just those passages most closely accordant
with the standard Wittgensteinian wisdom, thereby contriving to ignore or
discount a whole range of other, more acutely problematic (yet perhaps more
revealing) passages that would get in the way of any such fideist approach.

Hence the very different kind of reading that results when this presumption is
lifted, and interpreters – some of them taking a lead from Derrida – explore the
possibilities that are opened up by a more heterodox yet no less rigorous,
exegetically precise or philosophically searching account. It is here – in the space
of what Derrida calls 'a certain relationship, unperceived by the writer, between

what he commands and what he does not command of the patterns of the language he uses' – that there exists one point of entry for linguistic-philosophical reflection on the scope and limits of our freedom. Such reflection is most apt to occur when we encounter those limits precisely in and through the exercise of that freedom, whether as critically alert readers seeking to make the best sense of texts (including their blind spots of 'unperceived' implication) or as thoughtful moral agents likewise aware of the conflicts that can always arise between willed and unwilled, intended and unintended, or volitional and non-volitional acts and consequences.[105] Thus, as Derrida remarks *à propos* Rousseau, 'the writer writes *in* a language and *in* a logic whose proper system, laws, and life his discourse by definition cannot dominate absolutely' since 'he uses them only by letting himself, after a fashion and up to a point, be governed by the system'.[106] As I have said, the 'ordinary-language' approach – Austin's in particular, though also Wittgenstein's when read from a certain (call it Derridean) angle – can take us some way toward the kinds of insight here in question Where it tends to fall short when not read in this way is through its over-reliance either on the sanction of customary usage or, as in the case of speech-act theorists like Searle, on the problem-solving power of system and method as applied to various presumptively normal or deviant samples thereof. For if one thing emerges from Derrida's engagement with Austin and his more prickly but none the less probing and instructive contretemps with Searle it is the strict impossibility of laying down any such strict, *a priori* conditions for 'normal' as opposed to 'deviant' speech-acts, or those that meet the requirement of sincerely or authentically saying what one means and those that for some specifiable reason fall short of that requirement.[107]

This is not for one moment to dismiss the claim that performatives such as promising, vowing, signing a pledge or plighting one's troth can be taken to involve such sincerity-conditions, or at any rate the regulative notion of mindedness to keep one's word. Nor is it for one moment to deny that there exist certain accepted criteria of what counts as a normal or appropriate context, despite Derrida's well-taken point about the sheer, open-ended multiplicity of contexts in which any given performative locution might carry its intended (or perhaps some unintended) force. His point is not to deny these self-evident truths with regard to the normative character of speech-act utterance as a matter of ethical, social or communal acceptance. Rather it is to stress the manifold ways in which performative commitments – even where undertaken with sincere intent, in good faith or with a will to meet their satisfaction-conditions 'come what may' – are always subject to certain unforeseeable turns of event, such as might considerably complicate the issue as to just what those conditions might now be or what would count as properly meeting them. Indeed, it is precisely this openness of speech-acts to reinterpretation as a result of future changes in context, circumstance or the speaker's obligation that gives sufficient room for the continued exercise of morally discriminate judgement. That is to say, it is what makes all the difference between acting responsibly in light of such considerations and acting merely in accordance with certain interpretative norms or with precepts of an abstract, non-case-sensitive nature whose effect may be to close off any possibility of just such reflective and intelligent moral thought. Here again, it can be seen how this issue with regard to the binding (or sometimes the non-binding) force of speech-act commitment is a version of the same issue – that is, between deontological, consequentialist and broadly communitarian conceptions of the good – that has preoccupied moral philosophers from Kant to the present. Moreover, by posing it in linguistic terms as a matter of the kinds and degrees of freedom or constraint that characterize our various communicative dealings, whether spoken or written, this approach focuses squarely on the question that Derrida raises with regard to our reading of philosophical and other texts.

Hence (to repeat) his general observation that such reading requires a due regard for authorial intention – in so far as we are able to discern it – since 'without this recognition and this respect, critical production would risk developing in any direction at all and authorize itself to say almost anything'. And yet, he continues, 'this indispensable guardrail has always only *protected*, it has never *opened*, a reading'.[108] What is centrally involved here – in his discussion of the 'logic of supplementarity' as it emerges throughout Rousseau's writings on language, music, nature versus culture, the social contract, ethics, law and other topics besides – is precisely that interplay of freedom and necessity, volition and constraint, or utterer's intention and communicated sense that enters into all adequate reckoning with issues of ethics and interpretation. It is a question, Derrida writes, 'of Rousseau's situation within the language and the logic that assures to this word or this concept sufficiently *surprising* resources so that the presumed subject of the sentence might always say, through using the "supplement", more, less, or something other than he would mean [*voudrait dire*]'.[109] 'Surprising', I would suggest, in just the way that like moral agents or those who have entered into some kind of speech-act commitment can sometimes be confronted with deviant, unforeseeable or suchlike anomalous contexts or situations whereby they may think themselves justified in taking an altered, perhaps less strictly self-binding but at any rate more context-sensitive view of what their standing obligations amount to. The most important point – and one borne out to convincing effect by Derrida's reflections on the topic – is not to confuse this none the less demanding and self-critical conception of moral responsibility with the various kinds of pragmatist, communitarian or wholesale contextualist approach that would relativize the process of ethical judgement to some given consensus of beliefs-held-true within this or that linguistic or cultural community. It is for just this reason, I have argued here, that philosophy of language had better go by way of a closer acquaintance with developments in the 'other', post-Kantian continental or mainland- European tradition if it is to gain a useful purchase on perennial issues such as that of free-will versus determinism.

NOTES

1   For some recent philosophical perspectives, see L. Jonathan Cohen, *An Essay on Belief and Acceptance* (Oxford: Clarendon Press, 1992); Ted Honderich, *A Theory of Determinism*, vol. 1: *The Mind, Neuroscience and Life-Hopes* (Oxford: Clarendon Press, 1988) and vol. 2: *The Consequences of Determinism* (Oxford: Clarendon Press, 1988); Martha Klein, *Determinism, Blameworthiness, and Deprivation* (Oxford: Clarendon Press, 1990); J.R. Lucas, *The Freedom of the Will* (Oxford: Clarendon Press, 1970); David Owens, *Reason Without Freedom: The Problem of Epistemic Normativity* (London: Routledge, 2000); Galen Strawson, *Freedom and Belief* (Oxford: Oxford University Press, 1986).

2   See for instance David Chalmers, *The Conscious Mind: In Search of a Fundamental Theory* (Oxford: Oxford University Press, 1996); Paul M. Churchland, *Scientific Realism and the Plasticity of Mind* (Cambridge: Cambridge University Press, 1979) and *Matter and Consciousness* (Cambridge, MA: MIT Press, 1984); Paul M. Churchland and Patricia S. Churchland, *On the Contrary: Critical Essays, 1987–1997* (Cambridge, MA: MIT Press, 1998); Jeffrey A. Gray, *Consciousness: Creeping Up on the Hard Problem* (Oxford: Oxford University Press, 2004); Joseph Levine, *Purple Haze: The Puzzle of Consciousness* (Oxford: Oxford University Press, 2002); Colin McGinn, *The Mysterious Flame: Conscious Minds in a Material World* (New York: Basic Books, 1999); William S. Robinson, *Understanding Phenomenal Consciousness* (Cambridge: Cambridge University Press, 2004); Quentin Smith and Aleksandar Jokic (eds.), *Consciousness: New Philosophical Perspectives* (Oxford: Oxford University Press, 2003).

3   Frank Jackson, 'What Mary Didn't Know', *The Journal of Philosophy* 83(5) (May 1986), pp. 291–5.

4   See especially Churchland, *Scientific Realism and the Plasticity of Mind*.

5   McGinn, *The Mysterious Flame*.

6   See especially Noam Chomsky, *Syntactic Structures* (The Hague: Mouton, 1957); *Current Issues in Linguistic Theory* (The Hague: Mouton, 1964); *Aspects of the Theory of Syntax* (Cambridge, MA: MIT Press, 1965); *Cartesian Linguistics: A Chapter in the History of Rationalist Thought* (New York: Harper & Row, 1966); *Studies on Semantics in Generative Grammar* (The Hague: Mouton, 1972).

7   Chomsky, *Cartesian Linguistics*.

8   See for instance Chomsky, *American Power and the New Mandarins* (New York: Pantheon, 1969); *At War with Asia* (Pantheon, 1970); *Problems of Knowledge and Freedom: The Russell Lectures* (New York: Pantheon, 1971); *Towards a New Cold War. Essays on the Current Crisis and How We Got There* (New York: Pantheon, 1982); (with Edward S. Herman) *Manufacturing Consent: The Political Economy of the Mass Media* (New York: Pantheon, 1988); *Necessary Illusions: Thought Control in a Democratic Society* (Boston: South End, 1989); *Language and Politics*, ed. Carlos P. Otero (Montreal: Black Rose Books, 1989).

9   See Note 8, above.

10 See especially Geoffrey Sampson, *Liberty and Language* (Oxford: Oxford University Press, 1979).

11 Noam Chomsky, 'A Review of B. F. Skinner's *Verbal Behavior*', *Language* 35(1) (1959), pp. 26–58.

12 W.V. Quine, 'Epistemology Naturalized', in *Ontological Relativity and Other Essays* (New York: Columbia University Press, 1969), pp. 69–90.

13 See especially Ludwig Wittgenstein, *Philosophical Investigations*, trans. G.E.M. Anscombe (Oxford: Blackwell, 1951).

14 Immanuel Kant, *Critique of Practical Reason and Other Writings in Moral Philosophy*, trans. Lewis White Beck (Chicago: University of Chicago Press, 1949).

15 Martin Heidegger, *Poetry, Language, Thought*, trans. A. Hofstadter (New York: Harper & Row, 1975).

16   In this connection, see Victor Farias, *Heidegger and Nazism* (Philadelphia, PA: Temple University Press, 1989); Tom Rockmore, *On Heidegger's Nazism and Philosophy* (Berkeley and Los Angeles: University of California Press, 1992); Richard Wolin (ed.), *The Heidegger Controversy: A Critical Reader* (Cambridge, MA: MIT Press, 1998); Julian Young, *Heidegger, Philosophy, Nazism* (Cambridge: Cambridge University Press, 1997).

17   See Heidegger, *Poetry, Language, Thought*.

18   For further discussion of these various developments, see Christopher Norris, *Resources of Realism: Prospects for 'Post-Analytic' Philosophy* (London: Macmillan, 1997); *New Idols of the Cave: On The Limits of Anti-Realism* (Manchester: Manchester University Press, 1997); *Language, Logic and Epistemology: A Modal-Realist Approach* (London: Macmillan, 2002); *Philosophy of Language and the Challenge to Scientific Realism* (London: Routledge, 2004).

19   See for instance Judith Greene, *Psycholinguistics: Chomsky and Psychology* (Harmondsworth: Penguin, 1972).

20   See especially Chomsky, *Studies on Semantics in Generative Grammar*.

21   See Notes 6 and 8, above.

22   For further argument to this effect, see Christopher Norris, 'Modularity, Nativism, and Reference-Fixing: On Chomsky's Internalist Assumptions', in *Language, Logic and Epistemology*, pp. 111–49.

23   Chomsky, *Lectures on Government and Binding* (Dordrecht: Foris, 1981).

24   See for instance Roland Barthes, *S/Z*, trans. Richard Miller (London: Jonathan Cape, 1975) and *Image Music Text*, trans. Stephen Heath (London: Fontana, 1977); Catherine Belsey, *Critical Practice* (London: Methuen, 1981); Sean Burke, *The Death and Return of the Author: Criticism and Subjectivity in Barthes, Foucault and Derrida* (Edinburgh: Edinburgh University Press, 1999); Michel Foucault, 'What is an Author?', trans. Donald F. Bouchard and Sherry Simon, in *Language, Counter-Memory, Practice*, ed. Donald F. Bouchard (Ithaca, NY: Cornell University Press, 1977), pp. 124–7; Robert Young (ed.), *Untying the Text: A Post-Structuralist Reader* (London: Routledge & Kegan Paul, 1981).

25   Michel Foucault, *The Order of Things: An Archaeology of the Human Sciences*, trans. Alan Sheridan (New York: Pantheon, 1970).

26   See especially Heidegger, *Kant and the Problem of Metaphysics*, trans. James S. Churchill (Bloomington, IN: Indiana University Press, 1962).

27   Immanuel Kant, *Critique of Pure Reason*, trans. Norman Kemp Smith (London: Macmillan, 1964).

28   Immanuel Kant, *Political Writings*, ed. Hans Reiss (Cambridge: Cambridge University Press, 1976) and *The Conflict of the Faculties*, trans. Mary J. Gregor (New York: Abaris Books, 1979).

29   See Notes 2, 3 and 4, above.

30   See Christopher Norris, *Minding the Gap: Epistemology and Philosophy of Science in the Two Traditions* (Amherst, MA: University of Massachusetts Press, 2000) and *Truth Matters: Realism, Anti-Realism and Response-Dependence* (Edinburgh: Edinburgh University Press, 2002); also entries under Note 18, above.

31   Wittgenstein, *Philosophical Investigations*; also Christopher Norris, 'The Limits of Whose Language? Wittgestein on Logic, Mathematics, and Science', in *Language, Logic and Epistemology*, pp. 66–110.

32   See especially Gordon Baker and P.M.S. Hacker, *Wittgenstein: Understanding and Meaning* (Oxford: Blackwell, 1983) and *Language, Sense and Nonsense: A Critical Investigation into Modern Theories of Language* (Oxford: Blackwell, 1984).

33   See Notes 2, 3 and 4, above.

34   See McGinn, *The Mysterious Flame*.

35   Note 31, above.

36   See Saul Kripke, *Wittgenstein on Rules and Private Language: An Elementary Exposition*

(Oxford: Blackwell, 1982); also Alexander Miller and Crispin Wright (eds.), *Rule-Following and Meaning* (Chesham: Acumen, 2002).

37 See McGinn, *The Mysterious Flame*.

38 See especially Dan Sperber and Deidre Wilson, *Relevance: Communication and Cognition*, 2nd edn (Oxford: Blackwell, 1995); also Asa Kasher (ed.), *Pragmatics: Critical Concepts*, 4 vols (London: Routledge, 1998).

39 J.L. Austin, 'A Plea for Excuses', in *Philosophical Papers* (Oxford: Clarendon Press, 1961), pp. 175–204.

40 Keith Graham, *J.L. Austin: A Critique of Ordinary Language Philosophy* (Hassocks, Sussex: Harvester, 1977).

41 Austin, 'A Plea for Excuses', p. 182.

42 Ibid., p. 184.

43 Richard Rorty (ed.), *The Linguistic Turn: Essays in Philosophical Method* (Chicago: University of Chicago Press, 1967).

44 See also Rorty, *Consequences of Pragmatism* (Brighton: Harvester, 1982); *Contingency, Irony, and Solidarity* (Cambridge: Cambridge University Press, 1989); *Objectivity, Relativism, and Truth* (Cambridge: Cambridge University Press, 1991); *Truth and Progress* (Cambridge: Cambridge University Press, 1998).

45 See William James, *Pragmatism: A New Name for some Old Ways of Thinking* (New York: Longmans, 1907) und *The Meaning of Truth* (New York: Longmans, 1909).

46 Bertrand Russell, 'William James's Conception of Truth', in Simon Blackburn and Keith Simmons (eds.), *Truth* (Oxford: Oxford University Press, 1999), pp. 69–82.

47 See W.K. Clifford, 'The Ethics of Belief', in *The Ethics of Belief and Other Essays* (New York: Prometheus Books, 1999), pp. 70–96.

48 On these developments in post-Kantian idealist thought, see especially Frederick C. Beiser, *The Fate of Reason: German Philosophy from Kant to Fichte* (Cambridge, MA: Harvard University Press, 1987); also Norris, *Minding the Gap* and *Deconstruction and the 'Unfinished Project of Modernity'* (London: Continuum, 2000).

49 John McDowell, *Mind and World* (Cambridge, MA: Harvard University Press, 1994); Robert C. Brandom, *Making It Explicit: Reasoning, Representing and Discursive Commitment* (Cambridge, MA: Harvard University Press, 1994).

50 See Christopher Norris, 'McDowell on Kant: Redrawing the Bounds of Sense' and 'The Limits of Naturalism: Further Thoughts on McDowell's *Mind and World*', in *Minding the Gap*, pp. 172–96 and 197–230.

51 See Note 50, above; also Norris, *Deconstruction and the 'Unfinished Project of Modernity'*.

52 See Note 36, above.

53 McDowell, *Mind and World*, p. 41.

54 Ibid., p. 95.

55 Ibid., p. 65.

56 Ibid., p. 77.

57 Ibid., p. 93.

58 Ibid., p. 125.

59 Ibid., p. 187.

60 See Hans-Georg Gadamer, *Philosophical Hermeneutics*, trans. David E. Linge (Berkeley and Los Angeles: University of California Press, 1977) and *Truth and Method*, trans. John Cumming and Garrett Barden (London: Sheed & Ward, 1979).

61 McDowell, *Mind and World*, p. 184.

62 Ibid., p. 126.

63 Ibid., p. 126.

64 Ibid., p. 65.

65 Ibid., p. 64.

66 P.F. Strawson, *Individuals: An Essay in Descriptive Metaphysics* (London: Methuen, 1959)

and *The Bounds of Sense: An Essay on Kant's Critique of Pure Reason* (London: Methuen, 1966).

67 McDowell, *Mind and World*, p. 182.

68 Ibid., p. 115.

69 Kant, *Critique of Practical Reason*.

70 Rorty, *Objectivity, Relativism, and Truth*.

71 Ibid., p. 81

72 Ibid., p. 81.

73 See especially W.V. Quine, 'Two Dogmas of Empiricism', in *From a Logical Point of View*, 2nd edn (Cambridge, MA: Harvard University Press, 1961), pp. 20–46 and Thomas Kuhn, *The Structure of Scientific Revolutions*, 2nd edn (Chicago: University of Chicago Press, 1970).

74 For a wide range of approaches, see Ruth F. Chadwick and Clive Cazeaux (eds.), *Kant: Critical Assessments*, 4 vols (London: Routledge, 1992) and Paul Guyer (ed.), *The Cambridge Companion to Kant* (Cambridge: Cambridge University Press, 1992).

75 See Gottlob Frege, 'Review of Edmund Husserl's *Philosophie der Arithmetik*', trans. E.-H. W. Kluge. *Mind* 81 (1972), pp. 321–37; also Gilbert Ryle, 'Phenomenology' and 'Phenomenology versus *The Concept of Mind*', in Ryle, *Collected Papers*, vol. 1 (London: Hutchinson, 1971), pp. 167–78 and 179–96; also – for a different perspective – Leila Haaparanta (ed.), *Mind, Meaning, and Mathematics: Essays on the Philosophical Views of Husserl and Frege* (Dordrecht and Boston: Kluwer, 1994).

76 See Note 36, above.

77 Austin, 'A Plea for Excuses', p. 181

78 See Note 75, above.

79 See especially Paul Ricoeur, *Freedom and Nature: The Voluntary and the Involuntary*, trans. Erazim Kohak (Evanston, IL: Northwestern University Press, 1966); *The Conflict of Interpretations: Essays in Hermeneutics*, ed. Don Ihde; trans. Willis Domingo et al. (Evanston, IL: Northwestern University Press, 1969); *Hermeneutics and the Human Sciences: Essays on Language, Action and Interpretation*, ed. and trans. John B. Thompson (Cambridge: Cambridge University Press, 1981); *From Text to Action: Essays in Hermeneutics II*, trans. Kathleen Blamey and John B. Thompson (Evanston, IL: Northwestern University Press, 1991).

80 See Jacques Derrida, *'Speech and Phenomena' and Other Essays on Husserl's Theory of Signs*, trans. David B. Allison (Evanston, IL: Northwestern University Press, 1973); *Of Grammatology*, trans. Gayatri. C. Spivak (Baltimore, MD: Johns Hopkins University Press, 1976); *Writing and Difference*, trans. Alan Bass (London: Routledge & Kegan Paul, 1978); *Dissemination*, trans. Barbara Johnson (London: Athlone Press, 1981); *Margins of Philosophy*, trans. Alan Bass (Chicago: University of Chicago Press, 1982).

81 Jacques Derrida, ' "Genesis and Structure" and Phenomenology', in *Writing and Difference*, trans. Alan Bass, pp. 154–68 (159).

82 Ibid., p. 157.

83 Derrida, *Writing and Difference*, p. 5.

84 Maurice Merleau-Ponty, *The Phenomenology of Perception*, trans. Colin Smith (London: Routledge & Kegan Paul, 1962), p. 389.

85 Maurice Merleau-Ponty, *Signs*, trans. Richard McCleary (Evanston, IL: Northwestern University Press, 1964), p. 46.

86 See Michael Dummett, *Truth and Other Enigmas* (London: Duckworth, 1978) and *The Logical Basis of Metaphysics* (London: Duckworth, 1991); also Norris, *Truth Matters* and Neil Tennant, *The Taming of the True* (Oxford: Oxford University Press, 1997).

87 See Note 36, above.

88 McDowell, *Mind and World*.

89 Michael Dummett, *The Origins of Analytic Philosophy* (London: Duckworth, 1993).

90 See for instance Edmund Husserl, *The Phenomenology of Internal Time-Consciousness*, trans.

James S. Churchill (Evanston, IL: Northwestern University Press, 1964); *Formal and Transcendental Logic*, trans. Dorion Cairns (The Hague: Nijhoff, 1969); *Logical Investigations*, trans. J.N. Findlay, 2 vols (New York: Humanities Press, 1970); *Ideas: General Introduction to Pure Phenomenology*, trans. W.R. Boyce Gibson (London: Collier Macmillan, 1975).

91 See Jacques Derrida, 'Signature Event Context', *Glyph* 1 (1975), pp. 172–97; John R. Searle, 'Reiterating the Differences', *Glyph* 1 (1975), pp. 198–208; Derrida, 'Limited Inc abc', *Glyph* 2 (1977), pp. 75–176; also Jacques Derrida, 'Afterword: Toward an Ethic of Conversation', in Gerald Graff (ed.), *Limited Inc* (Evanston, IL: Northwestern University Press, 1989), pp. 111–54.

92 See Austin, 'A Plea for Excuses'.

93 Ibid.

94 For further argument to this effect, see Michael Devitt, *Realism and Truth*, 2nd edn (Oxford: Blackwell, 1986) and Norris, *Philosophy of Language and the Challenge to Scientific Realism*.

95 See Notes 18, 30, 86 and 94 above; also – for defences of alethic realism with regard to abstract and other kinds of object – Jerrold J. Katz, *Realistic Rationalism* (Cambridge, MA: MIT Press, 1998) and Scott Soames, *Understanding Truth* (Oxford: Oxford University Press, 1999).

96 See Notes 11 and 24, above; also Ferdinand de Saussure, *Course in General Linguistics*, trans. Wade Baskin (London: Fontana, 1974).

97 Note 6, above.

98 See Graham, *J.L. Austin*.

99 Austin, 'A Plea for Excuses', p. 182.

100 Plato, *Phaedrus and Letters VII and VIII*, trans. Walter Hamilton (Harmondsworth: Penguin, 1961).

101 Derrida, *Of Grammatology*, p. 158.

102 See Norris, *Deconstruction and the 'Unfinished Project of Modernity'*; also *Derrida* (London: Fontana, 1987); *Against Relativism: Deconstruction, Critical Theory, and Philosophy of Science* (Oxford: Blackwell, 1997); 'Derrida on Rousseau: Deconstruction as Philosophy of Logic', in *Language, Logic and Epistemology*, pp. 16–65.

103 Derrida, *Writing and Difference*, p. 5.

104 See McGinn, *The Mysterious Flame*.

105 Derrida, *Of Grammatology*, p. 158.

106 Ibid., p. 158.

107 See Note 91, above.

108 Derrida, *Of Grammatology*, p. 158.

109 Ibid., p. 158.

Index